The Feminist Legislation Project

In this book, leading law academics along with lawyers, activists and others demonstrate what legislation could look like if its concern was to create justice for women.

Each chapter contains a short piece of legislation – proposed in order to address a contemporary legal problem from a feminist perspective. These range across criminal law (sexual offences, Indigenous women's experiences of criminal law, laws in relation to forced marriage, modern slavery, childcare and sentencing), civil law (aged care and housing rights, regulating the gig economy; surrogacy, gender equity in the construction industry) and constitutional law (human rights legislation, reimagining parliaments where laws are made for the benefit of women). The proposed laws are, moreover, drafted with feedback from a senior parliamentary draftsperson (providing guidance to contributors in a personal capacity), to ensure conformity with legislative rigour, as well as accompanied by an explanation of their reasons and their aims. Although the legislation is Australian-based, the issues raised by each are recognisably global, and are reflected in the legislation of most other nations.

This first feminist legislation project will appeal to scholars of feminist legal studies, gender and the law, gender studies and others studying or working in relevant legal areas.

Becky Batagol is Associate Professor in the Law Faculty at Monash University, Australia.

Kate Seear is Professor at the Australian Research Centre in Sex, Health and Society, La Trobe University, Australia.

Heli Askola is Associate Professor in the Law Faculty at Monash University, Australia.

Jamie Walvisch is Senior Lecturer in the Law School at the University of Western Australia, Australia.

The Feminist Legislation Project

Rewriting Laws for Gender-Based Justice

Edited by Becky Batagol, Kate Seear, Heli Askola and Jamie Walvisch

Routledge
Taylor & Francis Group
LONDON AND NEW YORK

First published 2024
by Routledge
4 Park Square, Milton Park, Abingdon, Oxon OX14 4RN

and by Routledge
605 Third Avenue, New York, NY 10158

Routledge is an imprint of the Taylor & Francis Group, an informa business

a GlassHouse book

British Library Cataloguing-in-Publication Data
A catalogue record for this book is available from the British Library

Library of Congress Cataloging-in-Publication Data
Names: Batagol, Becky, editor. | Seear, Kate, editor. | Askola, Heli, editor. | Walvisch, Jamie, editor.
Title: The feminist legislation project : rewriting laws for gender-based justice / edited by Becky Batagol, Kate Seear, Heli Askola, and Jamie Walvisch.
Description: Abingdon, Oxon [UK] ; New York, NY : Routledge, 2024. | Includes bibliographical references and index.
Identifiers: LCCN 2024004013 (print) | LCCN 2024004014 (ebook) | ISBN 9781032444994 (hardback) | ISBN 9781032445021 (paperback) | ISBN 9781003372462 (ebook)
Subjects: LCSH: Feminist jurisprudence. | Women—Legal status, laws, etc | Sex discrimination against women—Law and legislation.
Classification: LCC K349 .F463 2024 (print) | LCC K349 (ebook) | DDC 328.3/73082—dc23/eng/20240129
LC record available at https://lccn.loc.gov/2024004013
LC ebook record available at https://lccn.loc.gov/2024004014

ISBN: 978-1-032-44499-4 (hbk)
ISBN: 978-1-032-44502-1 (pbk)
ISBN: 978-1-003-37246-2 (ebk)

DOI: 10.4324/9781003372462

Typeset in Sabon
by Apex CoVantage, LLC

Contents

Contributors

Dr Amira Aftab is a Senior Lecturer at Macquarie Law School. Her research considers the intersection of law, policy, race, religion and gender with a particular focus on family dispute resolution, as well as domestic and family violence.

Dr Natalia Antolak-Saper is a Senior Lecturer in the Faculty of Law, Monash University. She has recognised expertise in the areas of comparative criminal law and procedure. Her research combines applied doctrinal research with a range of methodologies, and she works closely with stakeholders to achieve practical legal solutions to pressing criminal law issues.

Dr Heli Askola is a comparative lawyer and an Associate Professor at Monash Law Faculty. Her main areas of expertise relate to the legal regulation of migration and citizenship, and she has published extensively on trafficking in human beings, sexual and labour exploitation, forced marriage and violence against women.

Dr Becky Batagol is an Associate Professor of Law at Monash University. She is a socially engaged feminist academic whose work has real impact in the world, especially in relation to gender and family violence. Her academic practice centres on tackling difficult social problems and considering whether we can improve people's lives through law and policy reform.

Dr Rachael Burgin is a Senior Lecturer in Criminal Justice at Swinburne University of Technology, and the CEO of Rape and Sexual Assault Research and Advocacy (RASARA). Her research interests include legal responses to rape and sexual assault, consent law reform, gendered violence, feminist jurisprudence and the prevention of violence against women.

Professor Jennifer Burn AM is a Professor of Law and leads Anti-Slavery Australia at the University of Technology Sydney.

Professor Jonathan Crowe is Head of School and Dean of the School of Law and Justice at the University of Southern Queensland. He is Director of Research at Rape and Sexual Assault Research and Advocacy (RASARA).

James Dalmau is a senior legislative drafter in an Australian jurisdiction. His contribution to this project is made in his private capacity and not in his capacity as a public servant.

Dr Julie Debeljak is an Associate Professor at the Faculty of Law, the Director of the Higher Degree by Research Program for the Faculty of Law and an Academic Member of the Castan Centre for Human Rights Law, Monash University. She teaches and researches in the areas of comparative and international human rights law, domestic and comparative human rights instruments and constitutional law.

Rebecca Dickson is a PhD Candidate in the Law Faculty at Monash University, researching construction law reform. Rebecca also practises as a construction contracts and projects delivery lawyer in the role of Special Counsel at Pinsent Masons in Melbourne and a Senior Fellow in Construction Law at the University of Melbourne.

Kate Eastman AM SC is a barrister who practises in the areas of human rights, employment and public law.

Dr Asher Flynn is an Associate Professor of Criminology in the School of Social Sciences at Monash University and a Chief Investigator on the ARC Centre of Excellence for the Elimination of Violence Against Women (CEVAW), where she leads the technology workstream. Asher is an award-winning international researcher in policy and prevention concerning gendered and sexual violence, with a key focus on technology-facilitated violence.

Professor Valerie Francis worked as a civil engineer before entering academia and is now the Chair of Construction at the University of Melbourne. As a long-time advocate for women in engineering and construction, much of her research and industry engagement revolves around gender, wellbeing and work-life balance.

Professor Paula Gerber worked as a construction lawyer before entering academia and is now a Professor in the Law Faculty at Monash University. She was the founder of the National Association of Women in Construction (NAWIC) in Australia. She is an internationally renowned scholar in two disparate fields, namely, construction law and international human rights law.

Alexandra Heron was a Research Associate in the Women, Work and Policy Research Group, the University of Sydney Business School and an Associate Investigator at the Centre of Excellence in Population Ageing Research. Alex's PhD is in combining informal eldercare with paid work. She has worked as a lawyer and in legal and policy research and advice positions in the UK, Australia and France in both the public and private sectors and for non-government organisations.

Dr Jessie Hohmann is an Associate Professor at UTS Faculty of Law. As an internationally recognised expert on the right to housing in international law, she works to advance social justice through housing in her scholarship. Her expertise is regularly sought out by NGOs and governments.

Dr Balawyn Jones is a Lecturer at La Trobe Law School. She researches across the fields of domestic and family violence, Muslim women's agency, Indonesian law and society and the implementation of women's rights at the intersection of gender, religion and law.

Dr Nicole Kalms is an Associate Professor in the Faculty of Art Design and Architecture Founding Director of the Monash University XYX Lab, which leads national and international research in gender and place.

Professor Susan Kneebone is a Professorial Fellow, Senior Associate Asian Law Centre, and Research Affiliate, Peter McMullin Centre on Statelessness, Melbourne Law School. Susan researches and publishes on topics on forced migration. She is currently conducting research under an Australian Research Council grant on 'The Role of Community Sponsorship for Refugee Resettlement in Australia'.

Dr Dani Linder is a Bundjalung, Kungarykany woman from Grafton, New South Wales and a Senior Lecturer in the TC Beirne School of Law at the University of Queensland.

Bri Lee is an award-winning author, academic and activist. Her books include *Who Gets to Be Smart* (2021), *Beauty* (2019) and *Eggshell Skull* (2018). She is a PhD candidate at the University of Sydney Law School, where she has also lectured in media law.

Dr Krystal Lockwood is a Gumbaynggirr and Dunghutti woman from Armidale, New South Wales and a Lecturer in the School of Criminology and Criminal Justice at Griffith University, Queensland.

Professor Arlie Loughnan is Professor of Criminal Law and Criminal Law Theory at the University of Sydney. She works at the intersection of criminal law, legal history and legal theory. She is the author of *Self, Others and the State: Relations of Responsibility* (2020) and *Manifest Madness: Mental Incapacity in Criminal Law* (2012).

Dr Kcasey McLoughlin is a Senior Lecturer in Law at Newcastle Law School. Kcasey's research examines the importance not only of greater diversity in our public institutions but also the need to critically interrogate the gendered assumptions that pervade legal and political institutions. Her first book, *Law, Women Judges and the Gender Order: Lessons from the High Court of Australia* (2022), was awarded the Law and Society Association of Australia and New Zealand 2022 Most Outstanding Book Prize.

Dr Laura McVoy is an interdisciplinary researcher from RMIT University, Australia. Her research focuses on gender inequality, feminist theory and violence against women, in a range of organisational, institutional and policy contexts.

Liza J Miller practised law as a barrister and solicitor. She has more recently engaged in socio-legal empirical research examining aspects of sentencing.

Professor Jenny Morgan is a Professor of Law at the Melbourne Law School, University of Melbourne. Probably most well-known for her book with Reg Graycar, *The Hidden Gender of Law*, she has worked on issues of violence against women for most of her career.

Dr Sean Mulcahy is a Research Officer at the Australian Research Centre in Sex, Health and Society at La Trobe University. His current research examines the application of human rights law to marginalised populations, including LGBTIQA+ people.

Saxon Mullins is a survivor and Director of Advocacy at Rape and Sexual Assault Research and Advocacy (RASARA). Saxon was the recipient of the Australian Human Rights Commission's 2018 Young People's Human Rights Medal.

Dr Yee-Fui Ng is an Associate Professor and the Acting Director of the Australian Centre for Justice Innovation at Monash University, and was a 2021–22 Fulbright Scholar. Her research centres on the intersection between public law and politics, focusing on enhancing executive accountability.

Stephen Page is the Principal at Page Provan solicitors, Brisbane. Stephen was admitted as a solicitor in Queensland in 1987, to the High Court of Australia in 1989 and as a barrister and solicitor in South Australia in 2013. He is the 2023 Queensland Law Society President's Medal recipient.

Dr Tania Penovic is an Associate Professor at Deakin Law School. She has served as Deputy Director, and subsequently research group convenor in gender and sexuality, for the Castan Centre for Human Rights Law at Monash University and is the Senior Co-Chair in Women and Girls' Rights for Australian Lawyers for Human Rights (ALHR).

Professor Marilyn Pittard is the Interim Dean and a Professor of Law in Monash University's Law Faculty. Marilyn publishes extensively in labour and employment law, including from grant-funded research. She was recently part of a 'think tank' of industrial relations law experts exploring a new design for relations between business, employees and unions, resulting in *A New Work Relations Architecture* – a book proposing a model for regulating industrial relations, including new labour rights.

Professor Nola Ries is a Professor in the Faculty of Law, University of Technology Sydney. Nola is an experienced legal and social science researcher with expertise in law, health and ageing. She has a special interest in legal aspects of dementia and teaches subjects in elder and health law.

Dr Olivia Rundle is Senior Lecturer in Law, in the College of Arts, Law and Education, University of Tasmania. The positive and negative consequences of legal recognition of personal relationships is a particular area of scholarly interest for Olivia, who was once a recipient of parenting payment.

Professor Kate Seear is an Australian Research Council Future Fellow at the Australian Research Centre in Sex, Health and Society, La Trobe University and the author of multiple books and articles on law, gender, health, alcohol and other drugs. She is also a practising solicitor. Her most recent book is *Law, Drugs and the Making of Addiction: Just Habits* (2020), which won the UK's Socio-Legal Studies Association's History and Theory book prize.

Dr Ronli Sifris is an Associate Professor in Monash University's Faculty of Law and Deputy Director of the Castan Centre for Human Rights Law. Her research is predominantly focused on issues at the intersection of reproductive health and the law (at both the domestic and international level) including abortion, surrogacy, assisted reproduction and involuntary sterilisation.

Dr Lyndal Sleep is Senior Lecturer at the Queensland Centre for Domestic and Family Violence Research, Central Queensland University. She researches technology and social policy, with the aim of improving the safety of women and their children. Lyndal's PhD was on the couple rule in Australian social security law; she was also lead Chief Investigator in the ANROWS (2019) project 'Domestic Violence, the Couple Rule and Australian Social Security Law'.

Charlotte Steer has been a government lawyer, sessional university lecturer and tribunal member in New South Wales for 25 years.

The Hon Pamela Tate AM KC is an Adjunct Professor of Law at Monash University and a former judge of the Victorian Court of Appeal. She was Special Counsel to the Victorian Human Rights Consultation Committee that recommended the enactment of the *Charter of Human Rights and Responsibilities*.

Professor Margaret Thornton is an Emerita Professor at the Australian National University with particular expertise in feminist legal theory and discrimination. Her most recent book is *Law and the Quest for Gender Equality* (2023). She is a Fellow of the Academy of Social Sciences in Australia and a Foundation Fellow of the Australian Academy of Law.

Dr Ramona Vijeyarasa is an Associate Professor in the Faculty of Law at the University of Technology Sydney. Ramona is the Chief Investigator behind the Gender Legislative Index, a tool designed to promote the enactment of legislation that works more effectively to improve women's lives. Her work innovatively combines law, engineering and data science to reinvigorate decades-long debates about the law's role in addressing gender inequality.

Dr Jamie Walvisch is a Senior Lecturer at the University of Western Australia Law School. He is a criminal law scholar with a strong law reform background, having previously worked at the Law Reform Commission of Western Australia and the Victorian Law Reform Commission. His main research focus is the intersection between crime and mental health, particularly in the sentencing context.

Forewords

Natasha Stott Despoja AO

The law is often presented as objective – at least by those who have historically made it – as if there is a sort of inevitability to the laws and regulations that govern our lives and shape our society: that is, laws that reflect the male perspective and lived experience. Feminist legal scholarship has laid bare so many of the patriarchal assumptions and silences embedded in our law and in the judgments of our courts, which deny women justice and reinforce inequality. As *The Feminist Legislation Project: Rewriting Laws for Gender-based Justice* makes clear, meaningful change to achieve equality for women and gender-diverse people requires the imagination to conceive of a different way of doing things – and include a feminist perspective in our law-making.

Women have historically been, and unfortunately remain, a minority in almost all legislatures around the world, including Australia. Only approximately 26% of all national parliamentarians globally are women – an increase of just 11% since 1995 when I first became a Senator.[1] At 26, I was the youngest woman ever to enter Federal Parliament. At that time, 14.9% of the Parliament was female.

Almost three decades later, only 1% of parliamentarians in the world are women under the age of 30 – and only five countries have reached 50% or more women in the lower or single houses of parliament. Unfortunately, Australia is not one of them: it was only in 2010 that our Federal Parliament hit the internationally recognised level of 'critical mass' for women in politics – 30%. Today, it is 44.5%. At the current rate, gender parity amongst our federal politicians will not be achieved until 2063.

The composition of our Parliament matters. The laws that governments produce reflect the experiences, worldviews and blind spots of those in positions of power and our lawmakers.

I am heartened that women's representation continues to rise and that there is more diversity represented in our parliaments. In my maiden speech, I said: 'I look forward to the day when I look across this chamber from my seat and see such a diversity of faces – young people, old people, different ages, men and women, and the many cultures that make up our nation, including indigenous cultures – that we no longer have to strive for it'. We are certainly not there yet.

We need to ensure we continue to inspire and support future feminist lawmakers to consider putting themselves forward for office. Part of that is also acknowledging that our parliaments have not been safe spaces for women and marginalised groups, which includes accepting how this reduces participation and why we need to change it.

Walking those corridors of power as a 26-year-old, I felt both out of place and like I was exactly in the right place. I felt a huge sense of opportunity, but also a great sense of responsibility: I was intent on bringing my feminist perspective into the Parliament.

Despite my focus on legislation, throughout my time as a Senator I experienced relentless stereotyping and sexism, often in a brazen attempt to undermine my policy positions. Unfortunately, women in public life continue to be subjected to similarly hostile treatment. There were daily comments about my appearance – what I wore or how I wore it. Given the public reckoning over the culture in Parliament in 2021, it will come as no surprise to hear that during my time in politics I experienced unwanted touching, threats and intimidation. When I was criticised by other politicians, gender always found a way into the conversation, as though my being a woman was proof enough that I wasn't qualified or competent.

In the Senate Chamber, when I protested the invasion of Iraq I was the 'Handmaiden of Hussein'. When my party – renowned for having female leadership – did a deal, you could 'rent us by the hour'. I had one Senate colleague who, after my first child was born, referred to me as 'Mother' for the rest of my term. Every single Australian female parliamentarian will have their own laundry list of experiences like these and their own examples of the misogynistic insults and comments they have faced from fellow parliamentarians, in the media and online.

How women in parliament are treated, including in the media, matters. There is plenty to discourage women and gender-diverse people from entering politics, but encouraging participation is crucial if we are to progress feminist policy.

Parliamentary culture has rightly come under scrutiny, through a broader conversation led by brave young women. A reckoning is underway, and this is an important start towards creating a much-needed safe working environment in Parliament. It is only now, in 2023, that codes of conduct apply to all parliamentarians and staffers. This was a key recommendation in the *Set the Standard* report into Parliament's workplace culture, based on the critically important independent review led by then Sex Discrimination Commissioner, Kate Jenkins, in 2021.[2]

Workplace safety means that we can be focused on getting on with the real work: making sure that the legislation being passed is fit for purpose and gender-responsive.

Pursuing progressive policy that advanced gender equality mattered to me – from introducing Australia's first national paid parental leave legislation, to same-sex marriage and transparency in pregnancy counselling advertising to genetic privacy and a Bill for a human rights charter – all of which were informed by a feminist perspective.

There are also examples of important reforms that were a result of female parliamentarians coming together across party lines to achieve better outcomes for women. Women are not homogeneous, and certainly don't always work together or agree in a parliamentary or legislative context, but this experience strengthened my conviction that greater numbers of women and gender-diverse people in Parliament make a real difference to policy, ultimately leading to decision-making that better reflects the needs and concerns of all Australians.

I also recall examples that were not informed by lived experience or a gender perspective such as the 2006 Stem Cell Regulations, following the passing of the *Prohibition of Human Cloning for Reproduction and the Regulation of Human Embryo Research Amendment Act* 2006,[3] which sought to outlaw the exportation of embryos for research purposes. The definition was drafted so broadly that a pregnant person travelling overseas would be committing a crime. It was only when I threatened to disallow the Regulations in the Senate that the Government reconsidered the definition. This is just one absurd example of the kinds of laws and regulations we end up with when the people in the room don't have experience beyond the 'pale, male and stale'.

In 2006, I worked with a cross-party group of women to ensure RU486 (the abortifacient drug) would be more readily available to women, and no longer subject to ministerial discretion. A survey at the time found that more than 80% of Australians believed that a woman should have the right to choose whether or not she has an abortion.[4] The 2006 conscience vote that overturned the 'ban' on RU486 grew out of Democrat amendments. These became a cross-party, female-sponsored Private Members' Bill, and ultimately a win against primarily male legislators who sought to interfere with women's decisions about their own bodies.

This shows exactly why we need more women in our parliaments – and why the Australian Feminist Legislation Project is so important.

It was a great honour to serve in Australia's Parliament – and it is a great honour to continue my work and passion for feminist law-making through my role on the UN Committee on the Elimination of all Forms of Discrimination Against Women (CEDAW). I have big shoes to fill: I am just the second Australian CEDAW member. The first was the esteemed Elizabeth Evatt. Elizabeth's formidable list of achievements include a long list of 'firsts' – the first female judge of an Australian federal court, the first Australian elected to the UN Human Rights Committee and CEDAW Committee, the first female President of the Australian Law Reform Commission – and the first person to become Chief Justice of the Family Court. She has inspired me, and generations of Australian women, and demonstrates the importance of pioneering women who showed us that we can do it too.

CEDAW is responsible for monitoring the progress of States towards equality for women under the Convention on the Elimination of All Forms of Discrimination Against Women, responding to complaints against governments, and producing General Recommendations on international law, standards and best practices on women's rights, which are influential and are widely referred to as standard-setting documents which influence policy-making, law-making and court judgments around the world. We are currently drafting the Committee's 40th General Recommendation (GR40) on the equal and inclusive representation of women in decision-making systems to achieve better models of governance, which resonates with the work of this project.

The initiative of GR40 is grounded in the understanding that having equal representation of women in decision-making improves governance and outcomes. Even though the numbers are slowly improving, they are not improving fast enough. Women's participation in public and political life is under threat everywhere, despite their proven competences as leaders and agents of change for their countries and for the planet. Through our work on GR40, we are exploring the obstacles to equal participation, from gender-based violence to other forms of discrimination and stereotyping. While States continually reiterate their commitments to equal representation, the available data shows only symbolic improvement. This requires us to consider new and updated approaches to advance gender parity in all aspects of law-making and decision-making, as well as to promote and expand feminist, gender-transformative and inclusive laws and policies.

For our policies and laws to deliver justice to every Australian, our Parliament must reflect diversity in all its forms. In Australia, it is incumbent upon lawmakers to seek a broad range of perspectives – from women and gender-diverse communities, as well as from Aboriginal and Torres Strait Islander peoples, for whom laws are so often written *for* but not *with*. It is my belief that if we are to have any radical reimagination of our laws, and to create a fairer and more equitable society, the active participation of marginalised voices is indispensable.

The Australian Feminist Legislation Project prompts us to examine the ways in which laws have been developed in Australia, and demonstrates how feminist law-making could transform lives, enrich public discourse and lead to a safer and more equitable society. It is up to us to pick up where this book ends and transform the promise of these ideas into action.

Natasha Stott Despoja AO

Natasha Stott Despoja AO is a Professor in the Practice of Politics at ANU and an Expert Member of the UN Treaty Body, CEDAW. She is also a former Senator and was Australia's Ambassador for Women and Girls. She is a non-executive director of several not-for-profit organisations.

Professor Rosemary Hunter KC (Hon)

The feminist judgment projects, from which *The Feminist Legislation Project: Rewriting Laws for Gender-based Justice* takes its inspiration, began with the premise that while feminist legal scholarship had flourished in universities, there was not much evidence of its impact on legal practice and particularly on judicial decision-making. Thus, in rewriting decided cases from a feminist perspective – imagining a feminist judge sitting on the bench in the original case or on appeal – the feminist judgment projects show what a difference a feminist approach to judicial decisions could make, provide models of feminist decision-making and, as Cooper has observed,[5] prefigure what a more inclusive feminist future might look like. This is not to deny the existence of feminist judgments in the 'real world', as my own work has shown,[6] but to demonstrate the scope for a much more comprehensive approach to the achievement of substantive equality, legal subjectivity for those historically marginalised by law, and gender justice in all its intersectional forms.

The Australian Feminist Legislation Project, initiated at Monash University in 2017, sought to take a similar approach to legislation as opposed to judgments. Similarly, there already exists legislation inspired, fought for, promoted and sponsored by feminist activists and feminist legislators. There is, in fact, quite a lot of it in Australia and across the world. The recent English publication *Women's Legal Landmarks*,[7] for example, illustrates the remarkable legislative productivity of feminist movements over several centuries (a history which has been persistently occluded and which the book aims to recuperate). But continuing experiences of women's oppression through law, or their inability to obtain legal remedies or redress for gendered harms, demonstrate that as with feminist judgments, there is considerable scope for a more comprehensive infusion of feminist principles and concerns into the legislative process. The topics covered by the various chapters in this collection – constitutional and human rights, rape and sexual assault, reproductive labour, criminal injuries compensation, sentencing, modern slavery, migration law, access to work and working arrangements, housing, Family Dispute Resolution, social security payments and public facilities – are all areas in which laws could be more supportive of women's equality, autonomy and safety, including the interests of women from widely diverse backgrounds and life experiences. And there are many more areas likewise ripe for revision.

As the editors and several of the contributors note, however, reimagining and rewriting legislation from a feminist perspective is not a simple or straightforward process. First, legislative drafting is a very particular, and peculiar, genre of writing. The translation of feminist ideas into statutory form is even more challenging than translating feminist ideas into the form of a judgment, which engages in a process of reasoning to reach a conclusion on a legal and/or factual question raised in an individual case. A statute, by contrast, expresses a general rule in peremptory terms. How exactly the rule should be expressed so as to achieve the desired object and cover all the circumstances sought to be included, in a way that can be practically applied by courts, administrative actors and ordinary people, is often far from obvious. And in the process of converting an idea into a rule, there is a risk that something important is lost, including nuances, the ability to acknowledge and cater for differences and the original idea's radical or transformative potential. The project could have given up at this point and simply presented the feminist proposals for law reform in themselves, without also including draft Bills, an approach that has been adopted in other projects.[8] It is commendable that the participants in this project set themselves the far harder task of translation. The fact that they may not always have produced a successful translation, or one that satisfies the writer of the commentary on their draft Bill, is therefore not surprising, but even these attempts provide valuable lessons for would-be feminist law reformers.

Secondly, the project participants faced the challenge of how to communicate their outputs, and the reasoning behind them, to a wider audience. Again, this was a more challenging task than was the case in the feminist judgment projects. While a judgment has to use a certain style of argumentation and be based on specific forms of authority, at least it is discursive, has a linear structure and can include a narrative of the facts to draw the reader in and explain the significance of what is being decided. By contrast, a piece of legislation – and especially a piece of amending legislation – has none of these. It is a stark and minimal document, which very often doesn't speak for itself. It refers to something else that is not present: 'Section 41 of *XX Act* is amended as follows. Delete subsection (a), add subsection (ab) etc.' How can a reader make sense of this?

The mechanism adopted by the project has been to provide a Second Reading Speech to accompany and explain each amendment. This is an elegant solution, but it also poses its own challenges. A Second Reading Speech is another particular genre of address which has little in common with the traditional academic essay. So the contributors to this book set themselves the challenge of achieving two different forms of plausibility – a legible draft Bill and an 'authentic' Second Reading Speech. In fact, there is some bending of the conventions of Second Reading Speeches, but this is both understandable and, at times, illuminating in illustrating the difficulties of acknowledging feminist commitments and academic sources in parliamentary speeches.

One of the issues raised in the feminist judgment projects concerned the ethics of decision-making. Writing as an academic brings with it ethical obligations towards other academics (in acknowledging one's reliance on the work of others) and sometimes, when undertaking empirical research, towards the research participants whose experiences have contributed to one's research data. Writing as a judge appears to entail no ethical obligations towards academics (unattributed use of academic work seems to occur quite regularly), although feminist judgments generally have observed those obligations. However, judges do have important ethical obligations to the parties whose cases they are deciding, which feminist judges have taken seriously both in how they write about and address the parties (including losing parties) and in resisting the urge to instrumentalise parties and their cases to make a wider point. There are also ethical considerations towards others similarly – or differently – situated, who might be affected by the judgment. This more extensive ethical obligation is writ large in the case of feminist legislation. The legislator has to think carefully about the potential impacts of their statute, including not just those they intend to benefit, but those who might potentially be impacted negatively, or subject to unintended consequences. Is legislation framed too narrowly or too broadly? Does it go too far or not far enough? Where boundaries are drawn, who is included and who is excluded? In this context, the four ethical principles established by the project organisers to guide the thinking of participants, and described in Chapter 1, are very important. It would be interesting to see such a principled approach being applied in practice in governments' approaches to new policy and legislative initiatives.

Finally, as more general debates within feminist scholarship over the value and limitations of feminist law reform efforts might suggest, imagined feminist legislation is perhaps more open to disagreement or criticism from other feminists than imagined feminist judgments. In feminist judgments, the range of choices open to the feminist judge are generally not wide open. In some cases, it's possible that different feminist positions might yield different outcomes, but in other cases, there's an obvious injustice to be remedied in the particular case, or the facts of the case call forth a particular feminist response. The nature of judgment-writing is also inherently contingent: it's accepted that judges exercise choices, varying judicial views and judicial dissent are accepted, and a judgment is never the last word on anything. The stakes are higher when proposing legislation. Legislation operates at large, the range of choices available to the legislator is unlimited, while the nature of the legislative process means that opportunities for reform might be rare, with correspondingly greater pressure to 'get it right'. This perhaps also helps to explain why commentators take issue with some of the proposals contained in this book.

The fact that feminism is not monolithic, and might construct, analyse and seek to remedy gendered social problems in a variety of ways, could caution against any attempt to frame feminist legislation. Or it could be taken as an invitation for imaginative dialogue and debate which conscientiously grapples with disagreements and tries to reach results that are as well-considered and inclusive as possible. The editors and contributors to this book have taken the latter course, and in doing so, they advance our thinking in valuable ways. I applaud their tenacity and am delighted and grateful that they have made the effort.

Professor Rosemary Hunter KC (Hon)

Rosemary Hunter KC (Hon) is a Professor of Law and Socio-Legal Studies and Head of the Law School at the University of Kent. Professor Hunter's research interests lie broadly in feminist and socio-legal scholarship.

Notes

1 UN Women, 'Facts and Figures: Women's Leadership and Political Participation', *Women's Leadership and Political Participation* (Web Page, 18 September 2023) <https://www.unwomen.org/en/what-we-do/leadership-and-political-participation/facts-and-figures>
2 Australian Human Rights Commission, *Set the Standard: Report on the Independent Review into Commonwealth Parliamentary Workplaces* (Report, November 2021) https://humanrights.gov.au/set-standard-2021 .
3 *Prohibition of Human Cloning for Reproduction and the Regulation of Human Embryo Research Amendment Bill 2006* (Cth).
4 R. Gibson et al., *The Australian Survey of Social Attitudes* (Report, 2004).
5 See, for example, Davina Cooper, 'Crafting Prefigurative Law in Turbulent Times: Decertification, DIY Law Reform, and the Dilemmas of Feminist Prototyping' (2023) 31 *Feminist Legal Studies* 17, 18.
6 See Rosemary Hunter, 'Justice Marcia Neave: Case Study of a Feminist Judge', in Ulrike Schultz and Gisela Shaw (eds), *Gender and Judging* (Hart Publishing, 2013) 399; Rosemary Hunter and Danielle Tyson, 'Justice Betty King: A Study of Feminist Judging in Action' (2017) 40(2) *UNSW Law Journal* 778; Rosemary Hunter, 'Feminist Judging in the "Real World"' (2018) 8(9) *Oñati Socio-Legal Series* 1275; Rosemary Hunter and Erika Rackley, 'Feminist Judgments on the UK Supreme Court' (2020) 32 *Canadian Journal of Women and the Law* 85.
7 Erika Rackley and Rosemary Auchmuty (eds), *Women's Legal Landmarks: Celebrating the History of Women and Law in the UK and Ireland* (Hart Publishing, 2018).
8 See, for example, Peter Goodrich and Thanos Zartaloudis (eds), *The Cabinet of Imaginary Laws* (Routledge, 2021).

Acknowledgements

This book is the product of collective working in the true spirit of feminism: authors, commentators and editors have challenged each other and cheered one another on, all the while supported by friends and colleagues whose labour is largely invisible in this collection, but has made it all possible.

In Australia, it is ethical and just research practice to acknowledge the First Nations' lands that we live and work on. We do this to centre the ongoing impact of colonial structures and dispossession on Aboriginal and Torres Strait Islander peoples. We acknowledge this book was written on the unceded lands of many Aboriginal and Torres Strait Islander peoples across our nation. The editors of this project have worked on Wurundjeri, Bunurong, Boonwurrung and Whadjuk Noongar Country. We are deeply grateful to be able to contribute to the long history of knowledge-sharing on these lands.

In a book looking to reimagine and rewrite laws, we also acknowledge that the First Nations peoples of Australia had a complex system of lore (law) predating colonisation. We pay our respects to those elders – past, present and emerging – who upheld this traditional system of law – 'the lore'. Traditional lore is connected to 'The Dreaming' and provides rules on how to interact with land, kinship and community. This book, and its intention for a feminist rewriting of law, applies to the system of British colonial law brutally imposed on the land that has come to be known as Australia, and its traditional custodians. We acknowledge that this system of colonial law is intimately involved in the generation and exacerbation of inequality and harm for Aboriginal and Torres Strait Islander peoples.

First and foremost, we offer heartfelt thanks to James Dalmau, without whom we could not have completed this project. James generously gave his time and expertise to the project in a personal capacity, initially providing us with training and instructions on how to draft legislation before offering comprehensive, meticulous and enthusiastic feedback on every contribution. It is impossible to put his contribution into words, but we are so grateful this project found a friend and champion in James. If there are any flaws in the laws we have imagined and sought to bring to life, they are ours and ours alone.

As we note in the introductory chapter, the book started out as the brainchild of members of the Feminist Legal Studies Group based at the Faculty of Law at Monash University. The Faculty and University provided us with a rich intellectual environment and financial assistance to establish and run the project, for which we are grateful. As a co-convenor of that group (with Associate Professor Becky Batagol), Associate Professor Janice Richardson provided us with practical and scholarly support, as well as encouragement and ideas throughout the project. We learnt so much from Janice, as well as from our many friends and colleagues who took an interest in the project along the way. Thanks go to all of them, including Professor Patrick Emerton, Associate Professor Faith Gordon, Dr Madeleine Ulbrick, Dr Renata Alexander, Professor Rachael Field, Professor Jennifer Balint, Professor Thalia Anthony, Professor Beth Goldblatt and Associate Professor Linda Steele for coming to our workshops, providing scholarly advice and feedback, and helping to sustain our energies.

We learned so much and were challenged to do so much more by Professor Rosemary Hunter, then Professor of Law and Socio-Legal Studies at Queen Mary University of London (now Head of School at the University of Kent), at our first project workshop with her in October 2017. This project grows from the rich soil of the feminist judgment projects. As an editor of the Australian, UK and New Zealand feminist judgment projects and advisor to many others, Rosemary's involvement at the earliest stages, when we were establishing the boundaries of our project, and at the end, in writing one of the Forewords for this book, provided the personal and intellectual connection to the feminist traditions we are proud to be part of.

We are particularly indebted to Eliza Venville, who provided us with research assistance across the course of this project, helping to bring all aspects of the work together and keep us on track. Mish Freilich provided wonderful administrative support to our project in the early stages.

We are also grateful to Professor Tom Clark of Victoria University, who provided us with training on the history, nature and art of political speechwriting, inspiring us all to experiment with a new genre in the form of Second Reading Speeches.

Thanks also go to Colin Perrin, Naomi Round Cahalin and the entire team at Routledge for their belief in the feminist legislation project and their assistance in bringing it to fruition. We are also grateful to the anonymous peer reviewers for their insights and feedback.

Tim Roberts and Rebecca Wise provided us with excellent editorial and language assistance in preparing the book manuscript for publication.

We are privileged to have benefitted from two wonderful, thought-provoking Forewords from two pioneering women whose work has inspired us: Natasha Stott Despoja AO and Professor Rosemary Hunter. On this note, we also want to recognise participants in the many earlier feminist judgments projects around the world, as well as those working on Indigenous and queer judgments projects, whose imaginative, challenging, and passionate work has kept us motivated and made us hopeful that together we can make better worlds. We also give thanks to the many feminist legal scholars we have met along the way, including those who provided advice and inspiration on our work at conferences, workshops and other events.

Finally, we acknowledge the unbreakable connections between sex, gender and race, and the ways in which different forms of injustice (including those listed here, as well as many others) rely on and shape one another. As we explain in the introductory chapter, the idea for this book first emerged in 2017. As it so happens, two other important things happened that year. First, Australia finally achieved marriage equality after a long battle by LGBTQIA+ communities and a divisive national plebiscite in the form of a postal survey. Australians had been asked whether marriage should still be determined by sex or gender. Although the nation voted to change the law, and reforms quickly followed, both the plebiscite and the ensuing debate highlighted the heteronormative underpinnings and functions of law, and the way different forms of oppression (sex, gender and sexuality) rely on each other for meaning and reinforce one another. In that same year, a group of Aboriginal and Torres Strait Islander people, coming from all points of the land we now call 'Australia', met at Uluru for a historic National Constitutional Convention. There, they considered how we might address the many ways that Aboriginal and Torres Strait Islander people suffer as a legacy of colonisation, including through unacceptably high levels of incarceration, reduced life expectancy, increased infant mortality and more. The result of this historic Convention was the *Uluru Statement from the Heart*: a short but powerful statement which invites Indigenous and non-Indigenous peoples to come together 'in a movement of the Australian people for a better future'. The Statement calls for three things: constitutional reform through an Aboriginal and Torres Strait Islander Voice enshrined in the Constitution, treaty-making and truth-telling. At the time of writing, Australians had just comprehensively rejected a proposal at a Referendum on the first element of the Statement's invitation: constitutional recognition in the form of an Indigenous Voice to Parliament. The nature and tone of the debate was too often shameful and debased, riven with harmful, inaccurate claims about the history of this continent and the reasons why Aboriginal and Torres Strait Islander people suffer extreme, ongoing and in some instances worsening, disadvantage. At times, the debate touched upon issues of significance to women, including those around the role of Aboriginal and Torres Strait Islander mothers, gendered forms of violence, and the gendered effects of colonisation. The debate highlighted the ways that different forms of oppression and injustice intersect with and inform each other, and reminded us of important differences in the experiences of Indigenous and non-Indigenous women.

As Aboriginal and Torres Strait Islander people know all too well, we have a long way to go if we are to fully grapple with and address this country's colonial history. Although at times this book has felt like a long and arduous journey, it pales in comparison to the past 65,000 years of flourishing intergenerational Aboriginal and Torres Strait Islander life and, since colonisation, the fight for recognition, reconciliation and justice.

We therefore want to close by acknowledging the journey for justice among Aboriginal and Torres Strait Islander peoples. We stand in solidarity with you, in the search for a better future.

Becky Batagol, Kate Seear, Heli Askola and Jamie Walvisch

Individual Author Acknowledgments

Professor Jennifer Burn AM: I would like to acknowledge the dedicated team at Anti-Slavery Australia at UTS for their commitment to justice and advocacy for survivors of modern slavery.

James Dalmau: Many thanks to Dr Sophie Yates for her invaluable support.

Dr Kcasey McLoughlin: Thanks to Adrienne Ringin and Sarah Easy for research assistance.

Dr Sean Mulcahy: I acknowledge the many conversations on this issue over many years with the Victorian Pride Lobby, Transgender Victoria, Zoe Belle Gender Collective, Thorne Harbour Health, the Australian Gender Equality Council, WorkSafe Victoria and others. The views expressed in this chapter are my own.

Dr Tania Penovic and Dr Julie Debeljak: We are grateful to James Dalmau for sharing his expertise in statutory drafting and to Becky Batagol, Heli Askola, Kate Seear, Ronli Sifris, Paula Gerber, Charlotte Steer and Jessie Hohman for their helpful comments.

Professor Marilyn Pittard: Thanks to Professor Marian Baird for feedback on an early draft of the chapter.

Dr Ronli Sifris: I am grateful to James Dalmau for sharing his expertise in statutory drafting; to Stephen Page for his subject matter expertise and for providing the commentary for this chapter; and to Jenny Morgan, Marilyn Pittard, Patrick Emerton, Becky Batagol, Kate Seear and Charlotte Steer for their helpful comments.

Dr Ramona Vijeyarasa: Thank you to José-Miguel Bello-Villarino for his feedback on earlier drafts of this chapter.

Table of Amended Legislation

Jurisdiction	*Amended Law*	*Area(s) of Law*	*Chapter(s)*
All Australian jurisdictions	(new model law)	Construction Law Employment Law	17
Commonwealth	*Commonwealth Electoral Act 1918*	Constitutional Law Electoral Law Aboriginal and Torres Strait Islander Peoples and the Law Mental Health Law	4
Commonwealth	*Fair Work Act 2009*	Employment Law	16
Commonwealth	*Family Law Act 1975*	Family Law Alternative Dispute Resolution	13
Commonwealth	*Migration Act 1958*	Migration Law Family Violence Law	14
Commonwealth	*Migration Regulations 1994*	Migration Law Family Violence Law	14
Commonwealth	*Modern Slavery Act 2018*	Human Rights Law Corporations Law Crimes Compensation System	18
Commonwealth	*Social Security Act 1991*	Welfare and Social Security Law	11
Commonwealth	The Constitution of Australia	Constitutional Law Gender Equality	3
New South Wales	(new law)	Older People and the Law Housing Law	15
Queensland	*Criminal Code Act 1899*	Criminal Law Sexual Violence Law	7
Victoria	*Assisted Reproductive Treatment Act 2008*	Health Law Reproductive Law Human Rights Law	8
Victoria	*Building Regulations 2018, Building Code of Australia*	Construction Law Gender Diverse People and the Law Human Rights Law	10

(*Continued*)

Jurisdiction	*Amended Law*	*Area(s) of Law*	*Chapter(s)*
Victoria	*Charter of Human Rights and Responsibilities Act 2006*	Human Rights Law Gender Equality	5, 6
Victoria	*Sentencing Act 1991*	Sentencing Law Criminal Law	12
Western Australia	*Criminal Injuries Compensation Act 2003*	Criminal Law Crimes Compensation System	9

List of Acronyms and Abbreviations

ABS	Australian Bureau of Statistics
ACOSS	Australian Council of Social Services
ACTHRA	*Human Rights Act 2004* (ACT)
ACTU	Australian Council of Trade Unions
AEC	Australian Electoral Commission
AFLP	Australian Feminist Legislation Project
ALHR	Australian Lawyers for Human Rights
ALRC	Australian Law Reform Commission
ANROWS	Australia's National Research Organisation for Women's Safety
BCA	Building Code of Australia
BSR	Business for Social Responsibility
CALD	Culturally and linguistically diverse
CEDAW	Convention on the Elimination of All Forms of Discrimination against Women
CEVAW	Centre for the Elimination of Violence Against Women
CSS	Community Support Services
DDA	*Disability Discrimination Act 1992* (Cth)
FDR	Family Dispute Resolution
FDRP	Family Dispute Resolution Practitioner
FLA	*Family Law Act 1975* (Cth)
GALOP	Gay London Police Monitoring Group
GNTs	Gender-neutral toilets
ICCPR	International Covenant on Civil and Political Rights
ICESCR	International Covenant on Economic, Social and Cultural Rights
IFA	Individual Flexibility Agreements
IFV Panel	Independent Family Violence Panel
IVAWS	International Violence Against Women Survey
IVF	In vitro fertilisation
JJA	Juvenile Justice Authority
LGBTIQ	Lesbian, Gay, Bisexual, Trans and gender diverse, Intersex, Queer and questioning
NAWIC	National Association of Women in Construction

NCAT	NSW Civil and Administrative Tribunal
NES	National Employment Standard
OECD	Organisation for Economic Co-operation and Development
RASARA	Rape and Sexual Assault Research and Advocacy
RIS	Regulatory Impact Statement
STPP	Support for Trafficked People Program
TCF	Textiles, Clothing and Footwear
UKHRA	United Kingdom Human Rights Act 1998
UN	United Nations
UTS	University of Technology Sydney
VLRC	Victorian Law Reform Commission
WIEGO	Women in Informal Employment: Globalising and Organising
YWCA	Young Women's Christian Organisation, now known as YWCA Australia

Part I

The Australian Feminist Legislation Project

Chapter 1

Introducing the Australian Feminist Legislation Project

Kate Seear, Becky Batagol, Jamie Walvisch and Heli Askola

In 2017, members of the Feminist Legal Studies Group met in a chilly conference room at Monash University's Faculty of Law, surrounded by the magnificent banksia drawings of Monash University botanical artist Celia Rosser, and created the world's first feminist legislation project. The group was led by Associate Professors Becky Batagol and Janice Richardson and involved each of the editors of this book. As activist feminist scholars, working on a range of legal issues, and from different theoretical perspectives, we came together to consider what we might be able to contribute to enduring debates about the role of law in women's lives. Taking inspiration from the 'feminist judgments' projects worldwide, we began to wonder whether it might be possible not to rewrite *judgments* from feminist perspectives, but to rewrite legislation, regulations, constitutions and/or treaties from feminist perspectives. Might it be possible, in other words, to imagine a world where laws would be written with a specific focus on benefitting women and people of diverse genders – and could we advance this by actually rewriting legislation ourselves? It was through these discussions that the Australian Feminist Legislation Project (AFLP) was born.

The proposals in this collection draw upon Australian law. Nevertheless, they raise issues that are of international interest and significance. Contributions to this collection touch upon issues that have long been of concern to feminists, including questions about bodily autonomy and integrity, reproductive freedom, rights at work, safer housing, family violence response and prevention and legal accommodations for victims of family violence, and the proper recognition of women's role in caregiving. Even though the precise wording of legislation may differ between jurisdictions, several of the laws being addressed in this collection have similar or nearly identical counterparts in other countries, including other common law and Commonwealth jurisdictions. It is for this reason that the collection will be of interest to those outside Australia. We hope it might help spark other feminist legislation projects around the world.

DOI: 10.4324/9781003372462-2

In this chapter, we set out the processes used to develop and frame the contributions in the AFLP, and other guiding principles, including intersectionality,[1] valuing diverse voices and the use of collaborative approaches. We then set out the structure of the book, outlining the individual chapter contributions and format. We also address some of the complexities and challenges that the project has encountered along the way.

Building on Feminist Judgment Traditions

The AFLP builds on the traditions established in feminist judgment projects conducted around the world in England and Wales,[2] Australia,[3] the United States of America,[4] Northern Ireland and Ireland,[5] New Zealand,[6] Scotland[7] and India;[8] with work also underway in Africa. The feminist judgment projects are diverse, with different origins and motivations. For instance, the Canadian project emerged out of concerns a group of Canadian feminists had shared with each other about how the equality provision in the *Canadian Charter of Rights and Freedoms* was being interpreted by the Canadian Supreme Court. Clear that the Court's decisions were not working for women, and perhaps could or should have been done differently, the group eventually arrived at a question: 'So why don't we show [the Court] how it could have been done, what substantive equality would look like in those cases? Why don't we rewrite these decisions that are so wrong?'[9] The English project had a broader remit. Instead of focusing on Charter rights, as the Canadian project had done, contributors to the English project set out to identify important cases that might have been decided differently if approached from a range of feminist perspectives. The aim of that project was to 'inaugurate a new form of scholarship, one which seeks to demonstrate, in a sustained and disciplined way, how judgments could have been rewritten and cases could have been decided differently'.[10] The Australian Feminist Judgments Project sought to contribute 'an Australian perspective to the growing international literature that investigates the role that feminist legal theory might play in judicial decision-making'.[11] That project comprised a collection of what the editors described as 'alternative' judgments, in which the authors 'imagined the decision and the reasoning that might have been adopted if a feminist judge had heard the case'.[12] Of course, the reasons that these feminist judgments were thought to be needed have been explained in depth by the editors of the various collections we have mentioned. As the editors of the Australian feminist judgments project explained it:

> [F]eminist judgments projects aim to engage with the law as law *reform* projects, by demonstrating the ways decision-makers make choices about how to interpret and apply the law. For instance, the feminist judgments in this collection not only reason from the experience of women, but also importantly unmask seemingly neutral laws and show that prevailing approaches to fact-finding are contingent and often partial.[13]

Importantly, contributors to the various feminist judgments projects around the world have sought to rewrite judgments within certain constraints. For instance, the Australian project invited authors to 'write within the legal genre of decision-making to produce an "authentic" and legally plausible judgment'.[14] The Canadian project adopted similar parameters, so that authors were both 'pushing the law and, at the same time, staying within the limits of the law'.[15] Some of the Aboriginal and Torres Strait Islander authors who contributed to the Australian project 'challenged the Australian common law system as a way of deciding cases and as a genre of writing which is unable to tell their stories appropriately',[16] resulting in variations to the format of judgments that were produced.[17] Subsequently, a collection of Indigenous judgments involving even more critical engagement with the style of judicial decisions has been published.[18] Other emerging judgment projects are questioning formats even more, such as the Queer Judgments Project,[19] which will include opportunities for creative outputs including theatre performances and podcasts.[20]

The feminist judgments projects respond to enduring debates about the role of the law in women's lives.[21] Feminists have long debated questions such as: How can women's lives be made better through law? How can law account for the experiences of gender-diverse people? Is it possible to pursue feminist reform within existing systems, or is a radical remaking of those systems and structures needed?

A Legislative Focus

The AFLP brings together academics, lawyers and activists from across Australia, many of whom have personal experience of the issues under consideration, to amend existing legislation or draft new legislation or constitutional provisions with the explicit aim of supporting the needs and rights of women, non-binary, gender-diverse, intersex and transgender populations. Under the category of 'legislation', the project also includes contributions which amend delegated legislation or regulations, which are executive laws made under the authority of parliamentary statute. Initially, we envisaged that international and bilateral treaties (international agreements concluded between States in written form and governed by international law) would be part of the project, although no contributor in our project focused on treaty law. Contributions to this book span five jurisdictions across the Australian state, territory and Commonwealth (federal) governments.

Our legislative focus is the key departure from the feminist judgments projects. Within common law systems, legislation is an especially powerful site for feminist activism because it is in the parliament that novel proposals for law must emerge. This creates significant transformative potential for feminist legislation projects and gives feminist parliamentarians a magnitude of imaginative freedom denied to feminist judges, who are weighed down by the doctrine of precedent.

We think it is significant that the first feminist legislation project has emerged from Australia. Within the British constitutional tradition largely inherited by Australia, the doctrine of parliamentary sovereignty means that the democratically elected parliament is the location of ultimate decision-making authority in the legal system.[22] In Australia, because there is no national Bill of Rights in the Constitution or statute, feminist activists have historically focused on the legislative arena rather than using strategic litigation as practiced in other countries.[23]

Sceptical Pragmatism

At the nexus of academic work and activism, we position the AFLP within feminist legal theory as an effort of 'sceptical pragmatism'.[24] Armstrong defines sceptical pragmatism as an approach in which feminists are willing to engage with the law and law reform, despite concerns about the latter's risks and limitations. So, as Armstrong explains, sceptical pragmatists:

> . . . share with legal pragmatists an acceptance that law can, and in some instances must, be used in an instrumentalist sense to achieve some broader social goal, or to limit the erosion of existing entitlements, but they are sceptical because they appreciate the political limitations and practical difficulties associated with law reform.[25]

According to this approach, feminists cautiously engage with the legal system, utilising its methods, languages and processes, to demonstrate how gender equality can be achieved through law reform, while remaining simultaneously alert to the limitations of such reforms for radically transforming women's lives.[26] So, instead of *rewriting judicial judgments* with the aim of promoting justice for women and others who might benefit from feminist methods of decision-making, as the feminist judgments projects do, this project seeks to extend the possibility of feminist interventions in law to legislation itself. In this collection, *we amend existing legislation or draft new legislation* based on feminist perspectives and concerns. In essence, the project aims to take us beyond the observation that feminist law reform is needed, by demonstrating 'how feminist law-making can be done'.[27]

Radical Imagination

According to Mary Jane Mossman:

> [I]f feminism has a power to transform the perspective of legal method, it must be because it permits us 'a new way of seeing' both the reality of our present lives and a new way of imagining a better one.[28]

The project uses 'radical imagination' as a tool to catalyse feminist change.[29] This approach has also been called 'prefigurative' law reform, in the same category as youth parliaments, model United Nations assemblies and moot courts.[30] Imagination is a practice which enables us to slip the bonds of the flawed present to create an alternative past, present and future. It is part of the academic activist tradition we have wholeheartedly adopted from the feminist judgment projects.[31] According to Davina Cooper, reimagining 'involves deliberate practices of framing, interpreting, cutting and connection-drawing, as alternative histories and futures get posited'.[32] Radical imagination is a transformative research method, where the researcher must not only observe and report but also awaken, enliven and convoke change.[33] In this way, our work is connected with the broader feminist movement for gender equality.

Like the feminist judgments projects before it, the AFLP 'imaginatively uses the tools of law-making to attempt to transcend many existing limits of law to point the way towards a system that benefits women', and attempts to 'reimagine a world where laws are made specifically to benefit women, rather than placing women in a worse or regressive situation than what they experienced prior to the law's enactment'.[34]

Imaginative practice is an unusual method in academic research. As academics we found ourselves proficient at the critical analyses necessary to identify the problem with current laws, but all struggled to inhabit the voices of lawmakers to reimagine legislation that would address gender-based harm. Each author eventually arrived at their imagined feminist future in their Second Reading Speech and proposed Act by drawing upon past traditions and struggles around gender.

The Feminist Legislation Process

In the first stage of the project, members of the Feminist Legal Studies Group at Monash University's Faculty of Law met to discuss how the project might develop and unfold, and to identify what supports, if any, we might need to pursue our aim of rewriting legislation from feminist perspectives. Rosemary Hunter, then Professor of Law and Socio-Legal Studies at Queen Mary University of London (now Head of School at the University of Kent), and an editor of the Australian, UK and New Zealand feminist judgment projects, joined us for our initial workshop in October 2017 to provide guidance on setting out the parameters of the project.

It quickly became apparent that legislative drafting is a highly specialised legal skill which requires drafters to translate sometimes complex policy considerations and principles into a very specific technical form, comply with conventions of language and statutory interpretation and draft legislation with common law developments in relevant jurisdictions in mind, among other things. The editorial team was extremely fortunate to meet James Dalmau, a highly experienced parliamentary draftsperson, who agreed to volunteer his time to the project and advise us, in a personal capacity, on the practice of legislative drafting. Early in the process, James delivered a workshop on the principles of legislative drafting and offered to review each contribution to the project. James' contributions have been absolutely integral to the development of this collection, helping to ensure that the legislation we have produced conforms to the requirements of statutory drafting including being consistent with contemporary legislative style and demands for clarity. Writing with James, we discuss these various principles and requirements of feminist statutory drafting in more detail in Chapter 2.

A call for contributors was shared initially with scholars (tenured and fixed-term employees and graduate research students) at Monash University and then more widely with Australian feminist scholars through our networks in 2019. We initially envisaged in-person workshops and suggested it was desirable that contributors were Melbourne-based. Each contributor was invited to choose an issue of interest to them, and to identify opportunities for legislative reform.

Enacting Feminisms

Beyond the expectation that relevant reforms would be Australian, contributors were able to identify issues in any area of law that interested them, on any issue they considered feminist. The editors did not seek to define in advance what might make a contribution 'feminist', or to establish other rules about the areas of law that might be considered. As Margaret Davies cautions, it is meaningless to talk about 'feminism' as though it is a single body of thought when the experiences of gender-based harm which inform feminist theory are so disparate.[35] We were open to contributions that might be thought of as controversial from different feminist perspectives, including those proposals' treatment of agency, power or the State. We were also open to proposals that might impact groups differently, including for reasons of sexuality, race or class, or by virtue of being differently abled. Indeed, and as we discovered as the project unfolded, this is a constant tension when it comes to drafting legislation – trying to anticipate the effects of provisions on diverse populations, and how to manage, mitigate or eradicate such effects, including adverse effects, while still ensuring the spirit of the reforms is upheld.

This is a far more complex task than it might seem, and one that we all grappled with as the project unfolded. Recognising these challenges and potential tensions, we asked all authors to consider these possibilities in their work, and to explore ways that these impacts could be minimised (if relevant and possible). We also invited all authors to explicitly engage with any potential controversies in their contributions, and to justify their suggested approach.

To help guide our authors on the complexities and challenges of varied feminist approaches, we developed a set of guiding principles for the project, inviting all contributors to keep these in mind as they devised and revised their reforms. These were as follows:

1. We acknowledge that gender-based harm is not experienced by everybody in the same way.
   We will consider the intersectional impact of our law reform proposals, encompassing the extent to which forms of harm are experienced by or impact people differently, including because of their race, disability, religion, gender, age or other aspect of their being.

2. We recognise that Aboriginal and Torres Strait Islander peoples were the first sovereign Nations of the Australian continent and its adjacent islands, and possessed it under their own laws and customs.
   We will consider the impact of our law reform proposals upon Aboriginal and Torres Strait Islander peoples.

3. We seek to listen to and learn from those with personal experience of gender-based harm.
   Our law reform proposals will respond to those with personal experience of gender-based harm and will strive to incorporate personal experience of gender harm into the feminist lawmaking process.

4. Our work will be gender and trans-inclusive. We know that trans, non-binary, gender-diverse and intersex populations and others across the gender spectrum face high levels of persistent stigma and prejudice, as well as discrimination, overcriminalisation and high rates of violence. We acknowledge that many laws we are concerned with also impact adversely on trans, non-binary, gender-diverse and intersex populations and others across the gender spectrum, and we will consider these issues and explore them wherever relevant.
   We will consider the gender language we use in our law reform proposals and directly address the inclusion of trans, non-binary, gender-diverse and intersex populations and others across the gender spectrum.

These principles have been incorporated into both the methods and output of our project.

Project Methods

The task of each contributor was to *identify* legislation and/or regulations that adversely impact women (including cisgender and trans women), as well as gender diverse, non-binary and intersex people; *do the work* of reforming such legislation; *explain* why reforms are needed; and *describe* why those reforms are 'feminist'.

For each reform proposal, the authors have identified either a particular piece of legislation that needs reform, or a gap in the legislative framework that requires a new law to be written. The resulting contributions range from issues in criminal law (sexual offences, Indigenous women's experiences of criminal law, laws in relation to forced marriage, modern slavery, childcare and sentencing), civil law (aged care and housing rights, regulating the gig economy, surrogacy, gender equity in the construction industry) and constitutional law (equality amendments to the constitution, human rights legislation). Some laws, such as surrogacy, are specifically directed at the experiences of cisgender women (although they can also affect trans men as well as intersex, gender diverse and non-binary people), while others may apply more generally but have a disproportionate impact on women (such as aged care and housing rights).

Each proposal has the same three-part structure: a Second Reading Speech, a proposed Act and a commentary by other expert/s. Chapters have been paired so that the Second Reading Speech and proposed Act appear in a chapter adjacent to the commentary chapter. We developed this structure to replicate the actual process of lawmaking as much as possible. It also mirrors the structure of the feminist judgment projects which enables multiple feminist perspectives on the same law.

All contributors but one situate their reform proposals in 2024, the year this book was published. This demonstrates the immediacy of the problem of gender-based harm under the law and demonstrates how feminist lawmaking can be implemented immediately. One contribution, the *Constitution Alteration (Equality and Diversity) Bill 2048* (Cth) in Chapter 3, has a much later date because to be enacted, it first requires the full implementation of the *Uluru Statement from the Heart* (Voice, Truth and Treaty) across Australia.[36] Our grim assessment is that our nation is not yet ready to realise a racially equal and gender-equal feminist future.

In Chapter 2 we detail the theory and process of drafting feminist statutes.

Feminist Speechmaking

Each Second Reading Speech in our project contains an overview of the proposed reform and the rationale for it in plain language. A Second Reading Speech is given by a member of parliament when a Bill is introduced to the chamber. Its purpose is to summarise the proposed reforms clearly and simply so that they can be understood by non-experts and debated by parliamentarians.

Every participant in this project designed their legislation knowing it would be interpreted against what Margaret Thornton has named the 'androcentric standard'.[37] Each of us faced up to Carol Smart's dilemma, 'the certain knowledge that, once enacted, legislation is in the hands of individuals and agencies far removed from the values and politics of the women's movement'.[38] For this project, we chose to use Second Reading Speeches over 'explanatory memorandums' (which explain the proposed Act in detail, provision-by-provision) because they are more engaging to read. Second Reading Speeches also provide an important feminist interpretative standard in our project because of the critical legal function that such speeches serve in statutory interpretation.[39] In this way, the methodology of our project responds to powerful feminist criticisms of the pointlessness of law reform in an enduringly patriarchal world by providing tools to understand new laws.[40]

As politicians deliver Second Reading Speeches, they often employ rhetorical techniques including repetition. In order to assist us in writing our Second Reading Speeches, Professor Tom Clark of Victoria University delivered a workshop for contributors. He is one of Australia's foremost experts in the analysis of rhetorical and poetic practices in politics, as well as being a professional speechwriter. In this workshop, Tom outlined strategies typically used by politicians to persuade others and appeal to their constituents. Importantly, we encouraged our contributors to try and adopt these rhetorical devices in their chapters, so that the form of their contributions differed from standard academic writing found in journal articles and books.

Two contributions deviate from the parliamentary speech approach. Chapter 3 is a speech to a Women's Constitutional Convention, a meeting which draws on the format established between 1891 and 1898, when the entirely male colonial delegates met in public assembly to frame what would become Australia's Constitution. The Convention debates hold an important function as an interpretive aid to the Constitution and can be used if a High Court of Australia judge adopts an originalist method of constitutional interpretation.[41] Chapter 10 takes the form of a 'Regulatory Impact Statement'. This format is used because the proposed reforms were for regulations accompanying a statute, rather than reforms to the statute itself. Although it is not necessary to generate a Second Reading Speech while reforming regulations, an alternative statement outlining the impact of the proposed regulatory reform is needed in some jurisdictions. This statement is generally sent to Parliament's scrutiny committee and, like the Second Reading Speech, is accessible to members of the public.

In this project, we wanted to model what feminist Second Reading Speeches might look like. We supported gender-inclusive language, while also encouraging contributors to play with their Second Reading Speech formats by using techniques that are not commonly adopted by parliamentarians who deliver such speeches. These techniques included supporting claims through reference to scholarship, activism and direct quotes and accounts from people with personal experience of gender harm.

An especially important aspect of feminist speechmaking in this project is that many of the academics, activists and practitioners making them have personal experience of the gender harm they seek to address. Our project's guiding principles make clear our respect for input from people with personal experience of gender problems, and the vital role they play in legislative and regulatory reform. In some cases, those of us with personal experience of such issues have been willing to identify ourselves as such. Other contributors have personal experience of relevant issues but have chosen not to identify themselves in that way. We acknowledge that identity categories are not binary (i.e. expert/non-expert, or academic/lived experience) and that many people occupy multiple positions at once. We acknowledge and respect the privacy of all our contributors and reiterate the value of disclosure on our own terms.

Feminist Commentaries

We adopted the commentary model from the judgments projects to provide another feminist perspective on each reform. These commentaries include critical reflections on the advantages and disadvantages of the proposed reform, how it will work and any other issues the commentator considers important, such as whether subsequent and related reforms might be needed. Through these commentaries we offer a different and critical perspective on the reform being proposed, in recognition of the diversity of feminist perspectives on both substantive issues and the possibilities of law reform. Many of the commentaries in this book do not support the statute they respond to, demonstrating the breadth of feminist thought represented and accommodated in this volume. Commentaries draw from either personal experience of the relevant gender harm or a different feminist perspective. Some commentators, especially those with personal experience of the problem, have worked with a partner commentator.

Feminist Parliamentary Processes

Feminist legislation requires feminist processes to pass the legislation. In remaking the methods used to create statutes, we were responding to long-standing feminist calls to redefine the methods of law and to challenge the power of law to define and disqualify.[42]

We first imagined us gathering as a feminist parliament, much as the judges of the first judgment project imagined themselves the Women's Court of Canada.[43] However, the advent of the COVID-19 pandemic and the accompanying restrictions implemented across Australia forced us to imagine new ways of working together, at a distance, throughout this project. Because it was not possible to meet in person for the vast majority of the time the project was being progressed, we decided to meet regularly online, through a series of workshops. The need to adapt and work online in this way was a response to significant policy shifts in Australia, including major restrictions on freedom of movement, the imposition of quarantine measures, mask and vaccine mandates and increased policing.[44] All of the editors and many of our contributors were based in Melbourne, Australia during 2020 and 2021. Melbourne residents were subjected to one of the longest and strictest lockdowns in the world, which included restrictions on care and mandated home-schooling of children. These measures have prompted much reflection, including in our own work.[45] It is clear that the pandemic differentially impacted women with children and other caregivers, including as a result of requirements in many parts of the world that children remain at home, and because housework fell disproportionately on women.[46] The contributors to this collection were also significantly affected, often in gendered ways. The COVID-19 prevention measures were thus a tangible example of the way that legislative and regulatory reforms might impact differentially on women, and the challenges that parliaments face when having to consider reforms under time pressures. Such gendered effects might not be anticipated, or known, at the time. This project has thus been a cogent reminder of the challenges of making law in a gender-sensitive way, and of what it is like to experience laws that impact genders differently.

Our hope, then, of gathering as a 'feminist parliament' to workshop our ideas was still realised, but ours became a virtual parliament. In these workshops, all contributors were asked to present drafts of their work and receive feedback, including from our expert draftsperson and other feminists attending. These workshops served several purposes. They helped to ensure quality and consistency across the collection. They also served as an opportunity to share our experiences and knowledge about the drafting process with one another. In addition, they helped to foster collegiality and connectedness at an especially challenging time, and made the project feel like a truly collaborative effort.

Our processes in this project were a site for reflection and imagination about what feminist parliamentary processes might look like. Our first requirement of a feminist parliament was that it would be a safe place for all, especially for women and gender-diverse people. The drafting of our feminist legislation and speechmaking in this project took place in the wake of a major public debate about safety in the Australian Parliament, including after one former Liberal staffer made allegations that she had been sexually assaulted at Australia's Parliament House. The Australian Human Rights Commission later conducted a comprehensive investigation into parliamentary culture which found that '[parliamentary] workplaces are not safe environments for many people within them, largely driven by power imbalances, gender inequality and exclusion and a lack of accountability'.[47] An imagined feminist alternative reality was imperative. We also imagined that feminist parliamentary processes are collaborative rather than adversarial; involve genuine and deep engagement with ideas, as opposed to political partisanship; and are sustained by mentorship and solidarity. Feminist parliamentary processes also involve the courage to go beyond what is or what might seem possible, and require us to imagine futures where we actively bring to life that which has been largely perceived as unattainable until now. The guiding principles of this project reflect our ideas of a feminist parliament.

We would recommend that future feminist legislation projects adopt a similar workshop model, as much can be learned from sharing lessons with one another.

The Reforms

The book is divided into six Parts. Part 1 sets out the parameters of the project. As well as providing a unifying structure for the collection, we anticipate that this Part will be of great interest to readers who may be contemplating feminist legislation projects of their own.

Parts 2 to 6 of the book contain its law reform contributions. Rather than organising these reforms by areas of law, we group the contributions by a series of key themes that tie the collection together (while recognising some overlap between them). In setting out the collection in this way, we aim to shift the focus of readers from specific areas of law that need reform to problems *in* and *of* law, including the way the law handles bodies, sex and agency, or the law's role in facilitating or exacerbating gender-based dependence and independence.

Part 1: The Australian Feminist Legislation Project

This opening Part contains two chapters which document the theoretical inspirations for the book; our methods; key practical, political and methodological considerations and challenges; and principles of legislative drafting.

Chapter 2 sets out the principles of feminist statutory drafting. In writing this chapter, the editors are joined by James Dalmau, whose contribution is to write about the theory of statutory drafting and our practices in this project. A particular challenge that we encountered was how to draft laws that are 'feminist' enough. This chapter draws from both the theory and practice of statutory drafting, alongside our experiences of drafting legislation for the AFLP, to develop a set of principles and practices that are part of feminist statutory drafting.

Part 2: Constitutions, Institutions and Rights

Part 2 contains four proposed laws and focuses on realising fundamental rights for diverse women and those who experience gender-based harm. Each Bill recognises the complexity of women's lives and dismantles the structures of their subordination embedded in our foundational legal documents and institutions.

Chapter 3, by Kcasey McLoughlin and Yee-Fui Ng, proposes amendments to Australia's national Constitution to ambitiously reimagine representative democracy by altering the preamble, creating a right to equality, and requiring gender, sexual and race equality in all branches of federal government. Their Bill could only be passed after the Voice, Treaty and Truth aspects of the aforementioned 2017 *Uluru Statement from the Heart* has been implemented. Commentary on the proposal by Margaret Thornton in Chapter 3A critiques McLoughlin and Ng's constitutional amendment, raising the imperative of guidance for positive interpretation by judges.

Chapter 4, by Dani Linder, a Bundjalung, Kungarykany woman, focuses on the disenfranchisement of imprisoned Aboriginal women. The chapter proposes amendments to the provisions of the *Commonwealth Electoral Act 1918* (Cth) that disqualify electors from enrolling and voting at Commonwealth elections if they are prisoners serving a lengthy term of imprisonment or are deemed to be of 'unsound mind'. The accompanying commentary in Chapter 4A is provided by Krystal Lockwood, a Gumbaynggirr and Dunghutti woman, who focuses on the potential practical application of such proposed amendments from an informed Aboriginal woman's perspective.

Chapters 5 and 6, which are co-authored by Tania Penovic and Julie Debeljak, contain intertwined laws which aim to incorporate gender considerations into the application of human rights in the first Charter of Rights to be enacted by an Australian state parliament, the Victorian *Charter of Human Rights and Responsibilities Act 2006* (the '*Charter*'). In Chapter 5, led by Penovic, the *Charter of Human Rights and Responsibilities (Advancing Equality) Amendment Bill 2024* (Vic) will repeal provisions which undermine equality in the *Charter* and will introduce a number of new rights, alongside interpretive aids that embed a gender perspective into the examination of the scope of rights. The accompanying commentary in Chapter 5A, by Kate Eastman AM SC, argues that the reform fulfils the aims of the *Charter* for transformative equality by recognising the need to combat structural gender inequality and intersectional discrimination. Chapter 6, led by Debeljak, contains the *Charter of Human Rights and Responsibilities (Advancing Enforcement) Amendment Bill 2024* (Vic). In order to improve access to justice for women, this Bill will amend the *Charter* to clarify and strengthen its two main enforcement mechanisms: rights-compatibility of legislation and obligations of public authorities. This reform is considered in Chapter 6A by Pamela Tate AM KC, who argues that the focus on human rights enforcement is crucial for attainment of gender-specific rights.

Part 3: Bodies, sex and agency

Part 3 contains four proposed laws on the theme of 'bodies, sex and agency'. The chapters create new solutions for old problems around legal control of the bodies of women and gender-diverse people, including approaches that challenge myths about rape, agency, responsibility and autonomy. The statutes and regulations address gendered rape and violence myths which enable gender-based harm (Chapters 7 and 9); they provide women and those with a uterus with the agency to profit from their own labour and pregnancy (Chapter 8); they prevent gendered financial penalties for victims of violent crime (Chapter 9) and they require action to reduce discrimination against gender-diverse people (Chapter 10).

In Chapter 7, Jon Crowe, Asher Flynn and Bri Lee present the *Criminal Code Amendment (Sexual Offences) Bill 2024* (Qld), which will introduce an affirmative consent model law for sexual offences in the State of Queensland. Their reforms will better recognise the personal experience of rape and sexual assault victims, and respond to changing attitudes towards what constitutes appropriate and respectful sexual relations. The powerful commentary in Chapter 7A, from victim-survivors Saxon Mullins and Rachael Burgin, praises the reforms for their clarity and simplicity in removing the mistake of fact excuse in relation to consent (where the accused failed to 'check in' with the other person(s) to ensure they were consenting).

In Chapter 8, Ronli Sifris proposes to amend section 44 of the *Assisted Reproductive Treatment Act 2008* (Vic), to permit payments to surrogates to ensure they are compensated fairly for the reproductive labour inherent in gestating and birthing a child in the State of Victoria. The commentary in Chapter 8A by Stephen Page supports the amendments because they remove an exploitative attitude to surrogates, particularly in circumstances where all of the other professionals involved are compensated.

In Chapter 9, Kate Seear, Jamie Walvisch and Liza Miller aim to amend section 41 of the *Criminal Injuries Compensation Act 2003* (WA), to expressly prevent decision-makers from taking the conduct of a victim of crime into account when deciding whether to provide statutory compensation in Western Australia. The amendment is intended to demonstrate that groups such as women, Indigenous peoples and LGBTIQA+ populations are not responsible for the violence perpetrated against them. The commentary in Chapter 9A by Jenny Morgan focuses on victim-blaming in crimes compensation decision-making and the difficulty of drafting legislation that could remove misogynistic practices from legal processes.

In Chapter 10, Sean Mulcahy amends the *Building Amendment (National Construction Code Variations – Sanitary and Other Facilities) Regulations 2024* (Vic) to require all gender toilets in certain public buildings, including offices, department stores, shopping centres, restaurants, cafes, bars and similar buildings. In the collection's only regulatory impact statement, Mulcahy argues the change will reduce discrimination against gender-diverse people, who identify outside of the gender binary of female and male, and improve their health, safety, wellbeing, comfort and physical independence without reducing toilets for women and men. Nicole Kalms and Laura McVey's commentary in Chapter 10A challenges the new regulations for further privileging 'default male' needs, and puts forward an alternate needs-based approach for greater inclusion in the design and provisioning of public sanitary facilities.

Part 4: Caring, Dependents and In/dependence

Part 4 of the book focuses on the theme of 'caring, dependents and in/dependence'. The two proposed laws in this Part address inequalities in 'gender-neutral' laws that disproportionately affect women through caregiving.

In Chapter 11, Olivia Rundle, drawing on her own experience as a partnered recipient of a parenting payment, presents the federal *Social Security Amendment (Fair and Equal Treatment No 1 – Parenting Payment) Bill 2024* (Cth), which will remove the distinction between social security parenting payment applicants according to their relationship status as 'single' or a member of a 'couple'. This reform will address inequities, particularly for women, who are statistically most likely to be primary carers and reliant upon social security and/or financial support from a partner, and will support healthy relationships through reducing the risk of financial abuse. The commentary in Chapter 11A by Lyndal Sleep provides a historically contextualised and personal experience-informed critique of the couple rule while supporting its abolition.

In Chapter 12, Natalia Antolak-Saper presents the *Sentencing (Reducing Women in Custody) Bill 2024* (Vic), which moves beyond seemingly 'gender-neutral' sentencing laws to recognise the distinct needs of women involved in the criminal justice system. The amendments will introduce a presumption against sentences of imprisonment of 12 months or less and require courts to account for the likely impact of a sentence on the offender's dependent children. The commentary in Chapter 12A by Arlie Loughnan welcomes the Bill as a satisfactory middle ground between pragmatism and creativity, noting multiple failings of the criminal justice system for women and suggesting that more radical change would involve abolition or a wholesale shift from retribution to rehabilitation.

Part 5: Diversity, Dignity and Autonomy

Part 5 of the book contains three proposed statutes on the themes of 'diversity, dignity and autonomy', addressing multiple specific harms caused by the intersection of gender and personal attributes such as race and cultural background, religion, immigration status and older age. The proposed legislation offers autonomy and dignity to women and those who experience gender harm after separation, as migrants and aged care residents.

In Chapter 13, Amira Aftab offers the federal *Family Law (Family Dispute Resolution) Amendment Bill 2024* (Cth), to introduce a more culturally and religiously sensitive family dispute resolution process after separation for women from culturally and linguistically diverse backgrounds. In Chapter

13A, Balawyn Jones supports the inclusion of cultural and/or religious advisors in dispute resolution because they will challenge the 'neutrality' of mediation, a concept which is built on a presumption of 'whiteness' and value-laden cultural imperialism.

In Chapter 14, Heli Askola proposes another federal law, the *Migration Amendment (Preventing and Responding to Family Violence) Bill 2024* (Cth), to improve immigrant women's safety by ensuring that survivors of family violence are able to maintain legal residence in Australia even if they leave violent partners. The Bill also clarifies that forced marriage and dowry-related economic abuse constitute family violence in the migration context, requiring action to protect the survivors of such practices from loss of residency rights. In Chapter 14A, Susan Kneebone supports the proposed legislative and regulatory reforms because they recognise the reality of female migration and guard against double-exploitation of female migrants at the hands of both the State and their intimates, partners, families and communities.

In Chapter 15, Charlotte Steer moves the *Aged Care Rights Bill 2024* (NSW) to give aged care residents, who are most likely to be women, the same enforceable tribunal remedies as those who live in retirement villages, caravan parks, boarding houses, strata title and residential tenancies. This would enhance and protect the human dignity of older people, as envisaged under the proposed United Nations Convention on the Rights of Older Persons. The accompanying commentary in Chapter 15A by Nola Ries and Jessie Hohmann commends the Act for offering achievable law reform based on a model of dignity, autonomy and agency, but notes that many of the structural issues that lie behind poor care and conditions in residential aged care will not be addressed.

Part 6: Work, Exploitation and Power

In the final Part of the book, the reform Bills explore a series of important questions pertaining to 'work, exploitation and power'. Each draft statute presented in this section harnesses the power of the State to enhance the lives of those who work for, and whose work is used by, Australian businesses, especially women and those who experience gender harm.

In Chapter 16, Marilyn Pittard proposes to enable flexible work though the federal *Fair Work Act Amendment Bill 2024* (Cth) to provide a right to work from home and a right to 'disconnect' from the workplace after working hours. This will benefit employees with caring roles, who are most likely to be women. The commentary in Chapter 16A by Alexandra Heron welcomes the advent of flexible work rights but queries how the reforms will change resistant workplace cultures.

In Chapter 17, Paula Gerber and Rebecca Dickson address the longstanding problem of gender inequity in the Australian construction industries. The lack of female participation in these industries has long been seen as an issue that the private sector should address. However, recent data show that female participation rates in construction are going backwards, and that a hands-off approach by government is not working. Theirs is a model Bill (the only one in this collection) known as the *Gender Equity (Increasing Female Participation) Bill 2024* (Cth). It provides ambitious quotas for female participation that all contractors seeking to work on government projects must meet, and a strict compliance regime to ensure that the goal is achieved. The commentary in Chapter 17A by Valerie Francis is broadly supportive of the Bill, but raises important questions, including possible unintended consequences and timelines for implementation. Francis also asks whether it should be expanded to other sectors.

In Chapter 18, the final feminist legislation of the collection, Ramona Vijeyarasa moves the federal *Modern Slavery Amendment (Exploitation in the Supply Chain) Bill 2024* (Cth). This Bill amends the recent gender-blind national modern slavery laws to require medium- and large-scale companies to conduct gender-sensitive due diligence on risks of exploitation in their supply chains, as well as to collect gender-disaggregated data. The proposed Act establishes a robust accountability mechanism that will both catalyse a response by businesses and provide a redress mechanism for victims in recognition of their human rights violations. The commentary in Chapter 18A by Jennifer Burn AM supports the new modern slavery law for its ambition and practicality. Burn focuses on the advent of the national compensation scheme in the Act, which provides direct redress for individuals affected by exploitation.

Impact

As an act of feminist sceptical pragmatism, we intended that this project should demonstrate how feminist law reform can be done. By drafting Bills that are legally plausible at the same time as being socially ambitious, we intend that the reforms in this book can easily be adopted, complete with legislative provisions and a Second Reading Speech. This is our way of stepping off campus and catalysing feminist change.

The project has had an impact even prior to publication of this book, with several contributors having the opportunity to either share their work with legislators and policymakers, or to adopt the lessons from the project to provide guidance on other possibilities for feminist legislation that were not included in this collection. For example:

- In 2023, Becky Batagol, with her Monash colleague Dr Jess Mant, were approached by Zoe Daniel, the federal independent Member of Parliament for the seat of Goldstein, to write a Second Reading Speech for a major family law reform Bill that subsequently passed the Commonwealth Parliament.[48] Daniel MP's speech to the House of Representatives, along with the amendments proposed, all written by Batagol and Mant, followed the feminist speechmaking approach used in this book and adhered to each of the four guiding principles for the project.[49] This experience shows us that the feminist approach developed in this project will work in practice.

- Also in 2023, Sean Mulcahy's work (detailed in Chapter 10) was considered by WorkSafe Victoria in the development of its *Workplace Facilities and the Working Environment Compliance Code*,[50] which was published in December 2023. It has also been considered by Latrobe City Council in the development of its *Public Toilet Action Plan*.[51]
- Also in 2023, Julie Debeljak made a submission to the Commonwealth Joint Committee Inquiry into Australia's Human Rights Framework, drawing on the thinking behind her collaborations with Tania Penovic, appearing as Chapters 5 and 6 of this collection. At the time of writing this introductory chapter, the Committee's work was ongoing.
- An earlier version of the Bill drafted by Jon Crowe, Asher Flynn and Bri Lee for this project (later adapted to the version that appears in Chapter 7 of this book) was moved in the Queensland Parliament by Amy MacMahon MLA of the Greens in March 2021 (but defeated along party lines).

Conclusion

Our hope is that this collection will change not just legislation, but also the process of *making* legislation. We think that it will be of interest to policymakers, legislators, academics, students and people with personal experience of gender harm, both within and outside Australia. Although it focuses on domestic laws specific to Australia, the contributions touch upon longstanding debates and issues that have resonance far beyond our jurisdiction. Even though the precise wording of legislation that we are addressing in this collection may differ between jurisdictions, several of the laws we consider have similar or nearly identical counterparts in other countries, including other common law and Commonwealth jurisdictions.

The book speaks directly to the challenges of feminist law reform worldwide and invites and includes reflections on the possibilities for more feminist futures.

Notes

1 Following Kimberlé Crenshaw, 'Demarginalizing the Intersection of Race and Sex: A Black Feminist Critique of Antidiscrimination Doctrine, Feminist Theory and Antiracist Politics' (1989) 1(8) *University of Chicago Legal Forum* 139.

2 Rosemary Hunter et al. (eds), *Feminist Judgments: From Theory to Practice* (Hart Publishing, 2012).

3 Heather Douglas, Francesca Bartlett, Trish Luker and Rosemary Hunter (eds), *Australian Feminist Judgments: Righting and Rewriting Law* (Hart Publishing, 2014).

4 Kathryn Stanchi et al., *Feminist Judgments: Rewritten Opinions of the United States Supreme Court* (Cambridge University Press, 2016).
5 Máiréad Enright et al., *Northern/Irish Feminist Judgments: Judges' Troubles and the Gendered Politics of Identity* (Bloomsbury Publishing, 2017).
6 Elizabeth McDonald et al., *Feminist Judgments of Aotearoa New Zealand: Te Rino; A Two-Stranded Rope* (Bloomsbury Publishing, 2017).
7 Sharon Cowan et al., *Scottish Feminist Judgments: (Re)Creating Law from the Outside In* (Bloomsbury Publishing, 2019).
8 Aparna Chandra et al., 'Introduction: the Indian Feminist Judgments Project', *Indian Law Review* (2021) 5(3) 261.
9 Diana Majury, 'Introducing the Women's Court of Canada', *Canadian Journal of Women and the Law* (2006) 18, at 2.
10 Hunter et al. (n 2) 3.
11 Douglas et al. (n 3) 1.
12 Ibid.
13 Ibid 8, original emphasis.
14 Ibid 1.
15 Majury (n 9) 10.
16 Douglas et al. (n 3) 1.
17 H Loban, 'Australian Competition and Consumer Commission v Ramon Lal Keshow: Judgment', in H Douglas et al (eds), *Australian Feminist Judgments: Righting and Rewriting Law* (Hart Publishing, 2014) 180–7; Irene Watson, 'First Nations Stories, Grandmother's Law: Too Many Stories to Tell', in Douglas, Bartlett, Luker and Hunter (n 3) 46–53; Nicole Watson, 'In the Matter of Djappari (Re Tuckiar): Judgment', in Douglas et al. (n 3) 442, 451.
18 Nicole Watson and Heather Douglas, *Indigenous Legal Judgments: Bringing Indigenous Voices into Judicial Decision Making* (Routledge, 2021).
19 See: https://www.queerjudgments.org.
20 The Scottish Feminist Judgments project invited visual artists to participate to show how 'non textual and non academic images and interpretations of legal processes and decisions can help us understand the power and reach of law, as well as its ethical impact.' *Artists – Scottish Feminist Judgments Project* (Web Page), https://www.sfjp.law.ed.ac.uk/artists/.
21 See, for example, Moya Lloyd, '(Women's) Human Rights: Paradoxes and Possibilities' (2007) 33(1) *Review of International Studies* 91–103; Regina Graycar and Jenny Morgan, *The Hidden Gender of Law* (Federation Press, 2002); Inderpal Grewal, 'Women's Rights as Human Rights: Feminist Practices, Global Feminism, and Human Rights Regimes in Transnationality' (1999) 3(3) *Citizenship Studies* 337–54; Joan Wallach Scott, *Only Paradoxes to Offer: French Feminists and the Rights of Man* (Harvard University Press, 1996); Wendy Brown, *States of Injury: Power and Freedom in Late Modernity* (Princeton University Press, 1995); Hilary Charlesworth, 'What are "Women's International Human Rights"?' in Rebecca Cook (ed), *Human Rights of Women: National and International Perspectives* (University of Pennsylvania Press, 1994) 58–84; Adetoun O Ilumoka, 'African Women's Economic, Social, and Cultural Rights – Toward a Relevant Theory and Practice', in Rebecca Cook (ed), *Human Rights of Women: National and International Perspectives* (University of Pennsylvania Press, 1994) 307–25; Catharine A MacKinnon, *Toward a Feminist Theory of the State* (Harvard University Press, 1989); Carol Smart, *Feminism and the Power of Law* (Routledge, 1989); Margaret Thornton, 'Feminist Jurisprudence: Illusion or Reality' (1986) 3 *Australian Journal of Law & Society* 5–29.
22 Jeffrey Goldsworthy, *The Sovereignty of Parliament: History and Philosophy* (Oxford University Press, 2001) 3.

23 Graycar and Morgan (n 21) 442.
24 Following Susan M Armstrong, 'Is Feminist Law Reform Flawed? Abstentionists and Sceptics' (2004) 20(1) *Australian Feminist Law Journal* 43, 50.
25 Ibid 44.
26 Enright and colleagues describe a similar approach in the feminist law reform work of a group of Northern Ireland abortion activists who engaged in law reform 'tinged with irreverence for law and for state power': Mairead Enright, Kathryn McNeilly and Fiona de Londras, 'Abortion Activism, Legal Change, and Taking Feminist Law Work Seriously' (2020) 71(3) *Northern Ireland Legal Quarterly* 359, 369.
27 Becky Batagol and Ramona Vijeyarasa, 'Lighting the Spark: Reimagining the Statutory Landscape through the Feminist Legislation Project', in Ramona Vijeyarasa (ed), *International Women's Rights Law and Gender Equality: Making the Law Work for Women* (Routledge, 2021) 189.
28 Mary Jane Mossman, 'Feminism and Legal Method: The Difference It Makes' (1986) 3 *Australian Journal of Law and Society* 30, 48.
29 Max Haiven and Alex Khasnabish, *The Radical Imagination: Social Movement Research in the Age of Austerity* (Zed Books, 2014).
30 Davina Cooper and Flora Renz, 'Introduction to Special Issue: Decertifying Legal Sex—Prefigurative Law Reform and the Future of Legal Gender' (2023) 31 *Feminist Legal Studies* 1, 12.
31 Rosemary Hunter et al., 'Feminist Judgments: An Introduction' in Hunter, McGlynn and Rackley (n 2) 8.
32 Davina Cooper, 'Introduction' in Davina Cooper et al (eds), *Reimagining the State: Theoretical Challenges and Transformative Possibilities* (Taylor & Francis Group, 2019) 1, 2.
33 Max Haiven and Alex Khasnabish, *The Radical Imagination: Social Movement Research in the Age of Austerity* (Zed Books, 2014) 2.
34 Batagol and Vijeyarasa (n 27) 194.
35 Margaret Davies, *Asking the Law Question* (Thomson Reuters, 4th ed, 2017) 233.
36 The *Uluru Statement From the Heart* is an 'invitation to the Australian people from First Nations Australians' to participate in processes of reconciliation, truth-telling and treaty-making. The Statement is a consensus statement generated through the National First Nations Constitutional Convention held at Uluru, and contains a call for: an Indigenous Voice to Parliament to be enshrined in the Australian Constitution; followed by Treaty; and processes of truth-telling. For more on the Statement and the components of the invitation, see https://ulurustatement.org/the-statement. At the time of writing this chapter, Australia had just rejected a law reform proposal in a national Referendum to enshrine a Voice to Parliament in the Constitution.
37 Thornton (n 21) 9.
38 Smart (n 21) 164.
39 Eg *Acts Interpretation Act 1901* (Cth) s15AB(2)(f); *Interpretation of Legislation Act 1984* (Vic) s 35(b)(ii).
40 Smart (n 21) 160.
41 Gregory Craven 'Convention Debates' in Michael Coper, Tony Blackshield and George Williams (eds), *The Oxford Companion to the High Court of Australia* (Oxford University Press, 2001).
42 Mossman (n 28) 44–8; Smart (n 21) 165.
43 Majury (n 9).
44 Deborah Lupton, 'Special Section on "Sociology and the Coronavirus (COVID-19) Pandemic"' (2020) 29(2) *Health Sociology Review* 111–12.

45 Heli Askola, 'A Proportionate Response is the Maximal One? Economic and Social Rights During the Pandemic' (2022) 28(1) *Australian Journal of Human Rights* 118–38; Kay Tucker and Becky Batagol, 'Pandemic Pressures in Universities and their Libraries: A View from Australia' (2021) 21(3–4) *Legal Information Management* 129–45; Robin Banks, 'Australia's Human Rights Challenges in the Face of COVID-19' in Paula Gerber and Melissa Castan (eds), *Critical Perspectives on Human Rights Law in Australia, Volume 2* (Thomson Reuters, 2021) 17–61); Sarah Joseph, 'International Human Rights Law and the Response to the COVID-19 Pandemic' (2020) 11(2) *Journal of International Humanitarian Legal Studies* 249–69.

46 Lyn Craig and Brendan Churchill, 'Working and Caring at Home: Gender Differences in the Effects of Covid-19 on Paid and Unpaid Labor in Australia' (2021) 27(1–2) *Feminist Economics* 310–26; T Murat Yildirim and Hande Eslen-Ziya, 'The Differential Impact of COVID-19 on the Work Conditions of Women and Men Academics During Lockdown (2021) 28(S1) *Gender, Work and Organization* 243–49; Nalia Kabeer, Shahra Razavi and Yana van der Meulen Rodgers, 'Feminist Economic Perspectives on the COVID-19 Pandemic' (2021) 27(1–2) *Feminist Economics* 1–29.

47 Australian Human Rights Commission, *Set the Standard: Report on the Independent Review into Commonwealth Parliamentary Workplaces* (Report, 2021) 8.

48 *Family Law Amendment Act 2023* (Cth).

49 Commonwealth of Australia, *Parliamentary Debates*, House of Representatives, 10 May 2023, 3054–6 (Zoe Daniel, MP).

50 https://content-v2.api.worksafe.vic.gov.au/sites/default/files/2023-12/Compliance-code-Workplace-facilities-working-environment-2023-12.pdf.

51 https://yoursay.latrobe.vic.gov.au/toilets.

Chapter 2

Feminist Statutory Drafting

Becky Batagol, James Dalmau, Heli Askola, Kate Seear and Jamie Walvisch

Introduction

Feminist statutory drafting must come before feminist legislation. When we set out to investigate how to draft legislation according to feminist principles, we found excellent work on statutory drafting generally, as well as on feminist judging and feminist statutory interpretation, drawing from the feminist judgments projects.[1] Surprisingly, however, we found little work specifically focusing on feminist approaches to writing legislation.[2] This chapter aims to fill that gap, drawing on feminist theory, the theory and practice of statutory drafting and our experiences of drafting legislation for the Australian Feminist Legislation Project (AFLP), to develop a set of principles and practices for what we call *feminist statutory drafting*.

Legislative language, and the process of writing, applying and interpreting it, has been extensively criticised by many feminists.[3] Behind the feminist concern with legal language is an understanding of the gendered and harmful impact of law, as Mary Jane Mossman explains:

> the issue of non-discriminatory language in law needs to be understood in the context of power: power which is revealed in the relative access of women and men to leadership positions in law, in the subtle use of pictures which devalue women in legal and other publications, and in the patterns of speech of members of the legal profession which may undermine women's voices and fail to understand their experiences of harm.[4]

It is essential that we 'confront the reality that gender and power are inextricably linked'.[5] Accounting for gender in the legislative drafting process is thus key to realising equality before the law.[6] As we explain in Chapter 1, our aim in the AFLP was to produce socially ambitious but legally plausible Bills. We therefore needed to employ the conventions and practices of the highly specialised field of statutory drafting, while considering any additional (specifically feminist) principles of statutory drafting. In turn, feminist approaches to *statutory drafting* are informed by biased practices of judicial

DOI: 10.4324/9781003372462-3

statutory interpretation that have systematically disadvantaged women and those who experience gender harm, whether through increasing legislation's penal or pecuniary burdens on women or reducing its pecuniary or property benefit for them.[7] Every AFLP author drafted their Bill with the problem of patriarchal interpretation and adoption of the laws in mind.

This chapter commences by examining the task of legislative drafting, including the need for specificity and consistency. It then sets out the key challenges around statutory drafting identified by the project along with our responses to these, guided by James Dalmau, the technical advisor who assisted with legislative drafting.[8] Next, the chapter distils key messages from contributors' drafting experiences to develop a set of principles and practices for feminist statutory drafting. Our principles connect the plain language movement to feminist law reform efforts, maintaining that law reform efforts must be intelligible to a wide range of audiences in order to be effective. We also canvass the history and debates around gender and statutory drafting, including debates surrounding gender-neutral, gender-silent and gender-specific legislation, arguing that inclusive feminist drafting practices might use either 'gender-silent' or 'gender-specific' language. Finally, the chapter explores three specific feminist drafting techniques which pre-emptively strike against patriarchal statutory interpretation. Overall, the chapter aims to lay bare the process and methods utilised across the collection and provide guidance for future feminist legislation projects globally. We encourage others to analyse, critique and build on these non-exhaustive principles in their own work in the years ahead.

The Nature, Practices and Principles of Statutory Drafting

At its simplest, the purpose of legislation is 'to alter the law'.[9] Legislative drafting involves 'the crystallization and expression in definitive form of a legal right, privilege, function, duty, status or disposition'.[10] Legislation is not about identifying outcomes to which a legislator aspires, but about making specific changes to governing legal rules with the expectation that these changes will move us closer to a desired social goal. Recognising that it is the words of an Act that control human behaviour, and not the words of the Minister who proposed the legislation, we need to keep in mind that legislation 'outlasts and makes legally irrelevant all parliamentary debate'.[11]

Legislative drafting involves highly specific legal skills, different from those typically possessed by legal academics, barristers, solicitors or judges. The orthodox position is that legislative drafters should be trained on the job using an apprenticeship model,[12] and that producing competent autonomous drafters takes five to ten years.[13] Trained drafters must become familiar with a jurisdiction's statute book, adept at expressing legal rules clearly and precisely while being skilled at statutory interpretation. Legislation should ideally be simple, precise and logically organised. Crucially, legislation should be written for the least charitable reader. Several writers trace this idea back to *Re Castioni* (1891) 1 QB 167 (or at least explain it by reference to that case), where it was said that:

> It is not enough [for the drafter] to attain a degree of precision which a person reading in good faith can understand, but it is necessary to attain if possible to a degree of precision which a person reading in bad faith cannot misunderstand. It is all better if he [sic] cannot pretend to misunderstand it.[14]

Legislative drafters also need to ensure consistency within the statute being amended, and the jurisdiction's statute law more generally. For this reason, it is often said that drafters are 'guardians of the statute book'.[15] So, 'each new change in the law has to be meticulously knitted into the existing fabric'.[16] It is not enough to derive a form of words reflecting the desired change to the law, and to identify a place in the statute to put it. It is necessary to see whether any of the ideas embodied in those words are expressed differently in other parts of the statute. If they are, it is generally preferable to adopt and integrate the existing formulation. This is because a 'different way of expressing similar ideas risks being treated by courts [. . .] as creating a different meaning, especially in common law jurisdictions where precedent is king'.[17]

For all of these reasons, legislative drafting is best understood as a complex and highly skilled enterprise requiring extensive legal knowledge, generally involving input from multiple actors. For instance, in the Australian state of New South Wales, the drafting process typically unfolds as follows: a Minister decides to procure new legislation, submissions to Cabinet are prepared, Cabinet deliberations occur and Parliamentary Counsel is then instructed to draft the Bill. Public servants are involved throughout.[18] Staff will variously: brief the Minister on available options, provide drafters with instructions and distribute drafts for consultation (both within Government and externally). Drafts of legislation typically involve several drafters. Put simply, 'no *one* drafter ever produces a piece of legislation; a robust system of peer review and revision is often involved'.[19]

Built into this process is a distinction between 'policy thinking' and 'legal thinking';[20] the former undertaken by those with responsibility for policy, and the latter by those with responsibility for drafting. These are different exercises, requiring different skills. And they work best in dialogue with each other, with the back-and-forth between drafters and officials ideally leading to better, clearer, more refined policy outcomes.[21] Typically, this process also involves negotiation and the balancing of political objectives and legislative possibilities.[22] Consequently, according to the prevailing view and practical orthodoxy, those who determine policy should be separate from those who draft the law.[23] However, this is not quite so straightforward in practice, with the division between drafting and policy often blurred.

The Challenge of Statutory Drafting in the Australian Feminist Legislation Project

This project's aim – to produce hypothetical but legally plausible legislation – immediately emerged as ambitious: first, because the authors were entering into this endeavour without the established institutional frameworks and teams that typically facilitate legislative development; and second, because the project merged the usually separate roles of policymaker and legislative drafter. As Emily Grabham points out, in a feminist project, there may be considerable power in occupying both the legislative policy and drafting roles simultaneously.[24] While it is unusual to merge these divided roles, the division itself is not absolute or uncontroversial. There are two bases for seeing the boundary between these roles as being at least somewhat porous. The first concerns the nature of the drafting task, which it has been suggested 'is inherently political [and] inescapably demands policy choices by drafters'.[25] Indeed, drafters have a responsibility to shape policy so that it conforms to the rule of law.[26] In addition, it has been noted that legislative drafters are often affected by political realities.[27] They craft Bills with an eye to political exigencies, reflecting the political compromises that are thought to be necessary to ensure they will actually pass into law.

A more modest view is that drafters have a role in developing policy, but not in initiating or dictating it,[28] or originating or determining it;[29] they also 'must take every precaution against the unwelcome injection of [their] own views into the policy features of the Bill'.[30] George Tanner indicates the nature of the drafter's function in relation to policy by noting that, when policy problems emerge in the course of drafting:

> Drafters do not, as a rule, sit back and say 'This is a policy matter on which I have no view'. They have expertise in the area, will have become involved with the issues through the drafting process, and have a contribution to make.[31]

There is also an empirical basis for seeing the division between policy and drafting as porous. In some jurisdictions, the division is not rigidly observed. For example, jurisdictions with a less expansive public service (owing to their size or to other factors) may not have sufficient resources to limit the duties of public servants to only one of these domains. So,

> [i]t is not unusual for the [drafter] in a 'mini-state' to be presented with a 'policy vacuum' and be expected to fill it. [They] will, on such occasions,

> be expected to devise a legislative scheme alone or in collaboration with a departmental civil servant who, through no fault of [their] own, may be of little assistance.[32]

The line can also be blurred in the other direction: for example, in the European Union's legislative process, drafting can be carried out (at a first draft stage) by non-drafters.[33]

In the AFLP, participants needed to determine the policy and do the legislative drafting themselves. Proposing concrete legislative changes was ambitious, given the highly specialised nature of drafting. Most policy advocacy, including by legal academics, operates from a distance. In this project, however, the authors had to work from among the weeds of statutory text, and try to do so in the language that state power and authority routinely uses to manifest itself, without the usual years of tutelage. In 1996, Richard Evans quoted Ian Malkin as saying that lecturers could be 'perhaps a bit flippant' about legislation, with a tendency to criticise it without offering suggestions about how it could be better.[34] This project is a repudiation of that tendency.

As we explain in Chapter 1, James Dalmau provided invaluable guidance and training to support the feminist drafters with this task. James delivered an initial seminar in which he introduced the group to some drafting fundamentals and identified sources to which we could refer. The content for the introductory seminar drew heavily on James' own experience of legislative drafting. It was designed as a 'crash course', mindful that there are limits to what can be taught about drafting outside of either on-the-job training or an academic subject. It covered some high-level drafting principles (staying conscious of our audience, achieving directness, working out what change is required); different types of legislative sentences (commands, prohibitions, permissions, and declaratory provisions); useful drafting devices (including substantive definitions and subjective language in conditions precedent); principles of plain language drafting (such as word choice, sentence structure, active voice, explanatory aids); and available guidance materials (such as publicly available drafting manuals and relevant texts). James then offered advice to all authors on their drafts.

In what follows, we set out the key elements of feminist statutory drafting, drawing on previous work on gender and statutory drafting as well as what we have learnt from the AFLP. It is our hope that these elements will be taken up and extended by others in future projects around the world. We also lay out what we have learnt throughout the AFLP (including some common themes that emerged in discussions with James), and the main challenges of feminist legislative drafting (as well as the opportunities it presented).

Feminist Statutory Drafting: Key Elements

The three key elements of feminist statutory drafting we have identified are:

- plain language;
- inclusive gender language; and
- feminist interpretive aids.

Plain Language: Drafting for the Patriarchy

The plain language movement was developed in response to complex, lawyer-driven statutory language that attempted to set out the law precisely, with all exceptions and qualifications, in order to minimise uncertainty and reduce the risk of disputes.[35] Advocates of plain language argue that such complexity is unnecessary, because detailed policy can be expressed in plain statutory language (providing the policy aims behind the Act are clear). Plan language proponents maintain that clarity and precision of statutory language are complementary goals.[36] Plain language drafting thus uses simple, straightforward language, combined with an accessible legislative structure and style, to render legislation readily understandable to the public.[37]

The plain language movement emphasises the importance of making statutes intelligible to all citizens, not just the legal technical specialists who must draft and interpret legislation in the common law system. In doing so, it aims to improve access to justice, enhancing people's ability to understand the content of the laws governing their lives.[38] Globally, women face barriers in access to justice, especially with legal problems issues connected with violence.[39] In Australia, women with a disability, Aboriginal and Torres Strait Islander women and refugee and immigrant women face greater barriers to access to justice following experiences of violence.[40]

For these reasons, and given the influence of the plain language movement in Australia (where plain language has been a focus of legislative practices since the mid-1980s),[41] we decided that plain language was an important part of feminist statutory drafting. For feminist law reform to be effective, it must be intelligible to a wide range of non-specialist audiences, especially those who lack access to justice because of gender harm. Over the course of our project, we learned three key lessons about writing plain language feminist legislation.

First, to produce plain language Bills, it is necessary to be clear about the policy aims behind the legislation. According to Esther Majambere, the 'main cause of imprecision' in statutory drafting is not poor writing, but rather that the policy being implemented by the drafter is insufficiently clear to them.[42] This was a common issue for our contributors, who frequently deployed vague language because the relevant policy concept had not been adequately refined. Often this occurred because the 'policy thinking' and 'legal thinking' were being done by the same person. Accordingly, the first step in addressing this issue was for James to see whether further policy consideration was needed with the authors.

Second, 'open-textured' or vague language is often undesirable in legislation, especially where patriarchal interpretations of legislation are anticipated. This principle applies most strongly in the contexts of private law and criminal law, where there is a tendency 'to insist on clarity and certainty [. . .] specifically because adjudication by a court is the primary consequence of the inclusion of a proposition in that sort of law'.[43] In a feminist context, the desirability of avoiding vague language is amplified by statutory interpretation practices where 'words were defined as men wished them to be defined' by judges who, as Jocelynne Scutt puts it, '[because they] already had the rights, benefits and privileges conferred by laws, they had no overriding interest in ensuring that these rights, benefits and privileges were conferred upon those outside their sphere'.[44] There may, however, be contexts in which a degree of vagueness in the text might reflect an appropriate, considered decision to leave it to the judiciary to 'fill in' the meaning of the expression 'within defined boundaries'.[45] Consequently, where James identified the use of open-textured language (which was another common theme), he sought clarification on whether this was an intentional decision, given the ramifications of leaving such matters to judges' discretion.

Third, and as we noted earlier, legislation should be written for the least charitable reader, which in our case includes the anti-feminist reader. This is particularly crucial for feminist drafting, which seeks to secure the text against subsequent governments' desire to undo the reforms. For instance, Heli Askola's Bill specifically includes provisions that are aimed at making it harder for future governments to reverse the changes introduced by the Bill.[46] Askola includes a section in her Bill which makes plain that subsequent governments should not amend the Regulations to adopt narrower understandings of family violence.

The Bills we drafted use the plainest legislative language we could muster. With James' help, we were able to revise our draft legislation to ensure they would provide legal protections for, and be accessible to, women and those who experience gender injustice. In this way, we hope our project demonstrates how plain language statutory drafting can contribute to feminist efforts to improve access to justice for marginalised genders.

Inclusive Gender Language: The Promise and Problem of Neutrality

Another key consideration for feminist drafters is how to treat the gender of the subjects of the laws they devise and, in particular, should statutes incorporate specific references to gender, remain 'gender-neutral', or remove gender entirely? Of course, these questions have long been of concern to feminist scholars. In English-language jurisdictions, where grammatical gender is not assigned to each noun, there is a great deal of flexibility about gender language in statutes, because 'gender is not baked into our language'.[47]

Since the 19th century, under the 'masculine rule',[48] legislation was largely drafted using male pronouns.[49] People of all genders, including women, were simply subsumed under the catch-all descriptor of 'men', positioning men as the proper subjects and objects of law, rendering women as lesser beings (at best) and non-entities (at worst). The masculine rule was accompanied by a rule of statutory interpretation through which male pronouns were to be read as including women (i.e. a law targeting, capturing or addressing 'him' was taken to also target, capture or address 'her').[50] Over time, however, feminists called for changes to this approach, arguing that:

> the drafting of legislation in 'masculine' language, which is simply one example of a much more widespread use of such language, contributes to some extent to the perpetuation of a society in which men, and perhaps more significantly, women, see women as lesser beings.[51]

Our contributors were encouraged to similarly reflect on their language choices, to address and correct harmful gendered language in the statutes they were reforming. We also encouraged AFLP contributors to carefully consider the implications of the language used for trans, intersex, non-binary and gender-diverse people.[52] This acknowledges that non-binary, gender-diverse, intersex and trans people face persistently high levels of stigma, prejudice and discrimination, overcriminalisation and high rates of violence.[53] Laws aimed at protecting women often do not provide formal legal protection for trans and non-binary people.[54] Some of the current Australian laws targeted for reform in this project adversely impact intersex, gender-diverse, non-binary and trans populations.[55] We therefore viewed inclusive language as a key part of any contemporary feminist approach to statutory drafting because:

> [T]he trajectory of recent language changes to account for women's rights should guide and inspire the next wave of language transformation to take account of LGBTQIA+ rights. Just as drafting conventions shifted over time in North America and elsewhere to reflect women's changing legal status, we believe that legislative drafting should now change to reflect and support the legal status of transgender persons and the legal recognition of non-binary genders.[56]

Authors could choose to adopt gender-neutral, gender-silent or gender-specific language. Gender-neutral drafting was introduced in response to feminist advocacy against the masculine rule.[57] This form of drafting either avoids the use of personal pronouns, or uses the words 'he or she' or 'her or him'.[58] In the late 20th century, several Commonwealth nations adopted gender-neutral language for new legislation.[59] Current Australian federal statutory drafting directions require gender-neutral language.[60] This is accompanied by either two-way or all-gender interpretation rules, which require those reading statutes to read references to men, women or any gender to include every other gender.[61] However, gender-neutral drafting is not as comprehensive or inclusive as it could be. Non-binary and gender diverse people were not contemplated in the late 20th-century shift from the masculine rule approach to a binary gender, and proposals for the use of non-binary pronouns in legislation were ridiculed at the time.[62] For these reasons, all authors in the AFLP project chose inclusive gender language rather than gender-neutral drafting. This practice, which reflects the shift towards trans, intersex, non-binary and gender-diverse inclusion in feminist practice, contrasts with most Australian statute law, which continues to use 'he or she' or 'him or her'.

An alternative approach is to use 'gender-silent' language. Gender-silent drafting 'moves beyond male-female gender neutrality to implement an all-genders inclusive drafting style'. [63] It is a form of gender-inclusive language.[64] Advocates of this approach argue that it is an 'honorable way to treat one another in a non-binary world'.[65] Gender-silent drafting is an exacting approach, because 'it expresses with clarity, precision, and unambiguity if and where gender is relevant in legislation'.[66] Examples of gender-silent drafting include:

- Using plural pronouns to indicate a singular individual (eg 'they' or 'them' instead of 'he or she' or 'him or her');
- Repeating nouns to avoid personal pronouns altogether (eg 'The Minister may issue an authorisation to the holder of a licence that enables *the holder* to operate a store'); and
- Avoiding gendered nouns and verbs altogether (eg 'chair' instead of 'chairman').

Decertification – the abolition of legal sex status – is an important example of feminist law reform that requires gender-silent drafting, as proposed by Davina Cooper and Flora Renz.[67] According to Grabham, under a decertified approach, without any state-based system that categories and recognises people according to legal categories of gender, there are a number of drafting techniques that can enable legislation to remain utterly silent on gender.[68]

Most authors in the AFLP employed gender-silent drafting. For example, when legislating for gender diversity in government appointments, Kcasey McLoughlin and Yee-Fui Ng avoided gendered nouns altogether: 'Representation can never exceed more than 60% of one gender.'[69] Dani Linder uses the plural pronoun 'they' ('if they are a person who is detained in a hospital or in a secure facility') in her revision of the voter disqualification provision in the *Commonwealth Electoral Act 1918* (Cth).[70] Linder's use of the plural pronoun demonstrates the difficulty of retrofitting gender-inclusive language into existing statutes, as her proposed 'they' will sit somewhat uncomfortably in a provision which contains other subsections featuring binary pronouns ('not entitled to have his or her name placed or retained on any Roll or to vote').[71]

From feminist perspectives, both gender-neutral and gender-silent drafting techniques still carry potential dangers. There is a well-evidenced risk that ostensibly 'genderless' statutory language (whether gender-neutral or gender-silent) will generate gender-based harms by failing to properly recognise the gendered nature of the problem.[72] By not referring explicitly to all genders, for instance, the statutes might be interpreted in ways excluding particular, marginalised genders. For example, in the 'persons' cases of the late 19th and early 20th centuries, patriarchal judges interpreted the word 'persons' in different Acts to exclude women, thereby denying women entry to the medical and legal professions.[73] Therefore, feminist drafting cannot rely upon gender-neutral or gender-silent wording as a guarantee of gender rights.

In response, a third option – 'gender-specific' language – can also be used. Gender-specific drafting is usually used in very particular circumstances, targeting particular genders in circumstances where the law should only apply to those genders. Relevant examples might be found in reproductive policies that are applied to women and those who have uteruses, or laws designed to recognise the fundamentally gendered nature of family violence.[74] Gender-specific drafting has been advocated as a feminist approach that 'would have even more impact in drawing the users' attention to the specific position of women in gender specific legislative texts'.[75]

Some authors in the AFLP have used gender-specific language for certain provisions in Bills which otherwise use gender-silent drafting. For example, it is used by Ramona Vijeyarasa to require corporate accountability for gendered modern slavery, by defining gender-sensitive due diligence as 'meaningful engagement with women and girls and non-binary people as relevant stakeholders, in order to understand their concrete experiences'.[76] Gender-specific language is also used by Sean Mulcahy in regulations necessitating separate toilets for specific genders, by listing in the Regulations 'separate sanitary facilities for males and females and all gender sanitary facilities' and 'separate sanitary facilities for males and females'.[77]

As a principle and practice of feminist statutory drafting, the decision of which gender language approach to follow ultimately depends on the purpose of the Bill and the policy objectives it hopes to achieve. Whichever decision is made, feminist statutory drafting involves a heightened awareness of the importance and function of gender and language in legislation. Our experience in the AFLP shows that inclusive drafting practices might use either 'gender-silent' or 'gender-specific' language, depending on those aims. By using these techniques, drafters can avoid the perils of 'gender neutrality', explicitly including trans, intersex, non-binary and gender-diverse people. Either way, the fact that Australian legislative drafting guidance still prefers gender-neutral drafting shows that legal practice lags behind our imagined feminist future.

'Drafting for the Dickheads': Techniques for Assisting with the Interpretation of Feminist Legislation

As feminist drafters, all authors were acutely aware that they were sending their Bills into a patriarchal world where the work could be misinterpreted, misapplied or otherwise openly resisted, including by the least charitable or anti-feminist reader. Decades of feminist legal scholarship show that feminist law reform often fails to reduce gender harm and has unintentionally harmful gendered effects because of law's 'androcentric standard'.[78] In interpreting statutes, judges make normative choices about the selection of facts and precedents, in the determination of relevance and the categorisation of principles which reinforce and create gender harm.[79]

In this regard, James sought to 'stress test' the drafted provisions with the authors (usually in conference) to explore how the text might be leveraged by those with aims and objectives different from the authors'. That is, it is important to be 'reading the law with intent to subvert it', to ensure uncharitable or hostile readers 'cannot successfully twist the meaning to another purpose'.[80] That exercise often revealed where more needed to be said in the text to guard against an undesired interpretation. It also resulted in the consideration of three techniques for trying to safeguard the Bill against anti-feminist readers, and to respond to the androcentric standard. These techniques are interpretive aids designed to guide judicial and everyday users of law on the feminist principles behind the Act, in an attempt to reduce a harmful gendered statutory interpretation of the new law.

The first technique is to make a clear statement of feminist intent in the Second Reading Speech. Second Reading Speeches serve an important legal role in statutory interpretation by guiding future judicial interpretation of ambiguous legislative provisions.[81] An example of this technique can be seen in Julie Debeljak and Tania Penovic's Second Reading Speech. This directly addresses judges interpreting the *Charter of Human Rights and Responsibilities Act 2006* (Vic), as follows: 'Recognising that gender-related issues have too often remained invisible, [their provision] requires a consideration of gender issues' in the statutory interpretation process.[82]

The second technique is to include statements of guiding principle for decision-makers in the Bills. Under James' guidance, we learnt that statements of guiding principle can be helpful but can also carry risks. It is important to establish exactly why statements of guiding principle are considered desirable, and to consider how much confidence could be placed in those provisions having the desired effect, and *only* that effect. If legislation's primary purpose is to impose legal obligations, define legal rights and create legal prohibitions, legislated statements of guiding principle do none of these things. They may instead infuse the statute with text that might be called on to assist in interpreting other provisions. The risk here is that:

> Setting out an objective for a change to private law or for the imposition of a criminal liability will usually be challenged by a legislative drafter on the grounds that its only effect is to add an element of uncertainty to the interpretation of the carefully framed and specific rights and obligations created in the law.[83]

This is not to say that statements of guiding principle are impermissible or always risky. Rather, their risks need to be understood. The core question here is about the aim and effects of such provisions. An example of a Bill which uses guiding principles is that proposed by Jonathan Crowe, Asher Flynn and Bri Lee to address affirmative consent in sexual offences. Their Bill sets out several matters that courts must consider when interpreting and applying the relevant sexual offence provisions.[84]

The third technique is to provide explicit guidance to judges in the Bills about relevant matters that they may or may not consider when applying a relevant provision. The use of such explicit directives can help ensure that judges do not overlook a relevant matter (due, for example, to patriarchal blindness to that issue), or do not consider irrelevant matters that may undermine the desired policy objectives. An example of this technique is the Bill by Kate Seear, Jamie Walvisch and Liza Miller, which seeks to address the gendered, victim-blaming attitudes held by assessors who decide compensation payable to victims of crime. They propose inserting a new provision into the *Criminal Injuries Compensation Act 2003* (WA) which explicitly excludes particular gendered factors and assumptions from the decision-maker's considerations: 'The following things are not to be taken, under subsection (1)(a), to have contributed, directly or indirectly, to the victim's injury or death . . .'.[85]

The techniques used by authors in the AFLP, in both their Second Reading Speeches and their Bills, were pragmatic feminist drafting techniques designed to respond to the risk that statutes will be interpreted in ways that further the interests of men at the expense of women. Deployment of the three specific techniques of a statement of feminist intent in the Second Reading Speech, statements of guiding principle in legislation and provision of legislative guidance in decision-making demonstrates an awareness of the dangers of gender injustice, alongside a hope that transformative change may be possible.

Nearly 40 years ago, Margaret Thornton called for the development of new feminist legal methods to create a semblance of gender equality before the law.[86] The AFLP responds to this call by attempting to develop and adapt legislative drafting practices to help advance gender equality.

Throughout this project, we identified a key tension in feminist statutory drafting: there is a need to conform to the practices and philosophy of established legislative drafting conventions and create laws which subvert patriarchal legal systems, while nevertheless operating within them. There is doubtless much to be said about this tension, including whether these conventions and practices can be challenged further in future feminist legislation projects. In any event, the key principles of feminist statutory drafting we have identified in the AFLP involve:

1. *The use of plain language to provide legal protections for, and be accessible to, women and those who experience gender-based injustices. In this way, we hope our project demonstrates how plain language statutory drafting can contribute to feminist efforts to improve access to justice.*
2. *A heightened sensitivity towards language in the drafting process, including the importance of inclusive gender language, with resulting drafts shaped by preferred policy outcomes. The deployment of inclusive gender language in statutes can be done through two particular legislative drafting techniques: 'gender-silent' and 'gender-specific' provisions. By using these drafting techniques, feminist legislative drafters can avoid the perils of gender neutrality and explicitly include trans, intersex, non-binary and gender-diverse people.*
3. *The use of three techniques for assisting with the interpretation of feminist legislation, namely: a clear statement of feminist intent in a Second Reading Speech, the inclusion of statements of guiding principle, and the use of explicit directives for decision-makers. These were used by authors to guide judicial and everyday users of law on the feminist principles behind the Act, in an attempt to reduce the risk of harmful gendered statutory interpretation of the new law.*

We encourage future feminist legislation projects to develop and refine these principles.

Finally, we want to return to a point about ambition and politics, based on an observation James Dalmau made as the AFLP unfolded. Given that the project involved hypothetical legislation, we never had to accommodate political compromises. We could draft whatever we wanted, including legislation reaching further than might be possible in a real parliament. Despite this, James frequently found himself reminding all of us that we possessed the power to be more imaginative, ambitious and definitive. Hypothetical legislators do not need to 'decide between the risk of losing [their] bill and the responsibility for leaving the law obscure'.[87] Nevertheless, our tentativeness at times reflected our training within a patriarchal, androcentric, male-dominated system, revealing just how deeply embedded legal norms are, with some of us doubting whether we were going 'too far', asking for 'too much' or being 'too demanding'. We are indebted to James for encouraging us to be bolder, and to experiment with new ideas and possibilities.

This raises important questions for future feminist legislation projects – can we push the boundaries of feminist statutory drafting even further, in search of an even more ambitious feminist future? Whether we have stunted the feminist potential of our Bills by 'compressing feminist scholarship into a traditional jurisprudential framework'[88] can only be decided by others, long after we have released our laws into the wild.

Notes

1 Specifically feminist judging and statutory interpretation approaches are explored in Rosemary Hunter, 'An Account of Feminist Judging' in Rosemary Hunter et al. (eds), *Feminist Judgments: From Theory to Practice* (2010, Hart Publishing) 30; Rosemary Hunter et al., 'Judging in Lower Courts: Conventional, Procedural, Therapeutic and Feminist Approaches' (2016) 12(3) *International Journal of Law in Context* 337; and Kim Brooks, 'Feminist Statutory Interpretation' (2019) 16(2) *Pittsburgh Tax Review* 125.

2 We did, however, find this wonderful piece emanating from the Future of Legal Gender project by Emily Grabham, 'Exploring the Textual Alchemy of Legal Gender: Experimental Statutes and the Message in the Medium' (2020) 10(2) *feminists@law.*

3 See eg Marguerite E Ritchie, 'Alice Through the Statutes' (1975) 21 *McGill Law Journal* 685, 705 ('Alice Through the Statutes'); Marguerite E Ritchie, 'The Language of Oppression – Alice Talks Back' (1977) 23 *McGill Law Journal* 535 ('Alice Talks Back'); Jocelynne Scutt, 'Sexism in Legal Language' (1985) 59 *Australian Law Journal* 163; Ray Stilwell, 'Sexism in the Statutes: Identifying and Solving the Problem of Ambiguous Gender Bias in Legal Writing' (1983) 32 *Buffalo Law Review* 559; Sandra Petersson, 'Locating Inequality – The Evolving Discourse on Sexist Language' (1998) 32 *University of British Columbia Law Review* 55 ('Locating Inequality').

4 Mary Jane Mossman, 'The Use of Non-Discriminatory Language in the Law' (1994) 73 *Canadian Bar Review* 347, 371.

5 Mary Jane Mossman, 'Feminism and Legal Method: The Difference It Makes' (1986) 3 *Australian Journal of Law and Society* 30, 48 ('Feminism and Legal Method').

6 Ritchie, 'Alice Talks Back' (n 3) 544.

7 Stilwell (n 3). See also Grabham (n 2) 16.

8 As we explain in Chapter 1, James' involvement in the AFLP was in his personal capacity, not in his capacity as a public servant or as a representative of the drafting office for which he worked.

9 George Engle, '"Bills Are Made to Pass as Razors Are Made to Sell": Practical Constraints in the Preparation of Legislation' (1983) 4(2) *Statute Law Review* 7, 10.

10 Reed Dickerson, *The Fundamentals of Legal Drafting* (Little, Brown, 2nd ed, 1986) 3, cited in Donald L Revell, 'Enhancing the Legislative Process: The Value of the Legislative Drafter' (2011) 32(2) *Statute Law Review* 149, 154 ('Enhancing the Legislative Process').

11 Nigel Jamieson, 'Would a Parliamentary Counsel by Any Other Name Be More of a Law Draftsman?' (1982) 3(1) *Statute Law Review* 13, 15.

12 Dale Dewhurst et al., 'Producing Legislative Counsel: Ways and Means' (2012) 33(3) *Statute Law Review* 339, 342.
13 G P Nazareth, *Legislative Draftsmen: A Continuing Dearth* (Annex to Paper LMM (83) 6) in 'Commonwealth Secretariat, Meeting of Commonwealth Law Ministers, Colombo, Sri Lanka' 14–18 February 1983: Memoranda, Commonwealth Secretariat London 1983, 129, 131 cited in Serge Lortie, 'Providing Technical Assistance on Law Drafting' (2010) 31(1) *Statute Law Review* 1, 13.
14 Esther Majambere, 'Clarity, Precision and Unambiguity: Aspects for Effective Legislative Drafting' (2011) 37(3) *Commonwealth Law Bulletin* 417, 422; Sandra C Markman, 'Training of Legislative Counsel: Learning to Draft without Nellie' (2010) 36(1) *Commonwealth Law Bulletin* 25.
15 Andrew Flavelle Martin, 'The Duty of Legislative Counsel as Guardians of the Statute Book: "Sui Generis" or a Professional Duty of Lawyers?' (2021) 44(3) *Manitoba Law Journal* 116, 123.
16 Engle (n 9) 11.
17 Markman (n 14) 31.
18 Roewen Wishart, 'Public Servants, Legislation and the Parliamentary Balance of Power' (1993) 52(2) *Australian Journal of Public Administration* 196, 197–8.
19 Richard Evans, 'The Hand That Signed the Papers: Are Legislative Drafters Behind the Times?' (1996) 70(4) *Law Institute Journal* 12, 13 (emphasis added).
20 Revell, 'Enhancing the Legislative Process' (n 10) 153.
21 Markman (n 14) 34.
22 Stephen Laws, 'Giving Effect to Policy in Legislation: How to Avoid Missing the Point' (2011) 32(1) *Statute Law Review* 1.
23 John Ewens, 'Legislative Draftsmen: Their Recruitment and Training' (1983) 57(10) *Australian Law Journal* 567.
24 Grabham (n 2) 42.
25 David A Marcello, 'The Ethics and Politics of Legislative Drafting' (1995) 70(6 Part B) *Tulane Law Review* 2437, 2439.
26 Ronan Cormacain, 'Legislation, Legislative Drafting and the Rule of Law' (2017) 5(2) *The Theory and Practice of Legislation* 134 citing Robert Seidman, 'Drafting for the Rule of Law: Maintaining Legality in Developing Countries' (1987) 12 *Yale Journal of International Law* 84, 86.
27 Engle (n 9) 9.
28 V C R A C Crabbe, 'The Ethics of Legislative Drafting' (2010) 36(1) *Commonwealth Law Bulletin* 11, 16.
29 Elmer A Driedger, *The Composition of Legislation* (The Department of Justice of Canada, 2nd ed, 1976) xv cited in Pius Perry Biribonwoha, 'The Role of Legislative Drafting in the Law Reform Process' (2006) 32(4) *Commonwealth Law Bulletin* 601, 604.
30 Reed Dickerson, *The Fundamentals of Legal Drafting* (Little, Brown and Company for the American Bar Association, 1965) 9 cited in Biribonwoha (n 29) 604.
31 George Tanner, 'The Role of Parliamentary Counsel' [1999] *New Zealand Law Journal* 423, 424.
32 T W Cain, 'The Legislative Draftsman in a Small Jurisdiction' (1993) 19(3) *Commonwealth Law Bulletin* 1237, 1238.
33 William Robinson, 'Accessibility of European Union Legislation' (February 2011) *The Loophole* 79, https://www.calc.ngo/sites/default/files/loophole/feb-2011.pdf .
34 Evans (n 19) 14.
35 Commonwealth Association of Legislative Counsel, 'Drafting Laws in Plain English: Can the Drafter Win?' (1986) 12(2) *Commonwealth Law Bulletin* 560, 562; Victorian Law Reform Commission and the Law Reform Commission of

Victoria, *Plain English and the Law: The 1987 Report Republished with a New Preface* (2017, Report No 9) 34.

36 Victorian Law Reform Commission and the Law Reform Commission of Victoria (n 35) 33–4.

37 Brian Hunt, 'Plain Language in Legislative Drafting: Is It Really the Answer?' (2002) 23 *Statute Law Review* 24, 24–5, 32.

38 Yaniv Roznai and Nadiv Mordechay, 'Access to Justice 2.0: Access to Legislation and Beyond' (2015) 3(3) *The Theory and Practice of Legislation* 333, 355.

39 Ana Speed et al., 'Stay Home, Stay Safe, Save Lives? An Analysis of the Impact of COVID-19 on the Ability of Victims of Gender-based Violence to Access Justice' (2020) 84(6) *The Journal of Criminal Law* 539; Christine Coumarelos, 'Quantifying the Legal and Broader Life Impacts of Domestic and Family Violence' (2019) 32 *Justice Issues* 1; Tamsin Bradley and Janet Gruber, 'VAWG Mainstreaming in Access to Justice Programmes: A Framework for Action' (2018) 28(1) *Development in Practice* 16.

40 Jane Maree Maher et al., *Women, Disability and Violence: Barriers to Accessing Justice: Final Report* (Australia's National Research Organisation for Women's Safety, Paper No 2, 2018); Zhigang Wei and Hugh M McDonald, 'Indigenous People and Legal Problem Resolution' (2018) 55 *Updating Justice* 1; Larissa Behrendt 'Aboriginal Women and the Criminal Justice System' (2002) 14(6) *Judicial Officers' Bulletin* 41; Cathy Vaughan et al., *Promoting Community-Led Responses to Violence Against Immigrant and Refugee Women in Metropolitan and Regional Australia: The ASPIRE Project* (Australia's National Research Organisation for Women's Safety, State of Knowledge Paper No 7, 2015).

41 Commonwealth Association of Legislative Counsel (n 35) 561.

42 Majambere (n 14) 421.

43 Laws (n 22) 12.

44 Scutt (n 3) 172.

45 Lord Hailsham, 'Addressing the Statute Law' [1985] *Statute Law Review* 4, 7.

46 Chapter 14 by Heli Askola.

47 Donald Revell and Jessica Vapnek, 'Gender-Silent Legislative Drafting in a Non-Binary World' (2020) 48(2) *Capital University Law Review* 103, 128.

48 Scutt (n 3).

49 Petersson, 'Locating Inequality' (n 3) 57.

50 Sandra Petersson, 'Gender Neutral Drafting: Historical Perspective' (1998) 19(2) *Statute Law Review* 93 ('Gender Neutral Drafting'); Christopher Williams, 'The End of the "Masculine Rule"? Gender-Neutral Legislative Drafting in the United Kingdom and Ireland' (2008) 29(3) *Statute Law Review* 139.

51 'Avoidance of "Sexist" Language in Legislation' (1985) 11(2) *Commonwealth Law Bulletin* 590, 590 ('Avoidance of Sexist Language'). Revell and Vapnek (n 47) 107–8.

52 The fourth 'guiding principle' we developed for the AFLP stated our commitment to 'consider the gender language we use in our law reform proposals and directly address the inclusion of trans, non-binary, gender-diverse and intersex populations and others across the gender spectrum'. See Chapter 1 by Kate Seear, Becky Batagol, Jamie Walvisch and Heli Askola.

53 Jaclyn White Hughto et al., 'Transgender Stigma and Health: A Critical Review of Stigma Determinants, Mechanisms, and Interventions' (2015) 147 *Social Science & Medicine* 222; Monica Campo and Sarah Tayton, *Intimate Partner Violence in Lesbian, Gay, Bisexual, Trans, Intersex and Queer Communities: Key Issues* (Child Family Community Australia, Australian Institute of Family Studies, 2015).

54 Ayden Scheim et al., 'Intersecting Inequalities in Access to Justice for Trans and Non-binary Sex Workers in Canada' (2023) 20(3) *Sexuality Research & Social Policy* 1245.
55 See eg Chapter 10 by Sean Mulcahy; Chapter 10A by Nicole Kalms and Laura McVey; and Chapter 18 by Ramona Vijeyarasa.
56 Revell and Vapnek (n 47) 105.
57 Scutt (n 3).
58 Petersson, 'Gender Neutral Drafting' (n 50). Four methods of removing masculine personal pronouns were canvassed by the Australian government in 1985 which were drafting in the plural, using plural pronouns (they, their, them, themselves), using the one and oneself pronouns and avoiding the use of pronouns entirely by repeating relevant nouns: see 'Avoidance of Sexist Language' (n 51) 590–1.
59 In British legislation prior to the 1850s, gender-silent drafting was widely used where the 'they' pronoun was used to refer to all people when not applying provisions specifically to men or women. See Petersson, 'Gender Neutral Drafting' (n 50).
60 Peter Quiggin, *Drafting Direction No. 2.1: English Usage, Gender-Specific and Gender-Neutral Language, Grammar, Punctuation and Spelling* (Office of Parliamentary Counsel, Commonwealth of Australia, Release 4.4, 2016) paras 15–16.
61 Petersson, 'Gender Neutral Drafting' (n 50) 37–46.
62 'Avoidance of Sexist Language' (n 51) 591.
63 Revell and Vapnek (n 47) 126.
64 Helen Xanthaki, 'Gender Inclusive Legislative Drafting in English: A Drafter's Response to Emily Grabham' (2020) 10(2) *feminists@law* 5–6.
65 Revell and Vapnek (n 47) 146.
66 Xanthaki (n 64) 10.
67 Davina Cooper and Flora Renz, 'Introduction to Special Issue: Decertifying Legal Sex—Prefigurative Law Reform and the Future of Legal Gender' (2023) 31 *Feminist Legal Studies* 1.
68 Grabham (n 2) 37–40.
69 Constitution Alteration (Equality and Diversity) Bill 2048 (Cth) cl 3, in Chapter 3 by Kcasey McLoughlin and Yee-Fui Ng.
70 Commonwealth Electoral Amendment (Addressing the Disenfranchisement of Aboriginal Women in Prisons) Bill 2024 cl 7 in Chapter 4 by Dani Linder.
71 *Commonwealth Electoral Act 1918* (Cth) s 93(8)(a).
72 Ritchie, 'Alice Through the Statutes' (n 3) 705.
73 Scutt (n 3).
74 *Family Violence Protection Act 2008* (Vic) preamble which states: 'that while anyone can be a victim or perpetrator of family violence, family violence is predominantly committed by men against women'.
75 Xanthaki (n 64) 6.
76 Modern Slavery Amendment (Exploitation in the Supply Chain) Bill 2024 (Cth) cl 1, schedule 1 in Chapter 18 by Ramona Vijeyarasa.
77 Building Amendment (National Construction Code Variations – Sanitary and Other Facilities) Regulations 2024 (Vic) cl 5 in Chapter 10 by Sean Mulcahy.
78 Margaret Thornton, 'Feminist Jurisprudence: Illusion or Reality?' (1986) 3 *Australian Journal of Law and Society* 5, 20; Carol Smart, *Feminism and the Power of Law* (Taylor & Francis Group, 1989) 160. See also 'Feminist Speech Making' in Chapter 1 by Kate Seear, Becky Batagol, Jamie Walvisch and Heli Askola.
79 Mossman, 'Feminism and Legal Method' (n 5) 42.
80 Alain Songa Gashabizi, 'In Pursuit of Clarity: How Far Should the Drafter Go?' (2013) 39(3) *Commonwealth Law Bulletin* 415, 416–7, citing A W Seidman

et al., *Legislative Drafting for Democratic Social Change: A Manual for Drafters* (Kluwer Law International, 2001) 255, 261.

81 See eg *Acts Interpretation Act 1901* (Cth) s15AB(2)(f); *Interpretation of Legislation Act 1984* (Vic) s 35(b)(ii).

82 Chapter 6 by Julie Debeljak and Tania Penovic.

83 Laws (n 22) 14.

84 Criminal Code Amendment (Sexual Offences) Bill 2024 (Qld) cl 347B in Chapter 7 by Jonathan Crowe, Asher Flynn and Bri Lee.

85 Chapter 9 by Kate Seear, Jamie Walvisch and Liza J Miller.

86 Thornton (n 78) 21.

87 Courtenay Libert, *The Mechanics of Law Making* (Colombia University Press, 1914) 18–19, 22–23 quoted in Marcello (n 25) 2453.

88 Thornton (n 78) 23.

Part II

Constitutions, Institutions and Rights

Chapter 3

Re-writing and Re-imagining Rights

Enshrining Gender Equality in Australia's Constitution

Kcasey McLoughlin and Yee-Fui Ng

Commonwealth of Australia

Women's Consitutional Convention

Hansard

2048

OLD PARLIAMENT HOUSE, CANBERRA

The CHAIRWOMEN (Hon Kcasey McLoughlin and Hon Yee-Fui Ng) –

Delegates, our proposal is at once modest and radical. It is a call to action to enshrine gender equality as a basic democratic value in Australia's Constitution. Unlike the Constitutional Conventions of years past, women have set the agenda at this convention. Crucially, we acknowledge that our draft proposals are simply the beginning of the conversation, and leave open the space to hear from (and include) the perspectives of all delegates.

We stand before you today acknowledging both the power and limitations of law. We seek to enshrine gender equality as a basic democratic value in Australia's Constitution in three distinct yet interconnected ways – through the crafting of a new preamble, the inclusion of an 'equal protection clause', and amendments to the mechanisms by which political and legal authority is to be assigned. This Convention is about remedying the exclusionary and masculinist ethos of our nation's founding document, which our proposed amendments seek to address.

But first, some history – both recent and not-so-recent – to justify our proposal. Australia's Constitution was drafted *by* and *for* white cisgender men at a series of conventions during the 1890s. It is not a majestic document, drenched in the language of human rights or equality. Rather, the framing of

DOI: 10.4324/9781003372462-5

this document is marred by an intrinsic racist and masculinist ideology. The language used operated from the outset to exclude First Nations people from what would become known as Australia, despite their existence on the territory for at least 65,000 years prior to English colonisation.

Women too were excluded from the business of nation-building, although the omission was qualified. Some non-Indigenous women at least were made citizens – a characterisation not afforded to First Nations people of any sex. However, it must be noted that this concession was less about equality and more about 'white women's common link with their menfolk' and the reality that two states had already given women the vote.[1] Therefore, 'within this masculine federation women would have to be citizens'.[2]

In many ways, this cavalier approach to women's citizenship highlights the matters that the drafters, now sometimes called 'the founding fathers', determined to be of real concern. The drafters envisioned a federal system of government assigning legislative power, demarcating the separation of powers and the judiciary's role within the Constitutional framework. As Professor Margaret Thornton has argued, their concern was in delineating powers within the new federation, not with individual rights.[3] This approach aligned with the dominant viewpoint of the time, informed by the works of AV Dicey and James Bryce, that civilised nations did not need to expressly provide for individual rights. Why? Because, so the story goes, they were already provided for by the common law and principles of responsible government.[4]

Perhaps father did *not* know best, after all? Certainly, by contemporary standards, this logic is dubious. These are self-serving lies that the law tells about itself. What about those for whom the common law and principles of responsible government held no such promise? It rankles that those who possessed rights might then decide that such rights were unnecessary for those who were – by virtue of their legal status as effectively non-persons – deliberately excluded from the drafting table.

As is only proper, this Convention follows the adoption of the Treaty with First Nations people, which brought the full Uluru Statement from the Heart to fruition after far too long. The Treaty has finally recognised the special status that ought to have always been afforded to the traditional custodians of this land. Explaining the gendered and racialised consequences of unceded sovereignty, Professor Aileen Moreton-Robinson, a Goenpul woman from Minjerribah, explains how the myth of terra nullius 'functioned as a truth within a race war of coercion, murder and appropriation carried out by white men in the service of the British Crown'.[5]

How have women fared in this Constitutional system? Importantly, as much as women were excluded from the formal Constitutional drafting process, they were neither indifferent nor absent. Feminist scholars such as Professor Helen Irving have done important work examining women's contributions to nation-building by bringing this history to the fore.[6] Feminist scholars have also demonstrated how women's exclusion shaped the

Constitution in significant ways. Women were failed on two key and interconnected fronts. First, they were barred from the conception phase of the document. Second, by extension, the resulting document did not acknowledge women's perspectives and lives, or imagine that they would exercise authority within the Constitutional framework. As Professor Kim Rubenstein explains, the exclusion of women from this process not only amounted to a failure to conform to the principle of representative democracy, but it also institutionalised and legitimised women's ongoing exclusion.[7]

Of course, we must acknowledge that today's Convention is certainly not the first occasion on which women have sought to shape Australia's Constitutional framework. Indeed, it was feminist scholars who agitated for the Women's Constitutional Convention in January 1998, a few days before the official Constitutional Convention. This event was organised by key women's groups: the Women's Electoral Lobby, YWCA, National Women's Justice Coalition, Women into Politics and Australian Women Lawyers. Although the Women's Constitutional Convention was not afforded official power, it provided an important opportunity for women's voices to be heard. As the tagline on its now-archived website read:

> One hundred years ago men gathered to draft the Australian Constitution. Now, for the first time, women from all sections of society will have the opportunity to contribute their perspective. [8]

Within this diverse assembly of 300 women, commonalities of topics for agitation presented themselves: support for a republic (subject to a number of principles), support for a Constitutional Bill of Rights (or alternatively, a Legislative Bill of Rights), electoral reform (including dedicated seats for Aboriginal and Torres Strait Islander peoples), the entrenchment of proportional representation and the implementation of processes to ensure an escalation of women being appointed to the High Court were persistent themes.

The Women's Convention agreed that a new preamble should include the following:

- The Australian people to be the source of authority for the Constitution;
- Commitment to peace and the environment;
- Acknowledgment of Aboriginal and Torres Strait Islander occupation, rights and culture and a statement of regret for past injustices;
- Affirmation of multiculturalism, equality between women and men and between races and a commitment to human rights and the freedoms of representative democracy.

By some measures, the Women's Convention was a success. For example, Professor Marion Sawer (one of the initiators) observed that 'delegates proceeding to the Constitutional Convention were empowered by the collective agenda of the Women's Convention, which was tabled by the Chair of the Constitutional Convention.'[9] However, the extent to which those delegates were able to set the agenda was limited. It was in the final two matters – that is, acknowledgment of Aboriginal and Torres Strait Islander rights and culture and a statement of regret for past injustices and the recognition of gender equality – that the Women's Convention and the official People's Convention parted ways.[10] (In any case, history records that the recommendations arrived at did not at that time translate into Constitutional reform.)

As we know, the exclusion of women, Aboriginal people and Torres Strait Islander people from Australia's Constitution was already well-entrenched a century before the preamble was up for debate. Nonetheless, the Constitutional Convention's explicit exclusion of these groups speaks volumes.

This is the unfinished business that we must now address.

Can this gendered and racialised sovereignty be remade and reimagined? We believe so. Although the past cannot be remade, we can reimagine the future.

Yet with the lessons of the past reverberating, one might ask: why pursue Constitutional reform? This is a pertinent question, particularly as our national history has demonstrated the difficulty of achieving Constitutional change through referendum. We acknowledge that the path to Constitutional reform to include those who have traditionally been ignored (and indeed, subjugated) by law and its institutions can be especially bruising. We saw this in the Constitutional reform process drawn from the Uluru Statement from the Heart, which began with the Voice Referendum. Our national ambivalence about rights and reluctance to embrace change (perhaps best expressed by the phrase 'if it ain't broke, don't fix it') certainly gives some insight into the challenges ahead.

But the Constitution *is* broken, and we need to fix it.

Here, we must look beyond our own shores. There has been a 'participatory turn' and acknowledgement that Constitutions have important work to do in the global gender equality project.[11] Tacit in these initiatives to utilise Constitutions is an acknowledgement of the 'power and importance of constitutions' as 'their content and design can have a major impact on women's lives and opportunities – making them a critical target in the quest for gender equality.'[12] As the United Nations Global Gender Database further explains:

> A well-designed constitution may allow women to recognize and assert their rights, enjoy full and equal citizenship, participate in their country's political decision-making and have access to public roles and offices on an equal footing with men. A constitution may, alternatively, obstruct women's equality and agency, making it difficult for them to enjoy rights and freedoms.[13]

Women's foundational exclusion from Constitution-making has shaped Constitutions the world over and is certainly not a uniquely Australian experience, with many Constitutions obstructing rather than bolstering women's agency in numerous ways. Yet it is perhaps fair to say that the Australian experience remains unique on two fronts. First, the limited provision of express rights means that the type of creative litigation strategies that have been pursued elsewhere in the world have not been workable in this country. For example, the innovative litigation strategy most famously associated with Ruth Bader Ginsburg in the United States, which extends the protection afforded by the 14th Amendment, is not available to vulnerable Australians because no such rights-based protection is included in our Constitution.[14]

Yet constitutions new and old now include explicit declarations regarding sex (and in some instances, gender) equality. Australia is also in the unique position of having the benefit of being able to survey reform efforts elsewhere in the world. A brief catalogue underlines Australia's exceptionalism:

- The French Constitution of 1946 identifies the equality of women and men in the third paragraph of the preamble, stating: 'The law guarantees women equal rights to those of men in all spheres.'[15] This declaration comes only after the two earlier decrees of inalienable rights to each human and the category demarcating a section on political, economic, and social principles.
- Akin to France, Germany's Constitution also places the equality of women and men early in the piece, with Article 3 stating: 'All persons shall be equal before the law . . . men and women shall have equal rights'.[16] Article 3 also places responsibility on the State to 'promote the actual implementation of' equality and, in direct opposition to Australia, finalises the Article with an all-encompassing 'no person shall be favoured or disfavoured because of sex, parentage, race, language, homeland and origin, faith, or religious or political opinions . . . or disability'.[17]
- India, another former British colony, emphasised the equality of its people in Article 15 where it is specifically noted that discrimination on the basis of sex (or religion, race, caste or place of birth, for that matter) is prohibited by all actors – the State as well as its citizens.[18] In Article 16, it also specifically addresses equality in employment.
- The Constitution of Canada not only enshrines equality between men and women but also features a Charter of Rights and Freedoms as well as a separate part dedicated to the rights of the Aboriginal People of Canada.[19]
- The South African Constitution (as of 1997) places equality as the third topic under Chapter 2: The Bill of Rights. In much the same way as Germany, sex is listed alongside other personal attributes.[20]

These options present this Convention, and therefore Australia, with a surfeit of riches when it comes to embedding gender equality in our Constitution. Granted, we also acknowledge that none of these Constitutional reform projects has produced a feminist utopia or remedied gender inequality. But how could any law eradicate patriarchy? The law is but one of many tools we have at our disposal, establishing norms of behaviour while shaping identity and culture. When it comes to the Constitution, the law has enormous potential to shape women's lives. For example, it can limit the state's power to pass discriminatory laws, empower the State to pass laws which enhance gender equality and set out the processes by which legal and political power will be allocated.

Reimagining our Constitution requires the principles of gender equality to be properly embedded from design to execution. In other words, this convention process needs to itself reflect the kinds of ideals we seek to embed in the Constitution. First, at the structural stage of deciding who gets to be in the room – *this* room – where the Constitution is redrafted, the inclusion of women and gender-diverse people is the bare minimum. Looking at the sea of faces before us, we are proud that women constitute a majority of delegates here today. We note that all delegates have been democratically elected, with express provision to ensure adequate representation across our rich and diverse communities. However, the inclusion of such members of society must represent the floor, not the ceiling.

Such a process also involves properly grappling with the consequences of our history, and the fact that many women and marginalised groups will understandably be sceptical about what Constitutions can do for them. In the words of Professor Ruth Rubio-Martin:

> [O]nly by taking into account women's tradition of political disempowerment (including their traditional exclusion from constitution-making) and the effects of its legacies on women do we create the possibility of fully grasping the forms, the strategies, but also the challenges that women are encountering in participating, and having their participation translate into power, in official and unofficial sites of constitution-making.[21]

Women must be in the room, yes, but their participation must also be meaningful. We wish to explain the choices made, while leaving open the discursive space for debate – our proposals are the beginning of the discussion, not the end. We draw upon our feminist forbears' ideas expressed at the 1998 Convention and earlier, while leaving open the possibility that a new generation will offer fresh perspectives. It is essential that we hear (and embed) the voices and perspectives of all women, not as some homogenous group, but instead acknowledging the rich differences between and among them.

Perhaps astoundingly, we find ourselves here with an opportunity to debate our Constitution at a reconstituted Women's Convention. We have a range of options before us about how to proceed. What are they? Pondering the possibilities of a different way of doing things, Professor Kathleen Sullivan, lawyer and former Dean of Stanford Law School, asked, albeit in the context of the United States: '[W]hat choices would a hypothetical set of feminist drafters face if they were to constitutionalize women's equality from scratch?' She then pondered the jurisprudential choices feminist drafters might face in crafting a Constitutional provision for women's equality:

> Such drafting would require choosing: (1) between a general provision favouring equality or a specific provision favouring sex equality, (2) between limiting classifications based on sex or protecting the class of women, (3) between reaching only state discrimination or reaching private discrimination as well, (4) between protecting women from discrimination or also guaranteeing affirmative rights to the material preconditions for equality, and (5) between setting forth only judicially enforceable or also broadly aspirational equality norms.[22]

Our overarching proposal is that any amendment to our Constitution must embed gender equality. This should not be controversial. It is now almost half a century since Australia signed the UN Convention on the Elimination of All Forms of Discrimination against Women (CEDAW), which was ratified in 1983. Article 2(a) of CEDAW [23] required States Parties '[t]o embody the principle of the equality of men and women in their national Constitutions or other appropriate legislation'. And yet, this principle is not embodied in our Constitution (although we do acknowledge the enactment of the *Sex Discrimination Act 1984* (Cth)).

Starting with the preamble, we seek to embed broadly construed aspirational equality norms into our Constitution. This is significant, not least because we currently have no preamble, at least not in the sense envisioned here. The proposed preamble acknowledges this land's original custodians, who existed prior to colonisation and continue to exist to this day. Further recognising the particular exclusion of migrant women, the preamble also acknowledges, recognises and values the people of Australia's cultural, religious, racial and linguistic diversity while celebrating the central tenets of multiculturalism. Reflecting our overarching concern to embed gender equality as a basic democratic value, our reimagined preamble recognises the equality of all genders and races, affirming the commitment to human rights and freedoms of representative democracy. Gender inequality inhibits sexual and reproductive rights; as a key determinant underpinning the gender-based violence mentioned in the preamble, it also inhibits people's right to a life free from gender-based violence and sexual and reproductive rights.[24] Recognising the need to avoid reproducing the gender binary, while also acknowledging the ways in which gender shapes all our lives, we have deliberately used the term 'gender' in this part and throughout.

We see this preamble as an aspirational statement. Although it would not be justiciable, it would nonetheless be invoked as a tool of Constitutional interpretation. As the then-Chairman of the Kenya Law Reform Commission, Kathurima M'Inoti, pointed out, although there are some similarities between preambles to ordinary statutes and Constitutions (in explaining the rationale underpinning the legislation), Constitutional preambles are 'primarily addressed to the people's emotions, collective memories and dreams rather than to the rational, organisational or legal sense of the citizen; it mirrors the founders' world view, their sense of national history and future'.[25] As M'Inoti simply put it, 'the preamble may be perceived as the conscience of the constitution'.

Although we do not see the revised preamble as explicitly creating justiciable rights, our position is that it will be used as a tool of judicial interpretation to understand the framers' (that's us!) intentions. Importantly, we want to emphasise that we do not see amendments to the preamble as a substitute for substantive amendments even though our preamble goes further than the substantive amendments.

In terms of justiciable rights to be included in the text of the Constitution, we emphasise that an express 'equality' provision is now commonplace in constitutions of the 21st century. Such a provision would bring Australia into line with other States of comparable societies and legal systems. We see a judicially enforceable 'right to equality provision' (modelled on approaches adopted elsewhere in the world) as an appropriate means of limiting classifications based on both sex and gender (and other attributes, to give the widest protection possible). We might recall the feminist litigation strategy in the United States, whereby Ruth Bader Ginsburg successfully argued that sex was a protected category as it is analogous to race. Our thinking is to include such a provision (but explicitly widening the list of protected attributes so no analogy is necessary) as a means of protecting minority rights through restraining state power. While the United States' experience has demonstrated that this is an imperfect mechanism, it is nonetheless workable.

Delegates, detractors might argue that such an equality provision will empower judicial activism and lead to excessive litigation (a 'lawyer's field day') in the High Court. These tired arguments have been invoked to prevent the extension of legal protections and rights for generations. Maintaining the status quo is not neutral. Rather, it upholds existing power relations. Judges will do what they have always done. If we, the people, decide to change the text of the law, then label us as activists, not the judges who will be tasked with interpreting the laws subject to accepted principles. Indeed, the equality provision we have proposed is by some measures a nod to pragmatism and compromise, insofar as it seeks to effect formal rather than substantive equality.

Finally, representation is the cornerstone of participation in democracy. Although we think it important both that the Commonwealth has the power to enact laws upholding gender equality *and* that its legislative power is limited, it is *also* important that our legal and political institutions reflect the populations from which they are drawn. Our proposed Constitutional amendment therefore also includes a gender quota (reflected as a ceiling).

Gender quotas are neither unique nor novel. For example, France and Rwanda have introduced proportional representation lists and reserved seating, respectively. Haiti, Congo and Tunisia have introduced candidate quotas for their electoral parties.[26] Globally, there is an agreement that women should hold at least 30% of decision-making positions, a notion agreed to in the Beijing Declaration,[27] which envisioned gender equality in all dimensions of life. Its strategic objectives included women's equal access to, and full participation in, power structures and decision-making positions. While the States so far suggested have been concerned with enforcing the gender binary, it is proposed that Australia, in recognition of current social understandings, is not restricted in this way. Our amendment frames this requirement to avoid reproducing a gender binary, instead using a phrase such as 'representation can never exceed more than 60% of one gender'.

To say that there is hesitancy around the concept of quotas is to perhaps underestimate the extent of reluctance, at least in some quarters. This hesitancy is often explained by a commitment to the merit principle, with opponents of quotas arguing that they will see unqualified people promoted. These tired old arguments do not square with experience. Let us be clear – for most of our nation's history, a de facto quota system has operated in favour of men in every branch of power. Until 2010, every Prime Minister was a man. Until 1987 every High Court Judge, a man. Until the 1940s, every parliamentarian, a man. Until the 1960s, every Minister, a man. And let us be clear – progress has been glacial for all of these firsts, even in the aftermath.

We therefore think it is essential to reframe how we conceptualise quotas.

Rather than focusing on quotas as a means of addressing the underrepresentation of women and other minority genders, let us focus instead on quotas as a means of addressing the overrepresentation of men. As Professor Rainbow Murray has argued, the traditional conception of quotas 'perpetuates the status of men as the norm and women as the "other"' and means that 'women are subject to heavy scrutiny of their qualifications and competence, whereas men's credentials go unchallenged'.[28] Setting a ceiling for any given gender avoids the overrepresentation of any single one.

We believe 60% of a given gender strikes the correct balance. This is because it provides some leeway in terms of the gendered composition of Parliament – which might constitute a majority of women in the future – but not to the extent of men's historically disproportionate representation. We acknowledge that a numerical quota will only be introduced in respect of gender (in recognition of the composition of society). To prevent these reforms privileging a select group of women, however, it is also important to ensure representation across geography, class, race, disability and sexuality. We call upon delegates to help us build this representation into our proposed reforms.

We acknowledge the intersectional impact of our gendered constitution (and indeed, our proposal) upon different women, including those who experience different gender harm because of their race, disability, religion, gender, age or other aspect of their being. This acknowledgement shaped not only the process of appointing delegates, but also our proposals, which go beyond enshrining gender equality. We have sought to protect other attributes beyond gender because our proposal stems from an intersectional feminism, which seeks to ensure that remedying the overrepresentation of men does not simply shift to representing a privileged class of white women. Mechanisms which ensure that our legal and political institutions better reflect the populations from which they are drawn only serve to enhance the legitimacy of those institutions.

There are, of course, matters left unaddressed in the modest proposal we put before you today. For example, we have not addressed several matters which have a direct bearing of the kind of society which enshrines gender equality as a basic democratic value. It is obvious that how our head of state is chosen – a hereditary monarchy headed up by a foreign head of state – does not befit the kind of modern democracy we are seeking to shape. Similarly, the current legislative powers of the Commonwealth government reflect the political concerns and lives of predominantly wealthy, white men at the turn of the last century. We might point to those matters which are absent from s 51, but have shaped women's lives in profound ways: reproductive rights, violence against women, discrimination and ex-nuptial children are all matters which come to mind. Experience tells us that the lack of explicit Commonwealth legislative authority has generated workarounds – some matters have remained the purview of the states, others through the referral of states' powers, and in still other instances through an expansive interpretation of existing powers. Delegates to this Convention will be addressing these and other matters over the next few days, and we are excited to hear their proposals.

More broadly, we acknowledge that there are some very real tensions in ensuring that such an approach does not simply reproduce the masculinist status quo. Are potential reforms merely tinkering at the edges, one might ask? The answer is yes. As Audre Lorde so powerfully put it, 'the master's tools will never dismantle the master's house'.[29] It would be preferable to begin again, and perhaps this is the recommendation this Convention will reach. And if so, we hope some of these features will find their way into the new Australian Constitution. And if not, the proposed amendments might be incorporated into our existing Constitutional framework – a stop-gap, if you will.

We think the case is made for the need for a Constitution which truly encompasses the notion of the will of the people: that promise that sits at the very heart of the democratic tradition. If there were ever any doubt that women are people (and indeed, our history records those doubts in infamy), it is now time to remedy that exclusion. It is time to act to ensure that gender equality is secured as a basic democratic value in Australia's Constitution, and that all people are properly represented *in* and *by* our Constitution irrespective of their gender.

We thank delegates for their attention at this Convention today.

The Parliament of the Commonwealth of Australia

HOUSE OF REPRESENTATIVES

Constitution Alteration (Equity and Diversity) Bill 2048

A Bill for an Act to alter the Constitution to enshrine gender equality as a basic democratic value and to promote gender equality and racial diversity, including equal integration, equal influence and gender equality in all functions in society on the basis of equal status of all persons irrespective of gender

The Parliament of Australia, with the approval of the electors, as required by the Constitution, enacts:

1 Short title

This Act may be cited as the *Constitution Alteration (Equality and Diversity) Act 2048.*

2 Preamble

Repeal the section, substitute:

We the people of Australia, as free and equal citizens –

Recognise the Aboriginal peoples and Torres Strait Islander peoples, the First Australians who were the original inhabitants of this territory, whose lands, winds and waters we all now share; and pay tribute to their unique values, and their ancient and enduring cultures, which deepen and enrich the life of our community; and who remain an integral part of this nation's future;

Regret the injustices of our past; and

Affirm that we stand together as one united peoples;

Emphasising the unique gifts and talents of this diverse and multicultural society; and celebrate and value the cultural, religious, racial and linguistic diversity of the people of Australia;

Proclaiming the right of equality of all persons in all facets, including but not limited to sex, gender, sexual orientation, ability or disability, culture, religion, ethnicity, employment, education, pregnancy, language, birth, race, colour, marital status or age and the right to a life free from gender-based violence and sexual and reproductive rights;

Believe that Australia belongs to all who live in it.

We hereby, through our freely elected representatives, adopt this Constitution as the supreme law of Australia.

3 Equality and Diversity

After section 6, insert:

6A Right to Equality

All persons shall be equal before the law, and shall have equal rights. The State shall promote the actual implementation of equality; and must not deny to any person within its jurisdiction the equal protection of the laws.

The enjoyment of the rights and freedoms shall be secured without unlawful discrimination on any ground such as sex, gender, race, colour, language, religion, political or other opinion, national or social origin, association with a national minority, property, birth or other status.

Note: Nothing in this section renders unlawful special measures for the benefit of persons on these grounds.

Section 43 of the Constitution is altered by inserting the following subsection after it:

43A Equality and Diversity

In selecting candidates for the House of Representatives and the Senate, political parties must endeavour to ensure that the composition of appointments reflects gender, sexual, and racial equality and diversity. Representation can never exceed more the 60% of one gender.

Section 64 of the Constitution is altered by inserting the following subsection after it:

64A Equality and Diversity

In appointing Ministers of State to administer departments of State of the Commonwealth, the Governor-General must endeavour to ensure that the composition of appointments reflects gender, sexual, and racial equality and diversity. Representation can never exceed more than 60% of one gender.

Section 67 of the Constitution is altered by inserting the following subsection after it:

67A Equality and Diversity

In the appointment of civil servants, the Governor-General in Council must endeavour to ensure that the composition of appointments reflects gender, sexual, and racial equality and diversity. Representation can never exceed more than 60% of one gender.

Section 72 of the Constitution is altered by inserting the following subsection after it:

72A Equality and Diversity

In appointing members of the judiciary, the Governor-General in Council must endeavour to ensure that the composition of appointments reflects gender, sexual, and racial equality and diversity. Representation can never exceed more than 60% of one gender.

Notes

1 Patricia Grimshaw et al., *Creating a Nation 1788–1990* (McPhee Gribble, 1994) 192.
2 Ibid.
3 Margaret Thornton, 'Legal Citizenship' in Wayne Hudson and John Kane (eds) *Rethinking Australian Citizenship* (Cambridge University Press, 2000) 111, 112.
4 Haig Patapan, 'The Dead Hand of the Founders? Original Intent and the Constitutional Protection of Rights and Freedoms in Australia' (1997) 25(2) *Federal Law Review* 211, 218.
5 Aileen Moreton-Robinson, 'Imagining the Good Indigenous Citizen: Race War and the Pathology of Patriarchal White Sovereignty' (2009) 15(2) *Cultural Studies Review* 61, 64.
6 Helen Irving, 'Fair Federalists and Founding Mothers' in Helen Irving (ed) *A Woman's Constitution?: Gender & History in the Australian Commonwealth* (Hale & Iremonger, 1996) 1.
7 Deborah Cass and Kim Rubenstein, 'From Federation Forward: The Representation of Women in the Australian Constitutional System' in Helen Irving (ed) *A Woman's Constitution?: Gender & History in the Australian Commonwealth* (Hale & Iremonger, 1996) 8, 18.
8 Women's Constitutional Convention, 'Sinclair Welcomes Outcomes' Media Release, 4 February 1998), http://www.womensconv.dynamite.com.au/mediaout.htm, archived at https://webarchive.nla.gov.au/awa/19990219193754/http://www.womensconv.dynamite.com.au/mediaout.htm.
9 Marian Sawer, 'Engendering Constitutional Debate' (1998) 23(2) *Alternative Law Journal* 78, 80.
10 George Williams, 'The 1998 Constitutional Convention – First Impressions', *Parliament of Australia* (23 March 1998), https://www.aph.gov.au/About_Parliament/Parliamentary_Departments/Parliamentary_Library/Publications_Archive/CIB/CIB9798/98cib11.
11 Ruth Rubio-Marin and Helen Irving, 'Introduction: Women as Constitution-Makers: The Promises and Challenges of Participation' in Ruth Rubio-Marin & Helen Irving (eds) *Women as Constitution-Makers: Case Studies from the New Democratic Era* (Cambridge University Press, 2019) 1, 2.
12 Ibid.
13 Christine Forster and Suki Beavers, United Nations Development Program, *Global Good Practices in Advancing Gender Equality and Women's Empowerment in Constitutions* (UNDP Report, 2016), https://docs.euromedwomen.foundation/files/ermwf-documents/8129_4.209.globalgoodpracticesinadvancinggenderequalityandwomen'sempowermentinconstitutions.pdf.
14 Kathleen Sullivan, 'Constitutionalizing Women's Equality' (2002) 90(3) *California Law Review* 735, 739.
15 *La Constitution du 4 octobre 1946* [French Constitution of 4 October 1946] Preamble.

16 *Grundgesetz für die Bundesrepublik Deutschland* [Basic Law for the Federal Republic of Germany] art 3.
17 *Grundgesetz für die Bundesrepublik Deutschland* [Basic Law for the Federal Republic of Germany] art 3.
18 *The Constitution of India 1950* art 15.
19 *Canada Act 1882* (UK) c 11, sch B pt I ('*Canadian Charter of Rights and Freedoms*') art 15(1); pt II Rights of the Aboriginal Peoples of Canada.
20 *Constitution of the Republic of South Africa Act 1996* (South Africa) ch 2.
21 Ruth Rubio Marin, 'Women and Participatory Constitutionalism' (2020) 18(1) *International Journal of Constitutional Law* 233, 236.
22 Sullivan (n 14) 747.
23 Convention on the Elimination of All Forms of Discrimination against Women, opened for signature 18 December 1979, 1249 UNTS 13 (entered into force 3 September 1981) art 2.
24 These material rights were (unsuccessfully) proposed in *Draft Political Constitution of the Republic of Chile July 2022*, ch 1, art 1(1), https://constitutionnet.org/sites/default/files/2022-09/International%20IDEA%20Translation%20Chile%202022%20Draft%20Constitution.pdf.
25 Kathurima M'Inoti, 'Constitutions and their Preambles' (2002) 17(2) *Wajibu* 11, 11.
26 *The Constitution of Haiti 1987*, art 17–1, 31–1–1; *The Constitution of the Republic of the Congo 2015*, art 15; *The Constitution of Tunisia 2014*, art 46.
27 UN Women, *Beijing Declaration and Platform for Action: Beijing +5 Political Declaration and Outcome* (Report 1995) art 119.
28 Rainbow Murray, 'Quotas for Men: Reframing Gender Quotas as a Means of Improving Representation for All' (2014) 108(3) *American Political Science Review* 520.
29 Audre Lorde, *Sister Outsider: Essays and Speeches* (Crossing Press, 1984) 112.

Chapter 3A

Commentary on Re-writing and Re-imagining Rights

Margaret Thornton

In view of Australia's tardiness in modernising its constitution, I congratulate Chairwomen Kcasey McLoughlin and Yee-Fui Ng for proposing that gender equality be enshrined in the Constitution. Indeed, proposals for a constitutional guarantee of gender equality have a long history, with Olympe de Gouges arguing for equal rights for women ('citizenesses') in her *Declaration of the Rights of Woman* in France in 1791, which was based on the revolutionary *Declaration of the Rights of Man and of the Citizen*. However, de Gouges was condemned as an 'impudent counterrevolutionary and unnatural being (a "woman-man")' and sent to the guillotine.[1] As there is no likelihood of McLoughlin and Ng suffering a similar fate, I suggest that they might have been a little more adventurous in their proposal.

Much of the focus of section 6A of the proposed legislation is devoted to equality and diversity in appointments to public office. While this is commendable, my concern is with the lack of specificity in the phrases 'equal before the law', 'equal rights' and 'equal protection of the laws'. While Julius Stone recognised that equality between all persons is the test of justice,[2] equality is also what he would term a 'category of indeterminate reference'. This compels a disproportionate reliance on judicial interpretation. Section 6A enjoins the State to 'promote the actual implementation of equality', but the meaning of 'actual' is unclear. If it means substantive rather than formal equality, this should be clarified.

Equality before the law, which McLoughlin and Ng advocate, is synonymous with formal equality and means treating everyone the same, regardless of gender, race, class, sexual orientation or other manifestation of difference, and accords with the conventional understanding of the rule of law within the Anglo-Australian legal tradition. Substantive equality, however, transcends the limitations of the formal interpretation by paying attention to the *result* of same treatment. In that case, equality may require multifaceted strategies; it does not lend itself automatically to equality of outcome.

Sandra Fredman advocates four overlapping aims that may be necessary to achieve substantive equality.[3] First, the cycle of disadvantage that disproportionately affects women or a particular identity group needs to be

DOI: 10.4324/9781003372462-6

broken; second, the dignity and worth of women or group need to be promoted to redress stigma; third, structural change to accommodate difference may be necessary; and fourth, full participation in society of women and/or group members needs to be the ultimate aim. McLoughlin and Ng recognise the importance of diversity in appointing personnel to public positions, but as Fredman suggests, substantive equality requires more. While the Constitution is a document that operates at a high level of abstraction to encompass multiple scenarios, Fredman argues that generalisations can leave too much discretion to judges or administrators in the interpretation of equality.

To illustrate the point, brief reference is made to the experience of the United States (US) Constitution. The 14th Amendment guaranteeing procedural equality was adopted in 1868 with the intention of ensuring civil and legal rights for the recently freed African-American citizens. However, the history of judicial interpretation reveals equality to be a contentious and uncertain term that is prone to be read down by conservative judges. Key cases, such as *Plessy v Ferguson*,[4] reveal that the prescript of equality was satisfied for the majority of judges by the highly discriminatory 'separate but equal' interpretation, which survived for more than 50 years before being overruled.[5]

If there is no guidance in the Constitution as to how judges are to interpret equality, should they adopt a formal or a substantive interpretation? That is, should an assessment be made at the starting point to determine whether equal opportunity prevails, or is the question one of equality of outcome, in which case remedial action might be necessary to overcome the history of differential treatment or disadvantage?

To illustrate the point, I turn to another key case that arose from the interpretation of equality in the US Constitution in the 1970s. Bakke was a white male applicant denied a place at the University of California Davis Medical School. He objected to the 16% set aside for racial minorities that had been introduced by the university as a substantive equality measure, as he had a higher entry score than some of the successful minority applicants.[6] The set-aside was struck down by the Supreme Court in a narrow 5–4 decision that led to a protracted and acrimonious debate regarding the meaning of equality and how it might be achieved.

Extrapolating from *Bakke* and seeking to avoid the impasse it created, the question for McLoughlin and Ng is: how should one interpret equality if there is no guidance in the constitution as to whether a formal or a substantive interpretation should be adopted?

It is apparent that judges cannot be relied upon to interpret positively the wording of the proposed constitutional amendment unaided in the absence of clear guidance, particularly when it comes to gender. After all, multiple judges of the British Empire seriously held for more than 60 years that women were not 'persons' for the purpose of admission to public and professional life, including legal practice.[7] While the proposed amendment is unlikely to result in such a bizarre outcome, the interpretation of equality in many facets of civil society will inevitably remain uncertain. We cannot expect an indeterminate term to speak for itself; nor can we rely on judges to be the sole arbiters of meaning without guidance.

Notes

1 Lynn Hunt, *Investing Human Rights: A History* (W W Norton, 2007) 171.
2 Julius Stone, *Human Law and Human Justice* (Maitland Publications, 1968) 332.
3 Sandra Fredman, *Discrimination Law* (Oxford University Press, 2nd ed, 2011) 25.
4 *Plessy v Ferguson* 163 US 537 (1896).
5 *Brown v Board of Education* 347 US 483 (1954).
6 *Regents of University of California v Bakke* 438 US 165 (1978).
7 Albie Sachs & Joan Hoff Wilson, *Sexism and the Law: A Study of Male Beliefs and Judicial Bias* (Martin Robertson, 1978). See also in *re Edith Haynes* (1904) 6 WAR 209.

Chapter 4

The Disenfranchisement of Aboriginal Women

Commonwealth Legislative Disability and Incarceration Disqualifications

Dani Linder

Extract from *Hansard* (Commonwealth of Australia)

Commonwealth Electoral Amendment (Addressing the Disenfranchisement of Aboriginal Women in Prisons) Bill 2024

Second Reading

HON DANI LINDER: I move:

That this Bill be now read a second time.

I rise today to speak on various amendments to the *Commonwealth Electoral Act 1918*, which I will simply refer to as 'the Act'.[1] Firstly, I propose an amendment to section 93 of the Act titled 'Persons Entitled to Enrolment and to Vote'. Specifically, I propose amendments to the Act which would do the following things:

1. Allow a person to vote in Commonwealth elections even if they are serving a sentence of imprisonment of three years or longer;
2. Allow a person to vote in Commonwealth elections if they are deemed to be of unsound mind and remove the Electoral Commissioner's right to object to enrolment on the basis of imprisonment or unsound mind (with some exceptions); and
3. Provide an excuse for a person who fails to vote at Commonwealth elections if their disability has prevented them doing so.

I acknowledge that the sections I've mentioned in the Act neither formally nor explicitly discriminate against persons according to their gender or race. In practice, however, the sections do indirectly contribute to the low voting political participation rates prevalent among Australia's most vulnerable, marginalised and disenfranchised citizens. Those citizens are people with

DOI: 10.4324/9781003372462-7

a disability, women, Aboriginal and Torres Strait Islander people, the homeless and those living in poverty in very remote and/or low socio-economic environments.

Of all those people, I find that in my experiences and observations of the Australian legal system, particularly as a Bundjalung and Kungarakany woman, the voices of Aboriginal women are far too often forgotten about or silenced. In fact, from my observations, Aboriginal women who experience discrimination and oppression across each of the intersectional categories I've outlined are at double the risk of being completely silenced and excluded from political participation and representation within the Australian electoral system.

It is for those reasons that I draw attention to the experiences of Aboriginal women and the important issues associated with those experiences. My hope is to provide Parliament with further context that justifies the need for the amendments to the Act that I propose today.

Drawing upon Aboriginal women's experiences is important for this Parliament to do, so that we can collectively commit to taking proactive steps that make space and provide a platform for Aboriginal women to be seen and heard. This is especially crucial when it comes to their participation and representation in law and policy decision-making processes that may affect their access to justice, political inclusivity and representation.

It is evident from the decade's worth of data that political exclusion of Aboriginal people, be it direct or indirect, is a somewhat accepted political norm in Australian society. This, however, is not what our representative democratic regime is meant to exemplify. The consequence of imposing such a high bar for a person's political participation, particularly Aboriginal women, has paved the way for further systemic racial and gender discriminatory issues that this group of people have been, and continue to be, subjected to.

It is therefore quite clear how the franchise is still limited for certain citizens in Australia, particularly for Aboriginal women who find themselves at most risk, compared to others, of being disqualified from voting at Commonwealth elections because they are serving lengthy terms of imprisonment or deemed to be of 'unsound mind'. As such, it's important to not only just consider my proposed amendments, but to vote yes on them as they will work to immediately to address these kinds of issues of disenfranchisement and in turn, contribute to enhancing Australia's democracy system so that everyone feels represented within it.

Allowing Prisoners to Vote

I'm going to start by addressing the prisoner disqualification provisions which I proposed repealing entirely. In doing so, I'm also going to highlight just some of the relevant contextual issues that are involved with this provision.

Specifically, section 93(8AA) disqualifies a person from voting in Commonwealth elections if they are serving a sentence of imprisonment of three years or longer. Now, while this disqualification applies equally to all persons who are serving a term of imprisonment of three years or more, it also comes with a variety of indirect gender and racial discriminatory issues for Aboriginal and Torres Strait Islander people – particularly Aboriginal women.

The High Court has also previously held that the wording contained within section 24 of the Australian Constitution, which grants Australian citizens an implied right to vote, does not guarantee universal suffrage. However, to exclude certain citizens from the franchise, the High Court has held that there must be 'substantial reasons' which are neither disproportionate nor inconsistent with choice by the people.[2]

So, what does this mean for citizens' electoral rights to participate?

Well, on that basis, electoral legislation has been deemed to allow for the disqualification of certain citizens from voting at Australian elections.

Such people include those who are infants, minors, persons of unsound mind and felons serving lengthy prison sentences. These are all considered to be 'substantial reasons' according to Australian common law standards.[3]

However, what poses an issue here is that the legal reasoning and justification behind the prisoner disqualification, which disqualifies prisoners from voting if they're serving a prison sentence of three years or more, only considers the length and serious nature of the offence committed by the prisoner.

Why is this problematic?

Well, this disqualification operates as a blanket ban applicable to *all* prisoners, excluding them from politically participating. Doing so fails to consider the disproportionate rates of Aboriginal people, particularly Aboriginal women, being streamlined at an early age toward institutionalisation, from detention centres to incarceration, relative to non-Indigenous Australians. The cause of this is widely understood to lie in the unhealed and unreconciled intergenerational traumatic experiences that remain unrecognised within Australia's formalised Western system of governance.[4]

Electoral legislation should consider other elements of a prisoner's identity prior to their disqualification, such as a person's cultural identity, gender and background. Every citizen, no matter what their identity, should have a free and equal opportunity to vote and be politically represented in Australia's democratic regime.

If we don't allow persons serving lengthy terms of imprisonment to vote, we really miss capturing the votes of many vulnerable citizens in society who are placed at the most risk of being disenfranchised from and disillusioned with the legal system.

Further, political participation rights form an important part of a person's connection to society and the exercise of civil rights. International standards[5] make it clear that such limitations placed upon a person's exercise of fundamental political rights add an additional and unnecessary layer of punishment on someone already punished and serving their sentence. Therefore, it is not appropriate for Commonwealth electoral legislation to further add to a state's administration of criminal justice, on a person who has committed a state-based offence, by disqualifying those persons from politically participating at federal elections.[6]

If anything, it is important for prisoners to maintain their political membership of their country's political community.[7] This is vital to ensure persons incarcerated, particularly those serving lengthy terms of imprisonment, form a better sense of civic responsibility and political inclusion that underpins citizenship rights and societal obligations.8 Therefore, while some crimes committed by sentenced offenders are worse than others, I maintain that political representation of those persons is still important if we as a society are to truly adhere to principles of democracy and the administration of criminal justice.

I'll also add that there is simply no evidence that further exclusion of a person from society politically – that is, through preventing them from voting, after they've already been sentenced for the crime they've committed incentivises the person to adhere to societal expectations and, most importantly, their legal obligations as a lawful citizen. In fact, I'd argue that it is usually those who are serving the lengthiest terms of imprisonment who require representation that will advocate for support that is rehabilitative, as well as a proactive approach that seeks to support those individuals as best as possible so that crimes warranting lengthy terms of imprisonment are prevented.

The preamble to the *Australian Citizenship Act 2007* (Cth) declares that Parliament recognises that Australian citizenship represents full and formal membership of the community of the Commonwealth of Australia, as well as that Australian citizenship is a common bond involving reciprocal rights and obligations.[9]

The reference to the reciprocity of rights and obligations is important in the context of membership of the community and Aboriginal women's exercise of their political participation rights. Why? Well because there are high statistics of Aboriginal women incarcerated in Australia every year and yet the current parliamentary rationale for temporarily disqualifying a person's right to vote is if they've engaged in antisocial behaviour and serious criminal conduct. In such cases, those persons are likely to be sentenced to a lengthy term of imprisonment. This would then, according to current electoral law, disqualify them from voting in an Australian election.

At this point, we must consider the complex contextual issues Aboriginal women face when it comes to being disproportionately incarcerated in Australian prisons, disproportionately sentenced to lengthier terms of imprisonment compared to non-Indigenous women and the history and present state of their disenfranchisement. When we consider such obstructions that limit an Aboriginal woman's ability to vote and be what's considered 'civically responsible', it's clear that their experiences with the law, be it in a criminal sense or political sense, are very different to others. Dispossession, racial discrimination and intersectional disadvantage are factors that place Aboriginal women at a greater risk in society of being disenfranchised in this way and such factors I'd argue justify why they, of all people, need political engagement, representation and continued access to the Australian political system through voting.

Since the handing down of the *Roach v Electoral Commissioner* High Court Case in 2007,[10] this Parliament missed a real opportunity to reform electoral legislation for the benefit of vulnerable and disenfranchised people.

The case of *Roach* saw Yuin woman Vickie Roach come before the High Court as a woman serving a lengthy term of imprisonment who was disqualified from voting at Commonwealth elections.

Roach challenged the electoral prisoner disqualification because, as she argued, this went against principles of representative democracy – specifically, the implied right to vote contained within sections 7 and 24 of the Australian Constitution.[11]

Yet despite those factors, the High Court upheld the disqualification of prisoners serving three years or more from Commonwealth elections; the Parliament has done nothing with that issue since.

Vickie Roach, however, is a textbook example of what many Aboriginal women in this country experience when it comes to domestic violence and intergenerational trauma that she's developed from being a survivor of the Stolen Generations.

She and other women and vulnerable incarcerated people like her should, at the very least, be able to access and exercise their voting rights.

Political participation forms an important part of a person's connection to society and their exercise of civil rights. This is also very much the view shared by international standards of political participation.[12]

Therefore, it is not appropriate for Commonwealth electoral legislation to further add to a state's administration of criminal justice to a person who has committed a state-based offence by disqualifying those persons from politically participating at Commonwealth elections.

This is particularly important when considering, for example, the experiences of Aboriginal women who are at high risk of suffering from poverty, homelessness, mental health problems or political and societal exclusion by virtue of residing on Country in often very geographically remote locations.

These factors are key contributors that place Aboriginal women at higher risk of being incarcerated compared to non-Indigenous Australians.

In fact, Aboriginal women are statistically proven to be Australia's fastest-growing prison population, occupying 34% of the overall female prison population despite comprising less than 2% of Australia's total population.[13]

As 80% of Aboriginal imprisoned women are also mothers,[14] most stories of Aboriginal children being placed into out-of-home care begin with the removal of their mother into adult incarceration.

We also must understand that most Aboriginal women incarcerated are not only sole carers to their own children, but also carers for other Aboriginal children from their community whose parents or grandparents have been deemed incapable of looking after them.

You can see just how far-reaching the damage can extend with Indigenous incarceration in Australia, but also precisely why Aboriginal people, particularly women, need to be politically engaged and able to vote for whoever represents their interests when it comes to law and policy reform on Aboriginal issues.

While Aboriginal women's incarceration rates continue to increase, I suggest that those people should be able to access and exercise their voting rights. Doing so enables those people to elect the political representative they think will most likely prioritise advocating for their rights. Such democratic representation is imperative in the context of reforming Australia's criminal justice system that oppresses and institutionalises Aboriginal women.

Until prisoners are given a voice, Australia's most vulnerable people will continue to be politically silenced by this Act and their issues will remain unresolved and left to the bottom of the agenda pile. Therefore, I move that we should vote Yes to repealing section 93 (8AA) of the Act.

Allowing Persons Deemed of 'Unsound Mind' to Vote

The next point I want to make relates to the proposed amendment of the 'unsound mind' disqualification in section 93(8)(a) of the Act. This section disqualifies a person from enrolling and voting at Commonwealth elections if they've been deemed to be of unsound mind.[15]

The disqualification is problematic as it leaves open the opportunity for its application – that is, the judgment of a person's ability to understand the significance of voting and how to vote – to be based on a discriminatory presumption. That discriminatory presumption is that people deemed to be of 'unsound mind' are incapable of voting and should be disqualified.

The Australian Human Rights Commission has previously criticised the wording of this disqualification as vague and lacking clarity in terms of how persons are categorised as being of 'unsound mind', as well as who decides on their status.[16]

That critique also acknowledges international standards of protecting the franchise of persons with disabilities found within the United Nations Convention on the Rights of Persons with Disabilities.[17] This exclusion was established during the 19th century in Australia during a time when exclusionary social policies were dominant and guided legislative drafting and political norms.[18]

Reflecting upon what I've just spoken about with the prisoner disqualification provision, including how it impacts Aboriginal women, I'd like to now draw your attention to some similar contextual factors to bear in mind when it comes to the 'unsound mind' disqualification.

While this section does not explicitly discriminate against persons according to their gender and cultural identity, it does have a real impact on Aboriginal and Torres Strait Islander people who are incarcerated – mostly Aboriginal women, whether they are incarcerated or not.

In their *Pathways to Justice* report of 2017, the Australian Law Reform Commission noted that Aboriginal people who are incarcerated are likely to be affected by mental illnesses and illiteracy issues.[19]

Historically, Aboriginal people were automatically deemed to be of 'unsound mind' under section 4 of the *Commonwealth Franchise Act 1902*. As that section showed, the original legislative electoral law presumption on Aboriginal people's mental capacity to exercise their rights to the franchise as citizens was exclusionary. Further, this presumption considered Aboriginal people as lacking the capacity and intelligence to understand political choice through voting at an election.[20]

Even though that section has since been repealed, there remain indirect possibilities where Aboriginal people may still experience racial discrimination by being deemed to be of 'unsound mind' for the purpose of disqualifying those persons from voting at Commonwealth elections.21 This is largely due to ever-present racial bias existent in many of Australia's institutions, laws and policies – particularly within Australia's healthcare system.[22]

The deeming of an elector (particularly those of Aboriginal descent) to be of 'unsound mind', which would disqualify them from voting at a Commonwealth election, provides doctors with power to certify those persons as being mentally or intellectually incapable to vote, from a systematic healthcare perspective where racial bias is present towards Aboriginal people.[23]

The section needs to better accommodate and have greater cultural sensitivity toward the ways in which Aboriginal people, particularly Aboriginal women, experience political and racial bias through discriminatory assumptions made about their mental capacity to make informed and intelligent political decisions that will affect their lives.

We need to recognise in Australian electoral legislation that most Aboriginal electors suffer from intergenerational trauma as a result of their dispossession following the Stolen Generations. Such traumatic events, and there are many, often lead to their incarceration through antisocial behaviour exhibited towards authorities.[24]

Those experiences of intergenerational trauma and dispossession, however, do not automatically negate Aboriginal people's ability to understand the importance of their right to vote and to exercise that right.

There have been many surveys conducted across Australia with Aboriginal women in prison which show that they experience high levels of psychological distress, depression and anxiety connected to social and emotional wellbeing, such as unresolved trauma, removal from their families as children and separation from their community.[25]

Additionally, qualitative research shows that this level of social and emotional disease is not considered to be exceptional by Aboriginal women; instead, it is the norm.[26]

However, intergenerational trauma, depression and an aggression towards authorities are factors that do not limit the political capacity and intelligence of a person to capably vote at an election.[27]

If anything, one would think those types of actions for a person from such a culturally disenfranchised background, particularly Aboriginal women, would empower them and positively impact their self-worth, both as an individual and as an Aboriginal person. In turn, this would lead to a better state of their mental health and wellbeing to some extent.

The 'unsound mind' disqualification should ultimately be amended so that it is narrower than its current definition. Section 93 (8)(a) should, in my opinion, reflect what has been introduced in similar electoral legislation in New Zealand. For example, the equivalent provision for section 93 (8)(a) in New Zealand is section 80 (c) of the *Electoral Act 1993* (NZ), which only applies to persons subject to a court order that declares their mental impairment[28] or a compulsory treatment order.[29]

Amending section 93 (8)(a) of the Act so that it has narrower scope to disqualify persons deemed of 'unsound mind' might clarify the process of determining a person's ability to vote in this context. I propose that section 93 (8)(a) of the Act be amended so that the disqualification is conditional. In other words, people under this section would only be disqualified if they are detained in a hospital or secure facility under their relevant state or territory mental health legislation and found by a court or judge to be mentally impaired and incapable of understanding the nature and significance of voting. In those circumstances, if after a reasonable adjustment plan has been considered by the AEC and the person's designated carer, it is agreed that such adjustments will have minimal to no improvement on the person's ability to vote, they will then be disqualified.

I propose that this approach to section 93 (8)(a) of the Act introduces a more thorough investigation and assessment of a person's ability to understand the voting process in Australian elections which might also assist in providing necessary data to the AEC when it comes to providing support services for vulnerable voters.

Removal of Objection to Enrolment for Prisoner and Unsound Mind Disqualifications

I also propose amendments to section 114 titled 'Objection to Enrolment' – specifically to subsection (3), which intersects with section 93.

Subsection (3) limits the Electoral Commissioner's right to object on the ground set out in section 93(8)(a). Given the ground contained in section 93(8)(a) is proposed to be repealed, this limitation will not be required, along with similar sections dealing with objections (including sections 113, 116 and 118).

Provide an Excuse for Persons with a Disability Who Fail to Vote on Election Day

Finally, I propose amendments be made to the 'compulsory voting' provision of the Act within s 245.

Specifically, I propose there be an insertion of a new subsection, namely 14A, which would provide a valid excuse for people who fail to vote at Commonwealth elections if their disability has prevented them from doing so. It would ensure that where this happens, they will not be subjected to the penalties set out in the Act.

This amendment is justified in light of:

- the financial vulnerabilities and poverty prevalent within Aboriginal families and communities;
- the challenging family structures that exist within Aboriginal families and how Aboriginal women are usually the sole providers of their own children and often, other children in their community; and
- the fact that Aboriginal women are the highest incarcerated group of people in the world who are also vulnerable to suffering from trauma, mental health issues, cognitive issues and illiteracy issues.

The intent behind the proposed insertion of subsection (14A) is to provide an additional 'valid and sufficient reason' for the failure of an elector to vote at Commonwealth elections if their disability has prevented them from doing so. In turn, this would ensure that electors who are prevented from voting for Commonwealth elections are not subject to penalties outlined within section 245 of the Act.

It is inappropriate to subject such vulnerable persons to penalties which requires them to take further administrative action to validate their circumstances while trying to juggle all of their other oppressive life struggles.

Again, elections need less red tape and more support of vulnerable disenfranchised people.

The insertion of this new subsection within s 245 of the Act might better provide the type of support and electoral attitude affected constituents need.

And finally, as a way of providing clarity within the Act around the term 'disability' (as there currently exists no definition for this term), I propose the insertion of a new subsection – that is, 14B within s 245 – with a term for 'disability', and that this new term be a broad and more inclusive term similar to the term set out in section 4 of the *Commonwealth Disability Discrimination Act 1992* (the DDA) definition of 'disability'.

As I mentioned earlier, this proposed amendment seeks to ensure all electors with disabilities who are prevented from voting at Commonwealth elections aren't subject to penalties under section 245 if they are unable to vote because of their disability.

I commend this Bill to the House.

The Parliament of the

Commonwealth of Australia

HOUSE OF REPRESENTATIVES

Commonwealth Electoral Amendment (Addressing the Disenfranchisement of Aboriginal Women in Prisons) Bill 2024

A Bill for an Act to amend the *Commonwealth Electoral Act 1918* to address the disenfranchisement of Aboriginal women in prisons and for related purposes

The Parliament of Australia enacts:

1 Short title

This Act may be cited as the *Commonwealth Electoral Amendment Act 2024*.

2 Commencement

(1) Each provision of this Act specified in column 1 of the table commences, or is taken to have commenced, in accordance with column 2 of the table. Any other statement in column 2 has effect according to its terms.

Commencement information

Column 1	Column 2	Column 3
Provisions	**Commencement**	**Date/Details**
1. The whole of this Act	The day after this Act receives the Royal Assent	

Note: This table relates only to the provisions of this Act as originally enacted. It will not be amended to deal with any later amendments of this Act.

(2) Any information in column 3 of the table is not part of this Act. Information may be inserted in this column, or information in it may be edited, in any published version of this Act.

3 Schedules

Legislation that is specified in a Schedule to this Act is amended or repealed as set out in the applicable items in the Schedule concerned, and any other item in a Schedule to this Act has effect according to its terms.

Schedule 1 – Amendments

Part 1 – Disqualification of persons serving a sentence of imprisonment of 3 years or longer

Commonwealth Electoral Act 1918

1 Section 93(2)

Omit "subsections (3), (4), (5) and (8AA)", substitute "subsections (3), (4) and (5)".

2 Section 93(8AA)

Repeal the subsection.

3 Section 208(2)(b)

Omit 'day; and', substitute 'day.'.

4 Section 208(2)(c)

Repeal the paragraph.

5 Section 221(3)(a)

Omit 'election; or', substitute 'election.'.

6 Section 221(3)(b)

Repeal the paragraph.

Part 2 – Disqualification of persons of unsound mind

Commonwealth Electoral Act 1918

7 Section 93(8)(a)

After 'voting', insert 'if they are a person who is detained in a hospital or in a secure facility under the person's residing state or territory relevant mental health legislation and has been found by a court or a judge to be mentally impaired and incapable of understanding the nature and significance of voting, provided that a reasonable adjustment plan has been considered by the Electoral Commission and the person's designated carer, and the Electoral Commission and the person's designated carer agree that even if the plan is implemented, the person is likely to remain incapable of understanding the nature and significance of voting'

Part 3 – Objection to enrolment

Commonwealth Electoral Act 1918

8 Section 113 (definition of *private objection*)

Omit 'subsection 114(1), (1A) or (1B)', substitute 'subsection 114(1) or (1B)'.

9 Section 114(1)

Omit ', other than the ground specified in paragraph 93(8)(a),'.

10 Section 114(1A)

Repeal the subsection.

11 Section 114(3)

Repeal the subsection.

12 Section 116(4)

Repeal the subsection.

13 Section 116(6)

Omit ', except one under subsection 114(1A),'.

14 Section 118(1A)

Omit 'other than one under subsection 114(1A)'.

15 Section (118) (3)

Omit 'an objection under subsection 114(1), (1A) or (2)', substitute 'an objection under subsection (1) or (2)'.

Part 4 – Compulsory voting

Commonwealth Electoral Act 1918

16 After subsection 245(1)

Insert:

(14A) Without limiting the circumstances that may constitute a valid and sufficient reason for not voting, the fact that an elector has a disability that prevented the elector from voting constitutes a valid and sufficient reason for the failure of the elector to vote.

(14B) In subsection (14A), ***disability***, in relation to an elector, means:

(a) total or partial loss of the elector's bodily or mental functions; or
(b) total or partial loss of a part of the body; or
(c) the presence in the body of organisms causing disease or illness; or
(d) the presence in the body of organisms capable of causing disease or illness; or
(e) the malfunction, malformation or disfigurement of a part of the elector's body; or
(f) a disorder or malfunction that results in the elector learning differently from a person without the disorder or malfunction; or
(g) a disorder, illness or disease that affects a person's thought processes, perception of reality, emotions or judgment, or that results in disturbed behaviour.

Notes

1 Version No 27 (Compilation Date 18 February 2022) <https://www.legislation.gov.au/Details/C2022C00074>.
2 *Roach v Electoral Commissioner* (2007) 233 CLR 162, [8] (Gleeson CJ).
3 *A-G (Cth) ex rel McKinlay v Commonwealth* (1975) 135 CLR 1, 642.
4 *Commonwealth Electoral Act 1918* (Cth) ss 93–7; Jennifer Fitzgerald and George Zdenkowski, 'Voting Rights of Convicted Persons' (1987) 11 *Criminal Law Journal* 11.
5 See, for example, the *International Covenant on Civil and Political Rights*, signed 16 December 1966 (entered into force 23 March 1976) arts 2, 25.
6 *Roach v Electoral Commissioner* (2007) 233 CLR 162, [10] (Gleeson CJ).
7 *Roach v Electoral Commissioner* (2007) 233 CLR 162, [11] (Gleeson CJ).
8 *Singh v Commonwealth* (2004) 222 CLR 322; *Hwang v Commonwealth* (2005) 80 ALJR 125; 222 ALR 83; Kim Rubenstein, *Australian Citizenship Law in Context* (Lawbook Co, 2002) [329].
9 *Australian Citizenship Act 2007* (Cth).
10 233 CLR 162.
11 *Constitution of the Commonwealth of Australia*, ss 7, 24.
12 See, for example, the *International Covenant on Civil and Political Rights*, opened for signature 16 December 1966, 999 UNTS X (entered into force 23 March 1976) arts 2, 25.

13 *Corrective Services, Australia: National and State Information About Adult Prisoners and Community-Based Corrections, Including Legal Status, Custody Type, Indigenous Status, Sex* (9 June 2022), https://www.abs.gov.au/statistics/people/crime-and-justice/corrective-services-australia/latest-release.
14 Schizophrenia Fellowship of NSW Inc, *Report on the Criminal Justice System in Australia* (Report, 2001) 24.
15 *Commonwealth Electoral Act 1918,* s 93 (8)(a).
16 Australian Human Rights Commission, *The Right to Vote Is Not Enjoyed Equally By All Australians* (1 February 2010), https://www.humanrights.gov.au/our-work/rights-and-freedoms/publications/right-vote-not-enjoyed-equally-all-australians.
17 Opened for signature 30 March 2007, 2515 UNTS 3 (entered into force 3 May 2008).
18 Trevor Ryan et al., 'Voting with an Unsound Mind: A Comparative Study of the Voting Rights of Persons with Mental Disabilities' (2016) 39(3) *UNSW Law Journal* 1038; Ien Ang and Jon Stratton, 'Multiculturalism in Crisis: The New Politics of Race and National Identity in Australia' (1998) 2 *TOPIA: Canadian Journal of Cultural Studies* 28; Bruce Kapferer and Barry Morris, 'The Australian Society of the State: Egalitarian Ideologies and New Directions in Exclusionary Practice' (Fall, 2003) 47(3) *Social Analysis* 85; Kay Anderson and Affrica Taylor, 'Exclusionary Politics and the Question of National Belonging' (2005) 5(4) *Ethnicities* 464.
19 Australian Law Reform Commission, *Pathways to Justice – Inquiry into the Incarceration Rate of Aboriginal and Torres Strait Islander Peoples* (Final Report No 133, 2017) 63.
20 *Commonwealth Franchise Act 1902*, s 4 (repealed).
21 *Commonwealth Electoral Act 1918,* s 93 (8)(a).
22 Angela Durey, 'Reducing Racism in Aboriginal Health Care in Australia: Where Does Cultural Education Fit?' (2010) 34(1) *Australian and New Zealand Journal of Public Health* 87–8.
23 Joint Select Committee on Electoral Reform, Parliament of Australia, *The Operation During the 1984 General Election of the 1983/84 Amendments to Commonwealth Electoral Legislation* (1986) 31 [3.39].
24 Human Rights and Equal Opportunity Commission, *Bringing them Home: Report of the National Inquiry Into the Separation of Aboriginal and Torres Strait Islander Children From Their Families* (Report, 1997) 154, https://www.humanrights.gov.au/sites/default/files/content/pdf/social_justice/bringing_them_home_report.pdf; Australian Law Reform Commission, *Pathways to Justice* (n 19) 66.
25 Justice Health & Forensic Mental Health Network, *2009 NSW Inmate Health Survey: Aboriginal Health Report* (Report, 2010) 8; James R P Ogloff et al., 'Assessing the Mental Health, Substance Abuse, Cognitive Functioning, and Social/Emotional Well-Being Needs of Aboriginal Prisoners in Australia' (2017) 23(4) *Journal of Correctional Healthcare* 398–411.
26 S Kendall et al., 'Holistic Conceptualizations of Health by Incarcerated Aboriginal Women in New South Wales, Australia' (2019) 29(11) *Qualitative Health Research* 1549–65.
27 Trevor Ryan et al., 'Voting with an Unsound Mind: A Comparative Study of the Voting Rights of Persons with Mental Disabilities' (2016) 39(3) *University of New South Wales Law Journal* 1060.
28 *Electoral Act 1993*, s 80 (c)(1)(i)(ii).
29 *Electoral Act 1993*, s 80 (c)(1)(iii).

Chapter 4A

Commentary on *The Disenfranchisement of Aboriginal Women*

Krystal Lockwood

This Bill addresses long-standing issues of First Nations disenfranchisement. Here, I first note the wider implications such reforms would bring, before outlining three significant points of how I believe these amendments would enhance the political inclusivity of Aboriginal women and their communities.

Wider Benefits

Initially, it is important to acknowledge this Bill's impact would extend far beyond Aboriginal women. The number of Aboriginal women impacted by prisoner disqualification laws is relatively small. Nearly half of custodial sentences for Aboriginal women are below six months, with the median length 18 months.[1] These are shorter than the median for Indigenous men (26 months),[2] as well as non-Indigenous men (48 months)[3] and women (36 months).[4] Although the number of those impacted by unsound mind disqualifications are harder to identify, the proposed amendments would undoubtedly benefit a wider cohort, including both Aboriginal and non-Aboriginal women and men.

The validity and impact of these disqualification laws have also been examined. An overwhelming finding is that flawed laws can underpin assumptions within a liberal democracy, and – as examined in this Bill – that such shortcomings can negatively affect impacted vulnerable populations.[5]

If this Bill passes, it would undoubtedly benefit a wider cohort. In saying this, it is important to note how this Bill would particularly benefit Aboriginal women, which would in turn impact their communities and wider society.

Ripple Effects Through First Nation Communities

Firstly, the nature of Indigenous familial relationships would result in a wide ripple effect from such laws. Many communities are matrilineal, or hold women in influential roles as Elders, Aunties, sisters and cousins.[6] Women are more likely to be in carer roles, thus tending to directly influence

DOI: 10.4324/9781003372462-8

underpinning values – including political engagement – giving Aboriginal women the greatest reach in their community. For Aboriginal women, disqualification laws would consequently have an effect well beyond those directly impacted.

However, much more work is needed to increase the franchise of Indigenous women and communities. Vickie Roach, who led the monumental *Roach* decision[7] in 2007, has since become frustrated with political processes and actively refrains from voting.[8] First Nations communities are collectivist,[9] and if vulnerable people within them are being excluded, there may be wider disengagement of civil participation. There is much work to be done – but empowering Indigenous women, rather than actively excluding them via disqualification laws, would lead to far greater benefits for the women and their communities.

The Insight from Lived Experience

An underlying assumption is that vulnerable Aboriginal women experiencing incarceration or poor health would lack a desire to engage in decision-making processes because of their experiences of being excluded from and by the Australian legal system. However, there is little evidence to support this. Engaging with Indigenous mothers who were incarcerated, Thalia Anthony and colleagues found their Indigenous mothers' primary concerns were a desire to make positive decisions about their lives and fulfil roles of responsibility within their communities.[10] Moreover, best-practice principles in healthcare are to empower people in care by ensuring they have decision-making powers,[11] preventing their adverse experiences from hindering the process of political engagement. Conversely, these experiences provide a first-hand experience of policy decisions, particularly when these policies and practices overlook vulnerable groups – a point exemplified by Vickie Roach's achievements.[12]

Indigenous Perspectives in Systems

Perhaps the most systemic issue this Bill could contribute to addressing is the failure to embed (or at least recognise) Indigenous ways of *knowing, being and doing* in law, policies and practices. At sentencing, there has been a tumultuous and piecemeal recognition of culture and considerations of Indigenous peoples' distinct experience. This has led to a 'weak' legal pluralism where the cumulative effect of settler colonialism on First Nations peoples is usually either overlooked or misunderstood.[13]

With Indigenous perspectives often neglected within healthcare, a lack of cultural competency in health professionals can have severe consequences. Moreover, Indigenous models of Social and Emotional Wellbeing are rarely understood or applied. These health concerns overlap considerably with the 'effectiveness' of the criminal justice system,[14] including applications of disqualification laws.

Conclusion

Aboriginal women who are incarcerated and women with complex health issues constitute vulnerable populations. When laws, policies and practices are made to support vulnerable populations, they create better outcomes for everyone. The proposed Bill would have notable impacts for Aboriginal women. Although relatively small numbers of women would be directly impacted by these changes, the pivotal roles played by Aboriginal women in their communities would lead to ripple effects across First Nations communities. Moreover, the lived experience of women would more likely inform rather than impinge on political engagement. In considering systems, the proposed amendments could address bureaucratic barriers that currently impede Indigenous perspectives in law and health. Overall, the propositions brought forward by this Bill would certainly enhance the political inclusivity of Aboriginal women, and in turn their communities.

Notes

1 Australian Bureau of Statistics, *Prisoners in Australia*, 2019 (Catalogue No 4517.0, 5 December 2019), https://www.abs.gov.au/statistics/people/crime-and-justice/prisoners-australia/2019; Lorna Bartels, *Sentencing of Indigenous Women* (2012) Brief No 14, Indigenous Justice Clearinghouse, 1–8.
2 Ibid 69.
3 Ibid 69.
4 Ibid 69.
5 Eg Lisa Hill and Cornelia Koch, 'The Voting Rights of Incarcerated Australian Citizens' (2011) 46(2) *Australian Journal of Political Science* 213–228; Trevor Ryan et al., 'Voting with an "Unsound Mind"? A Comparative Study of the Voting Rights of Persons with Mental Disabilities' (2016) 39 *UNSW Law Journal* 1038.
6 Patricia Dudgeon and Abigail Bray, 'Indigenous Relationality: Women, Kinship and the Law' (2019) 3(2) *Genealogy* 23.
7 *Roach v Electoral Commissioner* (2007) 233 CLR 162.
8 'How an Incarcerated Yuin Woman Took On the Electoral Commission and Won', *NITV* (Online, 13 May 2022), https://www.sbs.com.au/nitv/article/2022/05/03/how-incarcerated-yuin-woman-took-electoral-commission-and-won-1.
9 Patricia Dudgeon et al., 'Working Together: Aboriginal and Torres Strait Islander Mental Health and Wellbeing Principles and Practice' (2014) Telethon Kids Institute, Kulunga Aboriginal Research Development Unit, Department of the Prime Minister and Cabinet (Australia).
10 Thalia Anthony, Gemma Sentance and Larissa Behrendt, '"We're Not Being Treated Like Mothers": Listening to the Stories of First Nations Mothers in Prison' (2021) 10(3) *Laws* 74.
11 Michael L Wehmeyer and Karrie A Shogren. 'Self-Determination and Choice'. In: Singh, N. (eds) *Handbook of Evidence-Based Practices in Intellectual and*

Developmental Disabilities. Evidence-Based Practices in Behavioral Health (Cham: Springer, 2016), 561–584. https://doi.org/10.1007/978-3-319-26583-4_21.

12 *Roach v Electoral Commissioner* (2007) 233 CLR 162.

13 See Nicole Watson and Heather Douglas (eds) *Indigenous Legal Judgments: Bringing Indigenous Voices Into Judicial Decision Making* (Routledge, 2021).

14 Chelsea Watego et al., *Partnership for Justice in Health: Scoping Paper on Race, Racism and the Australian Health System* (Lowitja Institute, 2021).

Chapter 5

Re-Charting the Victorian Charter of Human Rights

Advancing Equality in Human Rights Legislation

Tania Penovic and Julie Debeljak

Extract from *Hansard* (Parliament of Victoria)

Charter of Human Rights and Responsibilities (Advancing Equality) Amendment Bill 2024

Second Reading

HON TANIA PENOVIC and HON JULIE DEBELJAK: We jointly move:
That the Bill be now read a second time.

Victoria's *Charter of Human Rights and Responsibilities Act 2006*[1] was the first legislative charter of rights to be enacted by an Australian state government. This landmark legislation has now been fully in force since 1 January 2008. Since then, we have reviewed the Charter's operation and examined the degree to which it has addressed gendered harms. Recognising its limitations, this parliament has committed to ensuring that the Charter operates as an instrument for empowering women and eliminating gender inequality. The Charter of Human Rights and Responsibilities (Advancing Equality) Amendment Bill 2024 is the culmination of our commitment.

The Bill strengthens the rights set out in the Charter, derived from the International Covenant on Civil and Political Rights (known as the ICCPR), to respond to women's lived experiences. Recognising the indivisibility and interdependence of human rights and the need to dismantle patriarchal structures which generate inequality, the Bill introduces rights enshrined in the International Covenant on Economic, Social and Cultural Rights (known as the ICESCR) and Convention on the Elimination of All Forms of Discrimination against Women (known as CEDAW).

Rights cannot be realised without effective remedies for breach. For this reason, the Bill is accompanied by the Charter of Human Rights and Responsibilities

DOI: 10.4324/9781003372462-9

(Advancing Enforcement) Amendment Bill 2024 (Advancing Enforcement Bill) through which the Charter's enforcement mechanisms will be clarified and strengthened. Working together, these Bills will refashion the Charter as a vehicle for advancing substantive gender equality.

Illuminating Gendered Harms

While recognising that some rights must never be limited, through the insertion of s 7(2B) the Bill embeds a gender perspective for examining the scope of rights and when rights may be limited under the Charter. This approach accords with the rights set out in CEDAW and the gender mainstreaming strategy adopted by United Nations (or UN) institutions and treaty bodies to shed light on gendered harms.[2]

A determination of when rights may be limited under section 7(2) must take account of the extent to which a right has been enjoyed by persons of different genders and the gendered impacts of limitations on the right. Section 7(2) assessments must also consider whether the enjoyment of the right has been undermined by social and cultural patterns of conduct. This will enable gender-based prejudices and misconceptions which sustain inequality to be exposed and eliminated. By bringing this framework into the determination of what is 'compatible with human rights', section 4 of the Advancing Enforcement Bill incorporates gender considerations into the application of human rights. This includes the development and scrutiny of legislation, statutory interpretation and conduct of public authorities.

Some members of this parliament have questioned whether legislation is a suitable means of addressing social and cultural patterns of conduct. It is abundantly clear that legislation has a key role to play. The Bill will provide a framework for dismantling gender-based stereotypes and assumptions which have informed the conduct of public authorities (including law enforcement, prosecutors, courts and tribunals), made women's lived experiences invisible and undermined the realisation of rights.[3]

Rigid assumptions about appropriate or acceptable behaviour have seen women all too often disempowered and disbelieved. They have had an especially pernicious effect where gender-based violence is alleged. The UN Committee which supervises CEDAW's implementation has found that stereotyped views about credible responses, ascribed to an imagined 'ideal victim', have driven gender-based violence,[4] hindered accountability[5] and undermined the impartiality and integrity of the justice system.[6] Such misconceptions must be identified and repudiated.

Dismantling Structural Inequality

Beyond gender stereotyping, the root causes of inequality include patriarchal power structures and systemic discrimination. The Bill will require the rights to non-discrimination and equality before the law to be interpreted with reference to these root causes, with a view to achieving substantive gender equality. It will provide a framework for our government, parliament, public authorities, courts and tribunals to recognise the complexity of women's lives and dismantle the structures of their subordination.

The Bill abandons the erroneous assumption that discrimination is confined to a single attribute and recognises the reality that discrimination may arise on intersecting grounds. Those who experience intersectional or entrenched discrimination may not be in a position to pursue complaints, and individual complaints cannot dismantle structural and systemic inequality. This Bill will establish a framework for the adoption of special measures to address specific manifestations of inequality that require comprehensive solutions. One of these manifestations is gender-based violence.

Eliminating Gender-Based Violence

Gender-based violence is Australia's most pressing human rights issue. It affects our entire community, is exacerbated by intersectional disadvantage and is experienced at high rates by some women, including Aboriginal women, culturally and linguistically diverse women, lesbian and transgender women and women with disabilities.[7] Gender-based violence is a key contributor to the burden of disease, poverty and problematic drug use, and a cause of intimate partner homicide,[8] with the COVID-19 pandemic seeing violence in the home rise in frequency and severity.[9]

Gender-based violence has been recognised as a key driver of women's subordination and a critical obstacle to achieving substantive gender equality.[10] The Bill recognises that the obligation to exercise due diligence to prevent, investigate and punish acts of gender-based violence is not confined to the conduct of state actors. It extends to violence perpetrated by non-state actors in the private sphere, including in the home.[11] Comprehensive measures to combat gender-based violence and support victim-survivors will be adopted in collaboration with victim-survivors, including Aboriginal women and others with lived experiences of intersectional disadvantage, in line with the maxim of 'nothing about us without us!'[12] In light of the ongoing legacy of colonisation, this maxim has particular pertinence for the rights of Aboriginal people.

Advancing the Rights of Aboriginal People

The perspectives of Aboriginal people have remained largely absent from the formulation and implementation of policies affecting their lives. Aboriginal women have been particularly marginalised and subjected to discriminatory policies devised without hearing their voices or considering their perspectives.

While gender-based violence is pervasive across the whole of society, nationally Aboriginal women are up to 3.4 times more likely to be sexually assaulted, 32 times more likely to be hospitalised due to family violence, and ten times more likely to be killed than non-Aboriginal women.[13] Yet structural discrimination, cultural ignorance and stereotyping have been defining features of their treatment by successive governments and parliaments, public authorities, courts and tribunals.

The past decade has seen the rate of imprisonment of Aboriginal persons almost double,[14] with Aboriginal women now representing the fastest-growing cohort in Victoria's prisons.[15] Most Aboriginal women in prison have experienced intersectional disadvantage and physical or sexual abuse. Victim-survivors of gender-based violence are often mistaken for perpetrators, denied the support they need and detained without conviction for minor non-violent crimes.[16]

The imprisonment of Aboriginal mothers has resulted in child removal, a form of gender-based violence[17] that perpetuates the shameful and racist legacy of the Stolen Generations. Children have been removed to out-of-home care, which is a recognised pathway to offending that sustains the cycle of intergenerational disadvantage and incarceration.[18] This cycle must end.

The Bill prohibits forced assimilation and destruction of culture, adopting a multi-pronged approach to ending Aboriginal disadvantage which accords with international standards, including the UN Declaration on the Rights of Indigenous Peoples and the Bangkok Rules on Women Offenders and Prisoners ('Bangkok Rules').[19] The UN Declaration calls on states to recognise the right of Aboriginal peoples and individuals to participate in decision-making in matters that affect their rights, including the adoption of measures to ensure full protection from violence and discrimination. The Bangkok Rules address the rights and needs of women in the criminal justice system and call for gender-sensitive alternatives to incarceration.

Drawing on these standards, the Bill makes significant amendments to the right to liberty and security of person. It requires that the arrest, detention or imprisonment of Aboriginal persons be used only as a measure of last resort, considering all relevant factors, including the high number of unsentenced prisoners held on remand for minor offences associated with the effects of poverty and intersectional disadvantage.

The overrepresentation of Aboriginal people in the criminal justice system will, like gender-based violence, be addressed by comprehensive measures developed and adopted under the leadership of Aboriginal women. These measures will include diversionary programs and cultural training for public officials, including police, correctional services and members of parliament, courts and tribunals. More broadly, the Bill combats racism, stereotyping and misogyny through the implementation of the right to education, a very important enhancement which we will explain later in this speech. But first, we will outline some other rights in the Charter which, like the right to liberty and security of person, have been strengthened to address abuses suffered predominantly by women.

Enhancing Existing Rights

In this Bill, a gender-sensitive approach in line with the Bangkok Rules will be an express corollary of the right to humane treatment when deprived of liberty. Protection from torture and cruel, inhuman and degrading treatment will be strengthened to ensure that all non-consensual medical procedures are prohibited. This amendment will advance the government's commitment to ending rights-abusive practices, such as so-called 'normalising' surgeries on intersex minors and the involuntary sterilisation of women and girls with disabilities.[20]

While non-consensual medical treatment breaches human rights, so too does conduct which undermines a person's access to medical treatment of their choice. The right to privacy is amended to remove any doubt that access to medical care falls within its purview.[21] The harassment of women outside clinics providing abortion by strangers seeking to interfere with their healthcare access has sometimes been rationalised as an exercise of religious freedom, premised on a misunderstanding of sections 7(2) and 14(1). The Bill amends section 14 to ensure that religious freedom is properly understood: while every person has the right to adopt a religion or belief of their choice, the freedom to demonstrate that religion or belief is not a license to undermine the rights and dignity of others, including the growing number of Victorians who do not adhere to a religion.[22]

Our commitment to protecting rights which may be undermined by religiously motivated conduct is further demonstrated by the enactment of Part 9A of the *Public Health and Wellbeing Act 2008* (Vic) and the *Change or Suppression (Conversion) Practices Prohibition Act 2021* (Vic). The Bill makes it clear that the conduct proscribed by these Acts breaches the fundamental rights of others. It communicates the message that such conduct is not a permissible exercise of a person's freedom to demonstrate their religion or belief.

The Bill removes paragraphs (4) and (5) of section 38 which gave religious bodies acting as public authorities the imprimatur to undermine the rights of Victorians, particularly women and LGBTIQ people, by invoking religious doctrines, beliefs or principles. As observed by Ahmed Shaheed, who served as the UN Special Rapporteur mandated to advance religious freedom, 'it is difficult to justify the accommodation of religious beliefs when the consequences are discriminatory and impose harm on others, especially on groups that may have long faced discrimination and marginalization.'[23]

Protecting Victoria's Diverse Families

The Bill strengthens the protection of families and children, recognising the diversity of families in Victoria and the equality of rights and responsibilities in marriage. In accordance with CEDAW and statements of international policy consensus,[24] it introduces the right of every person to decide freely and responsibly on the number and spacing of their children. Alongside the right to privacy, this right is too often challenged in the context of medical treatment. It is challenged not only by persons purporting to exercise their right to religious freedom, but also by intimate partners and others who seek to control another person's reproductive decision-making. Known as reproductive coercion, this behaviour is a form of gender-based violence which we are committed to eliminating.

Introducing Economic, Social and Cultural Rights

Our ability to address gender-based violations, such as reproductive coercion, has been limited by the Charter's exclusive focus on civil and political rights. Noting the indivisibility and interdependence of human rights, the civil and political rights set out in the Charter cannot be fully realised in the absence of mutually reinforcing economic, social and cultural rights. For example, the right to health is a corollary of the enjoyment of other human rights, including the right to life, while education underpins numerous rights, including the freedom of expression and the right to take part in public life. CEDAW recognises that the task of eliminating discrimination against women cannot be confined to civil and political rights, but must extend to the realisation of economic, social and cultural rights. Violations of economic, social and cultural rights have a gendered effect.[25] The COVID-19 pandemic has amplified the feminisation of poverty and highlighted the urgency of expanding the Charter to embed rights enshrined in the ICESCR and CEDAW.

A right to work and work-related rights will address the persistent problem of gender-based discrimination, harassment and inequality in the workplace and paid economy. Women carry a disproportionate burden of casual and insecure work which has been significantly affected by COVID-19 related job losses,[26] and many cannot secure sufficient paid employment to enjoy an adequate standard of living, including safe and adequate housing. Although the Commonwealth and states share legislative responsibility for social security, the fiscal reality is that the Commonwealth controls this area of regulation and service provision. Accordingly, this Bill does not address the right to social security but enshrines a right to housing. This right extends to the provision of gender-sensitive emergency accommodation, informed by the stark reality that gender-based violence is a leading cause of homelessness for women and their children.[27]

As the COVID-19 pandemic has demonstrated, human rights cannot be enjoyed without the right to health services, including physical and mental health treatment and care. An integral part of the right is access to sexual and reproductive healthcare, premised on the freedom to make decisions regarding one's body and entitlement to unhindered access to comprehensive services, goods and information.[28] Obstacles to the right's realisation include gender-based violence, a lack of information and education, discrimination, poverty and under-resourcing. To ensure that our public resources are directed to the right's fulfilment, all publicly funded health service providers will be required to provide comprehensive services within their area of operation without discrimination on religious or other grounds. Access to health services is a fundamental human right.

So too is the right to education, which lies at the heart of this Bill. In addition to primary and secondary education, the Bill recognises the right to post-secondary education and training, including vocational, higher, adult, community and further education. The right to education will play a critical role in creating a society in which rights are understood and actively respected, protected and fulfilled. As we have already mentioned, cultural training will form part of the Bill's response to addressing the ignorance, misogyny and racism which have informed interactions between all arms of government and Aboriginal people. More broadly, it will help dismantle stereotypes and misconceptions that sustain inequality.

Challenging existing and often entrenched views is essential but difficult. Preventing such views from taking hold is a more effective and sustainable way to build respect for human rights. Accordingly, the Bill's enactment will see Victorians educated from the earliest appropriate age to gain an understanding of and respect for human rights, gender equality and respect for Aboriginal people, including the role played by Aboriginal women in maintaining and strengthening the cultural heritage and survival of the world's oldest civilisation. By embedding such education in formal curricula at all educational levels, the state of Victoria will inculcate a human rights culture which will underpin the realisation of all rights in the Charter.

Repealing s 48

The Charter was the result of a public consultation regarding how to better protect rights in Victoria by the Human Rights Consultation Committee. Section 48 of the Charter did not appear in the draft instrument prepared by the Consultation Committee and was inserted at the behest of the Catholic Church.[29] Its inclusion coincided with the removal of section 9(2) of the Consultation Committee's draft, which stated that '[f]or the purpose of this Charter, the right to life is protected from the time of birth.'

Restrictions on abortion have been recognised as inconsistent with a number of the rights enacted in the Charter.[30] Section 48 sought to prevent the application of those rights from liberalising abortion access, leaving the question of reforming abortion law as 'a matter of ongoing political and legal debate in Victoria without the possibility of it being resolved' under the Charter.[31] That debate took place two years after the Charter's enactment and saw this Parliament legislate to uphold reproductive autonomy. Beyond decriminalising abortion, the *Abortion Law Reform Act 2008* (Vic) addresses the perennial problem of health practitioners barring access to abortion on religious grounds. It prioritises the autonomy and rights of patients seeking abortion over health practitioners' freedom to demonstrate their religion or belief. It does so by requiring those with a conscientious objection to abortion to disclose that objection and refer patients to a health practitioner who does not conscientiously object (known as the 'obligation to refer').

An examination of compatibility with the Charter would have concluded that Victoria's abortion legislation is consistent with human rights guarantees. It would also have found that the obligation to refer constitutes a reasonable and demonstrably justifiable limitation on religious freedom in accordance with section 7(2). But s 48 prevents such an examination from taking place. Having intervened to stop the Charter from affecting any law applicable to abortion, the Church could not invoke its provisions to challenge the legislation. Church representatives have lobbied the Commonwealth Attorney-General to enact legislation to override the obligation to refer,[32] observed the unanticipated effect of section 48 and called for its removal.[33]

The section should indeed be removed. It stands as a reminder of the vulnerability of women's rights to the interventions of patriarchal religious bodies. It undermines the inalienability of human rights by carving out an exclusion that privileges religious doctrines over the rights of Victorians to make autonomous decisions about their own bodies. The Bill restores subsection 9(2) as originally drafted and repeals section 48, which should never have been enacted.

We commend the Bill to the House.

PARLIAMENT OF VICTORIA

Introduced in the Assembly

Charter of Human Rights and Responsibilities (Advancing Equality) Amendment Bill 2024

A Bill for an Act to amend the **Charter of Human Rights and Responsibilities Act 2006** to strengthen the protection of human rights and advance gender equality.

The Parliament of Victoria enacts:

Part 1 – Preliminary

1 Purpose

The purpose of this Act is to amend the **Charter of Human Rights and Responsibilities Act 2006** to:

(a) strengthen the protection of human rights;
(b) embed a gender perspective in the application of human rights;
(c) eliminate gender-based stereotypes and misconceptions;
(d) advance substantive gender equality by combating structural inequality and intersectional discrimination;
(e) combat gender-based violence;
(f) advance the rights of Aboriginal people, with a particular focus on the persistent marginalisation and intersectional disadvantage experienced by Aboriginal women; and
(g) introduce new rights to give effect to certain provisions of the International Covenant on Economic, Social and Cultural Rights and the Convention on the Elimination of All Forms of Discrimination against Women.

2 Commencement

This Act comes into operation on the day after the day on which it receives Royal Assent.

3 Principal Act

For the purposes of this Act, the **Charter of Human Rights and Responsibilities Act 2006** shall be called the Principal Act.

Part 2 – Dismantling structural gender inequality

4 Definitions

(1) In section 3(1) of the Principal Act, **insert** –

'***discrimination*** in relation to a person, means direct or indirect discrimination (within the meaning of the **Equal Opportunity Act 2010**) on the basis of one or more attributes set out in section 6 of that Act;
gender-based violence has the meaning given in section 3A;
gender-sensitive has the meaning given in section 3B;
human rights mean the civil and political rights and the economic, social and cultural rights set out in Part 2;
sexual harassment has the same meaning as in section 92 of the **Equal Opportunity Act 2010;**
substantive gender equality means gender equality within the meaning of the **Gender Equality Act 2020;**'.

(2) In section 3(1) of the Principal Act:
(a) The definition of ***discrimination*** is **repealed.**
(b) The definition of ***human rights*** is **repealed.**

5 **New sections 3A and 3B inserted**
After section 3 of the Principal Act, **insert** –

'3A Meaning of gender-based violence

(1) For the purposes of this Charter, ***gender-based violence*** means violence that is directed against a woman because she is a woman or that disproportionately affects women, including lesbian, bisexual and transgender women.
(2) Without limiting subsection (1), gender-based violence includes all acts of violence that result in, or are likely to result in, physical, sexual, psychological or financial harm or suffering to women, including coercion or arbitrary deprivation of liberty and threats of such acts, whether occurring in public or private life.

3B Meaning of gender-sensitive

For the purposes of this Charter, a thing is gender-sensitive if it takes account of the distinctive needs and lived experiences of persons of the same gender with a view to achieving substantive gender equality.'.

6 **What is a public authority?**
After section 4(1)(c) of the Principal Act, **insert** –
'(ca) a registered funded agency within the meaning of the **Health Services Act 1988**, including a registered funded agency that is a hospital controlled by a religious denomination; or'.

7 **Human rights-what they are and when they can be limited**
In section 7(2), after 'A human right', **insert** 'other than a human right referred to in subsection (2B).'.

After section 7(2) of the Principal Act **insert** –

'(2A) A determination of whether a limitation is reasonable and demonstrably justifiable under paragraph (2) shall take into account the following:

(a) the extent to which the right has been enjoyed by persons of different genders, recognising that male paradigms of power have been an obstacle to the achievement of substantive gender equality and human rights;
(b) the purpose underlying and impact of the limitation on persons of different genders, recognising that a gender-neutral approach to the application of human rights fails to address gendered harms experienced predominantly by women; and
(c) the social and cultural patterns of conduct which undermine the enjoyment of the right with a view to eliminating misconceptions and prejudices based on:

  (i) the idea of the inferiority or superiority of any of the sexes;
  (ii) stereotyped roles for all genders; and
  (iii) expectations as to how a person who alleges a breach of human rights should behave in order to be considered credible.

(2B) The following human rights must not be subject (under law) to any limits –

(a) The right set out in section 8(1);
(b) The right set out in section 9;
(c) The right set out in section 10;
(d) The rights set out in sections 11(1) and (2);
(e) The right set out in section 14(1) except to the extent that it includes the freedom set out in section 14(1)(b);
(f) The right set out in section 14(2);
(g) The right set out in section 21(8); and
(h) The rights set out in section 27.'.

8 Recognition and equality before the law

(1) After section 8(1) of the Principal Act **insert** –

'(1A) It is the intention of this Parliament that the following sub-sections be interpreted to advance substantive gender equality, having regard to the underlying causes of gender inequality, including patriarchal power structures and gender stereotyping.'.

(2) After section 8(4) of the Principal Act **insert** –

'(5) Without limiting sub-sections (2), (3) and (4), a reference to discrimination includes discrimination on intersecting grounds, such as sex, Aboriginality, gender identity, sexual orientation and disability.

(6) Without limiting subsection (4), discrimination is not constituted by measures taken to identify and address systemic inequality and intersectional discrimination, including the measures set out in sections 8A(3) and 21(10) of the Principal Act.'.

9 **New section 8A inserted**
After section 8 of the Principal Act, **insert** –

'**8A Gender-based violence**

(1) Every person has the right to protection from gender-based violence.
(2) Gender-based violence is a violation of human rights, irrespective of where it occurs and by whom it is perpetrated.
(3) The State must develop and implement measures for:

(a) the prevention, investigation and punishment of gender-based violence; and
(b) the provision of support services and resources to victim-survivors of gender-based violence; and
(c) the provision of reparations to victim-survivors of gender-based violence.

(4) The development and implementation of the matters specified in subsection (3):

(a) must be done in collaboration with victim-survivors of gender-based violence; and
(b) to the extent that the development or implementation concerns Aboriginal women, must be done in collaboration with, and under the leadership of, Aboriginal women.'.

Part 3 – Strengthening Rights

10 **Right to life**
At the end of section 9 of the Principal Act, **insert** –

'(2) For the purpose of this Charter, the right to life is protected from the time of birth.'.

11 **Freedom from torture and cruel, inhuman or degrading treatment**
In section 10(c) of the Principal Act –

(a) for 'experimentation or treatment' **substitute** 'experimentation, treatment or procedures';
(b) after 'full, free and informed consent', **insert** 'including where the person lacks capacity to give that consent.'.

12 Privacy and reputation
In section 13 of the Principal Act –

(a) at the end of paragraph (b), for 'attacked.' **substitute** 'attacked; and';
(b) after paragraph (b) **insert** –

'(c) to obtain medical treatment of their choice without coercion, harassment or interference.'.

13 Freedom of thought, conscience and religion
After section 14(1) of the Principal Act **insert** –

'(1A) However, the freedoms set out in subsection (1) do not permit discrimination against, or otherwise limit the rights of others, including those who hold different religious beliefs and those who do not adhere to a religion.'.

14 Protection of children and families

(1) In section 17(1) of the Principal Act, after the word 'families' **insert** 'take diverse forms and'.
(2) After section 7(1) of the Principal Act **insert** –

'(1A) Every person has the right to:

(a) decide freely and responsibly on the number and spacing of their children; and
(b) have access to the information, education and means to enable them to exercise the right set out in paragraph (a).

(1B) Every person has the same rights and responsibilities with regard to marriage, both during marriage and at its dissolution.'.

15 Cultural rights
In section 19 of the Principal Act, **insert** –

'(3) Aboriginal persons have the right not to be subjected to forced assimilation or destruction of their culture, including child removal.'.

16 Right to liberty and security of person
After section 21(8) of the Principal Act, **insert** –

'(9) The arrest, detention or imprisonment of Aboriginal persons shall be in accordance with the law, and shall be used only as a measure of last resort, taking account of all relevant factors, including the following:

(a) the seriousness of the person's conduct;
(b) the person's background, including cultural background, ties to family and place, parenting and caring responsibilities and cultural obligations;

(c) the need to reduce the disproportionately high number of Aboriginal women in prison, having regard to the impact of incarceration on women and their children, families and communities;
(d) the need to recognise the harms associated with the removal of Aboriginal children into out-of-home care, which shall be a last resort, having regard to the right in section 19(3) and recognised links between out-of-home care, offending and incarceration;
(e) the need to recognise the implications of gender-based violence for women's contact with the criminal justice system, and ensure that victim-survivors are recognised, provided with culturally appropriate support services and not mistaken for perpetrators; and
(f) the need for non-custodial penalties and bail to be prioritised in all cases, recognising the high number of unsentenced prisoners held on remand for minor non-violent offences associated with the effects of poverty, discrimination, and the legacy of colonisation.

(10) Having regard to the overrepresentation of Aboriginal people in the criminal justice system, the state must develop and implement measures in collaboration with Aboriginal women and men, to:

(a) implement gender-sensitive alternatives to imprisonment, including diversionary programs and rehabilitation; and
(b) provide cultural training for public authorities working within the administration of justice.'.

17 Humane treatment when deprived of liberty
After section 22(3) of the Principal Act, **insert** –

'(4) All persons deprived of liberty must be provided with:

(a) gender-specific healthcare services equivalent to those available in the community; and
(b) the facilities and materials required to meet their hygiene needs.

(5) A gender-sensitive approach shall be adopted to ensure that all persons deprived of liberty are treated with humanity and respect for the inherent dignity of the human person in the context of personal searches.'.

Part 4 – Economic, Social and Cultural Rights

18 New sections 27A, 27B, 27C and 27D inserted
After s 27 of the Principal Act, **insert** –

'27A Right to work and other work-related rights

(1) Every person has the right to work, including the right to choose their occupation or profession freely.

(2) Every person has the right to enjoyment of just and favourable conditions of work.
(3) Every person has the right to form or join a work-related organisation, including a trade union, with the objective of promoting or protecting their economic or other social interests.
(4) Every person is entitled to enjoy these rights without direct or indirect discrimination or sexual harassment.

27B Right to housing

(1) Every person has the right to have access to adequate housing, including facilities essential for health, security, comfort and nutrition.
(2) Every person has the right to gender-sensitive emergency accommodation, services, goods and facilities.

27C Right to health services

(1) Every person has the right to access health services, including sexual and reproductive health services and mental health care, without discrimination.
(2) Every health or related service shall provide comprehensive health services within its area of operation without discrimination.
(3) In subsection (2), health or related service shall have the same meaning as in Part 6 of the **Health Services Act 1988**.

27D Right to education

(1) Every child has the right to have access to primary and secondary education appropriate to the child's needs without discrimination.
(2) Every person has the right to have access, based on the person's abilities, to post-secondary education and training that is equally accessible to all.
(3) So far as it is possible to do so within their subject matter, accredited courses at all levels must provide education directed to:

(a) the development of an understanding of and respect for human rights, and the acquisition of skills and knowledge consistent with internationally recognised human rights, including an understanding that discrimination is a breach of human rights;
(b) the development of an understanding of and respect for Aboriginal people and their diverse spiritual, social, cultural and economic relationship with their traditional lands and waters, including respect for the significant role played by Aboriginal women in maintaining and strengthening their cultural heritage;
(c) the elimination of prejudices and practices based on stereotyped gender roles or the idea of the superiority or inferiority of any of the sexes;

(d) the development of an understanding of and respect for substantive gender equality, mutual respect, non-violent conflict resolution in interpersonal relationships and the right to personal integrity, grounded in the understanding that gender-based violence breaches human rights irrespective of where it occurs and by whom it is perpetrated; and

(e) ensuring the health and wellbeing of families, including education, information and advice on family planning, and recognition of the common responsibility of all persons in the upbringing, care and development of their children.

(4) In this section, *accredited* and *course* have the meanings they have in the **Education and Training Reform Act 2006.**'.

Part 5 – Miscellaneous Amendments

19 Conduct of public authorities
Section 38(4) and (5) of the Principal Act are **repealed.**

20 Section 48 repealed
Section 48 of the Principal Act is **repealed.**

21 Repeal of this Act
This Act is **repealed** on the first anniversary of its commencement.

Notes

1 *Charter of Human Rights and Responsibilities Act 2006* (Vic), https://content.legislation.vic.gov.au/sites/default/files/2022-06/06-43aa015%20authorised.pdf.
2 See generally UN Office of the Special Adviser on Gender Issues and Advancement of Women, *Gender Mainstreaming: An Overview* (United Nations, 2002).
3 Committee on the Elimination of Discrimination Against Women, *General Recommendation 33 on Women's Access to Justice,* UN Doc CEDAW/C/GC/33 (23 July 2015) ('*General Recommendation 33*').
4 Committee on the Elimination of All Forms of Discrimination against Women, *General Recommendation No 35 on Gender-Based Violence against Women, Updating General Recommendation No 19,* UN Doc CEDAW/C/GC/35 (14 July 2017) ('*General Recommendation 35*').
5 Ibid; Committee on the Elimination of Discrimination against Women, Views: Communication No 18/2008, 46th sess, UN Doc CEDAW/C/46/D/18/2008 (22 September 2010) [3.5.1], [8.5] ('*Vertido v Philippines*').
6 Committee on the Elimination of Discrimination Against Women (n 3) [26].
7 Australian Institute of Health and Welfare (AIHW), *Family, Domestic and Sexual Violence in Australia: Continuing the National Story* (Report, 5 June 2019), 70–115.
8 Ibid, 44–50.
9 Monash Gender and Family Violence Prevention Centre, *Responding to the 'Shadow Pandemic'* (8 June 2020), 6.

10 Committee on the Elimination of Discrimination Against Women (n 4) [10].
11 See for example Committee on the Elimination of Discrimination Against Women (n 4) [24(b)].
12 See for example the *Lima Declaration of The World Conference of Indigenous Women* (30 October 2013).
13 Australian Institute of Health and Welfare (AIHW), *Family Violence among Aboriginal and Torres Strait Islander People* (Report, 1 November 2006).
14 See generally Australian Bureau of Statistics, Prisoners in Australia, 24 February 2023, https://www.abs.gov.au/statistics/people/crime-and-justice/prisoners-australia/latest-release.
15 Victorian Government, *Aboriginal Cohorts Under Justice Supervision*, undated, https://www.aboriginaljustice.vic.gov.au/the-agreement/aboriginal-over-representation-in-the-justice-system/aboriginal-cohorts-under-justice.
16 Ibid; Australian Bureau of Statistics (n 14); Australian Law Reform Commission, *Pathways to Justice – Inquiry into the Incarceration Rate of Aboriginal and Torres Strait Islander Peoples* (Report, 28 March 2018) [11.18]–[11.44].
17 UN General Assembly, *Report of the Special Rapporteur on Violence against Women, Its Causes and Consequences on Her Mission to Australia*, UN Doc A/HRC/38/47/Add.1 (17 April 2018) [45]–[46].
18 See Australian Law Reform Commission (n 16) 24.
19 *UN Rules for the Treatment of Women Prisoners and Non-Custodial Measures for Women Offenders (Bangkok Rules),* UN General Assembly (21 December 2010), A/RES/65/229.
20 See for example CEDAW Committee, *Concluding Observations on the Eighth Periodic Report of Australia*, UN Doc CEDAW/C/AUS/CO/8 (25 July 2018) [26(c)], [26(d)]; Committee on the Rights of Persons with Disabilities, *Concluding Observations on the Combined Second and Third Periodic Reports of Australia,* UN Doc CRPD/C/AUS/CO/2–3 (15 October 2019) [34(a)], [34(b)].
21 See for example Human Rights Committee, *Views: Communication No 1608/2007*, UN Doc CCPR/C/101/D/1608/2007 (28 April 2011) 11 [9.3]; Human Rights Committee, *CCPR General Comment No 28: Article 3 (The Equality of Rights between Men and Women)*, UN Doc CCPR/C/21/Rev.1/Add.10 (29 March 2000) [20]; CEDAW Committee, *General Recommendation No 24: Article 12 of the Convention (Women and Health)*, UN Doc A/54/38/Rev.1, chap. I (1999) [12(d)].
22 Regarding the nationwide decline in religiosity, see Neil Francis, *Religiosity in Australia* (Rationalist Society of Australia, 2021).
23 Special Rapporteur on Freedom of Religion or Belief, *Gender-Based Violence and Discrimination in the Name of Religion or Belief, Report of the Special Rapporteur on Freedom of Religion or Belief*, A/HRC/43/48 (24 August 2020) [71].
24 CEDAW art 16(1)(e), International Conference on Population and Development, 'Programme of Action' (Cairo, September 1994), Principle 8; Fourth World Conference on Women, *Beijing Declaration and Platform for Action*, UN Doc A/CONF.177/20 [223].
25 See generally *Montréal Principles on Women's Economic, Social and Cultural Rights* (December 2002).
26 Workplace Gender Equality Agency, *Gendered impact of COVID-19* (October 2020), https://www.wgea.gov.au/publications/gendered-impact-of-covid-19.
27 AIHW (n 7) 35.
28 Committee on Economic, Social and Cultural Rights, *General Comment No 22 on the Right to Sexual and Reproductive Health*, UN Doc E/C.12/GC/22 (2 May 2016) 1.

29 Gary Rivett, 'Catholic Maternity Wards "Face Closure" if Abortion Law Passes', *ABC News* (24 September 2008), https://www.abc.net.au/news/2008-09-23/catholic-maternity-wards-face-closure-if-abortion/520158.
30 See for example Human Rights Committee (n 21); *Whelan v Ireland,* HRC Communication No 2425/2014, UN Doc CCPR/C/119/D/2425/2014 (11 July 2017).
31 George Williams, 'The Victorian Charter of Human Rights and Responsibilities: Origins and Scope' (2006) 30 *Melbourne University Law Review* 880–905, 896.
32 See Jill Stark, 'Abortion Law Under Challenge', *Sydney Morning Herald* (8 May 2009); 'Pressure Rises Over Victorian Abortion Laws', *CathNews* (20 April 2009).
33 Catholic Church of Victoria, *Submission to the Scrutiny of Acts and Regulations Committee in relation to the Charter of Human Rights and Responsibilities Act 2006* (1 July 2011) 2, 16, 26, 31.

Chapter 5A

Commentary on *Re-charting the Victorian Charter of Human Rights*

Advancing Equality

Kate Eastman AM SC

Our understanding of human rights looks back to the *Magna Carta* of 1215, the English Bill of Rights of 1689, the French *Declaration on the Rights of Man and of the Citizen* of 1789 and the US Constitution and Bill of Rights of 1791. These ancient instruments are products of political conflicts, designed to quell disputes and distribute political and economic power by and for men. Rights in this form were irrelevant to women's lives. To the extent women had rights, it was only in the context of their relationship with men, typically their fathers, husbands and brothers. The ancient instruments are androcentric and assume the rights and freedoms that served male interests should be sufficient to serve women's interests. Yet, these instruments have influenced the development of laws to protect human rights. The consequence is those laws continue to speak to the male experience and the patriarchal social and political structures. Such laws overlook the realities of women's lives in all domains – civil, political, economic, social and cultural.[1]

The *Charter of Human Rights and Responsibilities Act* 2006 (Vic) ('the *Charter*') is influenced by the ancient instruments in how human rights are described and what rights are considered worthy of protection. The *Charter* draws on the rights that have historically protected men's interests in public domains concerning civil, political and economic affairs. The *Charter* does not reflect more contemporary expectations that human rights should be transformative and that opportunities, institutions and systems should no longer be grounded in historically determined male paradigms of power and life patterns.[2]

Transformative equality requires changing social and cultural structures and patterns that entrench inequality, including gender inequality.[3] It means women should be involved in designing the form and scope of rights that speak to their experiences. For example, recognising the intersectional experiences of women and girls, as well as recognising a right to live free of gender-based violence and that gender-based violence is a form of discrimination.[4]

The *Charter of Human Rights and Responsibilities (Advancing Equality) Amendment Bill* 2024 gives the *Charter* a clear purpose to advance gender equality by recognising the need to combat structural inequality and

DOI: 10.4324/9781003372462-10

intersectional discrimination.[5] In effect, it is a recognition that the *Charter* aims for transformative equality.

Part 2 – *Dismantling Structural Gender Inequality* – addresses power and equality. Noting that some rights, such as the right to life, must not be limited, the Bill embeds a gender perspective into the examination of the scope of rights under the *Charter*. If a human right is to be restricted or limited in some way, before any limitation is imposed, it will be necessary to take account of the extent to which the right has been enjoyed by people of all genders and the gendered impacts of limitations on the right.

Part 3 – *Strengthening Rights* – reframes existing rights based on the ancient instruments to reflect women's lives and experiences. By doing so, it challenges the androcentric framing of civil and political rights. For example, forced sterilisation of women with intellectual disability will be recognised as torture, cruel, inhuman or degrading treatment contrary to s 10(c) of the Charter. Women with intellectual disability should have choice and control about their bodies. Women with intellectual disability will have the right to determine for themselves how to manage menstruation, contraception, their sexual health, pregnancy and decisions about when or whether to have children.

In Part 4 – *Economic, Social and Cultural Rights* – the Bill draws on areas of key economic and social policy to support women's economic participation and security. Recognising women's right to work, housing, health services and education is key to achieving equality and challenging the feminisation of poverty. Part 4 recognises that the protection of women's civil and political rights is integrally connected to the protection of their economic, social and cultural rights. Section 27C(1) recognises every person has the right to access health services, including sexual and reproductive health services, without discrimination. Using the example above, for women with intellectual disability the right to reproductive health services without discrimination is integrally linked to securing their rights under s 10(c) of the *Charter*.

The Bill proposes freedom from gender-based violence as a human right. Treating gender-based violence as a violation of human rights engages with power – the power of men over women, as well as the state's power over women's lives. In this innovative approach, the proposed s 3A and s 8A recognising gender-based violence as a violation of human rights will require the Scrutiny of Acts and Regulations Committee to examine all Victorian Bills to consider how a proposed new law addresses gender-based violence.[6] It will require courts and tribunals to interpret Victorian laws[7] by reference to international instruments, including specific and more contemporary international laws and practices concerning women and girls. It will require the State of Victoria to develop and implement measures to address gender-based violence and provide support and resources for victim-survivors.[8] The shift from a reactive model being one that responds after violence has occurred to a proactive model with the aim of preventing gender-based violence is significant. It recognises the causes of gender-based violence are rooted in social and cultural structures that entrench gender inequality. Pro-active and systemic change is required to address gender-based violence in all settings.

The Bill recognises the importance of working with victim-survivors and amplifying their voices in the process of developing and implementing these measures, adopting an intersectional and collaborative approach which will be the key to its success.

Finally, the protection of human rights requires a framework to secure remedies for individuals and accountability for duty holders. In combination with the *Charter of Rights and Responsibilities (Advancing Enforcement) Amendment Bill* 2024, the Bill will require the duty holders to dismantle structural gender inequality, address gendered harms and provide effective remedies for violations experienced by women and girls.

Notes

1 Hilary Charlesworth et al., 'Feminist Approaches to International Law' (1991) 85 *American Journal of International Law* 613, 644.
2 Committee on the Elimination of Discrimination against Women, General Recommendation 25, on article 4, paragraph 1 of the Convention on the Elimination of All Forms of Discrimination against Women, on temporary special measures, 30th Sess UN CEDAW/C/GC/25 (12–30 January 2004) [10].
3 Committee on the Elimination of Discrimination against Women, *General Recommendation No 28 on the Core Obligations of States Parties under Article 2 of the Convention on the Elimination of All Forms of Discrimination against Women*, 47th sess, UN Doc CEDAW/C/GC/28 (16 December 2010) [22].
4 Committee on the Elimination of Discrimination against Women, *General Recommendation No 19 (1992) on Violence Against Women*, 11th sess (30 January 1992) [6].
5 See *Charter of Human Rights and Responsibilities (Advancing Equality) Amendment Bill 2024* (Vic) s 1(d).
6 See *Charter of Human Rights and Responsibilities Act 2006* (Vic) s 30.
7 See *Charter of Human Rights and Responsibilities Act 2006* (Vic) s 32.
8 See *Charter of Human Rights and Responsibilities (Advancing Equality) Amendment Bill 2024* (Vic) s 8A(3).

Chapter 6

Re-charting the Victorian Charter of Human Rights

Advancing Enforcement in Human Rights Legislation

Julie Debeljak and Tania Penovic

Extract from *Hansard* (Parliament of Victoria)

Charter of Human Rights and Responsibilities (Advancing Enforcement) Amendment Bill 2024

Second Reading

HON JULIE DEBELJAK and HON TANIA PENOVIC: We jointly move:
That the Bill be now read a second time.

We rise today to move amendments to the *Charter of Human Rights and Responsibilities Act 2006* (Vic) ('*Charter*').[1] The Advancing Enforcement Bill seeks to clarify and strengthen the two main enforcement mechanisms of the *Charter*. The first relates to rights-compatible interpretation of statutory provisions, with the amendments clarifying the meaning and effect of sections 7(2) and 32(1) and their interaction. The second relates to the obligation of public authorities to act and decide compatibly with rights under section 38(1), with the amendments improving the remedies available where public authorities violate those obligations under section 39.

This Bill complements the amendments proposed under the Charter of Human Rights and Responsibilities (Advancing Equality) Amendment Bill 2024 ('Advancing Equality Bill'), which strengthen and expand the rights guaranteed under the *Charter*. Those amendments seek to dismantle structural gender-based inequality, and to better promote and protect the rights of women and girls; however, those amendments alone cannot adequately advance gender equality. Gender-based reforms that broaden and strengthen the range and scope of rights guaranteed to women and girls are futile without reforming the mechanisms designed to enforce those rights. This Bill seeks to harness the transformative potential of rights by empowering women and girls to enforce their own rights.

DOI: 10.4324/9781003372462-11

As Canadian scholar Kent Roach notes, '[w]e live in a world rich with rights' but '[a]las, we live in a world poor in remedies'.[2] The realisation of rights requires effective enforcement, including effective remedies.[3] The United Nations Committee on the Elimination of Discrimination Against Women, or CEDAW Committee, recognises that the right to access to justice for women includes 'the provision of remedies for victims', with '[e]ffective access to justice optimiz[ing] the emancipatory and transformative potential of the law'.[4]

Article 2(3) of the *International Covenant on Civil and Political Rights*, known as the ICCPR, outlines the duty of states to provide remedies to victims of rights violations. The United Nations Human Rights Committee (HRC) notes that 'the obligation to provide an effective remedy . . . is central to the efficacy' of article 2(3), and 'attaches importance to States Parties' establishing appropriate judicial . . . mechanisms for addressing claims of rights violations under domestic law'.[5]

Although more effective enforcement mechanisms and remedies benefit everyone, enforcement mechanisms and remedies for women and girls are particularly important because they are more vulnerable to a range of violations of rights and they experience barriers to accessing justice on the basis of equality. The CEDAW Committee highlights that

> [d]iscrimination against women, based on gender stereotypes, stigma, harmful and patriarchal cultural norms and gender-based violence, which affects women in particular, has an adverse impact on the ability of women to gain access to justice on an equal basis with men.[6]

This Bill, and the accompanying Advancing Equality Bill, together will ensure that the *Charter* addresses the lived experience of women, men and those who fall outside the gender binary.

We now turn to the details of the amendments, starting with the rights-compatible interpretation of statutory provisions.

Amendments to sections 3 and 32

The meaning of section 32(1) of the *Charter* is unsettled, as is the interaction between the section 7(2) limitations provision and the section 32(1) statutory interpretation obligation. The purpose behind inserting the definition of 'compatible with human rights' and amending section 32(1) is to clarify the operation of, and interaction between, sections 7(2) and 32(1). In short, the new section 32(1) is intended to allow for remedial interpretation where 'possible', and the insertion of the definition is intended to make sure section 7(2) is part of assessing whether a statutory provision is 'compatible with human rights'. These two changes then alter the approach to section 32(1) rights-compatible interpretation.

Focussing on statutory interpretation, the courts have settled on section 32(1) being part of the ordinary process of statutory interpretation,[7] and merely a codification of the principle of legality.[8] This was not the intention of the *Charter*-enacting Parliament, and is problematic. The principle of legality is a frail shield because it is too easy for rights to be overridden by rights-*inconsistent* intentions of a later law-enacting Parliament, and it fails to adequately balance the intentions of the *Charter*-enacting Parliament – that is, rights-*compatibility* – with those of the law-enacting Parliament – that is, rights-*inconsistency*.[9]

This is clearly a problem with laws enacted *after* the *Charter* commenced. These laws must be accompanied by a section 28 Statement of Compatibility and be filtered through the section 30 parliamentary scrutiny committee process.

The parliamentary intention attributed to any law enacted *after* the *Charter*, and which is being interpreted under section 32(1), must account for the fact that the law-enacting Parliament has considered the rights-compatibility of the proposed laws under sections 28 and 30. A Parliament seeking to enact rights-*inconsistent* statutory provisions has many tools under the *Charter* to do so: its rights-limiting intentions can be conveyed by using clear and intended rights-limiting language in the statutory provisions, or by clearly indicating the incompatibility in the purposes provision of the statute, or by issuing a Statement of Incompatibility under section 28, or by using the section 31 override provision, or by a combination of each of these tools.

All of these tools support a culture of justification, transparency and accountability under the *Charter*. We ought not too readily assume the rights-*inconsistent* intention of a law-enacting Parliament where these tools are not utilised; nor should we too readily accept a clash between the rights-compatible intentions of the *Charter*-enacting Parliament and the intentions of future law-enacting Parliaments given that all new laws are filtered through a rights assessment.

The parliamentary intention attributed to any law enacted *after* the *Charter* and which is being interpreted under section 32(1) must account for the fact that the law-enacting Parliament has considered the rights-compatibility of the proposed laws under sections 28 and 30.

Turning to limitations, the operation of section 7(2) remains unclear, with some judges suggesting that section 7(2) has no role to play in assessing the compatibility of statutory provisions with rights. This was not the *Charter*-enacting Parliament's intention. Many guaranteed rights are not absolute, and rights need to be balanced against each other, as well as against other competing needs in society. Given the gender-blindness of many statutory provisions, the involvement of section 7(2) is vital to ensuring gender issues are part of the matrix of the judicial interpretation process.[10] Recognising that gender-related issues have too often remained invisible, section 7(2A) of the Advancing Equality Bill requires a consideration of gender issues in the section 7(2) process.

The principle of legality approach to section 32(1) and the unsettled role of section 7(2) have stifled enforcement of the *Charter*, as demonstrated by the lack of reliance on section 32(1) in litigation.[11] Individuals are not benefitting from rights-compatible statutory interpretation, and the courts are not performing their envisaged role of 'fixing' rights-incompatibility where it is 'possible' to do so through interpretation. It was the *Charter*-enacting Parliament's intention that the judiciary 'fix' rights-*incompatibility* wherever 'possible', rather than relying on the Parliament – with its already tight legislative timetable – to adjust legislation that can be adjusted through judicial interpretation. Parliament wanted individuals to benefit from rights-compatible interpretation of statutory provisions, and Parliament – retaining its sovereignty – can respond to any undesirable or unwanted judicial rights-compatible interpretations by way of later legislative amendment where necessary.

To ensure the intentions of this Parliament are made clear, we will more thoroughly explain the need for these amendments. We start by comparing the Victorian and British human rights laws.

The *Charter* and the *UKHRA*

Section 32(1) of the *Charter* was modelled on section 3(1) of the United Kingdom's *Human Rights Act 1998*, known as the *UKHRA*. They both require statutory provisions to be interpreted in a way that is compatible with the protected rights, with one condition: the *UKHRA* restricts the interpretation obligation to 'so far as it is possible to do so', whereas the *Charter* restricts the interpretation obligation to 'so far as it is possible to do so consistently with their purpose'.

The relevant difference[12] is that section 32(1) adds the phrase 'consistently with their purpose'. This additional phrase has split judicial opinion on the meaning and effect of section 32(1). On one view, 'consistently with their purpose' was intended to codify in the *Charter* the British jurisprudence on section 3(1) of the *UKHRA*.[13] On another view, the phrase enacted a different interpretive obligation altogether, with the Victorian Court of Appeal in *R v Momcilovic* (*VCA Momcilovic*) holding that 'consistently with their purpose' were 'words of limitation [that] stamped s 32(1) with quite a different character from that of s 3(1) of the *UKHRA*',[14] a view subsequently supported by a majority of the High Court of Australia.[15] For the Victorian Court of Appeal in *Momcilovic*, the significance of section 32(1) 'is that Parliament has embraced and affirmed [the principle of legality] in emphatic terms', codifying it so that the presumption 'is no longer merely a creature of the common law but is now an expression of the "collective will" of the legislature'.[16]

Approach to Interpretation

The *Charter's* legislative history supports the view that 'consistently with their purpose' was intended to codify the British jurisprudence – both by referring to that jurisprudence by name and using concepts from that jurisprudence in explaining the effect of the inserted phrase.[17] In order to be faithful to that legislative history, the approach to applying section 32(1) should be similar to the approach to applying section 3(1) of the *UKHRA* by the British courts.

It is the current Parliament's intention, through the amendment to sections 3 and 32(1), to adopt a similar approach to analysing rights-compatible interpretation to the one used under the *UKHRA*. This approach ensures that section 7(2) is part of assessing whether statutory provisions are 'compatible with human rights'; and is intended to allow remedial interpretation of statutory provisions, subject to the limitation of '[s]o far as it is possible to do so', which limits the judicial task to one of interpretation.

The approach requires an interpreter, say a judge, to first ask whether a statutory provision imposes a limit on rights. Second, if it does, the judge needs to ask whether the limit is justifiable under the section 7(2) limitation power or a limit specified within a right. Third, if the statutory provision imposes an unjustifiable limitation on a right, the judge should then consider whether the provision can be 'saved' through section 32(1) remedial interpretation, which requires the judge to alter the meaning of the statutory provision so that it is 'compatible with human rights'. Finally, the judge must then decide whether the altered interpretation that is compatible with human rights is 'possible'. There are two conclusions available here. If the rights-compatible interpretation is 'possible', this is a complete remedy to the rights issue. If the rights-compatible interpretation is not 'possible', the judge must consider whether to grant a non-enforceable Declaration of Inconsistent Interpretation under section 36(2).

Section 7(2)

Importantly, the section 7(2) analysis is now part of assessing whether a statutory provision is 'compatible with human rights'.[18] That is, section 7(2) analysis informs whether a statutory provision, according to ordinary statutory interpretation principles, *is* 'compatible with human rights' because any limitation on human rights is reasonable and demonstrably justified; or whether it *is not* 'compatible with human rights' because the limitation is unreasonable, demonstrably unjustified or both.

If the statutory provision is 'compatible with human rights', it should stand. If it is not 'compatible with human rights', only then should a remedial interpretation under section 32(1) be considered, and that remedial interpretation should only be the preferred interpretation if it is 'possible'. To avoid doubt, it is the intention of this Parliament that section 7(2) analysis be part of the overall process leading to a rights-*compatible* or a rights-*incompatible* interpretation.

More broadly, including section 7(2) analysis within the concept of 'compatible with human rights' recognises that not all rights are absolute and that the *Charter* does not protect rights in their absolute form. Under the *Charter*, justifiable limitations on rights are an expected and acceptable part of resolving conflicts between rights, and between rights and other competing values in a democratic society.

Section 32(1)

Equally as important, the section 32(1) interpretation obligation is now clearly intended to have a remedial scope. If a statutory provision imposes a limitation on a human right, but that limitation is reasonable and demonstrably justified under section 7(2), there is no violation of rights – the statutory provision can be given an interpretation that is 'compatible with human rights', it is applied, and parliamentary sovereignty is respected.

Conversely, if a statutory provision imposes a limitation on a human right, and that limitation is not reasonable or not demonstrably justified or both, there is a violation of rights. A section 32(1) remedial interpretation that allows a rights-compatible interpretation of the statutory provision is a complete remedy to what *otherwise* would have been a rights-*incompatible* interpretation of the statutory provision – provided that remedial interpretation is 'possible', with 'possible' limiting the judicial role to one of statutory interpretation.

The necessary constitutional limit on the judiciary's power of remedial interpretation comes from the phrase 'so far as it is possible to do so', not from the phrase 'consistent with their purpose'. What is 'possible' is judicial interpretation; what is not 'possible' is judicial acts of legislation. Again, the limiting effect of 'possible' preserves parliamentary sovereignty.

The British experience offers guidance. For example, Lord Chief Justice Woolf in *Donoghue* emphasised that when deciding whether a rights-compatible interpretation of a statutory provision is 'possible', the court's 'task is still one of interpretation'; and if the court must 'radically alter the effect of the legislation' to secure compatibility, 'this will be an indication that more than interpretation is involved'.[19]

In *Ghaidan*, Lord Nicholls indicated that 'possible' interpretation includes interpreting legislative language 'restrictively or expansively', 'read[ing] in words which change the meaning of the enacted legislation', 'modify[ing] the meaning, and hence the effect' of legislation, and implying words provided they 'go with the grain of the legislation'.[20] Conversely, Lord Nicholls indicated 'possible' interpretation would *not* extend to courts 'adopt[ing] a meaning inconsistent with a fundamental feature of legislation' or 'the underlying thrust of the legislation being construed', or implying words that did not 'go with the grain of the legislation'.[21]

The question of whether, how and when 'possibility' allows a court to depart from the statutory purpose of a law was also addressed. In terms of *whether*, Lord Nicholls acknowledged that section 3 '*may* require the court to depart from . . . the intention of the Parliament which enacted the legislation'; in terms of *how* and *when*, Lord Nicholls stated '[t]he answer . . . depends upon the intention reasonably to be attributed to the Parliament in enacting section 3.'[22]

Importantly, Lord Nicholls did not state that judges *must* depart from the legislative intention; rather, that judges *may* depart from such legislative intention, but *not* where to do so would *not* be considered 'possible' – that is, *not* where to do so would undermine the fundamental features of legislation, be incompatible with the underlying thrust of legislation, or go against the grain of legislation.[23] The judiciary will cross the line from proper judicial interpretation into *improper* judicial legislation where a section 3 interpretation is *not* compatible with the fundamental features, the underlying thrust and the grain of the legislation.

The inclusion of 'consistent with their purpose' in the *Charter* has diverted attention from the role 'possible' plays in limiting judicial power. Instead, 'consistent with their purpose' has become *the* limitation on judicial power, and it does not capture the nuance of the limits on the role of judges. It is difficult to conceive of a case where a rights-*compatible* interpretation was 'possible' because it supported the fundamental features, the underlying thrust, and the grain of the legislation, and yet that interpretation was *inconsistent* with the parliamentary intention.

Two important points follow. First, because 'consistent with their purpose' has not been treated by the judiciary here as a codification of this British jurisprudence, this phrase is being removed from section 32(1). Second, there is a renewed focus on 'possibility', with an emphasis on how Lord Nicholls' *obiter* comments place boundaries around the judicial power of interpretation, and indicate that section 32(1) does *not* sanction the exercise of non-judicial power – being acts of judicial legislation – by the courts.[24] To avoid any doubt, the concept of 'possibility' is intended to be the operative limit on judicial power under the *Charter*.[25]

This brings us to whether the phrase 'consistent with their purpose' should be retained to accommodate conflicting parliamentary intentions. At times, judges may be faced with the intention of the *Charter*-enacting Parliament that statutory provisions should be interpreted 'so far as it is possible to do so' compatibly with rights; and a later parliamentary intention to enact rights-inconsistent legislation. Removing 'consistent with their purpose' from section 32(1) means that the legislative purpose of the challenged law will not *automatically* be elevated above the *Charter*-enacting Parliament's purpose, and that each occasion of statutory interpretation will need to resolve the conflicting intentions within the boundaries of judicial interpretation. As currently drafted and applied, a rights-inconsistent parliamentary intention in a challenged law *too readily* overrides the rights-compatible parliamentary intention of the *Charter*-enacting Parliament.

Resolving conflicts will require close attention to whether the two intentions are in competition and, if so, whether they can be reconciled.

Take, for example, the case of *Ghaidan*, where the heterosexual definition of 'spouse' under the UK's *Rents Act 1977* was found to violate the article 8 right to home when read together with the article 14 right to non-discrimination of the *European Convention on Human Rights*.[26] The House of Lords 'saved' the rights-incompatible provision via section 3(1) of the *UKHRA* by interpreting the words 'living with the statutory tenant as his or her wife or husband' to mean 'living with the statutory tenant as *if they were* his or her wife or husband'.[27] Although rights-compatible interpretation of this type has been considered radical,[28] this view must be challenged.

First, Lord Nicholls did *not* propose that the *UKHRA*-enacting Parliament's intention expressed in section 3(1) in favour of rights-*compatibility* will *always* prevail over competing intentions of Parliament expressed in challenged legislation that is rights-*incompatible*, let alone *ever* prevail. Rather, his comments about competing parliamentary intentions are subject to the rules articulated about 'possible' interpretations – that is, what section 3(1) *does* and *does not* allow.[29] Second, in the pre-*UKHRA* equivalent case to *Ghaidan*,[30] 'traditional methods of statutory interpretation' were used to achieve a rights-compatible reading of the legislation without attracting the moniker of 'radical'.[31] Third, Lord Nicholls explicitly based his section 3(1) rights-compatible interpretation on the social policy underlying the challenged statute, demonstrating that the *ratio* of *Ghaidan* was grounded in a section 3(1) interpretation that was expressly demonstrated to be *consistent* with the purposes of the challenged law.[32]

The upshot is that, rather than *automatically* elevating the legislative intention of the law-enacting Parliament over the legislative intention of the *Charter*-enacting Parliament, both intentions must be recognised and an attempt made to reconcile them. This was achieved in *Ghaidan*, and a section 3(1) rights-compatible interpretation was 'possible' – that is, achieved within the boundaries of legitimate judicial interpretation. This does not undermine parliamentary sovereignty because of the dialogic structure of the *Charter*: Parliament can respond to unwanted or undesirable rights-*compatible* judicial interpretations by amending or enacting statutory provisions that clearly and explicitly adopt rights-*incompatible* purposes and explicit rights-*incompatible* statutory language, ideally being accompanied by a section 28(3)(b) Statement of Incompatibility or section 31 override.[33]

Where the law-enacting Parliament's intention is clearly rights-*incompatible* – say, where the purposes, text and context of the statutory provisions are explicitly and clearly rights-incompatible, or the statutory provisions are accompanied by a section 28(3)(b) Statement of Incompatibility – a rights-*compatible* interpretation will *not* be 'possible' within the boundaries of legitimate judicial interpretation. Attention then turns to whether an unenforceable Declaration of Inconsistent Interpretation should be granted under section 36(2).

Finally, to avoid any doubt, this Parliament considers that the rules of statutory interpretation under section 3(1) of the *UKHRA* that flow from the limitation of 'possible', and that are adopted under section 32(1) of the *Charter* by these amendments, are consistent with the common law and statutory rules of construction in Australia.

In the High Court's *Momcilovic* decision, Chief Justice French noted that judicial interpretation is 'an expression of the constitutional relationship between the arms of government', and referred to the 'constitutional tradition' that judges interpret legislation 'according to the intent of them that made it'.[34] His Honour stated that the 'duty of the court' is 'to give the words of a statutory provision the meaning that the legislature is taken to have intended them to have',[35] with legislative intention being ascertained by complying with the common law and statutory rules of construction.[36] Under common law rules, '[t]he meaning given to [statutory] words must be a meaning which they can bear';[37] subject to 'an exceptional case' where 'the common law allows a court to depart from grammatical rules and to give an *unusual* or *strained* meaning to statutory words where the ordinary meaning and grammatical construction would contradict the apparent purpose of the enactment', although 'the court is not thereby authorised to legislate.'[38]

In the same case, Justice Gummow refers to the constitutional limits of statutory interpretation, being that '[t]he duty of a court is to give the words of a statutory provision the meaning that the legislature is taken to have intended them to have'; but that

> [t]he context of the words, the consequences of a literal or grammatical construction, the purpose of the statute or the canons of construction *may* require the words of a legislative provision to be read in a way that *does not correspond with* the literal or grammatical meaning . . .

with the latter qualification 'apply[ing] *a fortiori* where there is a canon of construction mandated . . . by a specific provision such as s 32(1).'[39]

These principles are consistent with section 32(1) as amended. The section 32(1) limitation of 'possible' ensures that the judicial task remains within the constitutional realm of interpretation. Moreover, section 32(1) may require deeper thinking about statutory purpose, especially where there is an apparent conflict between a *Charter*-enacting purpose and a law-enacting purpose. However, section 32(1) does not sanction interpretations that undermine the fundamental features of legislation, are incompatible with the underlying thrust of legislation, or go against the grain of legislation – or, in short, that are inconsistent with statutory purpose. Further, Chief Justice French and Justice Gummow accept that ordinary meaning *may* need to give way to an alternative meaning. Acknowledging that a canon of construction may justify meaning *other than* the literal or grammatical meaning is *not* substantially different to the British jurisprudence. That section 3(1) 'allowed the court to depart from unambiguous meaning' was 'the most important premise in *Ghaidan*'.[40]

In sum, just as Chief Justice French considers that the common law rules of construction 'help . . . to define the boundaries between the judicial and legislative functions',[41] so too does the British experience help to define the boundaries between *possible* and *impossible* interpretation – which, in turn, helps to define the boundaries between *legitimate* judicial remedial interpretation and *illegitimate* judicial remedial legislation.

To conclude, if rights-*incompatible* legislation can be 'fixed' through judicial remedial interpretation that is 'possible', it provides a complete remedy for the person whose rights would otherwise be compromised, and saves Parliament the task of having to amend that legislation to be rights-compatible. This is an efficient division of labour between the two arms of government, and consistent with relevant constitutional roles.

We now move to our proposed amendments regarding the obligations on public authorities.

Sections 38 and 39 currently

Section 38(1) of the *Charter* imposes obligations on public authorities, by making it unlawful for them 'to act in a way that is incompatible with a human right' or 'to fail to give proper consideration to a relevant human right' when making a decision.

Section 39(1) imposes consequences for such unlawfulness. As currently drafted, section 39(1) does not create a freestanding cause of action or provide a freestanding remedy for individuals when a public authority engages in unlawfulness under section 38(1).[42] Rather than allowing a person alleging unlawfulness under section 39 to independently and solely claim for a breach of statutory duty with the statute being the *Charter*, section 39 requires a person to 'piggy-back' *Charter*-unlawfulness on to a pre-existing claim to relief or remedy, including any pre-existing claim to damages.[43] Section 39(3) provides that '[a] person is not entitled to be awarded any damages because of a breach of this Charter', with section 39(4) 'saving' pre-existing rights to damages beyond the *Charter*.

The amendments to section 39 are intended to extend the causes of action and remedies for unlawfulness under section 38(1) to include a freestanding cause of action and the inclusion of damages as a remedy. A freestanding cause of action supported by a freestanding remedy is an appropriate and effective legislative response to a public authority's failure to meet its obligations under section 38(1). Extending the causes of action and remedies through the section 39 amendments will address numerous weaknesses in the *Charter*'s enforcement regime.

First, section 39 as currently enacted undermines the enforcement of rights. To force an applicant to 'piggyback' a *Charter* claim on to a pre-existing relief or remedy adds unnecessary complexity to the vindication of rights claims against public authorities. This may result in victims of a rights violation receiving no remedy in situations where a 'piggyback' pre-existing relief or remedy is not available. Moreover, the complexity adds to the cost of *Charter* litigation, creating a disincentive for victims to pursue their rights claims.[44]

Secondly, all victims of rights violations are entitled to an effective remedy under article 2(3) of the *ICCPR*. Anything short of an unconstrained free-standing cause of action supported by a freestanding remedy fails to satisfy this obligation.

Extending remedies through the amendments to section 39 will also bring Victoria into line with comparable jurisdictions such as the United Kingdom. Under the *UKHRA*, a freestanding cause of action for breach of statutory duty is available where a public authority acts unlawfully.[45] Importantly, under section 8 of the *UKHRA*, a court may grant such relief or remedy, including damages, within its power as it considers just and appropriate.

The Australian Capital Territory now imposes obligations on public authorities in similar terms to section 38(1) of the *Charter*,[46] but adopted the UK position on remedies by allowing a freestanding cause of action against a public authority in its Supreme Court, in addition to allowing a person to rely on unlawfulness under the ACT's *Human Rights Act 2004* (*ACTHRA*) in any other legal proceeding.[47] However, similarly to section 39(3) of the *Charter*, the remedies provided by the *ACTHRA* exclude awards of damages.[48] The proposed amendments replicate relevant provisions of the *ACTHRA*,[49] but not its exclusion relating to damages, and bring the *Charter* into line with the *UKHRA*.

This Parliament also recognises that, in the absence of an *effective* remedy for *Charter* unlawfulness or an *inadequate* remedy under a pre-existing cause of action, the Supreme Court may craft a remedy by invoking its inherent jurisdiction. This has happened in New Zealand, where its *Bill of Rights Act 1990* does not expressly provide for remedies. The courts have filled the gap by developing two remedies for violations of rights – first, a judicial discretion to exclude evidence obtained in violation of rights; and second, a right to compensation if rights are violated.[50] This Parliament does not wish to leave this issue to the Supreme Court, but seeks to ensure that violations of human rights are met with appropriate, effective and adequate remedies.

In order to better protect the rights guaranteed in the *Charter*, this Parliament must clarify and strengthen these two enforcement mechanisms in the *Charter*.

We commend the Bill to the House.

PARLIAMENT OF VICTORIA

Introduced in the Assembly

Charter of Human Rights and Responsibilities (Advancing Enforcement) Amendment Bill 2024

A Bill for an Act to amend the **Charter of Human Rights and Responsibilities Act 2006** to advance the protection of human rights and clarify, strengthen and expand enforcement mechanisms.

The Parliament of Victoria enacts:

Part 1 – Preliminary

1 Purposes

The purpose of this Act is to amend the **Charter of Human Rights and Responsibilities Act 2006** to –

(a) advance the protection of human rights; and
(b) clarify, strengthen and expand enforcement mechanisms.

2 Commencement

This Act comes into operation on a day or days to be proclaimed.

3 Principal Act

For the purposes of this Act, the **Charter of Human Rights and Responsibilities Act 2006** shall be called the Principal Act.

Part 2 – Advancing Enforcement of Human Rights

4 Definitions

In section 3(1) of the Principal Act, **insert** –

'***compatible with human rights,*** in relation to an act, decision or statutory provision, means that the act, decision or statutory provision does not limit a human right or limits a human right in a manner and to the extent that is reasonable and demonstrably justifiable in accordance with section 7 of this Act;'

5 **Interpretation – amendment to s 32(1)**
In section 32(1) of the Principal Act, **delete** the words 'consistently with their purpose', so that it now reads:

'32 Interpretation

(1) So far as it is possible to do so, all statutory provisions must be interpreted in a way that is compatible with human rights.'

6 **Legal proceedings – amendments to s 39**

(1) For s 39(1) of the Principal Act, **substitute** –

'39 Legal proceedings

(1) This section applies if a person –

(a) claims that a public authority has acted in contravention of section 38; and
(b) alleges that the person is or would be a victim of the contravention.

(2) The person may –

(a) commence a proceeding in the Supreme Court against the public authority; or
(b) rely on the person's rights under this Act in other legal proceedings.

(3) The Supreme Court may, in a proceeding under subsection (2), grant the relief it considers appropriate.
(4) This section does not affect a right a person has (otherwise than because of this Act) to seek relief in relation to an act or decision of a public authority.'

(2) Section 39(3) and (4) of the Principal Act are **repealed.**

Part 3 – Miscellaneous amendments

7 **Repeal of this Act**
This Act is repealed on the first anniversary of its commencement.

Notes

1 *Charter of Human Rights and Responsibilities Act 2006* (Vic). This is Act No 43 of 2006; and the proposed amendments are based on Version 014 incorporating amendments as at 6 April 2020 (https://www.legislation.vic.gov.au/in-force/acts/charter-human-rights-and-responsibilities-act-2006/014.
2 Kent Roach, *Remedies for Human Rights Violations: A Two-Track Approach to Supra-national and National Law* (Cambridge University Press, 2021) 2.

3 All victims of human rights violations are entitled to an effective remedy under article 2(3) of the *International Covenant on Civil and Political Rights*, opened for signature 19 December 1966, 999 UNTS 171 (entered into force 23 March 1976).
4 Committee on the Elimination of Discrimination Against Women ('CEDAW Committee'), *General Recommendation No 33 on Women's Access to Justice*, UN Doc CEDAW/C/GC/33 (3 August 2015) paras 1–2.
5 Human Rights Committee, *General Comment No 31: The Nature of the General Legal Obligation Imposed on States Parties to the* Covenant, UN Doc CCPR/C/21/Rev.1/Add.13 (26 May 2004) para 15.
6 CEDAW Committee (n 4) paras 3, 8.
7 See Alistair Pound and Kylie Evans, *Annotated Victorian Charter of Rights* (Thomson Reuters, 2nd ed, 2019) CHR.32.80, CHR.32.100.
8 The principle of legality refers to the presumption that Parliament does not intend to interfere with fundamental common law rights, freedoms and immunities, except by clear and unambiguous language.
9 The word '(in)consistently' is used when referring to Parliament's purpose because the current wording of section 32(1) refers to 'consistently with their purpose'; whereas the word '(in)compatibility' is used when referring to ultimate judicial interpretation because the current wording of section 32(1) refers to 'compatible with human rights'.
10 Hilary Charlesworth, 'Human Rights as Men's Rights' in Julie Peters and Andrea Wolper (eds) *Women's Rights, Human Rights: International Feminist Perspectives* (Routledge, 1995) 103–13; United Nations Special Rapporteur on Violence against Women, *15 Years of the United Nations Special Rapporteur on Violence against Women, Its Causes and Consequences (1994–2009): A Critical Review* (Office of the UN High Commissioner for Human Rights, 2009) 10, 31.
11 See Julie Debeljak, 'The Fragile Foundations of the Human Rights Landscape: Why Australia needs a Human Rights Instrument' in Paula Gerber and Melissa Castan (eds) *Critical Perspectives on Human Rights Law in Australia: Volume 1* (Thomson Reuters, 2021) 39, 71; Bruce Chen, 'Revisiting Section 32(1) of the Victorian Charter: Strained Constructions and Legislative Intention' (2020) 46(1) *Monash University Law Review* 174, 187–88.
12 Another difference is that section 32(1) uses to 'be interpreted' whereas section 3(1) of the *UKHRA* uses the words 'read and given effect to'. Commentators have failed to attribute any significance to these differences in terminology: Priyanga Hettiarachi, 'Some Things Borrowed, Some Things New: An Overview of Judicial Review of Legislation under the Charter of Human Rights and Responsibilities' (2007) 7(1) *Oxford University Commonwealth Law Journal* 61, 83; Claudia Geiringer, 'The Principle of Legality and the Bill of Rights Act: A Critical Examination of R v Hansen' (2008) 6(1) *New Zealand Journal of Public and International Law* 59, 66. However, some judges have given them significance: see *R v Momcilovic* (2010) VSCA 50, [77] ('*VCA Momcilovic*'); *Momcilovic v R* [2011] 280 ALR 221, 378 [544] (Crennan and Kiefel JJ) ('*HCA Momcilovic*').
13 Most particularly *Ghaidan v Godin-Mendoza* [2004] UKHL 30 ('*Ghaidan*').
14 *VCA Momcilovic* (n 12) [74].
15 Six of seven High Court of Australia justices agreed that section 32(1) of the *Charter* was not analogous to section 3(1) of the *UKHRA*: see *HCA Momcilovic* (n 12) 37 [18], 50 [51] (French CJ); 210 [544], 217 [565]–[566] (Crennan and Kiefel JJ); 92 [170] (Gummow J); 123 [280] (Hayne J); 250 [684] (Bell J). See further, *Victoria Police Toll Enforcement & Ors v Taha and Others; State of Victoria v Brookes and Another* (2013) 49 VR 1; [2013] VSCA 37, 62 [190] (Tate JA).
16 *VCA Momcilovic* (n 12) [104].

17 Human Rights Consultation Committee, *Rights, Responsibilities and Respect: The Report of the Human Rights Consultation Committee* (Victorian Government, 2005) 82–3; Explanatory Memorandum, Charter of Human Rights and Responsibilities Bill 2006 (Vic) 23.
18 The amendment is consistent with recommendation 28(c) and 29 from the *2015 Charter Review*: Michael Brett Young, *From Commitment to Culture: The 2015 Review of the Charter of Human Rights and Responsibilities Act* 2006 (Victorian Government, 2015) 145–46, 148, 152–55 ('*2015 Charter Review*').
19 *Poplar Housing and Regeneration Community Association Ltd v Donoghue* [2001] EWCA Civ 595 [75]–[76].
20 *Ghaidan* (n 13) [32]–[33] (Lord Nicholls). Lord Rodger agreed with these propositions ([121], [124]), as did Lord Millett [67]).
21 Ibid [33]. Lord Rodger agreed with these propositions ([121]), as did Lord Millett ([67]). Justice Bell supported this approach to section 32(1) in *Kracke v Mental Health Review Board & Ors (General)* [2009] VCAT 646, [218].
22 *Ghaidan* (n 13) [30] (Lord Nicholls) (emphasis added).
23 See also *Sheldrake v DPP* [2005] 1 AC 264, [28]. For more on the British jurisprudence, see Julie Debeljak, 'Parliamentary Sovereignty and Dialogue under the Victorian Charter on Human Rights and Responsibilities: Drawing the Line Between Judicial Interpretation and Judicial Law-Making' (2007) 33(1) *Monash University Law Review* 9, 40–56.
24 See further Julie Debeljak, Submission to the National Consultation on Human Rights, *National Consultation on Human Rights Committee* (15 June 2009) 51–7 ('Submission to National Consultation').
25 Julie Debeljak, 'Who Is Sovereign Now? The Momcilovic Court Hands Back Power Over Human Rights That Parliament Intended it to Have' (2011) 22(1) *Public Law Review* 15, 30.
26 *European Convention on Human Rights*, opened for signature 4 November 1950, 213 UNTS 222 (entered into force 3 September 1953) arts 8, 14.
27 *Ghaidan* (n 13) [35]–[36] (Lord Nicholls); [51] (Lord Steyn); [129] (Lord Rodger); [144]–[145] (Baroness Hale).
28 Aileen Kavanagh, 'Unlocking the *Human Rights Act:* The "Radical" Approach to Section 3(1) Revisited' (2005) 3 *European Human Rights Law Review* 259.
29 That is, 'how far, and in what circumstances' the *UKHRA* intention overrides the intention of an enacting Parliament: *Ghaidan* (n 13) [30].
30 *Fitzpatrick v Sterling Housing Association Ltd* [2001] 1 AC 27.
31 Aileen Kavanagh, 'Choosing Between Sections 3 and 4 of the Human Rights Act 1998: Judicial Reasoning after Ghaidan v Mendoza' in Helen Fenwick et al. (eds), *Judicial Reasoning Under the UK Human Rights Act* (Cambridge University Press, 2007) 114, 142, fn 131. See Debeljak, 'Submission to the National Consultation' (n 24) 51–7.
32 See *Ghaidan* (n 13) [35].
33 Julie Debeljak, 'Rights Dialogue where there is Disagreement under the Victorian Charter' in Julie Debeljak and Laura Grenfell (eds), *Law Making and Human Rights: Executive and Parliamentary Scrutiny across Australian Jurisdictions* (Thomson Reuters, 2020) 267, 273–75; Julie Debeljak, 'Inquiry into the Charter of Human Rights and Responsibilities', Submission to the Scrutiny of Acts and Regulations Committee for the Four-Year Review of the *Charter of Human Rights and Responsibilities Act 2006, Victorian Parliament* (10 June 2011) 11–17.
34 *HCA Momcilovic* (n 12) 239 [37], 240 [38] (citations omitted).
35 Ibid 240 [38], citing *Project Blue Sky v Australian Broadcasting Authority* (1998) 194 CLR 355, 384 (McHugh, Gummow, Kirby and Hayne JJ) ('*Project Blue Sky*').

36 *HCA Momcilovic* (n 12) 240 [38], citing *Lacey v Attorney-General (Qld)* [2011] HCA 10 [43] (French CJ, Gummow, Hayne, Crennan, Kiefel and Bell JJ).
37 *HCA Momcilovic* (n 12) 240 [39], then quoting Lord Reid in *Jones v Director of Public Prosecutions* [1962] AC 635, 662.
38 *HCA Momcilovic* (n 12) 240 [40] (emphasis added).
39 Ibid 280 [170] (citations omitted) (emphasis added), citing *Project Blue Sky* (n 35) 384 [78].
40 See Aileen Kavanagh, *Constitutional Review Under the UK Human Rights Act* (Cambridge University Press, 2009) 94.
41 *HCA Momcilovic* (n 12) 241 [42].
42 *Director of Housing v Sudi* (2001) 33 VR 559 [215].
43 This has been referred to as the 'conditional and supplementary' nature of section 39(1): Ibid [96] (Maxwell P).
44 See Young, *2015 Charter Review* (n 18) 119–22.
45 This is in addition to a new ground of illegality under administrative law, and the ability to rely on the unlawful act in any other legal proceeding. See *R (on the application of Daly) v Secretary of State for the Home Department* [2001] 2 WLR 1622; and *Huang v Secretary of State for the Home Department; Kashmiri v Secretary of State for the Home Department* [2007] UKHL 11.
46 *Human Rights Act 2004* (ACT) s 40B ('*ACTHRA*').
47 Ibid s 40C(2).
48 Ibid ss 40C(4)–(5). Note that the inclusion of section 40C has not led to a proliferation of claims in the ACT courts: Young, *2015 Charter Review* (n 18) 126–7.
49 Ibid ss 40C(1), (2), (4)–(5).
50 ACT Bill of Rights Consultative Committee, ACT Legislative Assembly, *Towards an ACT Human Rights Act* (2003) paras 3.22–3.23.

Chapter 6A

Commentary on *Re-charting the Victorian Charter of Human Rights*

Advancing Enforcement

The Hon Pamela Tate AM KC[1]

Enforcement is the most important issue arising from Victoria's *Charter of Human Rights and Responsibilities* ('the *Charter*'). In their Charter of Human Rights and Responsibilities (Advancing Enforcement) Amendment Bill 2024, Associate Professors Debeljak and Penovic deal with this issue directly and creatively. Without effective forms of enforcement, there is little to gain by the introduction of gender-specific rights. It is within this context that Debeljak and Penovic set out to rewrite the *Charter* from a feminist perspective.

The *Charter* lacks a standalone cause of action. There is uncertainty as to the remedies available when a public authority has breached its obligation to comply with human rights or has failed to properly consider relevant human rights in its decision-making processes.[2] Although the *Charter* obliges the adoption of an interpretation of legislation that is compatible with human rights,[3] the potential for a court to provide an interpretation that in itself amounts to a remedy was significantly restricted by the High Court in *Momcilovic v The Queen* ('*HCA Momcilovic*').[4]

Debeljak and Penovic introduce a cause of action solely based upon an alleged breach of human rights. This places a proceeding for breach on an honest and independent footing without the technical difficulties arising from the need to 'piggyback' on another cause of action. The proceeding is restricted to those who allege they are, or would be, victims of the breach, while the jurisdiction is limited to the Supreme Court of Victoria.[5] This would enable women, including diverse women, to access the Supreme Court to allege, for example, that their right to the equal protection of the law has been breached. A victim may also rely on their *Charter* rights 'in other legal proceedings'. This should be read as including legal proceedings in all other jurisdictions, including the Victorian Civil and Administrative Tribunal and the County Court of Victoria, to ensure that those current avenues of access are not restricted.

The range of discretionary remedies is also expanded. The Supreme Court can award the relief it considers appropriate. Notably, this would include damages. There is no restriction of the type found in the UK's *Human Rights Act 1998* ('*UKHRA*'), where damages are not to be awarded unless necessary

DOI: 10.4324/9781003372462-12

to afford just satisfaction to the person concerned.[6] It may be implicit that the Supreme Court would first seek to ensure that the offending conduct stops, and minimum human rights standards are upheld in the future, before awarding damages. If a new and separate head of damages is to be recognised, available under the *Charter*, which does not seek to compensate for loss but is intended to vindicate a victim's rights, the amendments could state expressly that the available relief includes 'vindicatory damages'.[7]

The more difficult objective of the proposed amendments is to ensure that the *Charter* allows for the remedial interpretation of legislation. This goal is significant.

In 2004, the House of Lords held in *Ghaidan v Godin-Mendoza ('Ghaidan')*[8] that it was empowered by section 3(1) of the *UKHRA* to modify the meaning and effect of legislation to make it compatible with human rights, provided only that the meaning was 'possible' in that it was not inconsistent with a fundamental feature of the legislation.[9] This authorised a remedial reading of 'spouse' to include a same-sex partner, despite the legislation defining 'spouse' as a person 'living with the statutory tenant *as* his or her *wife* or *husband*'.[10] In effect, 'as' was interpreted to mean 'as if they were'. This permitted a person in a same-sex relationship to inherit a statutory tenancy when their partner died.

Section 3(1) of the *UKHRA* provides that '[s]o far as it is possible to do so, primary legislation and subordinate legislation must be read and given effect in a way which is compatible with [human rights]'. This stands in contrast to section 32(1) of the *Charter*, which provides that '[s]o far as it is possible to do so consistently with their purpose, all statutory provisions must be interpreted in a way that is compatible with human rights'.

In *HCA Momcilovic*, the High Court held that section 32(1) did not support 'strong' remedial interpretations of the type illustrated by *Ghaidan*.[11]

The proposed amendments seek to authorise the adoption of the remedial interpretation of legislation by two means: first, removing the requirement in section 32(1) that the interpretation of a statutory provision must be consistent with its purpose; and second, clarifying, by providing a definition of 'compatible with human rights', what amounts to a human rights-compatible interpretation, namely, one that imposes no limits on human rights or one that interferes with a human right in a reasonable and justified way, assessed by reference to the articulated proportionality criteria set out in the *Charter*.[12]

The second proposed amendment requires a careful assessment of whether there are interpretations that might interfere with a relevant human right to a lesser degree than an alternative interpretation. For example, in the circumstances of a case, the interpretation of the use by the police of force 'not disproportionate' to the objective to be achieved (say, an arrest) might include a consideration not only of the perceived threat to the officer but also of whether the arrest could have been effected while protecting a suspect's right to be treated with humanity and respect for the inherent dignity of the human person.[13] Directing a court to rigorously consider a range of alternative interpretations is an excellent proposal that may well bring about more human rights-compatible choices in construction.

The first proposed amendment is more contentious. It is implicit in section 3 of the *UKHRA* that the interpretation to be adopted is consistent with statutory purpose, as Debeljak and Penovic concede, yet this did not preclude the House of Lords from embracing a remedial approach. It is also accepted that section 32(1), as amended, will not sanction interpretations that are inconsistent with statutory purpose. The requirement to adopt a construction that achieves the purpose of a statutory provision is a fundamental canon of statutory interpretation in Australia.[14] The purposive requirement in section 32(1) assists in reinforcing the character of the exercise as a process of interpretation which may nevertheless demand a reading of words, in context, that deviates from literal or grammatical meaning.[15]

Opening the way to remedial interpretations might be better achieved by affirming that an assumption to be made when applying the interpretive obligation of section 32(1) is that Parliament intended to achieve a purpose that is compatible with human rights.[16] This would facilitate, for example, the interpretation of a mandatory requirement to impose on a 'third strike' offender the maximum term of imprisonment as subject to a limitation that it would not apply where the sentence would result in a breach of human rights.[17] This approach might involve not simply applying the principle of legality but also 'proactively seeking a rights-consistent meaning'.[18] The assumption would function as one of the rules of construction to determine the objective meaning of what Parliament has said.[19]

Associate Professors Debeljak and Penovic are to be congratulated for a thoughtful and serious analysis of complex legal issues. They have made a valuable contribution to an understanding of how human rights legislation can have a meaningful impact.

Notes

1 This commentary is confined to the amendments proposed by the Charter of Human Rights and Responsibilities (Advancing Enforcement) Amendment Bill 2024.
2 *Charter of Human Rights and Responsibilities*, ss 38(1), 39.
3 Ibid s 32(1).
4 *Momcilovic v R* (2011) 245 CLR 1; [2011] 280 ALR 221; [2011] HCA 34.
5 This reflects the *Human Rights Act 2004* (ACT) s 40C.
6 *Human Rights Act 1998* (UK) s 8(3).
7 See *Lewis v Australian Capital Territory* (2020) 271 CLR 192, 229–34 [104]–[121] (Gordon J; Gageler J agreeing 206 [22]), 248–51 [153]–[159] (Edelman J; Kiefel CJ and Keane J agreeing at 200 [2]), [2020] HCA 26, where the High Court rejected a head of 'vindicatory damages' at common law.
8 *Ghaidan v Godin-Mendoza* [2004] 2 AC 557, [2004] UKHL 30.
9 Ibid 572 [33] (Lord Nicholls), 601 [121] (Lord Rodger). This was before the enactment of same-sex marriage legislation.

10 Emphasis added.
11 *HCA Momcilovic* (n 4) 37 [20] 48–50 [47]-[50] (French CJ), 89 [155] (Gummow J; Hayne J agreeing at 123 [180]), 211 [546] (Crennan and Kiefel JJ), 250 [684] (Bell J).
12 *Charter* (n 2) s 7(2).
13 Ibid s 22(1), *Gebrehiwot v Victoria* (2020) 287 A Crim R 226, 264 [140]; [2020] VSCA 315.
14 *Project Blue Sky Inc v Australian Broadcasting Authority* (1998) 194 CLR 355; [1998] HCA 28. See, eg, *Interpretation of Legislation Act 1984* (Vic) s 35(a).
15 *HCA Momcilovic* (n 4) 92 [170] (Gummow J; Hayne J agreeing at 123 [180]).
16 *Fitzgerald v The Queen* [2021] 1 NZLR 551, 578 [56] (Winkelmann CJ); [2021] NZSC 131.
17 Ibid 596 [128]–[30], 597–98 [135] (Winkelmann CJ), 616–17 [203], 622–23 [219] (O'Regan and Arnold JJ), 629–30 [247]–[48], 630 [250] (Glazebrook J).
18 Ibid 578 [56] (Winkelmann CJ).
19 See *Zheng v Cai* (2009) 239 CLR 446, 455–56 [28]; [2009] HCA 52; *Lacey v Attorney-General (Qld)* (2011) 242 CLR 573, 591–92 [43]; [2011] HCA 10; Kenneth Hayne, 'Statutes, Intentions and the Courts: What Place does the Notion of Intention (Legislative or Parliamentary) Have in Statutory Construction?' (2013) 13(2) *Oxford University Commonwealth Law Journal* 271.

Part III

Bodies, Sex and Agency

Chapter 7

Implementing Affirmative Consent in Sexual Offences

A Model Law for Queensland

Jonathan Crowe, Asher Flynn and Bri Lee

Extract from *Hansard* (Parliament of Queensland)

Criminal Code Amendment (Sexual Offences) Bill (Qld) 2024

Second Reading

HON JONATHAN CROWE, HON ASHER FLYNN and HON BRI LEE: We jointly move –

That the Bill now be read a second time.

Rape and sexual assault cause significant and devastating harms to victims. Our Bill seeks to address Queensland's complex and outdated laws governing sexual violence by introducing vital reforms which better recognise the lived experience of victims of sexual violence and respond to changing attitudes towards what constitutes appropriate and respectful sexual relations.

The Bill has three main objectives. It aims to:

- uphold the fundamental right of every person to make decisions about their sexual behaviour and choose not to engage in sexual activity;
- protect children and persons with a cognitive impairment, mental illness or other vulnerability from sexual exploitation; and
- protect every person from unlawful threats or deprivation of their liberty.

To achieve these aims, we propose four main changes to add clarity to rape and sexual assault law and modernise outdated language:

1. Introducing guiding principles to recognise the unique nature of rape and sexual assault offences, which should be considered by the court and relevant criminal justice agents in dealing with these crimes;

DOI: 10.4324/9781003372462-14

2. Introducing a clear definition of consent as free and active agreement that embraces an affirmative consent standard, including a non-exhaustive list of consent-negating circumstances;
3. Replacing the outdated reference to 'carnal knowledge' in defining rape; and
4. Removing the problematic and outdated mistake of fact excuse in rape and sexual assault cases.

These changes build upon existing laws in other jurisdictions, including New South Wales, the Australian Capital Territory, Victoria, Tasmania, Canada and New Zealand. Importantly, the proposed legislation will advance existing rape law to ensure that perpetrators will not escape liability for rape where they mistakenly believed the other person was consenting. In this way, the Bill will enable Queensland to lead the way in sexual offence reform both in Australia and internationally.

Guiding Principles

There are a number of broad systemic problems in the criminal justice system's handling of rape and sexual assault. Sexual violence remains significantly underreported in Australia, with national survey data revealing 4 out of 5 Australian women did not report their sexual assault to police.[1] When complaints are made, a further winnowing occurs at the prosecution stage which sees between 15% and 20% of those accused of such crimes brought to trial,[2] with 3.5% ultimately convicted.[3] These figures demonstrate a fundamental problem with the law, as well as with current service delivery, support mechanisms and criminal justice processes for victims.

The law should play a distinct role in addressing these problematic figures by providing clear guidance on the circumstances in which rape and sexual assault occur and offering a clear definition of consent that reflects contemporary respectful sexual relations.[4] There are, of course, limits to what laws can achieve in bringing about social change. Nonetheless, the law can be used to classify what is and what is not acceptable conduct, and what is expected prior to and during sexual activity.

Too often, the complexity of rape is reduced to a simple narrative informed by 'rape myths', where rape is understood as a violent act committed by a stranger, generally because of risky activities by the victim (particularly women victims).[5] This leads us to assume a certain perspective on rape, and that victims (again, particularly women) are in some way responsible for preventing their own assaults. These assumptions are frequently evident in cases featuring circumstances at odds with the prevailing narrative, such as a delay in the victim reporting a rape or where the victim was intoxicated when they were assaulted.

The law also struggles to deal with rapes occurring in the context of an intimate relationship, or indeed most situations where the victim and perpetrator were known to each other. The persistence of 'rape myths' means that these assaults are often regarded as not meeting the stereotype that people associate with 'real rape'.[6] Given that most sexual crimes in Queensland (and Australia more broadly) occur in a residential location[7] and are carried out by someone known to the victim,[8] it is particularly troubling that the law has traditionally and consistently failed victims in these circumstances. The Bill seeks to address this.

The Bill begins by stating some key facts around rape and sexual assault victimisation. These are designed to counteract misconceptions of rape, including 'rape myths' and victim-blaming attitudes. Among other key principles, this section of the Bill requires courts to consider the following:

- There is a high incidence of sexual violence within society;
- Sexual offences are significantly under-reported;
- Sexual offenders are commonly known to their victims;
- Sexual offences most frequently occur in residential locations;
- There are common and legitimate reasons why victims of sexual violence may not physically resist an assault, including, but not limited to, physiological responses to aggression and fear of escalating or prolonging the attack;
- Sexual offences often occur in circumstances where there is unlikely to be any physical signs of an offence having occurred; and
- There are common and legitimate reasons why victims of sexual violence may not immediately report an assault to police or another party and a failure to make an immediate report, on its own, does not discredit an allegation.

The Bill also seeks to place rape and sexual assault victimisation in context. Globally, an estimated 35% of women have experienced either physical and/or sexual intimate partner violence, or sexual violence by a non-partner (not including sexual harassment) in their lifetime.[9] The Australian Bureau of Statistics reports that 19% of Australian women experience some form of sexual violence in their lifetime, while 8 out of 10 victims of sexual violence are women.[10] Similarly, the most recent victimisation data from the Australian Bureau of Statistics finds that women make up 84% of reported sexual violence victims in Australia.[11]

Broader patterns of sexual victimisation are also evident on the basis of age,[12] cognitive and physical impairment,[13] sexuality,[14] as well as Indigeneity, ethnicity and cultural and linguistic diversity.[15] The Bill's guiding principles place these experiences in context by stating that 'a significant number of sexual offences are committed against women, children and other vulnerable persons, including persons with a cognitive impairment or mental illness'.

Definition of Consent and Rape

Rape and sexual assault occur when sexual penetration or sexual touching takes place without consent.[16] Consent continues to be the primary issue at play in rape trials. The way consent is understood also contributes to low reporting rates for rape and sexual assault, as well as high attrition rates throughout the investigation and prosecution process. The Bill seeks to clarify the meaning of consent in law by providing a clear definition of consent as 'free and active agreement' using an affirmative consent standard, as well as defining what constitutes 'active agreement' to limit any confusion as to what this might look like.

An affirmative consent standard requires that a person demonstrates an ongoing willingness to engage in a sexual act, either verbally or through their actions.[17] Affirmative consent diverges from 'traditional' understandings of consent, which require a victim to express non-consent or actively resist a sexual act. It instead places the onus on each party to take active steps to ensure the other party is consenting before and during the sexual encounter.[18] In other words, the focus is on the *communication* between the parties. This approach better reflects the realities of sexual violence victimisation, where it is a common and understandable response for victims to freeze, shut down and/or stay silent during their assault.[19]

Under an affirmative consent standard, consent cannot be implied from the victim's (perceived) behaviour in the hours or days prior to the act, nor can it be inferred, for example, from previous consensual sexual encounters.[20] This provides a clear message that consent must be present at the time of the sexual act and must continue while the act itself continues. It addresses concerns around sexist discourses and outdated rape myths which imply if the victim had acted differently, 'the perpetrator would not have thought she "wanted sex" and would therefore not have raped her'.[21] By reducing the opportunities for these 'implied consent narratives' to function at trial,[22] the Bill directly challenges victim-blaming attitudes.

An affirmative consent standard also recognises that if one party to a sexual act departs from the agreed sexual conduct – for example, if consent was premised on the person wearing a condom, which they later remove – there is no requirement on the victim to revoke consent or express non-consent. Each party must continue to ensure the other person consents throughout the entire sexual encounter.

This approach, in which sexual consent is based on ongoing active agreement by all parties, is achieved in this Bill by stating that 'consent means free and active agreement to an act by a person with the cognitive capacity to give consent'. It is further reflected in provisions stating that:

- active agreement requires consent to have been expressed immediately before and during the sexual encounter;
- active agreement to a sexual act cannot be expressed hours, days or weeks prior to the sexual act occurring;

- active agreement cannot be implied. It must be clearly and positively expressed;
- each person engaging in sexual penetration or sexual touching must take steps to find out whether the other person consents to each sexual act, and to ensure that they continue to consent throughout the sexual encounter.

This Bill makes a substantive change to the law by providing these clear definitions of active agreement, seeking to counteract a system that allows victims to be blamed for their rape or sexual assault.

The Bill also provides a clear, but non-exhaustive, list of consent-negating circumstances that can be used by the courts to better understand the circumstances in which consent *cannot* be present, regardless of the perpetrator's claims the victim was consenting. This includes circumstances such as submitting due to force, fear, threats, intimidation or perceived or actual authority,[23] as well as circumstances such as where the victim is substantially affected by alcohol or another drug, or asleep or unconscious when any part of the sexual act occurs.

The Bill also includes a non-exhaustive list of circumstances in which the victim is unable to understand the nature of the sexual act, or where the victim submits because they are misled about a material fact, in the absence of which they would not have submitted.[24] This includes, for example, being misled about:

- the sexual nature of the act;
- the identity of any other person involved in the act;
- the purpose of the act (including medical, hygienic, veterinary, agricultural or scientific purposes);
- gifts or payment promised in relation to the act; or
- condom use by any other person involved in the act.[25]

In cases where any of these consent-negating circumstances can be established, the perpetrator should be found guilty of rape.

The current definition of rape in Queensland makes use of the common law term 'carnal knowledge',[26] an obscure and gendered term which has been replaced in other Australian jurisdictions.[27] This definition reflects the traditional understanding of rape as confined to penetration of the vagina by the penis, but has long been expanded to include other forms of sexual penetration. Because the offence of rape is now gender-neutral, this outdated and confusing terminology should not be retained.

Mistake of Fact Excuse

The Bill will eliminate the mistake of fact excuse[28] for the issue of consent in cases of rape and sexual assault. This excuse undermines the free and active agreement definition of consent now enshrined in the law. It also perpetuates harmful and false rape myths, allowing these myths to wrongfully become the focus of the trial.[29]

Under the mistake of fact excuse, a perpetrator can argue that even if the victim did not consent to the sexual act, they honestly and reasonably, but mistakenly, believed that they did and therefore should be found not guilty.[30] As recent research into the Queensland case law shows, this excuse has a number of undesirable consequences.[31] The main concern is that it undermines the way Queensland law construes the notion of free and active consent, by allowing factors such as the victim's social behaviour, relationship to the perpetrator or lack of overt resistance to be raised by the perpetrator in order to avoid liability.

There are several reasons why a victim may not resist or express lack of consent to a sexual act, even though they are unwilling to engage in it. First, they may be afraid due to the express or implicit threat of physical violence. Second, they may be affected by the 'freezing response' that is a common psychological reaction to aggression or trauma.[32] Third, they may be inclined to pacify the aggressor, rather than confronting them directly.[33] And fourth, they may rationally judge that it is safer not to 'fight back', rather than risk escalating or prolonging the encounter.

Many cases feature a combination of these factors, each of which indicates a lack of consent. It is important the law clearly acknowledges this, especially since recent Queensland case law shows that a perpetrator is more likely to be able to rely on the mistake of fact excuse if the victim did not clearly resist their advances.[34] Even if the victim *did* resist, other factors (such as subsequent passivity or the exchange of money) can support the excuse. This troubling reasoning has been approved by the Court of Appeal, even where there is a clear power imbalance between the parties.[35]

These cases show how rape myths and social expectations around sexual behaviour influence the mistake of fact excuse, even though they do not establish consent. Victims who go along with the perpetrator's advances under duress, who express affection after an assault has commenced in an attempt to placate a perpetrator, who experience a freezing response or do not vigorously resist or who have an ongoing financial, employment or other relationship with the perpetrator may find that these factors are considered relevant when the mistake of fact excuse is raised.

The excuse has also led to problematic results when applied to cases involving impaired capacity – such as intoxication, cognitive impairment or linguistic incapacity – by either the perpetrator or the victim. The effect of intoxication on the mistake of fact excuse effectively means the perpetrator can say, 'I was so drunk I thought they were consenting'. Intoxication of the victim also lowers the bar for the excuse – meaning that, effectively, the perpetrator can say, 'They were so drunk I thought they were consenting'. This argument can succeed even where the victim was, in fact, so intoxicated that they were incapable of giving consent.[36]

The cumulative effect of these interpretations is that where the perpetrator and victim are both intoxicated, the bar for establishing the excuse may be very low. The criminal law does not generally accept intoxication as an excuse for, or a mitigation of, bad behaviour. Driving is a good example of people having criminal liability for their actions, despite being voluntarily drunk or affected by drugs.

A further factor that can lower the bar for the mistake of fact excuse is the cognitive impairment of the perpetrator or victim (or both). As with intoxication, cognitive impairment on the part of either party tends to favour the perpetrator where the mistake of fact excuse is concerned. The perpetrator's cognitive impairment can lower the bar for the excuse by making their mistake more likely to be honest and, to a limited extent, reasonable. However, the victim's cognitive impairment also lowers the bar by enabling the perpetrator to contend that they misunderstood the victim's resistance. Again, as with intoxication, this argument can succeed even where the victim's incapacity casts doubt on their ability to have consented in the first place.

Our legal system contains special provisions to prevent perpetrators who do not have the cognitive capacity of an adult from being tried like other adults.[37] Judges also have a large discretion when sentencing someone with a different mental capacity, so they are not punished excessively given their difference.[38] Given these allowances, the mistake of fact excuse is not the best way to accommodate cognitive differences when doing justice.

Cases involving a perpetrator who is not proficient in the same language as the victim (regardless of whether that language is English) may also present an opportunity for a mistake of fact excuse, as counsel are able to paint a picture of 'grey areas' and 'miscommunications' that might otherwise seem unrealistic or unlikely. Linguistic incapacity being used to bolster mistake of fact arguments is at odds with the law not requiring a victim to 'fight back' to establish a lack of consent, placing extra pressure on victims to fight back harder if the perpetrator doesn't speak their language. In many cases, there is also a clear power imbalance between the victim and perpetrator which is exacerbated by the language difference. Indeed, several recent Queensland cases suggest that vulnerable victims who do not speak the same language as the perpetrator may be deliberately targeted for rape.[39]

The Bill responds to these problems by specifically and clearly removing the mistake of fact excuse in rape and sexual assault cases. The language used is based on similar wording elsewhere in the *Criminal Code*.[40]

Conclusion

In conclusion, this Bill introduces an affirmative model of consent for sexual relations, thereby addressing confusion around what constitutes consent. Further, the Bill seeks to rectify the damage caused by the mistake of fact excuse in rape and sexual assault cases, which undermines an affirmative consent model by shifting responsibility for the rape on to the victim and their behaviour.

There are several key benefits of the Bill, including increased clarity on the definition of consent and directly challenging outdated rape myths that have continued to infiltrate the law and the criminal justice process. The Bill will improve justice experiences for rape and sexual assault victims, as well as providing a vehicle to change problematic social attitudes that perpetuate victim-blaming. It does this by placing the onus on each party to a sexual act to seek *ongoing* agreement from anyone with whom they wish to engage in sexual penetration or touching.

Ultimately, this Bill makes significant improvements to Queensland's sexual offence laws.

We commend the Bill to the House.

Queensland

Criminal Code Amendment (Sexual Offences) Bill 2024

A Bill

for

An Act to amend the *Criminal Code Act 1899* (Qld)[41]

The Parliament of Queensland enacts –

1 Insertion of new sections 347A and 347B

Before section 348

insert –

Section 347A – Objectives of this chapter

The objectives of this chapter are –

(a) to uphold the fundamental right of every person to make decisions about their sexual behaviour and to choose not to engage in sexual activity;

(b) to protect the following persons from sexual exploitation –

   (i) children;

   (ii) persons with an intellectual, psychiatric, cognitive or neurological impairment or a combination of these; and

   (iii) other vulnerable persons.

Section 347B – Guiding principles

It is the intention of Parliament that in interpreting and applying this chapter, courts are to have regard to the following matters –

(a) there is a high incidence of sexual violence within society;

(b) sexual offences are significantly underreported;

(c) a significant number of sexual offences are committed against women, children and other vulnerable persons, including persons with a cognitive impairment or mental illness;

(d) sexual offenders are commonly known to their victims;

(e) sexual offences most frequently occur in residential locations;

(f) there are legitimate reasons why victims of sexual violence may not physically resist an assault, including, but not limited to, physiological responses to aggression and fear of escalating or prolonging the attack;

(g) sexual offences often occur in circumstances where there is unlikely to be any physical signs of an offence having occurred; and
(h) there are legitimate reasons why victims of sexual violence may not immediately report an assault to police or another person, and a failure to make an immediate report does not on its own discredit an allegation.

2 Section 348 (Meaning of *consent*)
Section 348(1)–(4) –
omit, insert –

(1) In this chapter –

(a) ***Consent*** means free and active agreement to an act by a person with the cognitive capacity to give consent.

(i) Consent to one act does not constitute consent to a different act, even where the acts are part of the same sequence of acts.

(b) ***Active agreement*** means that each person involved in an act takes steps to find out whether each other person involved consents to the act, and to ensure that they continue to consent for the duration of the act.

(i) Active agreement cannot be inferred from the circumstances of an act. It must be clearly and positively expressed.
(ii) Active agreement must be present immediately before and during an act. It cannot be inferred from words or actions made hours, days or weeks prior to the act occurring.

(2) There are circumstances in which a person does not consent to an act. These include, but are not limited to, the following –

(a) the person submits to the act due to force or the fear of force or harm of any kind, whether to that person or someone else or an animal;
(b) the person submits to the act due to threats or intimidation, whether physical, verbal or through control of the physical environment;
(c) the person submits to the act because they are unlawfully detained;
(d) the person submits to the act due to the exercise of actual or apparent authority;
(e) the person is asleep or unconscious when any part of the act occurs;
(f) the person is so affected by alcohol or another drug as to lack the cognitive capacity to consent to the act;
(g) the person lacks the cognitive capacity to understand the sexual nature of the act;
(h) the person submits to the act due to an incorrect belief, induced by or with the knowledge of any other person involved in the act, as

to any fact but for which the person would not have submitted to the act, including, but not limited to:

(i) facts about the sexual nature of the act;
(ii) facts about the identity of any other person involved in the act;
(iii) facts about the purpose of the act (including medical, hygienic, veterinary, agricultural or scientific purposes); or
(iv) facts about gifts or payment promised in relation to the act.

(i) the person submits to the act in the belief, induced by or with the knowledge of any other person involved in the act, that the other person will use a condom, and the other person does not do so or ceases to do so at any time during the act.

3 Section 348A (Mistake of fact in relation to consent)
Section 348A –
Omit.

4 Section 349 (Rape)
Section 349(2) –
omit, insert –

(2) A person rapes another person if –

(a) the person penetrates the vulva, vagina or anus of the other person to any extent with a thing or a part of the person's body without the other person's consent; or
(b) the person penetrates the mouth of the other person to any extent with the person's penis without the other person's consent.

After section 349(5) –
insert –

(6) Section 24 does not apply in relation to a belief of the person who performs an act referred to in subsection (2)(a) or (b) that the person on whom that act is performed is consenting to it.

5 Section 350 (Attempt to commit rape)
After section 350(3) –
insert –

(4) Section 24 does not apply in relation to a belief of the person who attempts to perform an act referred to in section 349(2)(a) or (b) that the person on whom that act is attempted is consenting to it.

6 Section 351 (Assault with intent to commit rape)
After section 351(3) –
insert –

(4) Section 24 does not apply in relation to a belief of the person who assaults another with intent to perform an act referred to in section

349(2)(a) or (b) that the person on whom that act is intended to be performed is consenting to it.

7 Section 352 (Sexual assaults)
After section 352(5) –
insert –

(6) Section 24 does not apply in relation to a belief of the person who performs an act referred to in subsection (1)(a) or (b) that the person on whom that act is performed is consenting to it.

Notes

1 Australian Bureau of Statistics, *Personal Safety Survey 2005 (Reissue)* (Catalogue number 4906.0, 21 August 2006).
2 Australian Bureau of Statistics, *Recorded Crime Victims Australia 2018–19* (Catalogue number 4510.0, 9 August 2020); K Daly, 'Restorative Justice and Sexual Assault: An Archival Study of Court and Conference Cases' (2006) 46(2) *British Journal of Criminology* 334; A Flynn, 'Sexual Violence and Innovative Responses to Justice: Interrupting the Recognisable Narratives' in A Powell et al (eds), *Rape Justice: Beyond the Criminal Law* (Palgrave Macmillan, 2015); Statewide Steering Committee to Reduce Sexual Assault, *Study of Reported Rapes in Victoria 2000–2003* (Report, 2004); Australian Institute of Criminology, 'Women's Experiences of Male Violence: Findings from the Australian Component of the International Violence Against Women Survey (IVAWS)', *Research and Public Policy Series, No 56* (Report, 1 January 2004), https://aic.gov.au/publications/rpp/rpp56.
3 Daly (n 2); Flynn (n 2).
4 See generally A Powell et al (eds), *Rape Justice: Beyond the Criminal Law* (Palgrave Macmillan, 2015).
5 Flynn (n 2). See also N Christie, 'The Ideal Victim' in E Fattah (ed) *From Crime Policy to Victim Policy* (Oxford University Press, 1988); S Estrich, *Real Rape* (Harvard University Press, 1988); L Pineau 'Date Rape: A Feminist Analysis' (1989) 8 *Law and Philosophy* 217.
6 For discussion, see A Powell et al, 'Meanings of "Sex" and "Consent": The Persistence of Rape Myths in Victorian Rape Law' (2013) 22 *Griffith Law Review* 456.
7 Australian Bureau of Statistics, *Personal Safety Survey* (Catalogue No 4906.0, 2016); A Moran, 'Patterns of Rape: A Preliminary Queensland Perspective' in P Easteal (ed) *Without Consent: Confronting Adult Sexual Violence* (Australian Institute of Criminology, 1993) 39–40, https://aic.gov.au/sites/default/files/publications/proceedings/downloads/20-moran.pdf.
8 Queensland Law Reform Commission, *Review of Consent Laws and the Excuse of Mistake of Fact* (Report No 78, June 2020) 42.
9 United Nations, 'Facts and Figures: Ending Violence Against Women', *UN Women* (United Nations, 2019), https://www.unwomen.org/en/what-we-do/ending-violence-against-women/facts-and-figures.
10 Australian Bureau of Statistics (n 1).
11 Australian Bureau of Statistics (n 2).
12 S E Baumgartner et al, 'Unwanted Online Sexual Solicitation and Risky Sexual Online Behavior Across the Lifespace' (2010) 31(6) *Journal of Applied Developmental Psychology* 439; N Henry et al, *Responding to 'Revenge*

Pornography's Prevalence, Nature and Impacts (Australian Institute of Criminology, 2019), http://crg.aic.gov.au/reports/1819/08-1516-FinalReport.pdf; A Powell et al, 'Image-Based Sexual Abuse' in W DeKeseredy and M Dragiewicz (eds) *Handbook of Critical Criminology* (Routledge, 2018).

13 M B Hossain et al, 'Are Female College Students who are Diagnosed with Depression at Greater Risk of Experiencing Sexual Violence on College Campus?' (2014) 25 *Journal of Health Care for the Poor and Underserved* 1341; I Khemka and L Hickson, 'Decision-Making by Adults with Mental Retardation in Simulated Situations of Abuse' (2000) 38 *Mental Retardation* 15; J A Snyder, 'The Link between ADHD and the Risk of Sexual Victimization Among College Women: Expanding the Lifestyles/Routine Activities Framework' (2015) 21 *Violence Against Women* 1364.

14 Australian Human Rights Commission, *Change the Course: National Report on Sexual Assault and Sexual Harassment at Australian Universities 2017* (Report, August 2017), https://www.humanrights.gov.au/sites/default/files/document/publication/AHRC_2017_ChangeTheCourse_UniversityReport.pdf; A Flynn and N Henry, 'Image-Based Sexual Abuse: An Australian Reflection' (2021) 31 *Women and Criminal Justice* 313; P R Sterzing et al, 'Social Ecological Correlates of Polyvictimisation Among a National Sample of Transgender, Genderqueer, and Cisgender Sexual Minority Adolescents' (2017) 67 *Child Abuse and Neglect* 1.

15 F Al-Yaman et al, *Family Violence Among Aboriginal and Torres Strait Islander Peoples* (Australian Institute of Health and Welfare, 2006); B Carlson, 'Indigenous Social, Cultural and Political Engagements on Social Media', paper presented at the QUT Creative Industries Indigenous Seminar Series, 2 June 2017, https://nowalls.qut.edu.au/wp-content/uploads/2017/05/Bronwyn-Carlson-Indigenous-Seminar-Presentation.pdf; H Douglas et al, 'Technology-Facilitated Domestic and Family Violence: Women's Experiences' (2019) 59 *British Journal of Criminology* 551; Office of the eSafety Commissioner, *eSafety for Women from Culturally and Linguistically Diverse Backgrounds: Summary Report* (Office of the eSafety Commissioner, 2019), https://www.esafety.gov.au/about-the-office/research-library/technology-facilitated-abuse.

16 *Criminal Code 1899* (Qld) ss 349, 352.

17 R Burgin, 'Persistent Narratives of Force and Resistance: Affirmative Consent as Law Reform' (2019) 59 *British Journal of Criminology* 296.

18 A Flynn and N Henry, 'Disputing Consent: The Role of Jury Directions in Victoria' (2012) 24(2) *Current Issues in Criminal Justice* 167.

19 J Crowe and B Lee, 'The Mistake of Fact Excuse in Queensland Rape Law: Some Problems and a Proposal for Reform' (2020) 39 *University of Queensland Law Journal* 1.

20 R Burgin and A Flynn, 'Women's Behavior as Implied Consent: Male "Reasonableness" in Australian Rape Law' (2021) 21 *Criminology and Criminal Justice* 334.

21 Ibid. See also E Craig, 'Ten Years after Ewanchuk: The Art of Seduction is Alive and Well: An Examination of the Mistaken Belief in Consent Defense' (2009) 13(3) *Canadian Criminal Law Review* 247.

22 Burgin and Flynn (n 20).

23 J Crowe and L Sveinsson, 'Intimidation, Consent and the Role of Holistic Judgments in Australian Rape Law' (2017) 42 *University of Western Australia Law Review* 136.

24 This mirrors the current law in Western Australia, Tasmania and the Australian Capital Territory. See J Crowe, 'Fraud and Consent in Australian Rape Law' (2014) 38 *Criminal Law Journal* 236, 239.

25 In a 'recent joint study between the Melbourne Sexual Health Centre and Monash University, one in three women and nearly one in five men' reported experiencing

non-consensual removal of a condom during sex. See B Chesser, 'Case in Victoria Could Set New Legal Precedent for Stealthing, or Removing Condom During Sex', *The Conversation* (16 August 2019), https://theconversation.com/case-in-victoria-could-set-new-legal-precedent-for-stealthing-or-removing-condom-during-sex-118343.

26 *Criminal Code 1899* (Qld) s 349.

27 See, for example, *Criminal Law Consolidation Act Amendment Act 1976* (SA); *Crimes (Amendment) Ordinance (No 5) 1985* (ACT); *Criminal Code Amendment (Sexual Offences) Act 1987* (Tas); *Law Reform (Decriminalization of Sodomy) Act 1989* (WA); *Criminal Code Amendment Act (No 3) 1994* (NT).

28 *Criminal Code 1899* (Qld) s 24.

29 Burgin (n 17); Crowe and Lee (n 19); J Crowe, 'Consent, Power and Mistake of Fact in Queensland Rape Law' (2011) 23(1) *Bond Law Review* 21; J Crowe et al, 'Affirmative Consent and the Mistake of Fact Excuse in Western Australian Rape Law' (2023) 50 *University of Western Australia Law Review* 284.

30 It is the prosecution's responsibility to negate the excuse if it arises on the facts. This creates the possibility of the mistake of fact excuse being raised on appeal, even if it was not argued at trial (or, indeed, directly contradicts the perpetrator's version of events). See, for example, *R v Elomari* [2012] QCA 27; *R v Soloman* [2006] QCA 244; *R v Cook* [2012] QCA 251. For detailed discussion of these cases, see Crowe and Lee (n 19).

31 Crowe and Lee (n 19).

32 See, for example, S D Suarez and G G Gallup, 'Tonic Immobility as a Response to Rape in Humans: A Theoretical Note' (1979) 29 *Psychological Record* 315; G C Mezey and P J Taylor, 'Psychological Reactions of Women Who Have Been Raped: A Descriptive and Comparative Study' (1988) 152 *British Journal of Psychiatry* 330; G Galliano et al, 'Victim Reactions during Rape/Sexual Assault: A Preliminary Study of the Immobility Response and its Correlates' (1993) 8 *Journal of Interpersonal Violence* 109.

33 See, for example, S E Taylor et al, 'Biobehavioral Responses to Stress in Females: Tend-and-Befriend, Not Fight-or-Flight' (2000) 107 *Psychological Review* 411; S E Taylor et al, 'Sex Differences in Biobehavioral Responses to Threat: Reply to Geary and Flinn' (2002) 109 *Psychological Review* 751.

34 QLRC (n 8) 41.

35 See, for example, *R v Dunrobin* [2008] QCA 116; *R v Kovacs* [2007] QCA 143. For detailed discussion of these cases, see Crowe and Lee (n 19).

36 See, for example, *R v CU* [2004] QCA 363, 5 (Jerrard JA); *R v SAX* [2006] QCA 397, [20] (Keane JA). For detailed discussion of these cases, see Crowe and Lee (n 19).

37 *Criminal Code 1899* (Qld) s 27.

38 *Penalties and Sentencing Act 1992* (Qld) s 18(a).

39 See, for example, *R v Kovacs* [2007] QCA 143; *R v Lennox* [2018] QCA 311.

40 *Criminal Code 1899* (Qld) s 365B. See also *Criminal Code of Canada* s 273.2.

41 *Criminal Code Act 1899* (Qld). The proposed amendments are based on the Act incorporating amendments as at 21 September 2022. https://www.legislation.qld.gov.au/view/html/inforce/2022-09-12/act-1899-009.

Chapter 7A

Commentary on *Implementing Affirmative Consent in Sexual Offences*

Saxon Mullins and Rachael Burgin

For survivors of sexual violence, the law has failed as a vehicle for justice. Conviction rates for rape and sexual assault are low, while attrition across various stages of the criminal justice process is high.[1] Survivors of sexual violence are not ignorant to the way they will be treated by the system. The 'second rape', or the experience of re-traumatisation in the criminal justice process, such as through cross-examination or police interviews, is a well-known phenomenon.[2] The symptoms of 'rape culture' which permeate society remind survivors that they may not be believed or might even be blamed for their own rape.[3] Against this backdrop, survivors are reluctant to report to the police.[4]

The origins of rape law reveal much about how we got to where we are today. Rape was criminalised to protect men's interests in women as wealth or status symbols.[5] When a woman was raped, her 'value' decreased and the law became a mechanism for men to 'recoup' losses.[6] Thus, rape was a property crime and women, the property. Gender played a central role in this dynamic of criminalisation. Only women could be raped, and only by men.[7] When the crime is considered in relation to its actual harm and to lived experience, this gendered element shifts. Anyone can be victimised, and anyone can perpetrate rape. Of course, patterns of sexual violence tell us that rape is overwhelmingly committed by men, and overwhelmingly committed against women.[8] Non-binary and trans people are also at heightened risk.[9] The law is only relatively recently catching up to the realities of these diverse lived experiences.[10] Society may be even further behind.

Changes to rape law to date have been championed by feminist activists. Each small step has been a hard win. These steps have contributed to significant change.[11] Yet, we retain a system that fails to treat survivors with something even adjacent to respect. Instead, the legal system is used against survivors, to belittle and demean them. Survivors are vilified and treated as if they are the ones on trial. This can include intrusive questioning into every facet of their lives.[12] Private communications from their text messages and emails can be admitted into evidence alongside counselling records and notes, once thought confidential.[13] This evidence goes to the core problem

DOI: 10.4324/9781003372462-15

of shaming women who dare to be active in sexual relationships, however distant or unrelated to the rape. Rape myths inform the legal argument playing out in a system supposedly concerned with 'truth'.[14]

While we have seen feminist law *reform*, we have not seen feminist *law*. Some would argue over whether such law can even exist. While they argue, sexual violence remains a plague on Australian society; another survivor is reporting to police; another survivor is cross-examined about whether they fought back or 'said no'.[15] Crowe, Flynn and Lee offer us a glimpse into what feminist law could do to improve survivors' experiences of the criminal justice system, as they reimagine Queensland rape law through a feminist lens.

This reimagining begins with proposing objectives and guiding principles for rape law in Queensland. These principles raise important reminders of the realities of sexual violence and challenge the myths and stereotypes about rape, rapists and survivors. Crucially, the guiding principles make direct reference to the reality that survivors '*may not physically resist an assault*'. Raising that someone 'didn't say no' is a key tactic in both legal settings and wider society to smear survivors' accounts of sexual violence.[16] It is established that 'freezing' in response to sexual violence is common. 'Tonic immobility' is the lesser-known sibling to the other involuntary physiological responses, 'fight or flight'.[17] But it is equally as legitimate. The denial of this response serves rape culture (and apologists) well. Women who freeze in response to an attack are labelled 'irrational'.[18] This is in fact a perfectly rational response, and one that can be credited as life-saving.[19] Fighting off an attacker may mean that further injury or even death is more likely.

Crowe, Flynn and Lee define consent as '*active agreement voluntarily given*'. These are critical pillars of affirmative consent, along with ensuring that the giving of consent is 'ongoing', as referenced in the Second Reading Speech. Importantly, the proposed legislation removes the excuse of mistake of fact in relation to consent. This means that a person who is accused of a sexual offence cannot act with impunity where they did not 'check in' with the other person(s) to make sure they were consenting. Failing to ascertain consent is not an excuse for rape. In defining active agreement as agreement that is '*clearly and positively expressed*', this legislation once again clarifies a point of contention both in the justice system and in wider society; that an affirmative consent model puts an undue burden on people wishing to engage in sexual activity. We hear time and again that affirmative consent legislation will restrict consensual relationships,[20] but here we are shown clearly that free, voluntary, active and ongoing consent is not difficult to interpret or hard to obtain. These changes not only legislate for affirmative consent, but do so with clarity and simplicity.

But this glimpse offered by the authors meets a hard geographical border and, like other attempts to reform the criminal law of rape in decades past, cannot prevent sexual violence. A broader system of social and cultural change is required to shift attitudes that facilitate rape. Changes to the law also have little impact on survivors' experiences with police, through the reporting and investigation of rape. For reforms such as those proposed here to be effective, they must also underpin police policy and procedure in relation to rape, and be supported by comprehensive training for police, prosecutors, judges and defence counsel.

Reform to the meaning of consent and to the legal boundary between 'rape' and 'not rape' must also be accompanied by challenges to legal practices, long assumed to be 'right', that prove to no longer serve the community that the law seeks to protect, or to reflect the state of knowledge about sexual violence. Evidence of an offender's 'good character' is considered in mitigation of their sentence, and even as 'proof' that they have not committed the offence. Yet, the good character of the victim-survivor is excluded from consideration, and defence counsel can, and do, propose that women have a motive to lie about sexual assault. If we are to develop a truly feminist law of rape, then we must turn our minds to these issues that plague the criminal rape trial.

What we need now is transformative, survivor-focused and evidence-based reform, such as what Crowe, Flynn and Lee have begun to envision. Such laws would have a significant impact beyond the criminal justice system, with a potential ripple effect into education, broader policy and societal views. Importantly though, these laws would facilitate the possibility of a fair trial for survivors. A trial that deliberates not on outdated notions of rape or of victimhood, but on the real ideals of a legal system and our cultural values. Once lagging behind, we can see a future where Queensland could be a world leader in sexual offence reform.

Notes

1 K Daly and B Bouhours 'Rape and Attrition in the Legal Process: A Comparative Analysis of Five Countries' in M Tonry (ed.), *Crime and Justice: A Review of Research* (University of Chicago Press, 2010); New South Wales Law Reform Commission (NSWLRC), *Consent in Relation to Sexual Offences* (Report No 148, September 2020) 23–4 [2.40]–[2.43].

2 L Madigan and N Gamble, *The Second Rape: Society's Continued Betrayal of the Victim* (Lexington Books, 1991); N Funnell et al., 'Survivors Speak: How the Criminal Justice System Responds to Sexual Violence' (2019) 31 *Bond Law Review* 21, 39–41.

3 See for example, N Gavey, *Just Sex?: The Cultural Scaffolding of Rape* (Routledge, 2005). For discussion about the impact of rape culture on rape prevalence and criminal justice responses, see M A Baum et al., 'Does Rape Culture Predict Rape? Evidence from U.S. Newspapers, 2000–2013' (2018) 13 *Quarterly Journal of Political Science* 263.

4 Australian Institute of Criminology, *Non-Reporting and Hidden Recording of Sexual Assault: An International Literature Review* (Canberra, Office of the Status of Women, 2003); Australian Bureau of Statistics (2017) *Personal Safety Survey*. Canberra: Australian Government Publishing Service.

5 R Burgin, 'Persistent Narratives of Force and Resistance: Affirmative Consent as Law Reform' (2019) 59 *British Journal of Criminology* 296; J A Bennice and A Resick, 'Marital Rape: History, Research, and Practice' (2003) 4 *Trauma, Violence, & Abuse* 228.
6 Burgin (n 5); D Dripps, 'Beyond Rape: An Essay on the Difference Between the Presence of Force and the Absence of Consent' (1992) 92 *Columbia Law Review* 1780.
7 Burgin (n 5); S Weare, '"Oh You're a Guy, How Could You be Raped by A Woman, That Makes No Sense": Towards A Case for Legally Recognising and Labelling "Forced to Penetrate" Cases as Rape' (2018) 14(1) *International Journal of Law in Context* 110.
8 Australian Bureau of Statistics, *Recorded Crime Victims Australia 2018–19* (Australian Government Publishing Service, 2019) and Australian Bureau of Statistics, *Recorded Crime – Offenders 2013–14* (Australian Government Publishing Service, 2015).
9 Kirby Institute, *The 2018 Australian Trans and Gender Diverse Sexual Health Survey: Report of Findings* (Report, 2019).
10 P N S Rumney, 'In Defence of Gender Neutrality within Rape' (2007) 6(1) *Seattle Journal for Social Justice* 481.
11 See R Burgin and A Flynn, 'Women's Behavior as Implied Consent: Male "Reasonableness" in Australian Rape Law' (2021) 21 *Criminology and Criminal Justice* 334; J Quilter, 'Getting Consent "Right": Sexual Assault Law Reform in New South Wales' (2021) 46(2) *Australian Feminist Law Journal* 225.
12 Burgin (n 5); Burgin and Flynn (n 11).
13 O Smith, 'Narratives, Credibility and Adversarial Justice in English and Welsh Rape Trials' in U Andersson et al. (eds) *Rape Narratives in Motion* (Palgrave Macmillan, 2019).
14 A Powell et al., 'Meanings of "Sex" and "Consent": The Persistence of Myths in Victorian Rape Law' (2013) 22(2) *Griffith Law Review* 456.
15 *The Guardian*, 'Jarryd Hayne Tells Rape Trial Alleged Victim "Never Said No"' (30 November 2020), https://www.theguardian.com/australia-news/2020/nov/30/jarryd-hayne-tells-trial-alleged-victim-never-said-no; K Fuller, 'Jack de Belin Rape Trial Told "Nothing Was Consensual That Night", as Alleged Victim Cross-Examined' (Australian Broadcasting Corporation, 9 November 2020), https://www.abc.net.au/news/2020-11-09/jack-de-belin-rape-trial-hears-more-details-from-alleged-victim/12863580.
16 See, for example, *R v L******* [2017] NSWCCA 279.
17 S D Suarez and G G Gallup, 'Tonic Immobility as a Response to Rape in Humans: A Theoretical Note (1979) 29 *Psychological Record* 315.
18 Burgin (n 5).
19 J Crowe and B Lee, 'The Mistake of Fact Excuse in Queensland Rape Law: Some Problems and Proposals for Reform' (2020) 39(1) *The University of Queensland Law Journal* 1.
20 NSW Bar Association, 'Consent Proposals Could Result in Significant Injustice' (Media Release, 25 May 2021).

Chapter 8

Compensation in the Context of Surrogacy

A Feminist Perspective on the Insistence on Altruism

Ronli Sifris

Extract from *Hansard* (Parliament of Victoria)

Assisted Reproductive Treatment Amendment Bill 2024

Second Reading

HON RONLI SIFRIS: I move:

That the Bill be now read a second time.

This is a Bill to amend section 44 of the *Assisted Reproductive Treatment Act 2008* (Vic),[1] which prohibits a surrogate from receiving 'any material benefit or advantage as a result of a surrogacy arrangement'. It should be noted that in addition to removing the prohibition on compensation, this amendment bill also mandates that the surrogate's actual costs be covered by the intended parents. This Second Reading Speech focuses on the question of compensation, as this is the more contentious aspect of the amendment. While I occasionally use the term 'women', I choose to use gender-neutral language where possible (recognising that people who do not identify as women may also be surrogates). It follows that laws and policies should be framed to accommodate the full spectrum of gender identification.

You may be wondering: Why is this change needed? It is needed to ensure that surrogates are compensated fairly for the reproductive labour inherent in gestating and birthing a child; as well as to rectify the current unacceptable situation in which everyone involved in a surrogacy arrangement is paid for their services except for the person who is assuming the highest risk – the surrogate – who is expected to act for free. It is also aimed at reducing the number of people travelling overseas to access surrogacy in jurisdictions where protecting the rights of all parties may be an ancillary consideration.

DOI: 10.4324/9781003372462-16

Victoria has been a leader in health law reform: I am proud to say that we were the first Australian State to decriminalise abortion! We are now a leader in reforming our law relating to surrogacy.

What Is the Problem with the Prohibition on Compensation?

The current ban on compensating surrogates is problematic for three key reasons. First, it encourages reproductive tourism. Second, this approach creates an illusory and damaging dichotomy between compensation and altruism. Third, it perpetuates the age-old tradition of failing to pay for 'women's work'.

Reproductive Tourism

Compensated surrogacy is currently prohibited throughout Australia.[2] This generally means that surrogates cannot receive financial compensation beyond the expenses associated with the fertility treatment and pregnancy. The fact that compensated surrogacy is illegal throughout Australia, but is legal elsewhere, has created fertile ground for reproductive tourism to flourish. In other words, banning compensated surrogacy doesn't prevent compensated surrogacy from happening – it just drives the practice elsewhere. This makes the perceived problem into someone else's, rather than effectively addressing any concerns at home.[3]

It is estimated that a whopping 75% of Australians entering into surrogacy arrangements do so overseas,[4] despite all the legal and other complexities they encounter by going down this path. They face the fear of not being allowed back into Australia with their child, coupled with the trauma of living their lives in Australia while knowing that they may need to get on a flight at a moment's notice should there be a problem with the pregnancy or the birth occur earlier than expected. This is nobody's first option – but for many Australians wanting to become parents, it is their *only* option. Australian laws and culture are driving desperate people overseas to become parents.

The following testimony from one such person communicates the heartache and desperation better than I can:

> Twenty years ago due to 'gross medical negligence' by a specialist I was given the mind numbing incredulous news that I would never be able to carry a baby . . . After many months of intensive counseling and medical preparation we attempted FIVE non commercial surrogacy (altruistic) using my girlfriend's womb. None of these attempts resulted in a pregnancy. It takes a certain type of person to become a surrogate and thus it was not as simple as going out and asking another friend to try for us (out of the goodness of their heart). Our last resort was to investigate Commercial surrogacy [overseas].[5]

As this testimony illustrates, surrogacy is an avenue for those who are out of other options. The persistent demonisation of intended parents who access compensated surrogacy arrangements unfairly buys into a fictional narrative that has been propagated for years by those opposed to surrogacy.

This prompts the question: Should Victoria persist in its insistence on prohibiting compensated surrogacy? In my view, the answer is clearly NO! A properly regulated compensated surrogacy framework represents a more ethical approach to the regulation of surrogacy than the outright prohibition which currently exists. Victoria needs to act to change both law and culture in order to make surrogacy more accessible back home, to prevent it being driven underground and overseas. Without introducing some form of compensation, 'the current status of Australia as one of the world's largest exporter[s] of intended parents for surrogacy per capita is likely to remain. The only solution is to allow surrogates to be paid.'[6]

'Compensation' and 'Altruism' Are not Mutually Exclusive

Stopping reproductive tourism is not the only reason Australian surrogates should be compensated; the current approach also creates an illusory and damaging dichotomy between compensation and altruism. Just because someone is *not* being paid does not mean that they are acting out of altruism, and just because someone *is* being paid does not mean that they are bereft of it. For example, many people become nurses out of a feeling of altruism and a desire to help others, but it would be outrageous to suggest that they should not be compensated for their labour. A surrogate may believe that they deserve to be compensated appropriately for their reproductive labour while at the same time being primarily motivated by altruism. To date, there has been a refusal to avoid simplistic and binary categorisations of surrogacy as either 'commercial' or 'altruistic'.

Professor Anita Stuhmcke, Dean of the UTS Faculty of Law, has also expressed concern at the binary categorisation of surrogacy as either compensated or altruistic. She has argued that 'the creation of altruistic surrogacy and commercial surrogacy is a fiction of law', and that

> labelling of a surrogacy arrangement as altruistic or commercial evolves from normative assumptions as to desirable public policy rather than evidence of the reality of the practice. It follows that the binary model ignores nuances and alternative truths, such as surrogate mothers either benefiting or suffering exploitation regardless of the amount of money paid.[7]

The refusal to acknowledge that a surrogate may be motivated by altruism while desiring compensation is unfair and dishonest. Further, such a perspective ignores the practical reality that friends or family of those for whom pregnancy remains out of reach may be subjected to enormous pressure to become an 'altruistic' surrogate. For example, one Australian fertility specialist has commented that

> Everyone gets their knickers so much in a twist about commercial surrogacy, but . . . one of the things that we are starting to see is some really unpleasant pressure being put on close friends and relatives to act as surrogates because commercial surrogacy is banned.[8]

We also have anecdotal evidence of a 'black market' for compensated surrogacy, which is clearly less than desirable.[9]

Linking altruism with a lack of compensation does not make sense, and positioning 'altruistic surrogacy' and 'compensated surrogacy' as mutually exclusive is a flawed proposition.[10] A person may believe that they deserve to be compensated appropriately for their reproductive labour while at the same time being primarily motivated by altruism.[11] It is time for Victoria to adopt a more nuanced approach to compensation in the surrogacy context.

Failure to Pay for 'Women's Work'

Another significant concern with the ban on compensation is its perpetuation of the traditional refusal to pay for 'women's work'. Given housework, childrearing and other care work has historically been gendered as well as unpaid, the elevation of 'altruism' in the surrogacy context reinforces these social expectations of women's unpaid labour and self-sacrifice. The work of housekeeping and childrearing continues to fall disproportionately on women while remaining largely invisible and uncompensated.

Feminists have long been concerned with the fact that

> [t]he labor that women provide in their homes caring for children or running the household is not compensated. The value of this labor is not included in the gross national product. Childcare and housework which are disproportionately performed by women are thus systematically undervalued.[12]

There is a clear gender dimension to the refusal to compensate surrogates, given that the role of a surrogate is usually a distinctly gendered role; a cisgender man cannot be a surrogate. Transgender men and gender non-binary people with uteruses can of course also be surrogates, and should obviously be included in all legislative changes. Although it is unfortunate that the legislation retains the terminology of 'surrogate mother' rather than the simpler and more accurate term 'surrogate', such a change impacting multiple sections is one for another day. This amendment is focused solely on section 44 and the current prohibition on compensation. It should however be clear that the intention behind the change is one of inclusivity; surrogates who do not identify is women should also be compensated.

The failure to compensate surrogates perpetuates the patriarchal tradition of refusing to pay for 'women's work'. Not only do we live in a society where the gender pay gap remains in excess of 10%,[13] but in some spheres where women shoulder the overwhelming burden, the dominant voices seek to convince us that we shouldn't get paid at all.

In reality, fertility clinics in Australia charge thousands of dollars for people to access their services. For example, at both Monash IVF and Melbourne IVF, two of the state's leading fertility clinics, the estimated out-of-pocket costs for an initial IVF cycle amount to approximately $5,000.[14] This excludes the cost of so-called IVF 'add-ons' which are thought to bolster the chances of a successful pregnancy. As a result, many of those involved in providing surrogacy – the clinics, doctors, lawyers and counsellors – are compensated for their time and services, but not the person doing the most labour and taking the greatest risk. How is this fair?

To prevent individuals from charging for the service of gestating and giving birth to a child, when 'big business' may charge large fees for other assisted reproductive services, is unacceptable and discriminatory. To add insult to injury, this insistence on altruism is frequently argued to be for the surrogate's own benefit (for example, to prevent exploitation). This idea – that depriving a person of fair compensation is for their own benefit – is the height of paternalism.[15]

Debunking the Myth of Exploitation

I know that some people take the view that inherent in compensated surrogacy arrangements is the exploitation and commodification of the surrogate.[16] In this context, the analogy is often made to sex work, as some people argue that this too amounts to the exploitation of desperate and vulnerable people.[17] Yet in 2022, this Parliament decided to decriminalise sex work, recognising that it should be viewed and regulated in the same way as other work and that criminalisation amplifies stigmatisation, which has a negative impact on the very people the law purports to protect.[18]

The connecting of compensation with exploitation is problematic. We should not assume that people who become compensated surrogates do so out of financial desperation. Research has revealed that, at least in countries similar to Australia in a social, cultural and economic sense, concerns relating to exploitation of surrogates is unfounded. The vast majority of surrogates make an informed, autonomous decision to enter into a surrogacy arrangement. Regret is uncommon and, while surrogates tend not to be wealthy, they are also not motivated by financial distress.[19]

Many feminists such as myself argue that the right to autonomy enshrined in international human rights law includes the right to choose to be a surrogate. This right should be protected by the domestic laws of individual countries, which should include appropriate safeguards to ensure that such a decision is free and fully informed.[20] Autonomy in this sense does not necessarily mean that the *context* of decision-making is completely ignored in favour of a narrow focus on whether a person understands what is involved in being a surrogate and formally consents to doing so. Instead, it may include an approach that considers whether the context of a person's life, such as their family or financial circumstances, removes their capacity to make a meaningful decision to be a surrogate.

People experiencing intersectional disadvantage, for instance, may be especially susceptible to pressure by other people and circumstances to become a surrogate. For example, a migrant woman who does not speak English and who is also a victim of domestic violence may be coerced into this role. In such circumstances, it would be prudent to interrogate the 'consent' provided.

The question of whether a decision to be a surrogate is a free and fully informed decision is particularly controversial in the context of some developing countries, where the surrogate may not understand the relevant documentation or may be 'poor, illiterate and uninformed of her rights'.[21] In other words, it seems to be a statement of the obvious that the most harm is 'borne by those with the least economic resources and the least power – including women in other countries, where legal protections for women acting as surrogates may be insufficient to ensure their health, dignity and safety.'[22]

A surrogate is not exercising their right to autonomy if true informed consent is absent. So, in countries where the surrogate receives no clear explanation of the relevant risks, or if they cannot read the consent form or understand the relevant procedures to be carried out, informed consent is lacking and an autonomy-based argument will fail. This is one reason the exodus of Australians to access surrogacy in other countries raises concerning questions, and is precisely why Victoria should regulate compensated surrogacy and enable people to access rights-respecting surrogacy arrangements at home.

On a slightly different note, it would be remiss of me not to mention the concerns of some feminists that compensated surrogacy constitutes an unjustified commodification of surrogates and their bodies; the concern that compensated surrogacy treats the bodies of surrogates as objects to be bought and sold.[23] Whatever the theoretical merits of such an argument, concerns around commodification have been somewhat diluted by the absence of the predicted baby-making factories in countries such as the United States. With the predicted tangible harms of compensated surrogacy largely failing to materialise in the US, less tangible concerns relating to commodification and market inalienability have faded into the background.[24]

Further, the claim that surrogates who accept compensation for their labour are essentially allowing themselves and their bodies to be commodified undermines the lived experience of many surrogates who feel empowered and valued. This is especially so where surrogacy arrangements are facilitated to enable the surrogate to choose the intended parents with whom they work and are structured to encourage ongoing relationships between the surrogates and the families they have assisted.[25] This type of scenario makes it hard to see the difference between altruistic and compensated surrogacy from a commodification perspective. Clearly, the surrogate in such a circumstance is not being viewed as a mere incubator.

Finally, arguments around commodification muddy the waters of reproductive freedom in a way that may negatively impact abortion regulation. The commodification argument against compensated surrogacy is uncomfortably similar to the 'women-protective' arguments for banning abortion, dangerous ground for a feminist.[26] This Parliament decided to decriminalise abortion back in 2008, a debate that should not be revisited. As the American legal scholar Elizabeth Scott has argued: 'Endorsing paternalistic government restrictions on women's reproductive choices in [the surrogacy] context is incompatible with the broader feminist political agenda'.[27] Such restrictions do not make sense in the context of this Parliament, which so recently decriminalised sex-work in a clear vote for autonomy over paternalism.

In conclusion, the anxiety surrounding the prospect of legalising compensated surrogacy in Victoria is unfounded. The Victorian legal system has the framework and capability to regulate compensated surrogacy in a way that minimises the risk of exploitation while appropriately protecting the rights and interests of all involved. Doing so would make surrogacy more accessible at home, likely reducing the number of Victorians travelling overseas to access compensated surrogacy arrangements with all the associated risk and stress.

The Proposal

In drafting this Bill, I was mindful of concerns that the authorisation of compensation would translate into a capitalist free-for-all where desperate people are asked to pay obscene amounts of money to have a child. The last thing I want is for this amendment to increase the risk of exploitation that already attaches to people who are desperate to have a child.

I was also mindful of concerns that the authorisation of compensation may lead to an indecent 'ranking' of surrogates enabling different amounts to be paid for different surrogate attributes. Rather, the purpose of this Bill is to ensure that surrogates are compensated fairly for the reproductive labour inherent in gestating and birthing a child.

The amended section stipulates that surrogates must be reimbursed for the 'prescribed costs actually incurred' as a direct consequence of the surrogacy arrangement. This is a significant change from the current section, which simply allows surrogates to be reimbursed their 'prescribed costs'. The aim of this part of the amendments is to ensure that surrogates are not out of pocket from the surrogacy experience, and that a mechanism is included to allow surrogates (and their partners) to enforce this right to reimbursement. Prescribed costs are set out in the regulations and remain unchanged.

The amended section then stipulates that 'an intended parent *may* compensate' a surrogate for their reproductive labour (emphasis added). So while reimbursement of actual expenses is mandatory, compensation for reproductive labour is optional. In other words, so-called 'altruistic surrogacy' is still permissible, the legislation simply provides the option for payment to recognise 'the physical, mental and emotional experiences' of being a surrogate. The regulations will establish the details regarding such compensation, just as the regulations set out the details regarding what constitutes 'prescribed costs'. They may, for example, establish a cap on the amount of permissible compensation.

It is my strong hope, Madam Speaker, that this Bill achieves better protection and recognition of surrogates and increased opportunities for families to be established through surrogacy here in Australia.

I commend the Bill to the House.

PARLIAMENT OF VICTORIA

Introduced in the Assembly

Assisted Reproductive Treatment Amendment Bill 2024

A Bill for an Act to amend the **Assisted Reproductive Treatment Act 2008** and for other purposes.

The Parliament of Victoria enacts:

1 Purposes

The main purpose of this Act is to amend section 44 of the **Assisted Reproductive Treatment Act 2008.**

2 Commencement

This Act commences on the day after the day on which it receives the Royal Assent.

3 Section 44 substituted

For section 44 of the **Assisted Reproductive Treatment Act 2008**, substitute –

'44 Surrogacy costs

(1) An intended parent must reimburse:

(a) a surrogate mother for the prescribed costs actually incurred by the surrogate mother as a direct consequence of entering into the surrogacy arrangement; and

(b) a surrogate mother's partner (if her partner is a party to the surrogacy arrangement) for the prescribed costs actually incurred by the partner as a direct consequence of entering into the surrogacy arrangement.

(2) If there is more than one intended parent, both intended parents are jointly and severally liable for the reimbursement provided for by subsection (1).

(3) A surrogate mother, or her partner, may, by commencing proceedings in a court of competent jurisdiction, recover the prescribed costs actually incurred as described in subsection (1) as a debt owing to them.

(4) In addition, an intended parent may compensate a surrogate mother for her reproductive labour.

(5) For the purposes of subsection (4), ***reproductive labour*** means the physical, mental and emotional experiences of a surrogate mother as a result of anything done under a surrogacy arrangement, including trying to become pregnant, becoming pregnant, carrying a pregnancy, and giving birth to a child.

(6) Any payment for reimbursement or compensation made by an intended parent to a surrogate mother or her partner under this section must be in accordance with the regulations.

(7) Without limiting subsection (6), regulations made for the purposes of that subsection may specify:

  (a) the amount of compensation that may be paid for reproductive labour; and

  (b) the period within which reimbursement or compensation under this section must or may be made.'

4 Repeal of this Act

This Act is repealed on the first anniversary of its commencement.

Note

The repeal of this Act does not affect the continuing operation of the amendments made by it (see section 15(1) of the *Interpretation of Legislation Act 1984*).

Notes

1 *Assisted Reproductive Treatment Act 2008* (Vic). This is Act No 76 of 2008. The proposed amendments are based on the version incorporating amendments as at 15 August 2022. https://content.legislation.vic.gov.au/sites/default/files/2022-08/08-76aa028%20authorised.pdf>.

2 *Parentage Act 2004* (ACT) s 41; *Surrogacy Act 2010* (NSW) ss 8 and 23; *Surrogacy Act 2010* (Qld) s 56; *Surrogacy Act 2019* (SA) s 23; *Surrogacy Act 2012* (Tas) s 40; *Assisted Reproductive Treatment Act 2008* (Vic) s 44(1); *Surrogacy Act 2008* (WA) s 8; *Surrogacy Act 2022* (NT) s 48.

3 Kerry Petersen, 'Cross Border Commercial Surrogacy: A Global Patchwork of Inconsistency and Confusion' in Michael Freeman et al. (eds), *Law and Global Health* (Oxford University Press, 2014) 209, 211.

4 Department of Home Affairs, Applications for children born through overseas surrogacy for citizenship by descent, 2012–2020; Australia and New Zealand Assisted Reproductive Database (ANZARD), University of New South Wales, children born through gestational surrogacy in Australia and New Zealand, annual reports for calendar years 2012–2018.

5 Surrogacy Australia, Submission No 32 to House of Representatives Standing Committee on Social Policy and Legal Affairs, *Inquiry into Surrogacy*, February 2016, 8.

6 Stephen Page, 'Surrogacy in Australia – A Missed Opportunity', *BioNews*, (United Kingdom), 13 June 2016.
7 Anita Stuhmcke, 'The Regulation of Commercial Surrogacy: The Wrong Answers to the Wrong Questions' (2015) 23 *Journal of Law and Medicine* 333, 334.
8 Denise Rice, 'Surrogacy a Legal Maze', *The Sunday Times* (Perth), 17 June 2007, 68.
9 See, for example, discussion of the risks associated with online forums through which people connect in Michael Gorton, 'Helping Victorians Create Families with Assisted Reproductive Treatment', *Final Report of the Independent Review of Assisted Reproductive Treatment* (May 2019) 8.4 (regarding gamete donation) 9.7.2 (regarding surrogacy).
10 Anita Stuhmcke, 'The Regulation of Commercial Surrogacy: The Wrong Answers to the Wrong Questions' (2015) 23 *Journal of Law and Medicine* 333.
11 Karen Busby and Delaney Vun, 'Revisiting *The Handmaid's Tale*: Feminist Theory Meets Empirical Research on Surrogate Mothers' (2010) 26 *Canadian Journal of Family Law* 13, 52–55.
12 Julie Shapiro, 'For a Feminist Considering Surrogacy, Is Compensation Really the Key Question?' (2014) 89 *Washington Law Review* 1345, 1369.
13 See Australian Government, Workplace Gender Equality Agency, *Australia's Gender Pay Gap Statistics* (8 March 2022) https://www.wgea.gov.au/publications/australias-gender-pay-gap-statistics>.
14 Melbourne IVF, *Costs of IVF*, <https://www.mivf.com.au/ivf-costs/costs-of-ivf (June 2022); Monash IVF, *Treatment Costs*, https://monashivf.com/costs/treatment-ivf-costs (February 2022).
15 For a discussion of the disconnect between the fees charged by private fertility clinics in Australia and the insistence on altruistic surrogacy, see Jenni Millbank, 'Rethinking "Commercial" Surrogacy in Australia' (July 2014) *Bioethical Inquiry*.
16 Merryn Elizabeth Ekberg, 'Ethical, Legal and Social Issues to Consider When Designing a Surrogacy Law' (2014) 21 *Journal of Law and Medicine* 728, 733; Margaret Jane Radin, 'Market Inalienability' (1987) 100 *Harvard Law Review* 1849.
17 Sara L Ainsworth, 'Bearing Children, Bearing Risks: Feminist Leadership for Progressive Regulation of Compensated Surrogacy in the United States' (2014) 89 *Washington Law Review* 1077, 1084. Katha Pollitt, for example, uses the term 'reproductive prostitution': Katha Pollitt, *Reasonable Creatures: Essays on Women and Feminism* (1995, Vintage Books) 69.
18 *Sex Work Decriminalisation Act 2022* (Vic). See Second Reading Speech (13 October 2021).
19 Karen Busby and Delaney Vun, 'Revisiting *The Handmaid's Tale*: Feminist Theory Meets Empirical Research on Surrogate Mothers' (2010) 26 *Canadian Journal of Family Law* 13.
20 Ronli Sifris, 'Commercial Surrogacy and the Human Right to Autonomy' (2015) 23 *Journal of Law and Medicine* 365.
21 John Pascoe, Chief Judge of the Federal Circuit Court, Submission No 35 to House of Representatives Standing Committee on Social Policy and Legal Affairs, *Inquiry into Surrogacy*, February 2016, 11.
22 Sara L Ainsworth, 'Bearing Children, Bearing Risks: Feminist Leadership for Progressive Regulation of Compensated Surrogacy in the United States' (2014) 89 *Washington Law Review* 1077, 1107.
23 Margaret Jane Radin, 'Market Inalienability' (1987) 100 *Harvard Law Review* 1849.

24 For a discussion of this tension, see Elizabeth Scott, 'Surrogacy and the Politics of Commodification' (2009) 72 *Law and Contemporary Problems* 109.
25 Sharon Bassan, 'Different but Same: A Call for a Joint Pro-Active Regulation of Cross-Border Egg and Surrogacy Markets' (2018) 28(1) *Health Matrix* 334, 357–362.
26 For discussion of the women-protective rationale for restricting access to abortion, see Reva Siegel, 'The Rights' Reasons: Constitutional Conflict and the Spread of Women-Protective Antiabortion Argument' (2008) 57 *Duke Law Journal* 1641.
27 Elizabeth Scott, 'Surrogacy and the Politics of Commodification' (2009) 72 *Law and Contemporary Problems* 109, 144.

Chapter 8A

Commentary on *Compensation in the Context of Surrogacy*

Stephen Page

The vast majority of Australian children born via surrogacy are born overseas, with statistics indicating that 79% of children born through surrogacy are born overseas, while only 21% are born domestically.[1] For a number of reasons, it is clearly more desirable for surrogacy arrangements to occur in Australia than overseas. However, until surrogates are compensated appropriately, there will not be enough willing surrogates to tip the balance in favour of domestic surrogacy. Failing to encourage people to come forward as surrogates makes intended parents more likely to seek surrogacy overseas, thus potentially exploiting surrogates in developing countries in some cases. The moral imperative is to promote surrogacy in Australia as much as possible, thereby reducing the rate of overseas surrogacy. That said, it is also important to cap the amount of compensation offered to surrogates to minimise the risk of exploitation.

Having a clear cap sets out what Parliament or the Government considers a fair amount. That works to send a clear message regarding what is and what is not appropriate. The upside of putting a specific amount in law is that it makes policymakers' expectations transparent. It would be an amount that is not too low or too high at which exploitation of somebody might appear assumed. By having transparency, policy makers could feel comfortable about the amount offered. Of course, if the cap is too low, would-be surrogates will not come forward, and intended parents will still go overseas. My view is that approximately AUD $20,000 to AUD $30,000 in addition to out-of-pocket expenses would constitute reasonable compensation.[2]

Australia's insistence on 'altruistic' surrogacy is nonsensical for several reasons. For example, the lines between 'altruistic' and 'compensated' surrogacy are blurred, sometimes constituting the same conduct under a different name. For instance, surrogacy in Canada is classed as altruistic under the *Assisted Human Reproduction Act*, SC 2004, c 2. Nevertheless, the reimbursable expenses of surrogates in Canada commonly vary between C$20,000 and C$32,000. While the compensation offered to gestational carriers in the United States varies dramatically, a gestational carrier in, for example, Minnesota receives a base compensation of US$25,000. Despite this, surrogacy

DOI: 10.4324/9781003372462-17

in Minnesota is considered commercial, whereas surrogacy in Canada is considered altruistic. This seems like somewhat of an absurdity.

There is much guilt, appropriately enough, regarding the treatment of mothers 50 years ago when forced adoptions were common. There is, however, a danger in conflating the tragedy of forced adoption with compensated surrogacy. After all,

> surrogacy and adoption are separate and distinct ways for people to achieve parenthood. Surrogacy is a medical solution to infertility, whether the infertility is physiological or social (based on relationship status), and is, therefore, a method of reproduction.[3]

Adoption, on the other hand, 'is the transfer of legal responsibility over an existing child from one party (or the state) to another.'[4] The issue of payment to surrogates and the comparison between surrogates and mothers through adoption was dealt with decisively by the Supreme Court of California in the seminal case of *Johnson v Calvert*,[5] where the court stated that:

> Gestational surrogacy differs in crucial respects from adoption and so is not subject to the adoption statutes. The parties voluntarily agreed to participate in in vitro fertilization and related medical procedures before the child was conceived; at the time when Anna entered into the contract, therefore, she was not vulnerable to financial inducements to part with her own expected offspring. As discussed above, Anna was not the genetic mother of the child. The payments to Anna under the contract were meant to compensate her for her services in gestating the fetus and undergoing labor, rather than for giving up 'parental' rights to the child. Payments were due both during the pregnancy and after the child's birth.

The court went on to address the question of whether surrogacy involves exploitation of the surrogate, concluding that exploitation is not an inherent feature of a surrogacy arrangement.[6] The court makes several notable points. First, the analogies between forced adoption and gestational surrogacy are misleading. Second, the payments in a gestational surrogacy arrangement are not payments for the child per se, but rather for the work inherent in gestating and birthing a child. Third, the assumption that surrogacy automatically equals exploitation of the surrogate is false, carrying connotations of paternalistic and patriarchal approaches to women's wellbeing. I agree with this sentiment and posit that the approach set out in this revised legislation is distinctly feminist.

The idea that people cannot be compensated for being surrogates when they are the ones bearing all the risk prevents them from achieving equality. When doctors, lawyers, counsellors, embryologists and judges are all being paid as part of the surrogacy process, surely the people who assume all the risk can be as well. Why are they alone expected to shoulder the burden without compensation?

Further, it is patronising to assume that a person who seeks to be a surrogate cannot have autonomy in their decision making, especially in circumstances when they have had the benefit of psychological screening, independent legal advice and judicial oversight. Of course, there is a risk that women of disadvantage (such as those from culturally and linguistically diverse backgrounds or low socioeconomic backgrounds) may be taken advantage of; this is especially the case when forms of disadvantage intersect and compound. Having the current safeguards included in the legislation – independent legal advice, counselling and written agreement – is vital.

Having agencies should be another bulwark. This is one of the reasons why I believe that ethically run surrogacy agencies should be permitted, because they help facilitate appropriate screening of surrogates so that women who should not be surrogates – including those on Centrelink who may be motivated primarily by money – are excluded. In every case, care must be taken by lawyers and fertility counsellors to ensure as far as possible that there is informed consent on the surrogate's behalf, coupled with a lack of duress. In my view, ethically run surrogacy agencies increase the chances of informed consent while reducing the possibility of duress occurring. They ought to be run according to feminist principles of self-empowerment while following best practice guidelines.[7]

The expectation that people should not be compensated for being surrogates reflects an exploitative attitude toward them, particularly as all other professionals involved are compensated. The proposed legislation will allow people to be properly compensated for their role in gestating a child (if they choose to do so), consistent with empowering the surrogate to attain equal economic rights and rightfully achieving autonomy over their bodies. The legislation does not propose mandating compensation but surrogates would have the ability to choose to be compensated – a choice that is currently denied them by criminal law.

I would like to add the final point that in Australia the maternal death rate in 2020 was 5.5 deaths per 100,000 women giving birth.[8] People are aware that there are risks involved in being pregnant and giving birth. It is unreasonable, unjust and exploitative to expect a person to put themselves at risk by being pregnant and giving birth (which is not a risk faced by anyone else in the surrogacy process) without some form of compensation.

Notes

1 Australian and New Zealand Reproductive Database (ANZARD0, University of New South Wales, Annual Reports; and Department of Home Affairs, applications for Australian citizenship by descent via surrogacy, obtained by the author via freedom of information.

2 See Stephen Page, *Submission to the House of Representatives Standing Committee on Social Policy and Legal Affairs Inquiry into Surrogacy* (10 February 2016).
3 American Bar Association, *Resolution 112B Adopted by the House of Delegates* (8 February 2016).
4 American Bar Association, *Draft Position Paper on Proposed Hague Surrogacy Convention* (1 September 2013). https://pageprovan.com.au/american-bar-association-draft-position-paper-on-proposed-hague-surrogacy-convention/.
5 *Johnson v Calvert* 5 Cal 4th 87 (1993). http://law.justia.com/cases/california/supreme-court/4th/5/84.html, pp.96–97.
6 Ibid, p.97.
7 For an example of best-practice guidelines, see Society for Ethics in Egg Donation and Surrogacy, *Standards of Ethical Conduct for SEEDS Member Agencies* (2022). https://www.seedsethics.org/resources/Documents/Standards/Final%20Standards%20with%20Guidelines%20and%20intro.pdf.
8 Australian Institute of Health and Welfare, *Australia's Mothers and Babies: Maternal Deaths* (28 September 2023). https://www.aihw.gov.au/reports/mothers-babies/maternal-deaths-australia.

Chapter 9

Reconsidering the Role of the Victim in Criminal Injuries Compensation

Kate Seear, Jamie Walvisch and Liza J Miller

Extract from *Hansard* (Parliament of Western Australia)

Criminal Injuries Compensation Act Amendment Bill 2024

Second Reading

HON KATE SEEAR, HON JAMIE WALVISCH and HON LIZA MILLER: We jointly move:

That the Bill now be read a second time.

We rise today to move an amendment to the *Criminal Injuries Compensation Act 2003* (WA).[1] We propose an important amendment to section 41 of that Act, which currently states that in assessing the compensation payable to a victim of crime, the assessor must consider 'any behaviour, condition, attitude, or disposition of the victim that contributed, directly or indirectly, to the victim's injury or death'. This section allows the assessor, if they wish, to refuse to compensate victims due to their own behaviour, or to reduce the amount they are paid.

In our view, this section is deeply flawed. It can generate significant harms to victims of crime because it tells them that *they* might be responsible for the crimes perpetrated against them, and that every aspect of *their* behaviour will be scrutinised by assessors if they apply for compensation to support them in their recovery. In putting the spotlight so squarely on victims, it also has the potential to misshape public understandings of the nature and origins of crime, agency and responsibility. Additionally, it sends a very worrying message to perpetrators.

The section is also incompatible with – and has the potential to undermine – important reforms that we have recently made to our criminal laws, including abolishing the provocation defence for murder and manslaughter.[2] One

DOI: 10.4324/9781003372462-18

of the reasons this defence was abolished was because it operates unjustly against women;[3] and the same goes for section 41. The provision is wholly unnecessary and has not been subject to sufficient scrutiny over the many years it has been in place. We think that this speaks volumes about the way that deeply gendered ideas about agency and responsibility remain within the law. It is essential that we work together to remove such flawed concepts from the Western Australian legal landscape.

Why Do We Have Crimes Compensation Schemes?

To properly understand our concerns about section 41, we need to recall why we have crimes compensation schemes at all. These schemes have existed in Australia since the 1960s and in Western Australia since 1970. In the Second Reading Speech for the original Criminal Injuries (Compensation) Bill, the Honourable Mr Bertram described it as a 'humanitarian' and 'social' piece of legislation.[4] Such descriptions are broadly in keeping with how crimes compensation legislation is generally portrayed – it is thought of as 'remedial' or 'beneficial' legislation designed to 'support, rehabilitate or otherwise benefit victims of crime'.[5] It is sometimes also said to be a 'therapeutically symbolic gesture of collegiality and concern' by the community and the state, and potentially 'cathartic' for victims.[6]

The symbolic potential and power of crimes compensation legislation can be especially important in cases where no perpetrator is ever identified, charged or convicted. In these cases – many of which concern sexual abuse and assault, or family violence – the opportunity to have one's experiences as a victim formally recognised by a court or tribunal can be a rare and precious opportunity to have one's suffering and its effects acknowledged by an authority figure.

The importance of this recognition of the trauma that can be caused by crime is often emphasised by people who have gone through the crimes compensation process. For example, one victim of crime told the Victorian Law Reform Commission:

> [W]hat I wanted more than the dollars was acknowledgement. I merely wanted a tribunal to listen to my story and say to me, in words like these: We believe you. We acknowledge your pain and your trauma at the hands of an abusive and violent person.[7]

For many victims, this recognition will be the most they can ever hope for.

It is essential that we bear this context in mind today, as we reflect on the operation and effect of section 41.

Why Was Section 41 Included in the Act?

In advocating for the original crimes compensation Bill, Mr Bertram noted that the State had long done all it could 'reasonably do to punish those people who commit crimes', but regrettably, it had done 'very little to help those who suffer as a direct consequence of those crimes'.[8] He was of the view that things should change. He said that he did not think that people who, by pure mischance, found themselves caught up in a criminal activity, and who had been maimed for life or had their lives ruined, should be left to bear the whole of the burden. It was not their fault that they had been victimised – it was simply bad luck.[9]

While the government acknowledged that the Bill may not have been perfect, and might have even been only tokenistic in some respects – including because of the relatively small sums of compensation on offer – it took pride in the fact that the State was 'making a start', and because 'a most excellent and worth-while principle' was involved.[10]

Unfortunately, despite these admirable aims, the original 1970 Act empowered a court or judge, when assessing an application for compensation, to take into account 'any behaviour' by the victim that contributed, directly or indirectly, to the injuries they had suffered.[11] In other words, the idea that a victim could contribute to the crime against them was a feature of the Western Australian scheme from the outset.

There was no debate in either chamber about the inclusion of this provision, nor any discussion about the contributory behaviour of victims. In our view, this is revealing. The idea that a victim could contribute to a crime committed against them seems to have been viewed as totally uncontroversial at the time, and in need of no carefully articulated public policy rationale.

There are likely to have been various reasons for adding this provision to the Bill, including the view, common then and still common now, that some people – especially women, LGBTIQA+ populations and people of colour – are often at least partly to blame for crimes committed against them, including family and sexual violence, homophobic and transphobic hate crimes and racial violence.[12]

In 1982, when extensive reforms to the crimes compensation scheme were proposed, the government observed that it had 'always been regarded' as against the public interest for a victim to be paid out when they had contributed directly or indirectly to their injuries.[13] The opposition supported the apportionment of liability as a 'common-sense' approach, claiming, without evidence or further explanation, that:

> In many cases involving criminal compensation, the injuries sustained have been provoked or in some way contributed to by the injured party; in that case, some apportionment should be made, having regard to the level of blame of the injured party.[14]

This meant that the Act retained a provision which allowed the victim's potentially 'contributory' conduct to be taken into account in determining the remedy. Such a provision has been maintained in all subsequent versions of the Act, although with slight adjustments to its wording. These tweaks have not altered the substance of the provision, however, which has consistently allowed the tribunal to take into account the behaviour and conduct of the victim.

What Do We Know About the Use of Section 41?

The current wording of section 41 was enacted in 2003, when the criminal compensation scheme was once again overhauled. Crucially, the provision was passed with no discussion, even though one member indicated that they had questions about the contributory behaviour clause.

Section 41 appears in Part 4 of the Act, which sets out a number of 'matters governing compensation awards'. Apart from section 41, this Part of the Act includes provisions which *require* an assessor to refuse to award compensation if it is likely to benefit the offender, if the applicant did not assist investigators or if the injury was suffered as a consequence of committing an offence or when the person was committing a separate offence.

As a side issue, we note that these other provisions also raise many concerns from a feminist perspective. There may, for instance, be very legitimate reasons why someone who has been a victim of crime, especially family violence or child sexual abuse, is neither willing nor able to assist investigators; and the requirement that an assessor refuse to award compensation if it is likely to benefit the offender may cause difficulties for victims of family violence if their finances are linked with the offender's. Although these provisions cause us significant disquiet, they each raise unique philosophical and practical questions that are deserving of separate analysis. We acknowledge those issues here and encourage Parliament to explore them and consider further amendments to the Act. In this Bill, we solely focus our attention on section 41.

Section 41 takes us into distinctly different territory from the provisions we were discussing a few moments ago. It is not about whether the victim was injured while committing another crime, such as robbing a bank, nor is it about the victim's failure to assist the police or prosecution after the offence. It is about whether the victim might have somehow triggered, encouraged, incited or otherwise influenced the perpetrator to offend.[15] In other words, it is about the victim's contribution to the offender's criminal actions.

We know from the Annual Report of the Office of Criminal Injuries Compensation that section 41 is used to both reduce and refuse compensation awards. For example, the 2020–21 Annual Report tells us that over 5,500 applications were finalised in that financial year.[16] The report reveals that a total of 47 applications were reduced or refused during that year because of the victim's behaviour.[17] The data show that of the 20 applications which were refused for contributory behaviour, nine involved family and domestic violence. Of the 27 applications that were reduced, two involved family and domestic violence.

The 2019–20 Annual Report reveals a similar tale, with over 3,000 applications finalised during that year. Unfortunately, the data concerning section 41 is somewhat unclear in the report. Its text states that:

> Reductions for contributory behaviour, ranging from 5% to 50%, were made in 18 awards . . . Of these, 6 awards were reduced by 20% or less and 12 awards were reduced by over 20%. No application was refused for contributory behaviour. Five of the applications on which a reduction was made for contributory behaviour involved family and domestic violence.[18]

However, contrary to the assertion that no application was refused for contributory behaviour, a table earlier in the report states that 27 applications were refused for contributory behaviour, 18 of which involved family and domestic violence.[19] In any case, the key point is that section 41 is being used to reduce or refuse awards of compensation, including to victims of family and domestic violence.

It is important to note here that section 41 refers to any 'behaviour, condition, attitude, or disposition' of the victim that contributed to their injury or death. Case law has made it clear that this includes circumstances where the victim 'provoked' the offence. For example, in *Edmonds v Juniper*, the Court observed:

> An example of the 'behaviour, condition, attitude or disposition' of a victim referred to in section 41(a) might be, in an appropriate case conduct such as provocation whereby a victim may have acted wrongfully so as to deprive an offender of self-control and thereby induce the offender to commit an offence against the victim in the heat of the moment, before passion and temper have cooled.[20]

In another case, the Court went even further and held that an award may be reduced or refused due to the victim's 'provocative' behaviour, even if that behaviour would not satisfy the criminal law defence of provocation.[21] This was recently affirmed by the District Court, which stated that section 41 'is wider in its terms than the defences of provocation and self-defence', and that whether an award should be refused or reduced on account of one's 'behaviour, condition, attitude or disposition' is 'a matter of fact and degree to be determined in light of the particular circumstances'.[22]

Why Does Section 41 Need Reform?

It can be seen from these cases that section 41 draws us into the realm of provocation. In the criminal law context, the partial defence of provocation previously reduced the offence of wilful murder or murder to manslaughter.[23] It continues to provide a complete defence to a charge of assault.[24] However, the defence has been subject to a sustained and valid critique by feminists for many years now.[25] Some of the key criticisms include:

- The defence operates in a gender-biased fashion. It predominantly operates to excuse male anger and violence towards women. It is most often raised by men in the context of a relationship of sexual intimacy, in circumstances involving jealousy or a desire to retain control – such as where the man's partner leaves or threatens to leave.[26]
- The framing of the test for provocation, which requires a sudden violent loss of self-control to a triggering act, favours stereotypically male aggressive responses.
- Provocation condones violence. There is insufficient moral or legal reason for excusing people who do not control their violent impulses.

For these reasons, among others, the defence has now been abolished in most Australian jurisdictions. In its 2007 *Review of the Law of Homicide*, the Law Reform Commission of Western Australia recommended abolishing provocation as a defence to murder in this jurisdiction.[27] This recommendation was implemented by the Government in 2008.[28]

Although it was beyond the scope of its review, the Commission was of the provisional view that the defence of provocation should also be abolished in relation to non-homicide offences, and recommended that the Government conduct a review of the issue.[29] Unfortunately, this recommendation has not been implemented, with provocation remaining a defence to assault. While we consider the continued existence of the provocation defence to be unacceptable for the reasons outlined above, and advocate for its removal from the criminal law, here we want to focus on the crimes compensation context.

Crucially, while there is obviously a relationship between the criminal justice system and the crimes compensation system – in that they both relate to criminal acts – their focus is fundamentally different. The criminal justice system is penal in nature, seeking to assess the wrongfulness of a person's actions in order to determine an appropriate penalty. By contrast, the crimes compensation system is remedial in nature, seeking to repair the harm done to the victim.

Despite these differences, the kinds of criticism levelled at the defence of provocation in the criminal context apply equally to the crimes compensation context. For example:

- Section 41 is likely to operate in a gender-biased way, reducing or refusing awards to women who are the victims of male anger and violence.[30]
- The operation of the provision is likely to favour stereotypically male aggressive responses that involve a sudden violent loss of self-control to a triggering act.
- By reducing or refusing an award on the basis that the victim has 'provoked' the crime, section 41 implicitly condones violence. People should

be able to resist their violent impulses, no matter how they are treated. Victims should not be penalised for the offender's failure to do so.

In addition, by focusing on the victim's contribution to the offending behaviour, section 41 promotes a culture of victim-blaming. This is antithetical to the entire purpose of the crimes compensation scheme, which is about repairing the harm caused to victims by criminal actions. Regardless of any role the victim allegedly played in the encounter, they have suffered the same harm and should be treated with equal dignity and respect.

It is no answer to our concerns to say that the application of section 41 is so rare as to render the section inconsequential. As we explained at the outset, the availability of crimes compensation can be hugely important, both symbolically and materially, for victims of crime. The fact that one's own conduct will have been assessed and seen to have potentially caused the offence has the potential to result in significant psychological harm to victims, especially in cases involving sexual offending or family violence. Further, while the application of the section may be rare, the data do not reveal how often the issue is raised before an assessor and thus put to the victim, even if ultimately unsuccessful.

Importantly, even if provocation is not argued in a specific case, it is likely that lawyers advising applicants will nevertheless need to take them through section 41, explaining that their conduct must be assessed and could be deemed relevant to determining whether they are 'worthy' or 'deserving' of compensation, or whether they are considered somehow 'responsible' for the crime perpetrated against them. We know from work undertaken by the Victorian Law Reform Commission that these kinds of considerations might dissuade victims from applying for compensation, cause them distress or retraumatise and re-victimise them.[31]

The mere existence of the provision therefore has the potential to generate suffering and angst for potential applicants. It also has the potential to create doubt in the minds of victims about whether they were actually responsible for the crimes perpetrated against them, sending a troubling message to the community about blame and responsibility when it comes to criminal offending. These effects are, we suggest, not only at odds with the purportedly beneficial nature of the scheme, but also deeply concerning because of their potential to reproduce or reinforce outdated ideas of the kind we mentioned earlier about agency and responsibility, gender, sex, sexuality and race. The provision is also flawed because the assessment of the victim's contribution is arbitrary, lacks principle and is likely to be applied in highly value-laden and subjective ways, drawing on myths and stereotypes that the law should be working hard to eradicate rather than sustain.

We therefore propose an amendment that makes clear that provocation-type arguments cannot be made and will not be taken into account by courts in their assessment for compensation. The proposed amendment is designed to act as a clear repudiation of provocation as a matter of principle, acknowledging its harmful effects on various populations, including women. We also intend the amendment to be a clear statement of parliamentary support for the principle that groups such as women, Indigenous peoples and LGBTIQA+ populations are not responsible for the violence perpetrated against them, and that victim-blaming has no place in Australian society.

We commend the Bill to the House.

Western Australia

<u>LEGISLATIVE ASSEMBLY</u>

Criminal Injuries Compensation Amendment Bill 2024

A Bill for

An Act to amend the *Criminal Injuries Compensation Act 2003*

The Parliament of Western Australia enacts as follows:

1. Short title

This is the *Criminal Injuries Compensation Act 2024*.

2. Commencement

This Act comes into operation on the day on which this Act receives Royal Assent.

3. Act amended

This Act amends the Criminal Injuries Compensation Act 2003.

4. Section 41 amended

After section 41(1) insert:

(2) The following things are not to be taken, under subsection (1)(a), to have contributed, directly or indirectly, to the victim's injury or death –

(a) any behaviour that was engaged in by the victim to deprive, or in an attempt to deprive, the person who committed the offence of the power of self-control;
(b) any condition, attitude or disposition of the victim that indicated the victim intended that the person who committed the offence be deprived of the power of self-control.

(3) For the purposes of subsection (2), it does not matter whether:

(a) the behaviour, condition, attitude or disposition of the victim constitutes provocation within the meaning of the *Criminal Code Compilation Act 1913* section 245;
(b) the behaviour, condition, attitude, or disposition of the victim was likely to deprive an ordinary person of the power of self-control; or
(c) the person who committed the offence has raised the defence of provocation in the proceeding for that offence.

Notes

1 Version 03-f0–00. Currency start 1 July 2022. https://www.legislation.wa.gov.au/legislation/statutes.nsf/law_a6998_currencies.html.
2 *Criminal Code Compilation Act 1913* (WA) s 281 ('*Criminal Code*'), repealed by *Criminal Law Amendment (Homicide) Act* 2008.
3 Western Australia, *Parliamentary Debates*, Legislative Assembly, 8 May 2008, 2776 (Walker MP).
4 Western Australia, *Parliamentary Debates*, Legislative Assembly, 15 October 1970, 1307 (Bertram MP).
5 K Seear and S Fraser, 'The Addict as Victim: Producing the "Problem" of Addiction in Australian Victims of Crime Compensation Laws' (2014) 25 *International Journal of Drug Policy* 826, 828.
6 I Freckelton, 'Compensation for Victims of Crime' in H Kaptein and M Malsch (eds) *Crime, Victims and Justice: Essays on Principles and Practice* (Ashgate, 2004) 58, 58.
7 Victorian Law Reform Commission, *Review of the Victims of Crime Assistance Act 1996* (Report, July 2018) [7.35], quoting Submission No 36 (name withheld).
8 Ibid.
9 Ibid.
10 Ibid.
11 *Criminal Injuries (Compensation) Act 1970* (WA) s 4(2), repealed by the *Criminal Injuries Compensation Act 1982* (WA).
12 See, eg, A Wakelin and K Long, 'Effects of Victim Gender and Sexuality on Attributions of Blame to Rape Victims' (2003) 49 *Sex Roles* 477.
13 Western Australia, *Parliamentary Debates*, Legislative Council, 9 November 1982, 4851 (Medcalf MP).
14 Western Australia, *Parliamentary Debates*, Legislative Assembly, 9 November 1982, 4867 (Grill MP).
15 Section 41 might also be about whether the victim has directly or indirectly contributed to their own injury by, for example, having a pre-existing medical condition. That is not, however, the focus of this Bill.
16 Office of Criminal Injuries Compensation, *Annual Report 2020–21* (Department of Justice, Western Australia, 2021) 11.
17 Ibid 17.
18 Office of Criminal Injuries Compensation, *Annual Report 2019–20* (Department of Justice, Western Australia, 2020) 16.
19 Ibid 15.
20 *Edmonds v Juniper* [2016] WADC 7 [19].
21 *Puterangi* [2017] WADC 168.
22 *Savic v Duric* [2021] WADC 53 [78].
23 *Criminal Code* s 281, repealed by *Criminal Law Amendment (Homicide) Act* 2008.
24 *Criminal Code* ss 245–7.
25 See, eg, J Morgan, 'Provocation Law and Facts: Dead Women Tell No Tales, Tales are Told About Them' (1997) 21 *Melbourne University Law Review* 237; Victorian Law Reform Commission, *Defences to Homicide* (Options Paper, September 2003) ch 3; B Naylor and D Tyson 'Reforming Defences to Homicide in Victoria: Another Attempt to Address the Gender Question' (2017) 6(3) *International Journal for Crime, Justice and Social Democracy* 72. For an overview of the various criticisms in the Western Australian context, see Law Reform Commission of Western Australia, *Review of the Law of Homicide: Final Report* (2007) 210–4.

26 On the contexts in which the provocation defence is raised, see especially J Morgan, *Who Kills Whom and Why: Looking Beyond Legal Categories* (Victorian Law Reform Commission, 2002).
27 Law Reform Commission of Western Australia (n 25) 222.
28 *Criminal Law Amendment (Homicide) Act 2008*, repealing *Criminal Code* s 281.
29 Law Reform Commission of Western Australia (n 25) 223.
30 Due to the lack of first instance reporting of crimes compensation claims, it is difficult to know the extent to which this occurs. However, there is no reason to doubt that it will differ from the criminal law context.
31 Victorian Law Reform Commission (n 7).

Chapter 9A

Commentary on *Reconsidering the Role of the Victim in Criminal Injuries Compensation*

Jenny Morgan

When I was first asked to be involved in this feminist legislation project, I thought the proposed task would be much easier than that taken on in the feminist judgments project(s).[1] For instance, the writer of the legislation and Second Reading Speech would not be constrained by the judicial form – there would be no requirement to actually reach a decision and write in an authoritative judicial voice, an approach quite different to the more tentative critical voice of the academic. Nor would the drafters need to be constrained by the need to be effectively restricted to the information available to the court at the time the case was argued.[2] However, reading the Second Reading Speech and accompanying legislation I was asked to comment on, I realised the drafters were subject to their own restrictions.

Most obviously, a government introducing legislation has to adequately identify the social problem to which the legislation responds,[3] and I am not convinced that the drafters have done so. I should make it clear that this is an observation, *not* a criticism. That is, the drafters are restricted in the information available to them in order to establish that there is such a social problem. The relevant legislation is directed to the section of the *Criminal Injuries Compensation Act*, legislation which allows a decision-maker to reduce or refuse altogether an award of crimes compensation if it is decided that the victim's 'behaviour, condition, attitude or disposition' has contributed to the injury.[4] As the authors observe, there is a lack of first instance reporting of crimes compensation claims, which makes demonstrating the social problem difficult. However, the drafters do gather together what information is available, particularly relying on annual reports of the Office of Criminal Injuries Compensation, which do report some statistics relating to domestic violence.[5] These show that in 11 of 47 cases where an award of compensation was refused or reduced, the context was one of domestic or family violence, and in 2019–20, 23 of 47 award reduction or refusal cases were cases of domestic or family violence. However, we do not know anything else about the circumstances.

The focus of the Bill as drafted is on ensuring that the misogynistic criminal defence to provocation does not creep into the decisions on alleged

DOI: 10.4324/9781003372462-19

contribution in the criminal compensation field. However, once again I am not sure the evidence is there to establish that this is, or is likely to be, the most prevalent form of victim-blaming in domestic violence cases. I worry that a more prevalent domestic violence scenario when an award is likely to be reduced or refused is where the victim is seen as encouraging a perpetrator's violence by encouraging or allowing contact to occur in breach of an intervention order. This is the scenario in JDQ [2010] WADC 93 [18] where the victim was contacted by the offender, seeking a meeting 'to resolve the issues between them'. Such a meeting was in breach of the intervention order binding both parties. In considering section 41 factors, the Court noted:

> Despite having the protection of a violence restraining order and in flagrant disregard of the order to which she was subject she agreed to meet the offender in an isolated place and to go with him to other places where, if a physical altercation arose, she would be unable to obtain protection or assistance.

The Court reduced her award by one-third.

The difficulty with narrowly focusing on meeting with the offender in breach of an intervention order is that it fails to recognise the wider context. Ending an abusive relationship is best seen as a process, often taking a number of attempts.[6] To blame a victim who is injured in that process by reducing damages only exacerbates the harm, rather than ameliorating it.

That said, there is no doubt that provocation is seen by decision-makers as relevant to an award of compensation, as the Second Reading Speech documents. I also agree with the drafters that the history of victim-blaming encapsulated in the provocation defence should certainly be made irrelevant to decisions in this area, as well as to the law of homicide. So, how does the legislation attempt to exclude considerations relevant to the traditional criminal defence of provocation?

The Bill specifies that a decision-maker should not treat 'any behaviour that was engaged in by the victim to deprive the [perpetrator's] power of self-control' as contributing to the victim's injury or death. It thus focuses on a central element of the provocation defence – the perpetrator's loss of self-control.

It also focuses on another central element of the provocation defence: the behaviour of the victim which is said to provoke the perpetrator, and excludes it from consideration. However, it extends the exclusion to any condition, attitude or disposition of the ostensible provoker, thus ensuring the desired limitations on blaming the victim.

It is also important that the Bill ensures that behaviour which might be read as provocative, but does not fulfil the criminal law definition of provocation, is also excluded from consideration. The Bill does this adroitly in subsection (3).

However, the Bill could go further and, as the VLRC proposed in relation to the equivalent provisions in the *Victims of Crime Assistance Act* 1996, provide that

> a victim's 'contributory conduct', including any 'provocation' or 'disposition', should no longer be relevant to a decision-maker's determination of whether a victim should be entitled to financial assistance to assist in their recovery from a criminal act.[7]

One can only hope that this proposed legislation is followed by further legislation to remove, as far as possible, all victim-blaming provisions in the WA legislation.

Notes

1 See, eg, H Douglas et al. (eds), *Australian Feminist Judgments: Righting and Rewriting Law* (Hart Publishing, 2014).
2 These and other restrictions are discussed in Douglas et al (n 1) ch 2.
3 This is obviously most necessary in a situation where a government needs the support of the opposition or crossbench to pass legislation.
4 See section 41.
5 A change made on the recommendation of the Law Reform Commission of Western Australia: see Law Reform Commission of Western Australia, *Enhancing Laws Concerning Domestic and Family Violence* (Final Report, June 2014).
6 See, eg, D Anderson and D Saunders, 'Leaving an Abusive Partner: An Empirical Review of Predictors, the Process of Leaving, and Psychological Well-Being' (2003) 4(2) *Trauma, Violence and Abuse* 163.
7 Victorian Law Reform Commission, *Review of the Victims of Crime Assistance Act 1996* (Report, July 2018) 415 [15.147].

Chapter 10

Let Us Pee

Building Regulations for All-Gender Toilets

Sean Mulcahy

Building Amendment (National Construction Code Variations – Sanitary And Other Facilities) Regulations 2024

Regulatory Impact Statement

This Regulatory Impact Statement (RIS) examines proposed regulations to provide for requirements relating to all-gender sanitary facilities for the use of women and men as well as gender diverse people in certain public buildings, including accommodation, office buildings, shops, restaurants, carparks, warehouses, storage buildings, factories, healthcare buildings, schools, universities, sports facilities, nightclubs and aged care facilities.

'Gender diverse' is an umbrella term for a range of non-binary genders that are not exclusively female or male. Findings from the *Victorian Population Health Survey 2017* indicate that 1 in 500 Victorians identify as gender diverse. Further findings from the 2021 report *Private Lives 3: The Health and Wellbeing of LGBTQ People in Victoria* indicate that over three-quarters of trans and gender diverse Victorians reported unfair treatment to some degree because of their gender identity in the past 12 months.

In February 2022, the Victorian Government released *Pride in Our Future: Victoria's LGBTIQA+ Strategy 2022–32*. The Strategy includes commitments to consider the impact of laws when viewed from the perspective of gender, sexuality, sex characteristics and culture to help address all forms of discrimination faced by LGBTIQA+ people, and to ensure new laws include LGBTIQA+ experiences while considering potential impacts on LGBTIQA+ communities.

In line with these commitments, the Government has considered the new National Construction Code (the Code), which came into operation on 1 May 2023 and only stipulates sanitary facilities for females and males. The Government has considered this in line with the principles set down in the *Gender Equality Act 2020*, including the principle that gender inequality

DOI: 10.4324/9781003372462-20

may be compounded by other forms of discrimination or disadvantage that a person may experience based on their gender identity. This principle recognises that gender diverse Victorians may experience discrimination or disadvantage that compounds gender inequality. In this case, the Code does not stipulate non-binary facilities. In consideration of the Code's impact on gender diverse people, and to ensure that sanitary facilities are inclusive of those who identify outside of the gender binary, the Government has determined to develop additional requirements for all-gender facilities in certain Victorian public buildings (the focus of this RIS).

The Code is Australia's primary set of technical design and construction provisions for buildings, setting the minimum required level for the safety, health, amenity, accessibility and sustainability of certain buildings. It is adopted in Victorian law via Regulation 10 of the *Building Regulations 2018*. The Code recognises that the absence of adequate personal hygiene facilities can impact building occupants' amenity, including their health, physical independence, comfort and wellbeing, a situation which the Code is intended to safeguard against. The Code stipulates that a building is to be provided with suitable sanitary facilities for personal hygiene that are appropriate to the gender of the building occupants. While the Code provides for unisex facilities for people with a disability, it does not provide for general all-gender facilities. This raises a problem whereby gender diverse building occupants may be compelled to use facilities intended for people with a disability.

The Government has consulted Transgender Victoria, Victoria's leading body for trans and gender diverse advocacy. Transgender Victoria commented that the different needs of the gender diverse community and people with disabilities are not fairly addressed under existing regulations, as many members of both cohorts will be potentially relying on the use of a single unisex facility. The Code therefore has a potentially negative impact, both on gender diverse people and people with a disability. Again, the principle set down in the *Gender Equality Act 2020* – that gender inequality may be compounded by other forms of discrimination or disadvantage that a person may experience based on gender identity or disability – is instructive. If gender diverse people and people with a disability are compelled to use the same facility, this could compound inequality for both groups.

If adequate all-gender facilities are not provided, a range of costs could be incurred, such as:

- health costs associated with the impacts on mental health and wellbeing of a lack of adequate personal hygiene facilities;
- social disruption;
- economic loss from reduced participation of gender diverse people in public life;

- lost business and tourism arising from a lack of adequate all-gender facilities that may impact Victoria's ability to attract large sporting events, conventions and the like; and
- legal costs arising from potential lawsuits under non-discrimination laws.

In relation to legal issues, section 8(3) of the *Charter of Human Rights and Responsibilities Act 2006* recognises that every person is entitled to equal protection of the law without discrimination, including that based on their gender identity. Failing to provide adequate sanitary facilities for gender diverse people may thus amount to discrimination, even if it is indirect. Discrimination against building occupants because of their gender identity also creates a risk to their health and safety. The Government's objective is to ensure the health, wellbeing, comfort and physical independence of gender diverse people in relation to sanitary facilities in public buildings, through the most cost-effective means. It should be noted that these Regulations do not reduce the number of female and male sanitary facilities required under the Code. These will still be mandated in line with the Code, as will unisex facilities for people with a disability. The proposed Regulations would simply require the addition of facilities that include all genders.

The Government recognises that additional requirements may impose an additional cost on business. However, considering the above, the Government has decided to create a requirement under Victorian law for all-gender sanitary facilities in certain public buildings. The Government recognises the need for education about all-gender facilities and will be investigating options for a public education campaign to accompany these new Regulations.

What are the Main Features of the Proposed Regulations?

The proposed Regulations take the form of amendments to the *Building Regulations 2018*, with the new requirements contained in a new Part 8A. A high-level overview of the broad features of the proposed new requirements is provided below.

Formal Matters

The Regulations are made under the *Building Act 1993* and amend the *Building Regulations 2018* to provide for additional Victorian variations to Volume One of the National Construction Code (the Code), including any variations or additions in the Victoria Appendix to that Volume, relating to sanitary and other facilities. For example, the Victoria Appendix to Volume One includes variations on sanitary facilities in early childhood facilities, which are reflected in these Regulations.

The Regulations commence on the same date that the Code comes into operation and apply to sanitary and other facilities in Class 3 (accommodation), 5 (office buildings), 6 (shops and restaurants), 7 (carparks, warehouses and storage buildings), 8 (factories) and 9 (healthcare buildings, schools, universities, sports facilities, nightclubs and aged care facilities) buildings. They primarily apply to the design and construction of new buildings, but also to alterations of existing buildings. If the alterations relate to more than half the building's original volume, the entire building must be brought into conformity with these Regulations.

Updated Terminology

The Regulations use the term 'all-gender' facilities. The Australian Workplace Equality Index encourages businesses to have 'gender neutral' or 'all-gender' sanitary and other facilities. The term 'unisex' has been retained when referring to accessible sanitary facilities for people with a disability.

Shared Sanitary Facilities

The Regulations remove the provision in the Code for shared toilet facilities if most employees are of one sex and there are only two or fewer employees of another sex. This provision could detrimentally impact women's safety in male-dominated industries. However, they retain the stipulation in the Code that an all-gender toilet may be provided instead of separate male and female toilets if ten or fewer people are employed. This will reduce any cost impact on small businesses of complying with the Regulations. However, the Government will consult further to determine whether this provision is still fit for purpose given safety and privacy concerns that can arise from shared sanitary facilities.

The Regulations also remove the provision in the Code for shared sanitary facilities for resident patients in healthcare wards. Again, this provision could detrimentally impact women's safety, particularly women who may be vulnerable due to various medical conditions that may necessitate treatment or attendance at a healthcare facility.

Sanitary Product Disposal Facilities for All

The Regulations require that adequate means of disposal of sanitary products be provided in all sanitary facilities, not just facilities for use by women as under the Code. This recognises that men and gender diverse people may also use sanitary products, such as incontinence pads, and, in the case of some transgender men and gender diverse people, menstrual tampons, pads and liners. This will ensure dignity for men and gender diverse people who need to use sanitary products.

All-Gender Sanitary Facilities

The Regulations require that all-gender sanitary facilities be provided for Class 3, 5, 6, 7, 8 and 9 buildings, and that the number of all-gender facilities is to be calculated according to the total number of persons accommodated in the building, except where there are separate facilities for employees or participants and other occupants such as students, spectators and patrons. The Regulations generally require that there should be one all-gender sanitary facility incorporating a closet pan and washbasin for every 100 persons accommodated in the building, except for larger buildings such as department stores, shopping centres, restaurants, cafes, bars, schools, multiplex theatres and cinemas, art galleries, sports venues, churches, chapels, public halls and function rooms, which have higher ratios reflecting the higher number of persons accommodated therein, and single-auditorium theatres and cinemas, which do not require sanitary facilities under the Code if there are 50 or fewer patrons.

Ambulant and Accessible All-Gender Sanitary Facilities

The Regulations require that there be at least one all-gender sanitary compartment containing a closet pan suitable for a person with an ambulant disability, as well as an all-gender accessible unisex sanitary compartment containing a closet pan at each bank of toilets. The Regulations also require that there be an all-gender accessible unisex sanitary compartment containing a closet pan at each bank of toilets in a Class 10a building (which includes sheds, carports and private garages), ensuring dignity for gender diverse people with a disability. This will only apply to Class 10a buildings with toilets. The Regulations also extend the requirement for accessible sanitary compartments and showers to resident patients in healthcare wards, ensuring dignity for patients with a disability in healthcare settings.

Victoria

Building Amendment (National Construction Code Variations – Sanitary and Other Facilities) Regulations 2024

1 Objective

The objective of these Regulations is to amend the **Building Regulations 2018**[1] to provide for Victorian variations to the **Building Code of Australia** relating to sanitary and other facilities.

2 Authorising provisions

These Regulations are made under sections 7, 9, 261 and 262 of, and Schedule 1 to, the **Building Act 1993**.

3 Commencement

These Regulations come into operation on 1 January 2025.

4 Principal Regulations

In these Regulations, the **Building Regulations 2018** are called the Principal Regulations.

5 New Part 8A inserted

After regulation 134 of the Principal Regulations, **insert** –
'Part 8A – Sanitary and Other Facilities
135 Application of the requirement in the BCA Volume One relating to sanitary and other facilities
The BCA Volume One applies as if –

(a) for clause F4D3(4) there were **substituted** –

'(4) For the purposes of this Part, a unisex or all-gender facility comprises one closet pan, one washbasin and means for the disposal of sanitary products.';

(b) for clause F4D4(1) there were **substituted** –

'(1) Except where permitted by (3), F4D5(a) and F4D5(b), separate sanitary facilities for males and females and all-gender sanitary facilities must be provided for Class 3, 5, 6, 7, 8 and 9 buildings in accordance with Tables F4D4a, F4D4b, F4D4c, F4D4e, F4D4f, VIC F4D4g, F4D4h, F4D4i, F4D4j, F4D4k and F4D4l, as appropriate.';

(c) for clause F4D4(3) there were **substituted** –

"(3) If not more than 10 people are employed, separate sanitary facilities for males and females need not be provided.";

(d) clause F4D4(4) were **deleted;**
(e) for clause F4D4(6) there were **substituted** –

'(6) Adequate means of disposal of sanitary products must be provided in sanitary facilities.';

(f) clause F4D4(7) were **deleted;**
(g) for Table F4D4a there were **substituted** –

Table F4D4a Sanitary Facilities in Class 3, 5, 6 and 9 Buildings Other Than Schools

User Group	*Closet Pans*		*Urinals*		*Washbasins*	
	Design Occupancy	*Number*	*Design Occupancy*	*Number*	*Design Occupancy*	*Number*
Male Employees	1–20	1	1–10	0	1–30	1
	>20	Add 1 per 20	11–25	1	>30	Add 1 per 30
	–	–	26–50	2	–	–
	–	–	>50	Add 1 per 50	–	–
Female Employees	1–15	1	N/A	N/A	1–30	1
	>15	Add 1 per 15	N/A	N/A	>30	Add 1 per 30
All Gender	1–100	1	N/A	N/A	1–100	1
(Based on Total Number of Employees)	>100	Add 1 per 100	N/A	N/A	>100	Add 1 per 100

(h) for Table F4D4b there were **substituted** –

Table F4D4b Sanitary Facilities in Class 7 and 8 Buildings

User Group	*Closet Pans*		*Urinals*		*Washbasins*	
	Design Occupancy	*Number*	*Design Occupancy*	*Number*	*Design Occupancy*	*Number*
Male Employees	1–20	1	1–10	0	1–20	1
	>20	Add 1 per 20	11–25	1	>20	Add 1 per 20
	–	–	26–50	2	–	–
	–	–	>50	Add 1 per 50	–	–
Female Employees	1–15	1	N/A	N/A	1–20	1
	>15	Add 1 per 15	N/A	N/A	>20	Add 1 per 20
All Gender	1–100	1	N/A	N/A	1–100	1
(Based on Total Number of Employees)	>100	Add 1 per 100	N/A	N/A	>100	Add 1 per 100

(i) for Table F4D4c there were **substituted** –

Table F4D4c Sanitary Facilities in Class 6 Buildings – Department Stores, Shopping Centres

User Group	*Closet Pans*		*Urinals*		*Washbasins*	
	Design Occupancy	*Number*	*Design Occupancy*	*Number*	*Design Occupancy*	*Number*
Male Patrons	1–1200	1	1–600	1	1–600	1
	>1200	Add 1 per 1200	>600	Add 1 per 1200	>600	Add 1 per 1200
Female Patrons	1–300	1	N/A	N/A	1–600	1
	301–600	2	N/A	N/A	601–1200	2
	>600	Add 1 per 1200	N/A	N/A	>1200	Add 1 per 1200
All Gender	1–1200	1	N/A	N/A	1–1200	1
(Based on Total Number of Patrons)	>1200	Add 1 per 1200	N/A	N/A	>1200	Add 1 per 1200

(j) for Table F4D4d there were **substituted** –

Table F4D4d Sanitary Facilities in Class 6 Buildings – Restaurants, Cafes, Bars

User Group	*Closet Pans*		*Urinals*		*Washbasins*	
	Design Occupancy	*Number*	*Design Occupancy*	*Number*	*Design Occupancy*	*Number*
Male Patrons	1–100	1	1–50	1	1–50	1
	101–300	2	51–100	2	51–200	2
	>300	Add 1 per 200	101–150	3	>200	Add 1 per 200
	–	–	151–200	4	–	–
	–	–	201–250	5	–	–
	–	–	>250	Add 1 per 100	–	–
Female Patrons	1–25	1	N/A	N/A	1–50	1
	26–50	2	N/A	N/A	51–150	2
	51–100	3	N/A	N/A	>150	Add 1 per 200
	101–150	4	N/A	N/A	–	–
	151–200	5	N/A	N/A	–	–
	201–250	6	N/A	N/A	–	–
	>250	Add 1 per 100	N/A	N/A	>1200	Add 1 per 1200
All Gender	1–300	1	N/A	N/A	1–300	1
(Based on Total Number of Patrons)	>300	Add 1 per 200	N/A	N/A	>300	Add 1 per 200

(k) for Table F4D4e there were **substituted** –

Table F4D4e Sanitary Facilities in Class 9a Healthcare Buildings

User Group	*Closet Pans*		*Washbasins*	
	Design Occupancy	*Number*	*Design Occupancy*	*Number*
Male Patients	1–16	2	1–8	1
	>16	Add 1 per 8	>8	Add 1 per 8
Female Patients	1–16	2	1–8	1
	>16	Add 1 per 8	>8	Add 1 per 8
All Gender	1–100	1	1–100	1
(Based on Total Number of Patients)	>100	Add 1 per 100	>100	Add 1 per 100

(l) for Table F4D4f there were **substituted** –

Table F4D4f Sanitary Facilities in Class 9b Buildings – Schools

User Group	*Closet Pans*		*Urinals*		*Washbasins*	
	Design Occupancy	*Number*	*Design Occupancy*	*Number*	*Design Occupancy*	*Number*
Male Employees	1–20	1	1–10	0	1–30	1
	>20	Add 1 per 20	11–20	1	>30	Add 1 per 30
	–	–	21–45	2	–	–
	–	–	>45	Add 1 per 30	–	–
Female Employees	1–5	1	N/A	N/A	1–30	1
	>5	Add 1 per 15	N/A	N/A	>30	Add 1 per 30
All Gender (Based	1–100	1	N/A	N/A	1–100	1
on Total number of Employees)	>100	Add 1 per 100	N/A	N/A	>100	Add 1 per 100
Male Students	1–25	1	1–50	1	1–10	1
	26–75	2	51–100	2	11–50	2
	76–150	3	>100	Add 1 per 100	51–100	3
	151–200	4	–	–	>100	Add 1 per 75
	>200	Add 1 per 100	–	–	–	–
Female Students	1–10	1	N/A	N/A	1–10	1
	11–25	2	N/A	N/A	11–50	2
	26–100	Add 1 per 25	N/A	N/A	51–100	3
	>100	Add 1 per 50	N/A	N/A	>100	Add 1 per 75
All Gender	1–200	1	N/A	N/A	1–200	1
(Based on Total Number of Students)	>200	Add 1 per 100	N/A	N/A	>200	Add 1 per 100

(m) for Table F4D4h there were **substituted** –

Table F4D4h Sanitary Facilities in Class 9b Buildings – Theatres and Cinemas with Multiple Auditoria, Art Galleries and the Like

User Group	*Closet Pans*		*Urinals*		*Washbasins*	
	Design Occupancy	*Number*	*Design Occupancy*	*Number*	*Design Occupancy*	*Number*
Male Participants	1–20	1	1–10	0	1–10	1
	>20	Add 1 per 20	>10	Add 1 per 10	>10	Add 1 per 10
Female Participants	1–10	1	N/A	N/A	1–10	1
	>10	Add 1 per 10	N/A	N/A	>10	Add 1 per 10
All Gender (Based on Total Number of Participants)	1–100	1	N/A	N/A	1–100	1
	>100	Add 1 per 100	N/A	N/A	>100	Add 1 per 100
Male Spectators or Patrons	1–250	1	1–100	1	1–150	1
	251–500	2	>100	Add 1 per 100	>150	Add 1 per 150
	>500	Add 1 per 500	–	–	–	–
Female Spectators or Patrons	1–10	1	N/A	N/A	1–80	1
	11–50	2	N/A	N/A	81–250	2
	>50	Add 1 per 60	N/A	N/A	251–430	3
	–	–	N/A	N/A	>430	Add 1 per 200
All Gender (Based on Total Number of Spectators or Patrons)	1–500	1	N/A	N/A	1–500	1
	>500	Add 1 per 500	N/A	N/A	>500	Add 1 per 500

(n) for Table F4D4i there were **substituted** –

Table F4D4i Sanitary Facilities in Class 9b Buildings – Single-Auditorium Theatres and Cinemas

User Group	*Closet Pans*		*Urinals*		*Washbasins*	
	Design Occupancy	*Number*	*Design Occupancy*	*Number*	*Design Occupancy*	*Number*
Male Patrons	1–50	0	1–50	0	1–50	0
	51–250	1	51–100	1	51–150	1
	251–500	2	>100	Add 1 per 100	>150	Add 1 per 150
	>500	Add 1 per 500	–	–	–	–
Female Patrons	1–50	0	N/A	N/A	1–50	0
	51–110	3	N/A	N/A	51–150	1
	111–170	4	N/A	N/A	>150	Add 1 per 150
	171–230	5	N/A	N/A	–	–
	231–250	6	N/A	N/A	–	–
	>250	Add 1 per 80	N/A	N/A	–	–
All Gender (Based on Total Number of Patrons)	1–50	0	N/A	N/A	1–50	0
	50–500	1	N/A	N/A	50–500	1
	>500	Add 1 per 500	N/A	N/A	>500	Add 1 per 500

(o) for Table F4D4j there were **substituted** –

Table F4D4j Sanitary facilities in Class 9b Buildings – Sports Venues or the Like

User Group	*Closet Pans*		*Urinals*		*Washbasins*	
	Design Occupancy	*Number*	*Design Occupancy*	*Number*	*Design Occupancy*	*Number*
Male Participants	1–20	1	1–10	0	1–10	1
	>20	Add 1 per 20	>10	Add 1 per 10	>10	Add 1 per 10
Female	1–10	1	N/A	N/A	1–10	1
Participants	>10	Add 1 per 10	N/A	N/A	>10	Add 1 per 10
All Gender	1–100	1	N/A	N/A	1–100	1
(Based on Total Number of Participants)	>100	Add 1 per 100	N/A	N/A	>100	Add 1 per 100
Male Spectators	1–250	1	1–100	1	1–150	1
or Patrons	251–500	2	>100	Add 1 per 100	>150	Add 1 per 150
	>500	Add 1 per 500	–	–	–	–
Female Spectators	1–15	1	N/A	N/A	1–60	1
or Patrons	16–60	2	N/A	N/A	6 1–200	2
	61–120	3	N/A	N/A	20 1–350	3
	>120	Add 1 per 70	N/A	N/A	>350	Add 1 per 150
All Gender	1–500	1	N/A	N/A	1–500	1
(Based on Total Number of Spectators or Patrons)	>500	Add 1 per 500	N/A	N/A	>500	Add 1 per 500

(p) for Table F4D4k there were **substituted** –

Table F4D4k Sanitary Facilities in Class 9b Buildings – Churches, Chapels or the Like

User Group	*Closet Pans*		*Urinals*		*Washbasins*	
	Design Occupancy	*Number*	*Design Occupancy*	*Number*	*Design Occupancy*	*Number*
Male Patrons	1–300	1	1–200	1	1–250	1
	>300	Add 1 per 500	>200	Add 1 per 200	>250	Add 1 per 250
Female Patrons	1–150	1	N/A	N/A	1–250	1
	>150	Add 1 per 150	N/A	N/A	>250	Add 1 per 250
All Gender	1–300	1	N/A	N/A	1–300	1
(Based on Total Number of Patrons)	>300	Add 1 per 500	N/A	N/A	>300	Add 1 per 500

(q) for Table F4D4l there were **substituted** –

Table F4D4l Sanitary Facilities in Class 9b Buildings – Public Halls, Function Rooms or the Like

User Group	*Closet Pans*		*Urinals*		*Washbasins*	
	Design Occupancy	*Number*	*Design Occupancy*	*Number*	*Design Occupancy*	*Number*
Male Patrons	1–100	1	1–50	1	1–50	1
	>100	Add 1 per 200	5 1–100	2	5 1–200	2
	–	–	101–150	3	>200	Add 1 per 200
	–	–	151–200	4	–	–
	–	–	201–250	5	–	–
	–	–	>250	Add 1 per 100	–	–
Female Patrons	1–25	1	N/A	N/A	1–50	1
	26–50	2	N/A	N/A	51–150	2
	51–100	3	N/A	N/A	>150	Add 1 per 200
	101–150	4	N/A	N/A	–	–
	151–200	5	N/A	N/A	–	–
	201–250	6	N/A	N/A	–	–
	>250	Add 1 per 100	N/A	N/A	–	–
All Gender (Based on Total Number of Patrons)	1–250	1	N/A	N/A	1–250	1
	>250	Add 1 per 200	N/A	N/A	>250	Add 1 per 200

(r) for clause F4D5(c) there were **substituted** –

'(c) at each bank of toilets where there are one or more toilets in addition to an accessible unisex sanitary compartment at that bank of toilets, not fewer than one sanitary compartment suitable for a person with an ambulant disability for use by males, one sanitary compartment suitable for a person with an ambulant disability for use by females and one all-gender sanitary compartment suitable for a person with an ambulant disability, each in accordance with AS 1428.1, must be provided; and';

(s) for clause F4D6(1)(c)(ii) there were **substituted** –

'(ii) at each bank of sanitary compartments provided in common areas, not fewer than 1.';

(t) for clause F4D6(1)(d)(ii) there were **substituted** –

'(ii) where a storey has more than 1 bank of sanitary compartments, at not less than 50% of those banks."

(u) for clause F4D6(1)(e) there were **substituted** –

"(e) For a Class 10a building, at each bank of sanitary compartments, not fewer than 1.'

(v) clause F4D6(2) were **deleted**; and
(w) clause F4D7(2) were **deleted**.

Note

1 Reg 4: SR No 38/2018 as amended by SR Nos 75/2018, 100/2018, 180/2018, 40/2019, 116/2019, 21/2020, 42/2020, 83/2020, 101/2020, 73/2021, 128/2021, 50/2022 and 61/2022.

Chapter 10A

Commentary on *Let Us Pee*

Nicole Kalms and Laura McVey

Debates on the implementation of gender-neutral facilities extend across various sectors in both society and scholarship. What began in the realm of academic rhetoric and socio-cultural commentaries has increasingly shifted into legislation and architectural briefs.[1] Most urban planners argue that the provisions of public amenity (broadly defined as any toilet 'away from home') should be informed by the proportions and needs of the different sections of society.[2] Yet, in public spaces, gender-neutral amenity is viewed as the solution that can best resist bias and discrimination with segregated facilities increasingly criticised for excluding members of trans and gender-diverse communities. We argue that the proposed legislative changes for the provision of 'all gender', 'gender-neutral' or 'unisex' toilets (or GNTs) operate under an incorrect assumption that gender neutrality will lead to greater inclusion. This is evidenced in the proposed legislative changes which note that one in 500 people in Victoria identify as trans, but fail to acknowledge that one in two Victorians are women, and that these women will be impacted by this legislative change.[3] Through putting forward a needs-based redesign, our argument highlights that rather than offering inclusivity, GNTs will likely further penalise those already disadvantaged in current public amenity design: marginalised people.

Within the disciplinary context of urban design, architecture and planning the built environment, the implementation of GNTs may appear to reconcile the social and political complexity of gender identity, assignation, expression and appearance. Yet the implementation of legislation for GNTs will result in the further privileging of 'default male' needs.[4] This is because the built environment is not a tabula rasa: the design and retrofit of public places – including the provision of gender-neutral and/or all gender facilities – occurs within a complex system of existing public infrastructure and amenity. In this context, owners, property managers, governments and communities have limited space, are constrained by budgets and inevitably have an inconsistent commitment to quality public amenity or gender equality. The likely outcome of such proposed building amendments will result in *cosmetic* changes at best, mere rhetorical reworks at

DOI: 10.4324/9781003372462-21

Figure 10A.1 Typical examples of women's public sanitary facilities being repurposed as gender-neutral

Credit: Monash University XYX Lab.

worst, rather than a substantive public infrastructure redesign that delivers greater inclusion.

The proposed legislation will shape the retrofit of existing buildings as well as new construction. For many owners, property managers, governments and communities, there will be an additional cost to incorporate the proposed amendment. This will multiply the ad hoc arrangements where a sign and /symbol on an existing 'female' or 'disabled' toilet provides a 'gender-neutral' or 'all genders' amenity, leaving the men's facility intact (indeed doubling men's toilet options). This point is locally illustrated by Chloe Booker's article, which promotes the idea that 'workplaces wouldn't necessarily need to build new bathrooms, but could reconfigure existing ones as all-gender toilets at a low cost'.[5] Similarly, a recent 'all-gender access toolkit' published by the Good Night Out campaign in partnership with Galop *We All Need the Toilet! An All Gender Access Toolkit* – was accompanied with the comment: 'If you have a wheelchair accessible toilet, then you already have an all-gender toilet on the premises!'[6] This change erodes the limited dedicated space for certain users, and further neglects the needs of those already marginalised in urban design, architecture and planning of public amenities.[7]

So while GNTs may appear to offer more inclusivity for trans and gender-diverse people, we suggest in practice it requires all socio-culturally neglected groups (including trans and gender-diverse people as well as breastfeeding women, people with children, older people, homeless people and migrant and culturally diverse women) to adapt to an amendment that functions as an 'add-on' to an enduring structure that privileges antiquated notions of men's needs. Further, the ways in which systemic discrimination and everyday racism manifests for First Nations people (such as heightened risk of homelessness, household crowding, the likelihood of living in underserved communities lacking adequate housing maintenance and public infrastructure and being ostracised from freely using certain public areas) means they both face a disproportionate requirement to use public sanitation facilities, as well as suffering exclusion and control in the design, signage and placement of public facilities.[8] Within the context of public austerity, political lobbying and the increasing requirements for universal access design (that is, ensuring amenities can be accessed by people of all ages and abilities), there is a longer-term consequence where GNTs become the *only* provision. Taken together, already marginalised groups will be burdened by any design that continues to work without the material realities and practical uses of public facilities.

We therefore suggest that current reform proposals for inclusivity do not go far enough, and put forward the need for a more 'radical redesign'[9] of public sanitary facilities. Such a radical redesign, we argue, requires a needs-based design ethos based on users' requirements. This approach reiterates the importance of more inclusive design, but does so by considering and prioritising those most significantly and disproportionately impacted and neglected by current design.

A needs-based approach highlights that public facilities are more than basic amenities: they are multipurpose spaces shaped by social, cultural and spatial factors, which are often required to meet users' personal needs (including activities illegal in public settings such as smoking, drug use and sex) and biological needs (which are often sources of discomfort and shame).[10] The personal and biological needs of users may also be intersecting and can include breastfeeding, menstruation, incontinence, caring for a child or dependent adult and socially or culturally required cleaning (for reasons such as homelessness, faith-based rituals or in-transit needs). While not a focus of this commentary, the network of public toilets across cities and communities must meet the needs of the population; the distance people must travel to reach these is a key determinant of access and inclusion. Indeed, for some marginalised groups the intersectional and compounding nature of their socio-political disadvantage, including overcrowding in homes and unreliable, unsafe and substandard public sanitation facilities, points to the importance of public facilities that are designed with cultural competency for the needs of people and places.[11] Despite these critical needs, the quality and quantity of public sanitation facilities influence the likelihood of such groups of people to use – or frequently, avoid using – public sanitary facilities.[12]

In considering who most frequently requires public facilities and their needs, we argue the provision of spaces that support care, comfort and refuge is paramount. This would allow sanitary facilities to fulfil the unique function of being at once a public *and* a private space.[13]

Care

Women from culturally and religiously diverse backgrounds are neglected and frequently require sex-segregated and private spaces – including requiring privacy to wash and remove items of clothing, such as hijabs – and hence are unable to use gender-neutral facilities.[14] For decades, international students, for example, have been excluded from facilities provided in Australian universities, frequently reporting difficulty using standard facilities that lack a wet bathroom.[15]

For many women, public sanitary facilities are places where they access family and domestic violence materials as well as information about sexual harassment and assault. These messages function as a result of a sex-segregation context. While the provision of sanitary items is increasing in public sanitary facilities, a design focused on care would also include access to basic necessities such as wet wipes, diapers, tampons and pads and drinking water.

Comfort

Taking a care-focused approach would mean that the spatial configuration of public sanitary facilities, as well as the fixtures and fittings, would accommodate the ergonomic needs of pregnant women, children, people with mobility aids and larger people. In public spaces, users may be burdened with additional bags and children and the need to sit down to urinate, all of which require considerable space and time.[16] All toilets should be acoustically comfortable and maintain visual privacy.

Menstruation has been observed as a 'double burden' for women, in that it is both a biological and cultural experience resulting in their social and infrastructural invisibility. Randstad and colleagues state that 'the need to service sanitary bins also frames menstruation as an afterthought' lacking infrastructural consideration.[17] Bins are also required for sharps, diapers and incontinence pads. So, when bins are centrally considered as a part of a needs-based design, rather than being an afterthought, it is not only women but also parents, the elderly, those living with illness or addiction who also become prioritised in public infrastructure design.

Refuge

Ensuring safety and freedom from sexual violence in public sanitary facilities can be partially addressed through crime prevention,[18] but the construction of safe spaces is central and supports both comfort and care. Risk of assault and harassment has been found to be a critical consideration in women's decisions to use public sanitary facilities.[19] For example, women fear sexual assault as a result of predators' use of GNTs; although for some women this is based on previous personal experiences, studies have found many women are conscious of the dangers without having a prior history of assault.[20]

Safety is also a key concern for homeless people alongside care and comfort, with facilities required to be accessible 24 hours a day. The need for intersecting considerations of care, comfort and refuge is also reflected in public facilities being required by many to be quiet and private places to rest.[21]

Conclusion

'Critical scrutiny' is required to unpack 'what-is and a vision for what ought-to-be'[22] when redesigning building amendments for public sanitary facilities. The specific needs, revealed as social and cultural spaces of care, comfort and refuge, indicate a holistic radical redesign approach should be considered. In this commentary, we have put forward an alternate approach for greater inclusion in the design and provisioning of public sanitary facilities.

Notes

1 Meagan Tyler, 'Shared Bathrooms: Moving from Rhetoric to Redesign', *ArchitectureAU* (8 March 2021). https://architectureau.com/articles/shared-bathrooms-moving-from-rhetoric-to-redesign/.
2 Clara Greed, 'Join the Queue: Including Women's Toilet Needs in Public Space' (2019) 67(4) *The Sociological Review* 908; Clara Greed and David Johnson, *Planning in the UK* (Palgrave, 2015); Nicole Kalms, *She City: Designing Out Women's Inequity in Cities* (Bloomsbury, forthcoming).
3 Sara Ortiz Escalante and Blanca Valdivia Gutiérrez, 'Planning from Below: Using Feminist Participatory Methods to Increase Women's Participation in Urban Planning' (2015) 23(1) *Gender & Development* 113; Maryam Heidaripour and Laura Forlano, 'Formgiving to Feminist Futures as Design Activism' (Conference Paper, Design as a Catalyst for Change – DRS International Conference 2018, 25–28 June 2018). https://dl.designresearchsociety.org/drs-conference-papers/drs2018/researchpapers/41.
4 Caroline Criado-Perez, *Invisible Women: Exposing Data Bias in a World Designed for Men* (Vintage, 2019).
5 Chloe Booker, 'All-Gender Bathrooms Proposed for Victorian Workplaces and Footy Ovals', *The Age* (23 April 2021). https://www.theage.com.au/national/victoria/all-gender-bathrooms-proposed-for-victorian-workplaces-and-footy-ovals-20210420-p57ksw.html.

6 Good Night Out and Galop, *We All Need the Toilet! An All Gender Access Toolkit* (Good Night Out Campaign CIC, 2021). https://www.goodnightoutcampaign.org/wp-content/uploads/2021/03/toilets.pdf.
7 Gail Ramster et al., 'How Inclusion Can Exclude: The Case of Public Toilet Provision for Women' (2018) 44(1) *Built Environment* 52.
8 Elizabeth McDonald et al., 'Evaluating a Handwashing with Soap Program in Australian Remote Aboriginal Communities: A Pre and Post Intervention Study Design' (2015) 15(1) *BMC Public Health* 1188; Claire Smith et al., 'The Markers of Everyday Racism in Australia', *The Conversation* (24 January 2017). http://theconversation.com/the-markers-of-everyday-racism-in-australia-71152.
9 Tyler (n 1).
10 Fernanda Deister Moreira et al., 'On-Street Toilets for Sanitation Access in Urban Public Spaces: A Systematic Review' (2021) 70 *Utilities Policy* Article No 101186.
11 Nina Lansbury Hall et al., 'Safe Water and Sanitation in Remote Indigenous Communities in Australia: Conditions towards Sustainable Outcomes' (2022) 26(2) *Australasian Journal of Water Resources* 187; McDonald (n 8).
12 Evawani Ellisa and Linga Luana, 'Female Restrooms in the Tourist Destination: How the Socio-Spatial Conditions of Public Toilets Influence Women's Perception of Safety' (2022) 21(4) *Journal of Asian Architecture and Building Engineering* 1624; Siobhan M Hartigan et al., 'Why Do Women Not Use the Bathroom? Women's Attitudes and Beliefs on Using Public Restrooms' (2020) 17(6) *International Journal of Environmental Research and Public Health* 2053; Ramster et al. (n 7).
13 Ibid.
14 Ibid.
15 Isvet Amri Novera, 'Indonesian Postgraduate Students Studying in Australia: An Examination of Their Academic, Social and Cultural Experiences' (2004) 5(4) *International Education Journal* 475; Jan Schapper, 'The Writing Is on the Wall: The Text(Ure) of Women's Toilets in Australia' (2012) 19(4) *Gender, Place & Culture* 494.
16 Ramster et al. (n 7).
17 Ibid 99.
18 Ellisa and Luana (n 12).
19 Hartigan et al. (n 12); Sheila Jeffreys, 'The Politics of the Toilet: A Feminist Response to the Campaign to "Degender" a Women's Space' (2014) 45 *Women's Studies International Forum* 42.
20 Hartigan et al. (n 12).
21 Katherine Webber, 'We Need to Talk About Public Toilets', *Policy Futures: A Reform Agenda* (2021). https://stories.uq.edu.au/policy-futures/2021/we-need-to-talk-about-public-toilets/index.html.
22 Miriam, Kathy, 'Re-Thinking Radical Feminism: Opposition, Utopianism and the Moral Imagination of Feminist Theory' (PhD Thesis, University of California, Santa Cruz, 1998) iv. https://www.proquest.com/docview/304418169/abstract/CC4551E733EE4110PQ/1.

Part IV

Caring, Dependents and In/dependence

Chapter 11

Assessing Parenting Payment Applications by Parents' Individual Circumstances, not their Relationship Status

Olivia Rundle

Extract from *Hansard* (Commonwealth of Australia)

Social Security Amendment (Fair and Equal Treatment No 1 – Parenting Payment) Bill 2024

Second Reading

HON OLIVIA RUNDLE: I move:

That this Bill be now read a second time.

Reforming the 'Couple Rule' to Make Social Security Fair and Equal

The 'couple rule' provides social security recipients who are in a recognised couple relationship with less financial support than they would receive if they were not in a couple relationship. Bureaucrats apply the definition of a couple in section 4 of the *Social Security Act 1991*[1] to decide whether an applicant or recipient is partnered – and this decision has consequences for both the eligibility for and the quantum of payments. The couple rule creates vulnerability within relationships, as well as unfairness and inequity within the social security system. This Bill is the first of a series to be presented to address negative consequences of the 'couple rule'. As a consequence of this law reform agenda, all recipients of social security benefits will be assessed based upon their individual needs rather than their relationship status. It is part of this government's commitment to make social security payments fair and equal.

DOI: 10.4324/9781003372462-23

This Bill will change the approach to the parenting payment. It will result in single and partnered recipients of the parenting payment being treated equally. Eligibility for all primary carers of young children will be assessed on the basis of their individual circumstances, rather than whether they have an intimate partner or their partner's financial position.

Flawed Assumptions of the 'Couple Rule'

The justification for the differential treatment of partnered social security applicants is that a 'couple can share the cost of day-to-day living whereas a single person needs a relatively higher rate in order to enjoy the same living standard.'[2]

The rule assumes that marriages and 'marriage-like' relationships all involve equal sharing of and access to the resources of the parties to the relationship. It assumes that being in a couple includes being financially responsible for a partner.

The couple rule also assumes that people live in stable and happily interdependent nuclear families raising children of both partners. However, modern patterns of intimate relationships are often fluid, unstable and changeable.[3] Assumptions of relationships' stability and long-term financial interdependence are not evidence-based, but rather fictional ideas about how people live their lives.

The couple rule assumes that primary carers are provided for by their partner, regardless of whether or not their partner actually provides them with financial support.[4] In many circumstances, a recipient has no enforceable right to be financially supported by the person they are deemed to be in a couple relationship with.[5]

Social security claimants are often participating in ambiguous relationships because they are trying to manage with limited resources.[6] Their relationship might be ambiguous because they are trying to avoid stepping into the 'couple zone' with a person with whom they are romantically connected, or because they share a residence with another adult to reduce their living costs. The ambiguity may result in administrative findings that two people are a couple, resulting in financial detriment.

Abolishing the 'Couple Rule' Would be Fair and Equitable

It is unfair to assume that people in couple relationships have a financial advantage compared to people not in such relationships. It is also unfair to treat people in a couple relationship as being the only people who might be able to economise.[7]

This Bill acts upon recommendations that entitlement to social security should be assessed individually. The differential treatment of singles and couples in social security law has been the subject of considerable criticism from feminists,[8] welfare rights experts[9] and law reform bodies.

The 1994 Australian Law Reform Commission Report *Equality Before the Law: Women's Equality* documented the unequal position of women in Australian social security law, particularly sole parents. The ALRC expressed a view that entitlement to social security should be assessed individually,[10] a view which it noted again in its 2011 Family Violence Report.[11]

The current treatment of people who rely on social security benefits ties and assesses them together as a family unit. By contrast, people who pay tax are treated as individuals, regardless of their relationship status, which is only relevant for fringe aspects of taxation. This unequal treatment based upon income-earning capacity is inconsistent with the principle of a fair and equal society.

This Bill Responds to the Realities of Gendered Inequity

Women are less likely than men to be financially independent. In 2020, Australian women's full-time adult average weekly ordinary time earnings were 86% that of men's.[12] Women are three times more likely than men to be part-time or casual employees, and much more likely than men to take extended periods away from the paid workforce to care for young children.[13] Women are therefore more likely than men to rely upon either their partner or the state for financial support.

Expectations of dependence within couple relationships are deeply connected to the gender stereotype of woman as nurturing, passive, domestic, innately caring, vulnerable, weak and incompetent.[14] People of all genders may be the subject of this dependence upon their partner in a couple relationship due to taking on the role of primary caregiver of young children. This Bill is therefore drafted in gender-neutral terms, although in practice it will have a much greater impact upon women due to the far greater proportion of women receiving parenting payments. In 2020, for example, 95% of single recipients and 90.6% of partnered recipients were women.[15]

Current social security law exacerbates women's financial dependence by treating women with partners less favourably than if they were not partnered. This forces a group of people who are already financially disadvantaged into financial dependence within their relationship.[16]

This Bill does not address the social inequity of the disproportionate performance of care by mothers and inequities between parents where one is the 'primary' carer rather than the care being shared equally between them. It does not remove the reality that, in the words of Sharon Thompson, 'the family is a stabilizing force for structural inequality.'[17] Instead, the Bill acknowledges social realities and seeks to improve the situation of primary carers within the context of social inequity. In this way, it is an explicitly feminist piece of legislation.

Disadvantages of the 'Couple Rule'

Statistically, women are disadvantaged by the 'couple rule', which targets vulnerable women. Administrative Appeals Tribunal decisions about the 'couple rule' almost always involve women.[18] Many women do not challenge administrative findings that they have been living in a couple relationship. Consequently, many are found to owe a debt. These women are typically experiencing multiple problems and vulnerabilities, making an administrative appeal unfeasible.[19] Aboriginal and Torres Strait Islander people (8.9%),[20] people living in very remote areas (4.7%)[21] and migrants (4.2%)[22] are more likely than all Australians (1.4%) to receive parenting payment.[23] With most parenting payment recipients living in poverty (72%),[24] parenting payment recipients – particularly single parents – experience poorer mental health than the general population.[25] Further, caring for children limits parents' time to challenge debt allegations or adverse administrative decisions, or to seek help to do so.

Forcing a stay-at-home parent to rely on their partner for financial support increases the opportunity for financial abuse. Financial dependence exacerbates the power dynamic between primary carers and their partners.[26] This applies equally to parents who are married, de facto, in a couple relationship with their child's other parent or in a relationship with a person who is not the parent of their child.

Dr Lyndal Sleep from Griffith University has conducted a considerable amount of empirical work that demonstrates how people are negatively affected by the 'couple rule' in the social security context. In a 2019 ANROWS report,[27] Dr Sleep analysed Administrative Appeals Tribunal cases involving domestic violence and application of the couple rule between 1992 and 2016. Key findings included that victim/survivors were often found to owe a social security debt because their couple relationship was deemed to exist while they were being subjected to violence and control. This was based partly on evidence of the perpetrator's presence at their home, use of their property and other facts that also demonstrated coercive and controlling behaviour. Victim-survivors can be deemed financially dependent upon their abuser, particularly when they are trying to end the relationship and find a safer life for themselves and their children. They may be denied social security, found to owe a debt and sometimes even be prosecuted for fraud.[28] Take the example of 'Michelle', a culturally and linguistically diverse woman with physical and mental disabilities and four children including a baby.[29] Michelle relied upon her abusive ex-partner for support, despite his violent treatment of her, because she lacked an alternative support network in Australia and could not afford to return to her home country.[30] His support was interpreted as a continuation of their couple relationship, and Michelle was asked to repay the parenting payment she had received after their separation – further holding her back financially from being able to escape her violent situation.[31]

The Bill Will Abolish Invasive Scrutiny of Single Parents

Single applicants are currently subjected to scrutiny over whether or not they are actually single. A bureaucrat can evaluate the circumstances of a relationship between two people and declare it to be a couple relationship. Such assessments are subjective, open-ended and vague in application, despite their significance.[32]

Parenting payment (single) is the Centrelink benefit type most commonly prosecuted for fraud.[33] Many more parenting payment (single) recipients are investigated for fraud than are prosecuted, and investigations can lead to a large debt being determined. In Australia, 8.8% of imprisoned women have been convicted for a crime of fraud, deception and related offences,[34] most of these being mothers.

By abolishing the distinction between single and partnered parents, this Bill will avoid the costs of investigating relationship status. This will be a saving for the Department as well as parents, avoiding significant financial, time, stress and relationship costs that do not support parents or children, or provide the desired 'security' of the social security system.

Remedying Unequal Treatment of Single Parents

A single parent should not be treated more favourably than a partnered 'primary' carer for the same parenting work. Currently, the parenting payment enables one parent of children to be their 'primary' carer by providing a small independent income until their child reaches a certain age. The social benefits of supporting someone to perform a fundamental service for family and society warrant the payment of basic living costs to a young child's primary carer. This Bill will ensure that this opportunity is applied fairly and equitably to all parents who are primary carers, regardless of their relationship status.

Distinct eligibility tests and rates of payment apply to applicants who are single and those who are in a couple relationship. Single recipients are assessed using the ordinary income test, while partnered recipients are assessed using a modified version of the benefits income test.

Payments to partnered recipients have always been at a lower rate. When I received parenting payment, it was as a partnered parent; my partner had no income. Although we were sharing the work of parenting, only one of us could apply for parenting payment due to the 'primary' parent model, which prevents the payment being shared by both parents when they co-parent. Our family lived on my parenting payment, at a lower rate than had I been single. The parenting work being done, and therefore the benefit to society, was the same.

While partnered recipients are only eligible until their youngest child turns six, single recipients are eligible until their youngest child turns 14. Until 20 September 2023, single recipients were only eligible for parenting payment until their youngest child turned eight. The justification for raising the age was that '[b]y 14, children have typically settled into high school and need less parental supervision, and single parents are in a much stronger position to take on paid work'.[35] Those observations also apply to children of partnered 'primary' parents. Equal and fair treatment requires that partnered recipients be eligible to apply for parenting payment until their child turns 14.

The assets test restricts eligibility to applicants who own assets below a certain threshold. Currently, the assets test is more generous to single applicants than partnered applicants. In the current test, the relevant assets for partnered applicants include the value of assets owned by their partner. This creates a barrier for parents who are in a relationship with a person who owns assets, regardless of whether or not the applicant has any equitable interest in or use of them. The effect of this approach is to make some parents wholly financially dependent upon their partner by denying them eligibility for parenting payment. This increases stress, especially for blended families and re-partnered single parents, while creating conditions that enable financial abuse to occur.

What This Bill will Change in the Legislation

This Bill will remove the two existing payments 'pension parenting payment (single)' and 'benefit parenting payment (partnered)', replacing these with a single 'parenting payment' category. This Bill changes references to 'pension parenting payment (single)' to 'parenting payment' and repeals provisions specifically applying to 'benefit parenting payment (partnered)'.

Eligibility and rate of payment will be determined by a single set of criteria, applying the more generous approach currently taken for single recipients to all parenting payment recipients. Section 1068A will apply to all applications for parenting payment and includes the rate calculator. Section 1068B and the modules within it, which are the separate rate calculators for parenting payment (partnered), will be repealed.

Jointly owned assets will continue to be assessed according to the value of the applicant's interest in the asset, as provided in section 11(2). For the sake of clarity, a note will make clear that where an asset is owned as joint tenants, the person's interest in the asset will be an equal share with other owners, as if they were tenants in common with equal shares. This is consistent with the approach taken to joint tenancies in calculating capital gains tax.

The Bill's primary achievement is to equalise the treatment of applicants, regardless of their relationship status, while retaining existing approaches to parenting payment that currently apply to single applicants. The Bill does not introduce any new requirements.

This Bill extends eligibility of all parents until their youngest child turns 14. The existing paid workforce participation expectations, currently applying to single recipients from when their youngest child turns six, will apply to all recipients. This equality of expectation is in keeping with the fair and equitable aims of the reforms.

All parenting payment applicants will be eligible to apply for a pensioner concession card, support to participate in education and pharmaceutical allowance. Entitlements such as rent assistance and telephone allowance will be assessed by uniform criteria for all parenting payment recipients.

When this Bill is implemented, recipients of parenting payment will have greater certainty about their entitlements, without a change to their relationship status risking the reclassification of their parenting payment.

Cost Implications of this Bill

This Bill will make more primary carers of young children eligible for parenting payment, or entitled to a higher payment than they currently receive.

While the expansion of eligibility to a greater number of people is expected to increase the overall cost of parenting payment, this financial cost will be a worthwhile investment in supporting parents to raise young children with less financial stress. With early childhood experiences shaping children's development, this Bill supports investment in our country's future.

The financial costs of increased eligibility and rates of parenting payment made will be tempered by the fact that the Department will no longer need to conduct intrusive and expensive inquiries into the relationship circumstances of any parenting payment recipients.[36] We therefore anticipate that the Bill will ultimately be close to cost-neutral.

I commend this Bill to the House.

The Parliament of the Commonwealth of Australia

HOUSE OF REPRESENTATIVES

Social Security Amendment (Fair and Equal Treatment No 1 – Parenting Payment) Bill 2024

A Bill for an Act to amend the *Social Security Act 1991* (Cth), and for related purposes

The Parliament of Australia enacts:

1 Short title

This Act is the *Social Security Amendment (Fair and Equal Treatment No 1 – Parenting Payment) Act 2024.*

2 Commencement

1) Each provision of this Act specified in column 1 of the table commences, or is taken to have commenced, in accordance with column 2 of the table. Any other statement in column 2 has effect according to its terms.

Column 1	**Column 2**
Provision(s)	**Commencement**
1. Sections 1 to 3 and anything in this Act not elsewhere covered by this table	The day on which this Act receives the Royal Assent.
2. Schedule 1	The later of: (a) 1 January 2024; and (b) the day after this Act receives the Royal Assent.

3 Schedule(s)

Each Act that is specified in a Schedule to this Act is amended or repealed as set out in the applicable items in the Schedule concerned, and any other item in a Schedule to this Act has effect according to its terms.

Schedule 1 – Parenting payment

Social Security Act 1991

1 **Paragraph** 7(6AA)(b)

Omit 'pension PP (single), benefit PP (partnered)', substitute 'parenting payment'.

2 **Section 11**

After subsection (2) insert a note:

> Note: Where a person owns an asset as a joint tenant, for the purposes of calculating their interest in a particular asset, they will be treated as a tenant in common having equal shares with other joint tenants.

Repeal subsection (10AA); and
Repeal paragraph (10A)(d).

3 **Section 18**

Repeal the section, substitute:

> **18 Definition of parenting payment**
> In this Act, unless the contrary intention appears:
>
> *parenting payment* means payment whose rate is worked out under the Parenting Payment Rate Calculator in section 1068A.

4 **Subsection 19C(8)**

In paragraph (da) omit '; or', substitute '.'; and
Repeal paragraph (e).

5 **Paragraph 19D(5)(i)**

Repeal the paragraph.

6 **Section 23**

Omit the definition 'benefit PP (partnered): see section 18';
Omit the definition 'non-benefit PP (partnered): see section 18';
Omit the definition 'pension PP (single): see section 18'; and
In the definition of 'social security benefit' omit paragraph (f).

7 **Subsection 500(1)**

In paragraph (c) omit 'is not a member of a couple and'; and
In paragraph (d)(i) omit 'the person is not a member of a couple and'.

8 **Section 500D**

Omit paragraph (1)(b);
In paragraph (1)(c) omit '6', substitute '14'; and
Repeal subsection (2).

9 Section 500Q

In subsection (2) omit 'who is not a member of a couple';
In the subsection (2) Table heading omit 'for a person who is not a member of a couple'; and
Repeal subsections (3), (4) and (5).

10 Paragraph 500S(2)(b)

Omit 'pension PP (single) or a social security benefit other than a benefit PP (partnered)', substitute 'parenting payment'.

11 Section 500V

Repeal the section.

12 Section 501D

Repeal paragraph 501D(1)(a), substitute:

(a) because of the application of Module E of the Parenting Payment Rate Calculator, the person is receiving a parenting payment at a rate that has been reduced; or

Repeal paragraph 501D(2)(a), substitute:

(a) is satisfied that because of the application of Module E of the Parenting Payment Rate Calculator, the person is receiving a parenting payment at a rate that has been reduced; or

13 Section 503

Omit everything after 'A person's parenting payment rate is worked out using', substitute ' the Parenting Payment Rate Calculator at the end of Section 1068A (see Part 3.6A).'

14 Paragraph 1061A(6)(a)

Omit 'from benefit PP (partnered) to pension PP (single)'.

15 Section 1061ED

Omit paragraph (3) definition of 'annual payment rate', substitute:

annual payment rate means – if the person was receiving parenting payment on the last payday before the application for the advance payment was lodged – the rate at which the payment was payable under the Parenting Payment Rate Calculator to the person on that payday, disregarding any amount payable by way of remote area allowance.

16 Section 1061EE

Omit 'benefit PP (partnered), ' from the following:

Subsection (1);
Subheading to subsection (4); and
Subsection (4); and
Repeal paragraph (6)(a).

17 Paragraph 1061JU(4)(i)

Repeal the paragraph.

18 Section 1061PJ

Repeal paragraph (2)(dc) and subsection (2D).

19 Paragraph 1061PZG(1)(b)(ia)

In the paragraph and Note 1, omit ', newstart allowance or benefit PP (partnered)', substitute 'or newstart allowance'.

20 Section 1061Q

Repeal subsections (2D), (3A), (3G) and (3H);
In paragraph (3)(a), omit ', benefit PP (partnered)'; and
In paragraph (3F)(a), omit '(iv) benefit PP (partnered)'.

21 Section 1061ZA

Repeal paragraph (2)(b)(iv) and subsection (2D).

22 Paragraph 1061ZD(5A)(c)

Omit the paragraph.

23 Paragraph 1061ZDA(2)(c)

Repeal the paragraph.

24 Paragraph 1061ZEA(2)(ga)(ii)

Omit ', or who ceases to receive benefit PP (partnered)'.

25 Paragraph 1061ZEB(4)(ba)

Repeal the paragraph.

26 Paragraph 1061ZK(5)(f)

Repeal the paragraph.

27 Paragraph 1061ZMA(2)(ga)

Omit content up to 'the person is qualified for a health care card until', substitute 'the person continues to be qualified for the payment referred to in subsection 1061ZK(5)'.

28 Paragraph 1067F(1)(d)

Repeal item (xiii).

29 Section 1067G (Module L, Table)

Repeal item 26.

30 Paragraph 1067K(1)(d)

Repeal item (xii).

31 Section 1068A

In the heading, omit '– pension PP (single)'; and
Repeal subsections (1), (2) and (3), substitute:

(1) Parenting payment is worked out in accordance with the rate calculator at the end of this section.

32 Section 1068B

Repeal the section, including the calculator.

33 Paragraph 1070(f)

Omit the paragraph, substitute 'Parenting Payment Rate Calculator (parenting payments)'

34 Subsection 1210(4)

Repeal item 8 in the Table.

35 Paragraph 1224EA(d)

Omit ' or benefit PP (partnered)'.

36 Amendments of listed provisions

Further amendments

Item	*Provision*	*Omit*	*Substitute*
1	Paragraph 4(6A)(f)	Pension PP (Single)	Parenting Payment
2	Subsection 7(6AA) *first occurring*	pension PP (single)	parenting payment
3	Subsection 11(13)	pension PP (single)	parenting payment
4	Paragraph 19C(8)(da)	pension PP (single)	parenting payment

(Continued)

Further amendments

Item	*Provision*	*Omit*	*Substitute*
5	Paragraph 19C(8)(da)	Pension PP	Parenting Payment
6	Paragraph 19D(5)(h)	pension PP (single)	parenting payment
7	Section 23 definitions of 'social security pension' and 'special employment advance qualifying entitlement'	pension PP (single)	parenting payment
8	Subsections 500VA (1), (2) and (3)	pension PP (single)	parenting payment
9	Paragraph 514A(1)(a) and Note 1	benefit PP (partnered)	parenting payment
10	514C (Lump Sum Calculator, method statement, step 4)	pension PP (single)	parenting payment
11	Subsection 514D(2)	benefit PP (partnered)	parenting payment
12	Subsection 514D(3)	pension PP (single)	parenting payment
13	Subsection 514D(3), Note 3	pension PP (single) and benefit PP (partnered)	parenting payment
14	Section 514E (Lump Sum Calculator, method statement, step 4)	pension PP (single)	parenting payment
15	Chapter 2 Part 2.13A Division 1 Heading	pension PP (single)	parenting payment
16	Section 665A Heading and paragraph (a)	pension PP (single)	parenting payment
17	Paragraph 665M(a)	pension PP (single)	parenting payment
18	Paragraph 729(2)(bb)	benefit PP (partnered)	parenting payment
19	Section 1061ED Heading, subsection (1) and subsection (4) example	pension PP (single)	parenting payment

(*Continued*)

Further amendments			
Item	*Provision*	*Omit*	*Substitute*
20	Section 1061JC note (f) of definition of 'pharmaceutical allowance rate'	Pension PP (Single)	Parenting Payment
21	Paragraph 1061JU(4)(h)	pension PP (single)	parenting payment
22	Paragraph 1061PE(4)(d)	pension PP (single)	parenting payment
23	Paragraph 1061PJ(2)(d)	pension PP (single)	parenting payment
24	Subsection 1061Q(3E)	pension PP (single)	parenting payment
25	Section 1061ZDA Heading, paragraphs (1)(a) and (4)(b)	pension PP (single)	parenting payment
26	Paragraph 1061ZEA(2)(ga)(ii)	pension PP (single)	parenting payment
27	Paragraph 1061ZEB(2)(c)(ii)	pension PP (single)	parenting payment
28	Section 1061ZM paragraphs (1B)(a) and (3)(a)(i)	pension PP (single)	parenting payment
29	Paragraph 1067F(1)(d) item (x)	pension PP (single)	parenting payment
30	Point 1067G-B3A *wherever occurring*	Pension PP (Single)	Parenting Payment
31	Point 1067G-B3A	pension PP (single)	parenting payment
32	Section 1067G (Module L, Table), item 17	Pension PP (Single)	Parenting payment
33	Paragraph 1067K(1)(d), item (ix)	pension PP (single)	parenting payment
34	Point 1068-B1, Note 8	Pension PP (Single)	Parenting Payment
35	Point 1068-B5 *wherever occurring*	Pension PP (Single)	Parenting Payment

(*Continued*)

Further amendments

Item	*Provision*	*Omit*	*Substitute*
36	Section 1068A, Heading to the Calculator	Pension PP (Single)	Parenting Payment
37	Section 1068A (Module A), point 1068A-A1 and method statement, step 7	Pension PP (Single)	Parenting Payment
38	Paragraph 1070A(b)	Pension PP (Single)	Parenting Payment
39	Paragraph 1070E(a)	Pension PP (Single)	Parenting Payment
40	Subsection 1070M(1)	Pension PP (Single)	Parenting Payment
41	Subsection 1070T(1)	Pension PP (Single)	Parenting Payment
42	Subsection 1129(1A) and note	pension PP (single)	parenting payment
43	Section 1130B Heading	Pension PP (Single)	Parenting Payment
44	Section 1130B paragraphs (1)(a) and 2(b) *wherever occurring*	pension PP (single)	parenting payment
45	Section 1130C Heading, Subsections (1), (2) and subheading to (2), and (9)	pension PP (single)	parenting payment
46	Section 1159 paragraphs (1)(a) and (2)(a)	pension PP (single)	parenting payment
47	Subsection 1161(2)	pension PP (single)	parenting payment
48	Section 1190 (Table) column 2 of items 1, 24, 25, 28 and 29.	pension PP (single)	parenting payment
49	Section 1190 (Table) column 4 of items 1, 20 and 44	Pension PP (Single)	Parenting Payment
50	Subsection 1192(5AAA)	Pension PP (Single)	Parenting Payment

(*Continued*)

Further amendments

Item	*Provision*	*Omit*	*Substitute*
51	Subsection 1196(1)	pension PP (single)	parenting payment
52	Section 1210 paragraph (2A)(c) (iii) and subsection (4), item 7	pension PP (single)	parenting payment
53	Paragraph 1228B(1) (b)(v)	pension PP (single)	parenting payment
54	Paragraph 1237AAC(6)(b)	PP (partnered)	Parenting Payment

37 Application

The amendments made by this Schedule apply, on or after the commencement of this Schedule, in relation to a person who made a claim for parenting payment on or after 1 January 2018 that was granted on or after that date.

Notes

1 Compilation No 206 (currency start 1 January 2023), https://www.legislation.gov.au/Details/C2023C00030.
2 Australian Law Reform Commission (ALRC), *Family Violence and Commonwealth Laws: Improving Legal Frameworks*, Final Report No 117 (Report, November 2011) [5.16].
3 Australia's National Research Organisation for Women's Safety Limited (ANROWS), *Domestic Violence, Social Security and the Couple Rule* (Research Report, July 2019) 11.
4 Tamar Hopkins, 'Divorcing Marital Status from Social Security Payments' (2005) 30(4) *Alternative Law Journal* 189.
5 Ibid 191.
6 Kieran Tranter et al., 'The Cohabitation Rule: Indeterminacy and Oppression in Australian Social Security Law' (2008) 32(2) *Melbourne University Law Review* 698, 726.
7 Ibid; Hopkins (n 4) 189–90.
8 Terry Carney, 'Women & Social Security/Transfer Payments Law' (Legal Studies Research Paper No 10/93, Sydney Law School, October 2010); Tranter et al. (n 6) 700–1 discuss feminist critique of the rule.
9 Lyndal Sleep et al., 'The Cohabitation Rule in Social Security Law: The More Things Change the More They Stay the Same' (2006) 13(3) *Australian Journal of Administrative Law* 135, 144; Hopkins (n 4); Lyndal Sleep, 'Women Doubly Governed: Offering a Governmentality Analysis to Solve the Apparent Paradox of the Current Cohabitation Rule' (Conference Paper, Sociology for a Mobile World, The Australian Sociological Association, University of Western Australia and Murdoch University, 4–7 December 2006).

10 Australian Law Reform Commission (ALRC), *Equality Before the Law: Women's Equality*, Report No 69, Part II, 21 December 1994) [12.11].
11 ALRC (2011) (n 2) [6.7] where the earlier recommendation was noted.
12 Australian Bureau of Statistics, *Gender Indicators* (released 15 December 2020, reference period 2020). https://www.abs.gov.au/statistics/people/people-and-communities/gender-indicators-australia/2020.
13 Ibid.
14 Catharine A MacKinnon, 'Feminism, Marxism, Method, and the State: An Agenda for Theory' in David Kennedy et al. (eds), *The Canon of American Legal Thought* (Princeton University Press, 2006) 857.
15 Department of Social Security (DSS), *DSS Benefit and Payment Recipient Demographics – Quarterly Data December 2020*. https://data.gov.au/dataset/ds-dga-cff2ae8a-55e4-47db-a66d-e177fe0ac6a0/distribution/dist-dga-0429d083-d8d2-4fff-bc75-f9100e1723ad/details?q=.
16 Carney (n 8).
17 Sharon Thompson, 'Feminist Relational Contract Theory: A New Model for Family Property Agreements' (2018) 45(4) *Journal of Law and Society* 617, 622.
18 Tranter et al. (n 6) 726.
19 Ibid 728.
20 Australian Institute of Health and Welfare (AIHW), *Unemployment and Parenting Income Support Payments*. https://www.aihw.gov.au/reports/aus/228/employment/unemployment-and-parenting-income-support-payments, citing 2021 statistics.
21 Ibid.
22 Department of Social Services, National Centre for Longitudinal Data, *Building a New Life in Australia (BNLA): The Longitudinal Study of Humanitarian Migrants – Findings from the First Three Waves* (2017). https://dataverse.ada.edu.au/dataverse/DSSLongitudinalStudies 61, citing 2013–18 statistics.
23 AIHW (n 20).
24 Australian Council of Social Service and UNSW Sydney, *Poverty in Australia 2023: Who is Affected* (Poverty and Inequality Partnership Report No 20, 2023). https://povertyandinequality.acoss.org.au/poverty-in-australia-2023-who-is-affected/ 11, citing 2019–20 statistics.
25 Kim M Kiely and Peter Butterworth, 'Social Disadvantage and Individual Vulnerability: A Longitudinal Investigation of Welfare Receipt and Mental Health in Australia' (2013) 47(7) *Australian & New Zealand Journal of Psychiatry* 654.
26 Thompson (n 17) 631.
27 ANROWS (2019) (n 3).
28 ALRC (2011) (n 2) [6.2].
29 ANROWS (2019) (n 3) 35 citing AAT Matter No 2011/78.
30 Ibid.
31 Ibid.
32 Sleep et al. (n 9).
33 Australian Institute of Criminology, *Welfare Fraud in Australia: Dimensions and Issues* (Trends & Issues in Crime and Criminal Justice No 421, June 2011).
34 ABS (n 12).
35 Prime Minister of Australia, 'Extending the Financial Safety Net for Single Parents' (media release, 8 May 2023). https://www.pm.gov.au/media/extending-financial-safety-net-single-parents.
36 Greg Marston and Tamara Walsh, 'A Case of Misrepresentation' (2008) 17(1) *Griffith Law Review* 285, 287–8; Hopkins (n 4) 193.

Chapter 11A

Commentary on *Assessing Parenting Payment Applications by Parents' Individual Circumstances, not their Relationship Status*

Lyndal Sleep

I welcome this Bill and applaud its aim to address some of the impacts of the patriarchal and gender-inequitable aspects of the previous legislation, especially due to the 'couple rule'. It will make a tangible difference to the lives and life chances of Parent Payment (Single) recipients and their children. This is important. However, the gender-fractured impact of the couple rule[1] does not stop at Parent Payment (Single), but permeates through all payments administered by the *Social Security Act*. The couple rule is an umbrella rule that impacts most payment categories including Age Pension, Jobseeker Allowance, Youth Allowance, Disability Support Pension and others. The couple rule has negative impacts not just on single parents and their children, but also on people with disabilities, people who are currently unemployed, young people, older people and people in positions of intersectional disadvantage who experience two or more forms of marginalisation.

For example, women with disabilities were the second-largest category who had trouble with the couple rule in research that investigated AAT couple rule decisions that reported domestic violence.[2] This research showed that the couple rule has been applied where women with disability are dependent on care from the perpetrator, entrenching their vulnerability. A situation specific to women with disability at the intersection of domestic violence and the couple rule emerged in AAT Matter No 2011/23, where Mary[3] had taken out a Violence Restraining Order against her ex-partner and the father of her children. However, Mary also suffered from a number of psychological issues as well as renal issues, which meant that she often found it difficult to care for her children on her own. Mary did not have an extended family network that she could ask for help:

> [N]o siblings or even close friends, so her only recourse was to ask her estranged husband to help with the children, because she knew that they would be put in foster care otherwise.[4]

Indeed, this need for support was identified by her doctor in the AAT decision:

DOI: 10.4324/9781003372462-24

> I believe she can care for her children as a full-time parent in her current state, however she is in need of significant support. Most of this support comes from her husband [perpetrator]. In the past she has repeatedly told me she has needed her husband [perpetrator] even though he does not live with her. They have been separated for some years but [perpetrator] continues helping out at home whilst she was dealing with her anxiety and depression.[5]

Unfortunately, this meant that the perpetrator had 'lived at [Mary's] places quite a lot' because she had been 'sick quite a lot', which was interpreted by social security decision-makers as a relationship according to the couple rule.[6] This placed Mary in a particularly vulnerable position in relation to the perpetrator. While independent access to her own financial resources was an important safety factor for Mary, this application of the couple rule threatened to decrease or stop her payment. However, the abusive and controlling behaviour of the perpetrator, and Mary's particular vulnerability and dependence, was not considered a special condition when applying the couple rule. Mary was required to repay the full amount of debt incurred from claiming the single rate of payment.

Older women are also subjected to intersectional gendered harms that are entrenched and magnified by the couple rule. A situation specific to older women in AAT decisions of couple rule matters experiencing family violence emerged in my previous research, where violence was from a grown child or extended family member towards the older women.[7] For example, in AAT Matter No 2006/725, Robyn[8] had custody of her grandchildren, but was subjected to violence and threats from the children's father – her son. The son was also accused of sexual abuse of the children. Although Robyn and her husband James had never divorced, they had considered themselves separated for many years and the marriage over. According to a social worker's report included in the AAT decision, the need to protect Robyn and her grandchildren from her son's violence 'has emphasised [alleged partner James's[9]] need to reside in the home'.[10] According to the couple rule, the protection that James provided for Robyn was considered evidence for their possible continued relationship. This type of family violence resonates with the literature on elder abuse.[11] However, the couple rule, by denying financial support to Robyn while caring for her grandchildren and pressuring her to live without the sense of protection that came from residing with her ex-husband, added to the stress of her situation and placed Robyn and her grandchildren at greater risk of further harm.

The issue, as touched on in the Second Reading Speech, is that unlike Australian taxation law, the *Social Security Act* treats individuals who are in a 'relationship' as a single economic unit. This means that the member of a couple who is most marginalised from employment or economic resources, usually a woman, experiences access to social security payment dependent on the income and assets of their partner. As mentioned in the Second Reading Speech, in situations of domestic violence (including financial abuse), this ties a woman's access to social security payment to the income and assets of the perpetrator. It also means that when both alleged members of a couple are receiving social security payment, they receive the lesser 'coupled' payment rate. Because it is the couple rule that engrains this dynamic, the obvious solution is to abolish the rule and make *individuals* the assessable unit for the purposes of social security eligibility, regardless of the income and assets of any perceived 'partner'. This is a recommendation of recent research by Economic Justice Australia,[12] as well as my previous work on the couple rule with ANROWS.[13]

The couple rule's gendered harms do not stop at single parents. The couple rule harms women in various positions of intersectional disadvantage while entrenching marginalisation and interrupting the various ways that women arrange their lives to improve their sense of safety. Providing social security payment to people as individuals, regardless of their perceived relationship status, is an important step towards achieving gender equality in Australia. It aligns with current expectations of financial independence in relationships, and works towards acknowledging the care work that women who are outside the paid workforce often undertake which, to paraphrase Carole Pateman,[14] have always subsidised the welfare state by providing care for free. I view this Bill as a step towards gender equality in the *Social Security Act*, but look forward to future legislation that abolishes the couple rule from the eligibility criteria for all Australian social security payments. Assessing people's eligibility as individual economic units regardless of perceived relationship status is a necessary step towards reducing gender harms caused by social security legislation as well as important work towards moving away from the gendered assumptions and exploitations at the core of our welfare state apparatus.

Notes

1 *Social Security Act 1991* (Cth) section 4.3.
2 *Domestic Violence, Social Security and the Couple Rule* (ANROWS Research Report, April 2019).
3 Not her real name.
4 AAT Matter No 2011/23 [44 (f)].
5 AAT Matter No 2011/23 [43].
6 AAT Matter No 2011/23 [28].
7 Ibid n(2).
8 Not her real name.
9 Not his real name.
10 AAT Matter No 2006/725 [23 (b)].

11 See, for example, Australian Law Reform Commission, *Elder Abuse: A National Legal Response* (Final Report, 14 June 2017) 131; Rae Kaspiew and Rachel Carson, 'Elder Abuse in Australia' (2016) *Family Matters* 98, 64–73. https://search.informit.org/doi/10.3316/agispt.20172024.
12 Economic Justice Australia, *Debt, Duress and Dob-Ins: Centrelink Compliance Processes and Domestic Violence* (Report, November 2021).
13 *Domestic Violence, Social Security and the Couple Rule* (ANROWS Research Report, April 2019).
14 Carol Pateman, *The Disorder of Women: Democracy, Feminism and Political Theory* (Polity Press, 1989) 193.

Chapter 12

Gender and its Relevance to Sentence

Natalia Antolak-Saper

Extract from *Hansard* (Parliament of Victoria)

Sentencing (Reducing Women in Custody) Bill 2024

Second Reading

HON NATALIA ANTOLAK-SAPER: I move:

That the Bill be now read a second time.

This Bill proposes significant amendments to the *Sentencing Act 1991* (Vic) that aim to reduce the number of women in custody for non-violent offences. Women offenders are often imprisoned for non-violent offences, with a significant number receiving sentences of imprisonment of under 12 months. Such relatively short sentences may be extremely detrimental to the social structures supporting offenders, and fail to provide appropriate treatment for the underlying causes of their offending. The Government wants to ensure that imprisonment is truly a sanction of last resort, particularly for non-violent offences. This Bill therefore introduces a presumption against sentences of imprisonment for 12 months or less unless there are exceptional circumstances.

Sentences of imprisonment, even of short duration, can have devastating impacts on the children of prisoners. As women are overwhelmingly responsible for the care of children, this issue disproportionately affects women offenders. Under current law, the impact of a sentence on dependants can only be taken into account in 'exceptional circumstances'. This Bill removes that hurdle and requires the court to take into account the likely impact of a sentence on the offender's dependent children. Why should the children of caregiving offenders, facing separation from their parent as a result of the criminal justice system, be treated differently from children who are separated from their parents in the Family Court?[1] This is supported by the

DOI: 10.4324/9781003372462-25

introduction of a court-ordered pre-sentence report specifically addressing factors that may impact the dependent child.

Complementing these amendments, the government intends to introduce a further Bill reinstating a home detention regime for sentences of 12 months or less. This will allow the court to assist non-violent offenders to maintain their connection with family and community, helping to facilitate rehabilitation.

Although primarily aimed at addressing factors that negatively impact women offenders, these amendments are gender-neutral and achieve more just outcomes for all defendants, in particular those with dependent children, without compromising community safety.

Women in Prison

In recent years, Victoria has experienced a substantial increase in the use of imprisonment as a result of the former government's failed so-called 'tough on crime' policies. Between 2010 and 2020, the Victorian prison population increased by 58%. The percentage of women prisoners increased by 29% over that period. Although there was a significant decrease in 2020, this was likely due to the impact of COVID-19 on sentencing, such as an increase in trial adjournments and a preference by courts for non-custodial sentences to avoid associated health risks.[2] This decrease is, therefore, likely a result of responses to the pandemic and not indicative of a sustained decline in women prisoners. Indigenous women are also overrepresented in these figures, with 10% of women prisoners being Aboriginal or Torres Strait Islander.[3]

When women offend, their offences are more likely to be non-violent or less serious than men's. In 2017, the main serious charges or offences for most women prisoners in Victoria were drug offences, assaults and property offences other than burglary, while for men they were assaults, sex offences and drug offences.[4] In 2020, 37% of women prisoners were sentenced for property or drug offences as their most serious offence, compared to 23% of men.[5] Even where these prisoners are violent, they are often accompanied by significant mitigating factors that may result in a reduced sentence, for example, a history of abuse, substance dependency and mental illness. Further, the proportion of women imprisoned for homicide, sex offences, or robbery and extortion has decreased, suggesting that women are committing very serious crimes at a declining rate.[6]

Offences committed by women are more often the result of troubled lives than of a deliberate course of action. Many women prisoners present with what has been described as the 'triumvirate' of factors – a history of victimisation, including sexual abuse and family violence, substance dependency and mental illness.[7] They are also more likely to offend due to their relationships (for example, committing offences to support someone else's drug use).[8] In its paper, 'Women in the Victorian Prison System', the Department of Justice and Community Safety identified women prisoners as presenting with unique needs, including:

- 'the role that personal relationships, victimisation and trauma have in contributing to women's offending;
- women's complex and varied health needs, including chronic conditions and mental health concerns; and
- the extent to which substance abuse links with women's offending and reflects past victimisation and trauma.'[9]

Gender is not a generally a relevant consideration to sentencing.[10] However, courts should not ignore factors that are closely related to gender and which may impact on the hardship associated with a particular sentence. For example, pregnancy may make a term of imprisonment more onerous.[11] Similarly, a transgender woman who is required to serve a period of imprisonment in a men's prison will likely serve their time under more restrictive conditions than other prisoners.[12]

I am not suggesting that women should be sentenced more leniently simply because of their gender. This Government does not shy away from the need to imprison offenders who are a danger to the community. I simply highlight that as a class of offender, women are more likely to be committing non-violent offences, and would therefore benefit from treatment and maintaining social relationships. In 2020, 25% of female prisoners were serving a sentence of 12 months or less.[13] This indicates that these offenders are not necessarily a threat to the community and that other forms of community-based punishments can be imposed that allow the underlying causes of the offending to be addressed.

A Presumption against Short Sentences

Although short sentences may appear to be lenient, these terms are sufficiently long to disrupt the offender's home life, relationships and employment, but not long enough to develop strategies to readjust to life on the outside or receive treatment and/or access programmes. As the UK Ministry of Justice stated in its Female Offender Strategy:

> [s]hort sentences offer limited public protection and fail to offer time for meaningful rehabilitative activity. In some cases, short sentences can aggravate vulnerabilities and raise the risk of reoffending. Going into custody often causes huge disruption to the lives of offenders and their families, causing crises in employment, housing and contact with dependents.[14]

As women prisoners represent a relatively small percentage of the overall prisoner population, they may have less access to services and programs in the prison system.[15] The Government has acknowledged that many programmes and interventions are designed to provide support over a set period of time, making it difficult for individuals with short-term sentences to fully engage in these programmes and receive the necessary support which can reduce the risk of reoffending.[16] There is also some evidence that the shorter the sentence, the higher the rate of return to prison within a two-year period.[17]

Presumptions against short sentences are found in Scotland, where the initial provision applied to sentences less than three months; this was increased to 12 months in 2019.[18] Similar provisions are found in New South Wales, with a limit of six months,[19] and Western Australia, with a limit of 12 months. In its submission to the Parliamentary Inquiry into Victoria's Criminal Justice System, Victoria Legal Aid also supported the abolition of short sentences as being detrimental to prospects of rehabilitation.[20]

These reforms are not without criticism. There is a concern that such presumptions might lead to 'sentence creep', where offenders may be sentenced to a longer period of imprisonment to compensate for the abolition of short sentences.[21] Any reduction in custodial sentences must therefore be accompanied by investment in adequate and appropriate community-based options – such as home detention – as alternatives to short sentences. This Government believes that with appropriate alternatives, 'sentence creep' is not inevitable. For example, in Scotland, while there is ongoing debate as to whether the reforms have had the desired effect, recent statistics show a significant reduction in sentences of 12 months or less, mostly due to reductions in the number of shorter sentences rather than an increase in sentences of over 12 months.[22]

This Bill therefore amends the *Sentencing Act 1991* (Vic) to introduce a presumption against short sentences of 12 months or less, from which the sentencing decision-maker can deviate if no other method of dealing with the offender is appropriate.

The Impact of Sentencing on Dependants

The purposes of the criminal law are most clearly expressed in the sentencing of offenders. It is here that the community's condemnation of criminal behaviour is expressed, while making allowance for mitigating factors and the possibility of rehabilitation. The *Sentencing Act 1991* (Vic) provides the framework for this difficult balance, setting out the purposes and principles of sentencing, the considerations a court must take into account and the hierarchy of sentencing options. Although sentencing is an individualised process which takes into account the offender's personal characteristics and circumstances, gender is not a relevant factor in itself.

While it may be accepted that a woman convicted of a crime should generally be sentenced the same as a similarly situated man, this concept of neutrality poses a challenge in cases where gender has a legitimate bearing on either the nature of the offending or the impact of the sentence. One particularly relevant factor is the role of caregiver for dependent children. While the role of caregiver is of course not limited to women, the fact is that women are still disproportionately responsible for caring roles, particularly of children. In 2021, for example, 54% of families reported a woman was the main person looking after children, while 40% reported equal sharing of responsibility.[23] Only 4% of families reported a man to be the person who usually or always looked after the children, while 79.9% of parents were women in single-parent families.[24]

Given that caring for children disproportionately falls on women, it is therefore much more likely that the sentencing of a woman offender will have a detrimental impact on the offender's children. However, the profile of primary carer is quite different for sentenced prisoners. In 2018, while 70% of sentenced women reported being parents, the proportion reporting they were the primary carer for their children was only 25%.[25] This reflects the likely impact of socio-demographic factors that may lead to a significant number of female offenders losing their status as primary carer. For example, financial difficulties and unmanageable work burdens may mean that the primary carer role is passed to another family member.

Under the current law, the impact of a sentence on third parties such as families or dependants is not normally a mitigating factor. Such impacts can only be taken into account where the circumstances are 'highly exceptional'.[26] The standard for exceptional circumstances being considered as an aspect of mercy is very high, with Victorian authority suggesting it will be 'rare'.[27] This is an unacceptably high burden for a factor that may detrimentally impact the defendant's relationship with their child, and on the child's development. The incarceration of a parent may have significant negative effects on a child's development, with increased risk of adverse mental and physical health outcomes.[28]

Even short periods of parental imprisonment can be severely disruptive to a child's family life, education and housing.[29] A tailored approach to sentencing is required, given the range of factors such as a history of victimisation, including sexual abuse, and family violence, substance dependency and mental illness which are likely to form part of the parent's history. Indigenous women prisoners are also disproportionately more likely to be mothers and primary carers of children.[30] The incarceration of caregivers can be particularly damaging for Indigenous children, where the effects can be exacerbated by other forms of disadvantage.[31]

This Bill departs from the common law by introducing a new subsection 5(2K) of the *Sentencing Act 1991* (Vic) to allow the impact of a sentence on a dependent child to be taken into account in determining the sentence to be imposed. For example, this may have a bearing on whether a custodial or non-custodial sentence is imposed. The provision is based on an equivalent provision in the *Commonwealth Crimes Act* 1914, which has been held by the Victorian Court of Appeal to not require 'exceptional circumstances'.[32] The section does not, however, indicate the weight to be given to this factor, but the reality is that non-custodial sentences should be favoured for women who have dependent children.[33] This amendment applies only to dependent children. Impacts on other family members and dependents must be considered, if at all, where there are 'exceptional circumstances'.

Despite focusing on the impacts on the child, this amendment can also benefit the offender by supporting their relationship with the child, facilitating positive familial and social behaviours that may support rehabilitation. Although most likely to apply to women, the provision is gender-neutral, applying to any defendant with a dependent child. It is consistent with Article 17 of the *Charter of Human Rights and Responsibilities Act 2006* which provides that '[f]amilies are the fundamental group unit of society and are entitled to be protected by society and the State' – a right that is not forfeited on account of a criminal conviction.[34] It is also consistent with the United Nations Rules for the Treatment of Women Prisoners and Non-custodial Measures for Women Offenders, which provide that where possible a non-custodial sentence should be imposed when sentencing a child's sole or primary caretaker.[35]

Pre-Sentence Reports

This reform is further supported by the ability of the Court to order a pre-sentence report. Section 8A of the *Sentencing Act 1991* (Vic) currently provides the sentencing judge with a discretion to order a pre-sentence report, and such reports are mandatory in the context of certain penalties. The contents of a pre-sentence report are set out in section 8B. These reports are tailored to the circumstances of the offender. For example, it may provide information about the offender's family situation, education and background, medical and psychological history and assessed risk to the community. Given it is generally not a relevant consideration, there is currently no provision for a pre-sentence report to include information relating to the probable impact of the sentence on the offender's dependants. We therefore propose amending section 8B to include specific issues to be addressed in the report where the judge is taking the impact on dependants into account. A non-exhaustive list of factors is provided, based on factors contained in section 60CC of the *Commonwealth Family Law Act 1974* where a court is to determine the best interests of the child. It includes factors such as the views of the child, the actual nature of the relationship between the offender and their children, the extent to which the offender has been involved in caring for the child (and their capacity to do so in the future), the circumstances of the child (such as maturity) and the impact on the cultural wellbeing of the child, particularly in the case of Indigenous children.

This reform may have an impact on hearings due to delays and some additional costs while such reports are prepared. Suitable experts will also be required to bring specialist expertise to these assessments. However, we believe that such impacts are outweighed by the benefits associated with the sentencing judge having a more detailed picture of the likely impact on the child, information which is at least as important in the criminal as it is in the family jurisdiction.

Home Detention

Reducing the number of non-violent women offenders in custody is only part of the story. This must be accompanied by an increased focus on non-custodial sentencing options to support women offenders in the community.[36] As part of a broad suite of reforms, this Government is committed to reinstating the electronic monitoring home detention programme which was abolished in 2011 by the conservative Coalition Government. This is consistent with the Parliamentary Inquiry into Victoria's Criminal Justice System recommendation that home detention be considered as a non-custodial sentence that balances community safety with an offender's ability to access local rehabilitative services.[37]

The proposed reforms, which are the subject of a separate Bill, will be based on the Tasmanian model which introduced an electronic monitoring home detention programme in 2018.[38] It is proposed that home detention may be ordered instead of a term of imprisonment of 12 months or less, and will involve confining an offender to their place of residence, subject to a number of exceptions. Often viewed as a favourable alternative to imprisonment, home detention allows offenders to work and maintain connections with their families while avoiding the well-documented harms associated with institutional prisons.[39] Although not suitable for all offenders – where there is a risk of family violence, for example – it is often regarded as an appropriate sentence for women offenders, particularly those with dependent children. [40]

I commend the Bill to the House.

PARLIAMENT OF VICTORIA

Introduced in the Assembly

Sentencing (Reducing Women in Custody) Bill 2024

A Bill for an Act to amend the ***Sentencing Act 1991*** (Vic), and for related purposes.

The Parliament of Victoria enacts:

1 Short title

This Act may be cited as the *Sentencing (Reducing Women in Custody) Act 2024*.

2 Commencement

Each provision of this Act commences on the day on which this Act receives the Royal Assent.

3 Presumption against short sentence

After section 6AA of the **Sentencing Act 1991 (Vic) insert** –

'6AAB Presumption against short sentence

(1) A court must not pass a sentence of imprisonment for a term of 12 months or less on a person unless the Court considers that no other sentence is appropriate.

(2) Where a court passes such a sentence, the court must –

(a) state its reasons for the opinion that no other method of dealing with the person is appropriate; and

(b) have those reasons entered in the record of the proceedings.'

4 Impact of Sentence on Dependent Child

After section 5(2J) of the **Sentencing Act 1991 (Vic), insert** –

'5(2K)(a) Where the offender is the carer of a dependent child, in sentencing the offender the court must take into account the probable effect that any sentence or order under consideration would have on any of the person's dependent children.

(b) Where the carer is the primary carer, a sentence of imprisonment should not be imposed where the impact on dependants would make a custodial sentence disproportionate to achieving the sentencing objectives.'

In section 3(1) of the **Sentencing Act 1991** (**Vic**) **insert** –

'***child*** means a person who is under 18. Without limiting who is a child of a person for the purposes of this Act, someone is the child of a person if they are a child of the person within the meaning of the *Family Law Act 1975*.'

In section 3(1) Sentencing Act 1991 (Vic) insert –

'***primary carer*** for the purposes of section 5(2K) means the person who has the day-to-day responsibility for the care of the child.'

5 Pre-Sentence Reports

After section 8B(2) **Sentencing Act 1991** (**Vic**) **insert** –

'8B(3)(a) Where a court, in sentencing an offender, considers the probable effect of the sentence on the offender's dependent child or children, the court must order a pre-sentence report addressing this issue.

(b) Where a pre-sentence report is already required, these factors must be incorporated in that report.

(c) In addition to the matters set out in subsection (1), the report must include, where relevant:

(i) any views expressed by the child and any factors (such as the child's maturity or level of understanding) that the court thinks are relevant to the weight it should give to the child's views;
(ii) the nature of the child's relationship with the offender, their other parent and other persons (including any grandparent or other relative of the child);
(iii) the extent to which the offender has taken, or failed to take, the opportunity to participate in making decisions about major long-term issues in relation to the child; and to spend time with the child; and to communicate with the child;
(iv) the extent to which the offender has fulfilled, or failed to fulfil, their obligation to maintain the child;
(v) the likely effect on the child of any separation from the offender due to a period of imprisonment;
(vi) the capacity of the offender and any other person to provide for the needs of the child, including emotional and intellectual needs;
(vii) the maturity, sex, lifestyle and background (including lifestyle, culture and traditions) of the child and of

either of the child's parents, and any other characteristics of the child that the court thinks are relevant;
(viii) if the child is an Aboriginal child or a Torres Strait Islander child, the child's right to enjoy his or her Aboriginal or Torres Strait Islander culture and the likely impact any proposed sentence will have on that right;
(ix) the attitude to the child, and to the responsibilities of parenthood, demonstrated by the offender;
(x) any family violence involving the child or a member of the child's family; and
(xi) any other fact or circumstance that the court thinks is relevant.'

Notes

1 Shona Minson, *Maternal Sentencing and the Rights of the Child* (Oxford University Press, 2020) 3.
2 Department of Justice and Community Safety – Corrections Victoria, *Annual Prisons Statistical Profile* (30 June 2022).
3 Ibid.
4 Department of Justice and Community Safety, *Women in the Victorian Prison System* (Report, January 2019) 4.
5 Ibid.
6 Samantha Walker et al. (2019), *Characteristics and Offending of Women in Prison in Victoria, 2012–2018* (Crime Statistics Agency Research Paper, 7 November 2019) 6.
7 Lorana Bartels et al., 'Understanding Women's Imprisonment in Australia' (2020) 30(3) *Women and Criminal Justice* 204, 206.
8 Suzanne Smith and Stephen Whitehead, 'Problem-Solving Courts for Women: An Evidence and Practice Briefing', Centre for Justice Innovation (briefing, September 2021) 2.
9 Department of Justice and Community Safety, *Women in the Victorian Prison System* (report, January 2019) 3.
10 *R v Harkness* (2001) VSCA at [58] per Winneke ACJ, Ormiston and Callaway JJA.
11 *Dong v The Queen* (2016) VSCA 51.
12 *Palmer v WA* (2018) WASCA 225 at [71],[76] per Mazza JA, Mitchell JA and Allanson J.
13 Department of Justice and Community Safety, *Women in the Victorian Prison System* (Report, 2019) 3.
14 Ministry of Justice, *Female Offender Strategy* (Report, 27 June 2018) 17.
15 Bartels et al. (n 7) 204, 205.
16 Legislative Council Legal and Social Issues Committee, *Inquiry into Victoria's Criminal Justice System* (March 2022) vol 1, 549.
17 Ibid.
18 Justice Committee, *Presumption Against Short Periods of Imprisonment* (Scotland) Order 2019 (21 June 2019), Scottish Parliament.
19 *Crimes (Sentencing Procedure) Act 1999* (NSW) s 5.
20 Victoria Legal Aid, Submission No 159 to the Inquiry into Victoria's Criminal Justice System, *Towards a Fairer and More Effective Criminal Justice System for Victoria* (30 September 2021) 9.

21 Legislative Council Legal and Social Issues Committee, *Inquiry into Victoria's Criminal Justice System* (March 2022) vol 1, 550.
22 Scottish Government, *Criminal Proceedings in Scotland: 2020–2021,* Safer Communities Directorate (report, 21 July 2022). https://www.gov.scot/publications/criminal-proceedings-scotland-2020-21/pages/13/.
23 Department of the Prime Minister and Cabinet, National Strategy to Achieve Gender Equality (March 2023) Discussion Paper [4.2] 10.
24 Ibid.
25 Crime Statistics Agency, *Characteristics and Offending of Women in Prison in Victoria 2012–2018* (Research Paper, 2019) 15.
26 *Markovic v The Queen; Pantelic v The Queen* [2010] VSCA 105 at [13] per Maxwell P, Nettle JA, Neave JA, Redlich JA and Weinberg JA.
27 Ibid.
28 Legislative Council Legal and Social Issues Committee, *Inquiry into Children of Incarcerated Parents* (Final Report 4, August 2022) 26.
29 The Public Defenders (NSW), *Bugmy Bar Book,* 'Incarceration of Parents and Caregivers' 1.
30 Australian Law Reform Commission, *Pathways to Justice – An Inquiry into the Incarceration Rate of Aboriginal and Torres Strait Islander Peoples* (ALRC Report 133, December 2017) 349.
31 The Public Defenders (NSW), *Bugmy Bar Book,* 'Incarceration of Parents and Caregivers' 1.
32 *Mohamed v The Queen* [2022] VSCA 136 at [81]–[93] per Maxwell P, Emerton and Sifris JJA; *Rodgerson v The Queen* (No 2) [2022] VSCA 154 at [73] per Emerton P, Kyrou and T Forrest JJA.
33 Minson (n 1) 138.
34 Ibid.
35 United Nations Rules for the Treatment of Women Prisoners and Non-Custodial Measures for Women Offenders, UN Doc A/RES/65/229 (adopted by the General Assembly on 21 December 2010) ('the Bangkok Rules'), art 9.
36 Bartels et al. (n 7) 204, 215.
37 Legislative Council Legal and Social Issues Committee, *Inquiry into Victoria's Criminal Justice System* (24 March 2022) vol 1, xxvi.
38 Sentencing Act 1997 (Tas), pt 5A.
39 Amanda George, 'Women and Home Detention – Home is where the Prison Is' (2006) 18(1) *Current Issues in Criminal Justice* 79, 79.
40 Anti-Discrimination Commission of Queensland, *Women in Prison: A Human Rights Consultation Report* (Report, 2019) 96.

Chapter 12A

Commentary on *Gender and its Relevance to Sentence*

Arlie Loughnan

In the years since the turn of the 21st century, feminist judgments projects have proliferated across the world.[1] Into this field steps a novel project, centred on feminist lawmaking, which I understand is a world first. As the editors of the collection explain, by rewriting and reimagining original legislation and treaties through a feminist lens, the legislation project explores the effect of feminist theory on the decision-making of parliaments.This is a worthy and important project. Through it, we can imagine what might be possible if all parliamentarians were feminists!

The aim of this project is to reimagine a world where laws are made specifically to benefit women rather than ignoring, marginalising or even harming us. And the focus of attention on legislation and treaties is welcome: the rise of parliaments as law-making bodies is a feature of the modern era,[2] and, across the globe, parliaments are increasingly active lawmakers and statutes, codes, regulations and related sources of law are increasingly dominant features of our legal landscape. In the criminal law context in particular, parliamentary law-making has exploded in the decades since the 1970s, with heightened demands on parliaments arising from the victims' movement, popular punitiveness and other factors.[3]

Criminal sentencing has been a particularly popular site for legislative intervention. Across Australian jurisdictions, the judicial practice of sentencing those who have been convicted of a crime is now subject to a complex matrix of legislation. In my own jurisdiction of New South Wales (NSW), recent decades have seen the introduction of guideline judgments, mandatory minimum sentencing periods, changes to laws to increase maximum sentences, post-sentence preventive detention and numerous other initiatives.[4] Combined with changes in policing practices, these changes to the law have led to significant increases in prison numbers, and have had a particularly devastating effect on rates of incarceration of First Nations people.[5] At the time of writing this comment, NSW reached a record high with Indigenous people making up 29.7% of the adult custody population.[6] The picture of women's imprisonment numbers is also dire, having skyrocketed in recent years, and dwarfing even the sizable increases in men's imprisonment.[7]

DOI: 10.4324/9781003372462-26

The Sentencing (Reducing Women in Custody) Bill 2023, drafted by Natalia Antolak-Saper, is a welcome intervention into this depressing landscape. The Bill will amend the *Sentencing Act 1991* (Vic) and initiates two key changes in sentencing practice. First, it introduces a presumption against a sentence of imprisonment for 12 months or less for offenders convicted of non-violent offences. This ensures that it will only be in exceptional circumstances that an offender will be imprisoned for a short period, as another sentencing option should be employed instead. The Bill also notes the need for increases in the non-custodial sentencing options available to support offenders in the community, to make non-custodial options a real choice for courts. As the Bill makes clear, the presumption against short sentences applies to all offenders but will benefit women specifically: women are disproportionately sentenced to short periods of time in jail, during which they are unlikely to be able to access training or therapeutic options, and this has a well-documented negative impact on family, employment and housing.[8]

Second, using a pre-sentence report, the Bill allows the court to consider the impact of the sentence on the offender's dependent child or children. While likely to impact women specifically, this amendment is gender-neutral. This change means that it will no longer be the case that the impact on a child of a parent's imprisonment must be 'exceptional' to be considered by the sentencing judge and brings the criminal justice system into line with the family court system, which must consider the best interests of the child in adjudicating family disputes. While this change raises issues about fairness to offenders without dependants, it is a necessary development, noting as the Bill does, the disproportionate amount of unpaid care performed by women, and what we know about the particular issues that arise for First Nations women prisoners, 80% of whom are mothers.[9] As noted in the Bill, the effects of imprisonment on the children of prisoners are profound, and they represent yet another cost of imprisonment, which has been overlooked for too long.

This Bill represents a considered, positive and evidence-based attempt to alleviate some of the many problems replete in our criminal justice system, and it deserves strong and wholehearted support. Of course, like any persuasive argument for greater leniency and flexibility in the application of criminal laws, the Bill raises uncomfortable questions about whether the criminal justice system itself is fit for purpose in the current era. The prevalence of factors such as trauma, substance misuse, addiction, untreated mental illness, abuse, family breakdown, out-of-home care and homelessness in the lives of offenders raises uncomfortable questions about the real level of moral culpability of many individuals who come into contact with the criminal justice system.[10] On to this is overlaid the impacts of racism in policing, prosecution and other parts of the criminal justice system on its operation.[11] And in relation to women, to this must be added the problems of the criminal trial process and the poor fit between major defences like self-defence and women's offending.[12]

Once someone is convicted, the problems with sentencing that this Bill aims to address become apparent. In particular, the principle of individualised justice means that the focus of criminal sentencing must be on the offender,[13] obscuring and ignoring the structural aspects of offending. In the case of women offenders, these include gender discrimination and cultural misogyny, among other factors. The situation of women offenders is desperate, but, arguably, so is that of all prisoners, and, when measured in terms of cost-effectiveness and desistance from crime,[14] imprisonment as a punishment for crime is itself problematic. Abolitionists have made persuasive cases for the disutility of prison as a response to crime.[15] Short of abolition, or a radical change in our approach to punishment, away from retribution and toward genuine rehabilitation, the changes included in this Bill seem to be the best we can do.

The Sentencing (Reducing Women in Custody) Bill 2023 is an exercise in what Máiréad Enright has called 'as if' jurisprudence, in which authors carve out a path between pragmatism and creativity.[16] This Bill plots the value of legal paths not (yet) taken, and alternative futures that exist at this time only on an imaginary plane. But the urgency and gravity of the problems with imprisonment in Australia demands reconsideration of extant approaches to sentencing. It is to be hoped that this draft legislation will be part of any such reconsideration.

Notes

1 For an overview of feminist judging, see Rosemary Hunter et al (eds), *Feminist Judgments: From Theory to Practice* (Bloomsbury, 2010).

2 For a discussion of modernity, see Anthony Giddens, *The Consequences of Modernity* (Stanford University Press, 1990); Anthony Giddens, *Modernity and Self-Identity: Self and Society in the Late Modern Age* (Stanford University Press, 1991).

3 For discussion, see Luke McNamara et al. (2018) 'Theorising Criminalisation: The Value of a Modalities Approach' (2018) 7(3) International Journal for Crime, Justice and Social Democracy, 91–121.

4 See eg Julia Quilter, 'One-Punch Laws, Mandatory Minimums and "alcohol-fuelled" as an Aggravating Factor: Implications for NSW Criminal Law' (2014) 3(1) *International Journal for Crime, Justice and Social Democracy* 81–106.

5 See Don Weatherburn, 'Is Tougher Sentencing and Bail Policy the Cause of Rising Imprisonment Rates? A NSW Case Study' (2020) 53(4) *Australian & New Zealand Journal of Criminology* 563–84 and Indigenous Justice Clearinghouse, 'Sentencing Indigenous Offenders' (Research Brief No 7, 2010), respectively.

6 See Bureau of Crime Statistics and Research, 'NSW Custody Statistics: Quarterly Update March 2023'. https://www.bocsar.nsw.gov.au/Publications/custody/NSW_Custody_Statistics_Mar2023.pdf.

7 See Australian Institute of Family Studies, 'The Health and Welfare of Women in Australia's Prisons' (Report, November 2020). https://www.aihw.gov.au/getmedia/32d3a8dc-eb84-4a3b-90dc-79a1aba0efc6/aihw-phe-281.pdf.aspx?inline=true.

8 For a discussion in the context of Indigenous offenders, see Australian Law Reform Commission, *Pathways to Justice – An Inquiry into the Incarceration Rate*

of Aboriginal and Torres Strait Islander Peoples (ALRC Report No 133, December 2017) [7.151]–[7.169].

9 Sacha Kendall et al., 'Holistic Conceptualizations of Health by Incarcerated Aboriginal Women in New South Wales, Australia' (2019) 29(11) *Qualitative Health Research* 1549–65.

10 For a philosophical discussion of these issues, see Gary Watson. *Agency and Answerability: Selected Essays* (Oxford University Press, 2004) ch 8.

11 For discussion in relation to Indigenous youth in detention, see Thalia Anthony, '"They Were Treating Me Like a Dog": The Colonial Continuum of State Harms Against Indigenous Children in Detention in the Northern Territory, Australia' (2018) 7(2) *State Crime Journal* 251–77.

12 In the context of the criminalisation of women responding to violence, see Centre for Women's Justice, 'Making Self-Defence Accessible to Women Who Use Force Against Their Abuser: Learning From Reforms in Canada, New Zealand and Australia' (briefing, 2023). https://www.centreforwomensjustice.org.uk/stop-criminalising.

13 See for discussion in relation to sentencing Indigenous offenders, *Bugmy v The Queen* (2013) 249 CLR 571.

14 See Wai-Yin Wan et al., 'The Effect of Arrest and Imprisonment on Crime' (2012) 158 *Crime and Justice Bulletin* 1–18.

15 See Nicolas Carrier and Justin Piché, 'The State of Abolitionism' (2015) *Champ pénal/Penal field* XII. http://journals.openedition.org/champpenal/9164.

16 M Enright, 'Book Review: *Scottish Feminist Judgments: (Re)Creating Law from the Outside In*' (2021) 30 *Social & Legal Studies* 2.

Part V

Diversity, Dignity and Autonomy

Chapter 13

Navigating Cultural and Religious Needs in Family Dispute Resolution

Amira Aftab

Extract from *Hansard* (Commonwealth of Australia)

Family Law (Family Dispute Resolution) Amendment Bill 2024

Second Reading

HON AMIRA AFTAB: I move:

That this Bill be now read a second time.

Australia is promoted as a multicultural country. Yet, our institutions, including the law, do not always recognise diversity within our communities. This means the needs of different groups, especially women from diverse cultural and religious backgrounds, are often overlooked.

To address this gap in our legal system, particularly family law, this Bill introduces greater recognition and accommodation of women from diverse backgrounds. It is born out of a recognition of the impact Family Dispute Resolution (known as FDR) has on parties, especially women, from culturally and linguistically diverse (CALD) backgrounds and faith-based communities. I would like to note that CALD typically refers to people from non-English speaking backgrounds and/or people born overseas from countries where English is not the primary language – for this reason, I refer to faith-based communities separately. It is also important to note that Indigenous communities are a separate group with their own specific history, needs and interests that stand outside of this broad umbrella of CALD communities.

So, what is Family Dispute Resolution?

You will recall that in 2006, FDR provisions were introduced into the *Family Law Act 1975* (Cth) (*FLA*). In particular, we saw the introduction of compulsory FDR for parties seeking a parenting order.

DOI: 10.4324/9781003372462-28

FDR falls under the broad umbrella of private dispute resolution, which can take various forms including mediation, conciliation or arbitration, all of which aim to divert legal disputes about children from the courts. One advantage of these forms of private dispute resolution is that the non-legal needs and interests of parties can be considered, where courts are only able to apply the legal principles as outlined in the law.

Within an FDR process, a neutral third party, known as a Family Dispute Resolution Practitioner (or FDRP), is engaged to help parties resolve their dispute. An FDRP does not make a final decision, however, and the decisions are not binding until formalised in a legally binding agreement. Instead, the aim is to facilitate discussion and mutual agreement between the parties with the aim of avoiding litigation through the courts.[1] Where parties are unable to reach an agreement via FDR, they can only apply to the court once an FDRP certifies that a genuine attempt to resolve the matter through FDR has been made.

FDR was introduced for a number of reasons. Most importantly, it was seen to align more closely with the 'best interests of the child' principle that is embedded within our family law system.[2] Another perceived benefit of FDR is that it is more expedient and cost-effective for both parties. In addition to this, it draws on concepts of individual choice, and is often seen as 'autonomy-enhancing' and 'less adversarial' for both parties.[3]

There are, of course, benefits to these dispute resolution processes, such as greater self-expression and empowerment. At the same time, there is the risk they may place women in weaker bargaining positions. Where this happens, it can result in them being encouraged, or even coerced, to settle for a lesser outcome compared to what may be received through the adversarial process.[4]

Other concerns that may arise include a lack of appropriate safeguards to ensure women's interests are adequately protected in FDR processes; concerns regarding whether parties are effectively protected if domestic violence and/or safety concerns arise during the FDR process;[5] and the legal barriers faced by parties in accessing legal resources and advice.

While I recognise these concerns, the benefits to facilitative mediation – the most common model of FDR employed within the Australian family law system – often outweigh the risks. Not only is facilitative mediation designed to empower parties and give them a voice during the decision-making process, but it also allows parties to retain some control within the process while closely reflecting on their specific needs.[6]

The ability for parties to shape the decision-making process is particularly important for women from CALD and faith-based communities, as it offers an opportunity to raise their unique needs. The term 'women' is used in the context of discussing this proposed Bill, as it is individuals who identify as women within these communities that are often impacted by unequal outcomes. I note that this term is used in a gender-inclusive way, and importantly recognise the way that sexual orientation and gender identity intersects with culture, race and/or religion to shape the experiences of marginalised individuals or groups. With the potential to 'display inherently feminist values and principles' and empower women, FDR is a promising avenue to allow these women the much-needed opportunity to speak and be heard.[7]

Why does private dispute resolution, including our current FDR process, offer such empowering opportunities for the parties involved, especially women from diverse backgrounds? Well, it has a lot to offer those whose cultures the law is blind to, allowing family members to live and settle disputes according to their values, with reference to the law to the extent that they choose.[8] Where power imbalances are largely absent (or can be counteracted by an effective, competent and reflexive mediator), where consent is genuine, where decision-making is informed and where settlement of the dispute is consensual, FDR in the form of mediation has much to offer by way of equality and fairness.[9] Whether it provides legal justice, however, is a separate question.

A further question is whether parties from diverse communities, particularly women, would even look favourably on alternative dispute resolution processes.

My answer to this is 'yes'. While not all women may want more culturally appropriate services, there is evidence to suggest that many do. For example, various community consultations and parliamentary inquiries have shown us the barriers faced by Aboriginal and Torres Strait Islander communities in accessing mainstream family law processes, demonstrating a clear need for more culturally appropriate services.[10]

I would like to note that in response, as of 2022 we have new Family Dispute Resolution services for Aboriginal and Torres Strait Islander families. These services prioritise cultural healing and family restoration led by community processes. Equally importantly, however, this service delivery will conclude in 2026.

For this reason, we need to consider the measures I propose here today for longer-term and more sustainable reform to the FDR framework.

We also have examples of informal dispute resolution processes taking places at community level. This is most evident within faith-based communities, where we also see examples of these dispute resolution processes being embraced by women – mostly because of their less adversarial nature, but also due to their frequent alignment with cultural or religious processes around dispute resolution.

This reinforces the idea that these private dispute resolution processes allow women to exercise a level of agency in decision-making and engagement in resolving a dispute that is otherwise not allowed within formal legal processes before the courts.[11]

Fundamentally, FDR offers flexibility by allowing cultural and religious norms, as well as personal values, to guide the process. This is important when we consider the intersection of women's different cultural and religious identities.

Looking at the example of faith-based communities for a moment, religious people often find themselves subject to two different systems as they navigate family disputes in accordance with both state and religious laws and values. In a recent study, one Muslim woman noted that an Islamically valid divorce was important to her because she wouldn't consider the divorce to be complete without religious approval.[12]

Recognising and providing a space that accounts for the importance of religious values and norms in an individual's life creates the potential for more efficient dispute resolution – one which ultimately enhances the current FDR framework by drawing on the parties' common values.

It is also important to recognise that for a religious woman navigating the secular legal system, their notion of justice and their faith may directly conflict with that embedded within the state legal system. As a result, religious women may feel unseen, unheard, disenfranchised and disempowered by the secular process.[13] This reinforces why we need FDR to be more sensitive to the needs of women not only from diverse religious backgrounds, but also from CALD backgrounds.

Women within these communities may often turn to forms of informal dispute resolution processes taking place at the community level. This is not only due to these processes' cultural sensitivity and culturally specific knowledge that is currently lacking in mainstream services, but also because these women may not be comfortable bringing cultural or religious needs to the attention of the FDRPs that operate within the formal family law system.[14]

We know that CALD families may not understand or trust mainstream services, may face communication barriers and may be influenced by socio-cultural norms that emphasise informal community processes over 'mainstream help-seeking'.[15] In fact, some women find 'the court system is a frightening thing for people to enter into',[16] with one woman noting that 'Going to court wore me down – I felt alone and helpless'.[17] As a result, they often turn to community leaders (or Elders) as an avenue of redressing/resolving family disputes, a decision which is even more common among newly arrived migrant and refugee women.[18] This lack of knowledge, combined with the often-held fear of 'losing children' in a divorce, means that women will not access legal assistance – or if they do, it might be so delayed that it comes 'at the point of crisis'.[19]

There are many reasons why parties to turn to community processes over Australian family law processes based on cultural and religious barriers. One is that the understandings of divorce and parenting within Australian family law may not align with family values within cultural and religious communities.

Additionally, women may at times feel their partners or husbands are being manipulative or controlling within FDR sessions, but sense that this is not recognised or understood by the FDRPs due to a lack of cultural understanding. Essentially, FDRPs may lack the culturally specific knowledge to see or appreciate the presence of types of behaviour that are understood to be manipulative or controlling from a specific cultural perspective.[20]

Challenges also arise where community or cultural norms emphasise family privacy and discourage seeking outside help with family matters from mainstream family services. In these situations, the legal process is often seen as the 'last resort'.[21] This can be compounded where culturally (or socially) isolated women turn to their community for assistance out of familiarity, especially those women who have newly arrived in the country. This often leads to limited (if any) help-seeking outside the community. In a study exploring the experiences of Muslim women turning to community processes, one professional supporting Muslim women noted that 'they feel comfortable coming here because we give like a cultural lens, somewhere that they can culturally identify themselves with'.[22]

Women from CALD communities also require multiple services to assist them in navigating FDR, with the lack of service integration contributing to the barriers/difficulties encountered.[23] While the Bill does not necessarily resolve these particular issues more broadly within the family law system, it aims to address these barriers within FDR processes.

To do this, we clearly need to either have more qualified mediators from diverse backgrounds (that is, linguistic, ethnic, cultural and religious) or find an alternative to address this gap.

It is this gap that the Bill speaks to, with the aim of building on the *FLA*'s existing aims and policy, specifically the 2006 reforms that introduced compulsory FDR where parties are seeking a parenting order. Current family law services have been documented as being fundamentally insensitive or not open to the inclusion of cultural or religious values of women within CALD and/or religious communities.[24]

This need for greater sensitivity is made most obvious when contrasted to processes that have emerged within religious communities. These informal processes have proven to be successful in mediating family disputes, though they have their own shortcomings that should be addressed.[25] The provisions introduced by this Bill aim to bridge the gap between these informal processes and the state-provided legal system, and in doing so, go some way to addressing the shortcomings in both approaches.

While the mainstream model is positive in its facilitative nature led by a neutral, impartial mediator who encourages open and frank discussions, we need to recognise that its culturally specific focus on Western values and norms is at odds with the practices of people from more collectivist cultures where dispute resolution may involve other stakeholders.[26] The direct nature of mainstream negotiations presents difficulties for people who come from cultural backgrounds where such practice is not the norm, consequently causing stress that can discourage participation in state-based FDR processes.[27]

As mentioned earlier, there is an identified gap in the availability of culturally appropriate FDR services for Indigenous people within the Australian context – a shortcoming which was the key driver for the new FDR service introduced in 2022.

There is a need to address conflict resolution in ways that recognise not only parties' cultural values and beliefs, but also the priorities and governance structures shaped by their communities. For Indigenous parties, this includes recognising kinship protocols, respect for Elders and traditional owners, the use of ceremony, and particular understandings and approaches to gender.[28]

In responding to these specific needs, the provisions outlined in this Bill recognise not only the value of FDR within the family law system, but also the fact that informal processes of dispute resolution are often preferred by women within culturally, linguistically and religiously diverse communities.

What Does the Bill Propose to Improve Current FDR Processes?

The Bill considers the diverse needs of parties and introduces supports to strengthen the benefits and outcomes of FDR. It does this by shifting the current approach of FDR to emphasise the principles of co-mediation more than we currently do. In this proposed reform, a number of relevant and useful stakeholders, referred to as 'relevant specialist advisors' and 'specialist persons', enter the process to co-facilitate an appropriate and acceptable outcome for both parties.

While co-mediation is typically a model involving two or more mediators working together to help the parties resolve their conflict, this Bill's provisions do not rely on mediators or FDRPs alone. Instead, it looks to other experts or individuals that can offer valuable insight and support to ensure greater respect for and accommodation of the parties' cultural, linguistic and religious needs.

This approach is introduced for a number of reasons. Importantly, FDRPs mediating disputes are often unable to address power imbalances that may arise within the process, as there are concerns that these efforts would compromise their impartiality. Weighed against this, however, is the need to offer additional protections to vulnerable parties. Co-mediation 'carried out by an interdisciplinary, gender-balanced team has been found to be ideal and particularly important.'[29] While there may be concerns about the resource implications of this style, we must remember that the benefits outweigh any additional costs. Additionally, because dispute resolution is already far more cost-efficient than court processes, investing more to facilitate this model will have long-term cost benefits.

Additionally, the new model can help significantly in situations where the mediator's gender may be an issue – for example, a male mediator may intimidate or make women from religiously or culturally diverse backgrounds feel marginalised or uncomfortable.[30] A significant strength of the amendments is that they will enable various experts' skills to be combined and pooled, balancing the strengths and weaknesses among FDRPs.

Cultural, Linguistic and Religious Needs Assessment Screening – s 10KA(1)(a)

Under section 10KA(1)(a), bringing in relevant specialist advisors to the Family Dispute Resolution process is available where there are identified cultural, linguistic and/or religious needs of the parties to a family dispute. The appropriateness of doing so is determined by the FDRP during the existing intake processes, where FDRPs already assess the suitability of Family Dispute Resolution for the parties alongside determining the appropriate form of dispute resolution.

The *Family Law (Family Dispute Resolution Practitioners) Regulations 2008* (Cth) ('*Family Law Regulations*') already note in Regulation 25 that practitioners must ensure an assessment has been conducted in determining whether Family Dispute Resolution is appropriate. This is typically in relation to family violence screening, but also includes a number of other relevant factors – as such, assessment screening for cultural, linguistic and religious needs will be included as part of this pre-FDR process. An amendment will be made subsequent to this proposed Bill being passed to Regulation 25(2) to include cultural, linguistic and religious needs as part of relevant matters to be taken into account when determining suitability of FDR. Additional training will be mandated for FDRPs, and a framework will be implemented to provide a screening checklist, similar to the procedures around family violence screening.

Introducing a cultural, linguistic and religious needs assessment screening as a pre-FDR step is not such a novel idea, as the Federal Circuit and Family Court of Australia already 'employs family consultants to meet with Indigenous family members prior to commencement of dispute resolution',[31] during which they assess the cultural needs of the family and liaise with the FDRP. This has been found to be effective in supporting the parties during the FDR process as well as assisting the FDRP to better understand the needs and interests of the parties.[32] Expanding this approach and embedding it within the pre-FDR procedure is therefore a realistic avenue of reform.

Importantly, the cultural, linguistic and religious needs screening does not override or cancel out the family violence screening but will instead operate within the existing screening process. This will determine whether FDR is appropriate for the parties, and specifically what type of FDR approach is needed. While the presence of family violence leads to a determination that FDR is inappropriate for the parties, the cultural, linguistic and religious assessment screening is in place to help determine which model of FDR is most appropriate and will be most beneficial for the parties.

FDRPs will be the convenors of the FDR process, recognising their existing role as the facilitators of Family Dispute Resolution processes and fitting the proposed FDR model within the existing framework. Specialist advisors will work within the FDR process with the FDRP in an advisory capacity to help navigate the nuanced cultural and/or religious matters that arise. Importantly, the provision outlines that both parties must consent to this proposed new model of dispute resolution and the participation of relevant specialist advisors.

This proposal recognises that the participation of certain specialist advisors may raise concerns for parties – for example, if parties do not want cultural or religious norms to inform the process even if they identify as part of a particular cultural or religious community/background. It is important to note, as covered in Regulation 29(c)(i) of the *Family Law Regulations*, that parties already have a right to request that the FDR be terminated at any point during the process. This is a protection that will also cover the proposed FDR model. Similarly, FDRPs already have the ability to terminate an FDR if they are no longer satisfied that it is appropriate. With this existing power held by FDRPs in mind, the new provisions extend FDRPs' oversight as convenors of this process, to allow them to assess the appropriateness of a specialist advisor's participation within the process.

Australian Legal Practitioners – s 10KA(3)(a)

Section 10KA(3)(a) of the Bill ensures that parties are entitled to Australian legal practitioners involved in FDR. The legal practitioners that may be involved are specified to be those that are already engaged to advise any of the parties; however, an FDRP may recommend a lawyer to participate if parties do not have legal representation of their own. There is considerable value to involving legal professionals in the dispute resolution process.

The presence of legal practitioners can be beneficial in addressing and moderating the disadvantages or inequalities in bargaining power.[33] Not all FDRPs are legally trained, and it is not appropriate for them to provide individual legal advice to parties aside from general legal information and/or encouraging parties to seek legal advice if they have not already done so.

This lack of legal knowledge among FDRPs is recognised in studies looking at the preferences and engagement with dispute resolution by Muslim women. In this example, the research shows us that despite the religious process being what women in the community want, there are concerns about legal fairness. As religious processes are informal, guided by religious principles more so than the legal principles of Australian family law, so our challenge is bringing them together.[34]

There may be concerns that involving lawyers is inappropriate, as they are adversarial and their practices do not align with the principles of mediation. Given these issues, some FDRPs may be critical of lawyers being too involved.[35] However, we need to overcome the stereotype that lawyers are *only* adversarial, as they can also help protect vulnerable parties. This is especially important where lack of knowledge about law can be exploited for use against weaker parties.

Lawyers can play a significant and useful role as well as making valuable contributions through collaboration. This is particularly so in light of concerns that in the absence of legal representation or advocacy, it cannot be assumed that the parties are well-informed about the law when weighing up different settlement options.[36] Instead of being a representative for a particular party, the lawyer engaged by the FDRP as a specialist advisor is there to fill the legal knowledge gaps that a FDRP from a non-legal background may have.

Models that place the role of a legal advocate centrally within the process to provide advice and necessary information or answer questions are particularly helpful in preventing vulnerable parties (most often women) from being pressured into disadvantageous agreements.[37] These arrangements can also go some way to addressing barriers to legal resources and ensuring that parties are not agreeing to their rights being eroded. Legal practitioners can ensure that the options discussed are realistic as well as equitable from a legal perspective. This model can also be beneficial in ensuring that the agreements are made legally binding by following through with a consent order submitted to the court.

Interpreters – s 10KA(3)(b)

The participation of interpreters is already recognised and embedded within the Australian legal system. Organisations such as Family Relationship Centres and legal aid commissions, who also facilitate FDR processes, already offer interpreter services. The Bill explicitly outlines interpreters not because their involvement is new, but to emphasise the importance of providing adequate linguistic support to parties who may otherwise not realise this is available and is their right. In arranging and convening the conference, FDRPs can ensure that interpreters are lined up where needed.

Respected Member of the Community (Cultural and/or Religious) – s 10KA(2)(a)

The proposed Bill also recognises that there are currently limits on how many people can participate or be present during an FDR process. For example, the Legal Services Commission of South Australia notes that if a party brings a lawyer, then it is preferred that they do not bring any other support person. Recognising the way that current models of FDR are Western-centric in values and do not adequately recognise the nuanced cultural and religious needs of some parties to FDR, section 10KA(2)(a) introduces space for respected members of cultural and religious communities to be involved as part of the FDR conference.

The role of these individuals is to provide cultural or religious insight in order to make the process more inclusive. Importantly, these individuals are distinct from existing recognition of support persons that parties have traditionally been able to bring into a mediation. Support persons as they currently stand do not actively participate in the FDR process, they simply providing emotional support to a party while in mediation.

By contrast, individuals who participate as a specialist advisor, such as cultural or religious leaders, will act as an advisor to the FDRP on cultural or religious issues that may arise during the FDR process. As they are not there to represent a particular party, they in essence should be neutral and speak only to cultural and/or religious norms and values.

So who is a respected member of the community? Well, these individuals need to be respected and recognised as 'leaders' within their cultural or faith-based community. This means that they have to be part of a specific cultural or religious community organisation and/or other multicultural commission – for example, organisations including the Board of Imams Victoria, the Australian Lebanese Association, the South Australian Bangladeshi Community Association, the Equatoria Community and Welfare Association NSW.

Individuals will need to provide evidence of their involvement within the community and links to the community organisation in order to join a register that will be established for religious and cultural specialist advisors.

In assessing the cultural and religious needs of parties, FDRPs can only select cultural and religious leaders to participate as specialist advisors from this register. Fundamentally, respected members/leaders within cultural and religious groups can bring in necessary knowledge about cultural and religious values and norms to help guide the FDR process.

Cultural and/or Religious Community Support Services – s 10KA(2)(b)

Similarly, there is considerable value in involving cultural and/or religious community support services (CSS). For this reason, section 10KA(3)(b) permits the involvement of a CSS representative with the process. This may be welfare support services, but may also include counsellors who can not only advocate for parties, but also help them navigate the process. This is especially important where the FDRP must remain neutral and cannot assist or advocate for victims themselves. The types of organisations that may have a representative participate in FDR must be registered non-government organisations that provide support services within the community, for examples around health, counselling or family support. These organisations are often on the frontline of providing support and referrals to other support services, including legal services, and therefore may have a unique insight into individuals' needs.

Conclusion

This Bill addresses an important gap in existing FDR processes – our current failure to adequately recognise the needs of parties from diverse CALD and faith-based communities. Through the introduction of specialist advisors to aid FDRPs within FDR processes and shifting the current model towards a 'Family Dispute Resolution conference' based on a model of co-mediation, we can strengthen the benefits and outcomes of FDR. We can also ensure greater respect and accommodation of parties' identities and backgrounds, so that we can proudly say that we go beyond simply claiming Australia is a multicultural country to actually demonstrating how our state institutions recognise and adapt to diversity.

I commend this Bill to the House.

The Parliament of the Commonwealth of Australia

HOUSE OF REPRESENTATIVES

Family Law (Family Dispute Resolution) Amendment Bill 2024

A Bill for an Act to amend the *Family Law Act 1975* (Cth), and for related purposes

The Parliament of Australia enacts:

1 Division 3 – Family Dispute Resolution

Insert:

10KA Cultural, Linguistic and Religious Needs of Parties

(1) Family dispute resolution practitioners may engage with relevant specialist advisors in family dispute resolution where:

(a) There are identified cultural and/or religious needs of parties; and
(b) Both parties agree to relevant specialist advisors participating in the family dispute resolution.

(2) The following persons are considered relevant specialist advisors who may participate in family dispute resolution to advise on cultural and religious considerations:

(a) A respected community member of the relevant cultural and/or religious group; and
(b) A representative from a cultural and/or religious community support service.

(3) Parties to family dispute resolution are entitled to be supported by the following additional specialist persons in family dispute resolution:

(a) An Australian legal practitioner; and
(b) An interpreter.

Notes

1 John W Cooley, 'Arbitration vs. Mediation – Explaining the Differences' (1986) 69(5) *Judicature* 263.

2 Elizabeth Wilson-Evered and John Zeleznikow, 'The Evolution of Family Dispute and the Need for Online Family Dispute Resolution in Australia' in Elizabeth Wilson-Evered and John Zeleznikow, *Online Family Dispute Resolution* (Springer, 2021) 7.
3 Audrey Macklin, 'Multiculturalism Meets Privatization: The Case of Faith-Based Arbitration' in Anne C Korteweg and Jennifer A Selby (eds) *Debating Sharia: Islam, Gender Politics and Family Law* (University of Toronto Press, 2012) 100–1.
4 Samia Bano, 'Women, Mediation, and Religious Arbitration: Thinking Through Gender and Justice in Family Law Disputes' in Samia Bano (ed.) *Gender and Justice in Family Law Disputes: Women, Mediation and Religious Arbitration* (Brandeis University Press, 2017).
5 Australian Institute of Family Studies, *Evaluation of a Pilot of Legally Assisted and Supported Family Dispute Resolution in Family Violence Cases* (Commissioned Report, December 2012).
6 Rachael Field, 'A Call for a Safe Model of Family Mediation' (2016) 28(1) *Bond Law Review* 83; and Rachael Field and Angela Lynch, 'Hearing Parties' Voices in Coordinated Family Dispute Resolution' (2014) 36(4) *Journal of Social Welfare and Family Law* 392.
7 Rachael Field, 'Using the Feminist Critique of Mediation to Explore "The Good, The Bad and The Ugly" Implications for Women of the Introduction of Mandatory Family Dispute Resolution in Australia' (2006) 20(1) *Australian Journal of Family Law* 6; Samia Bano, 'Agency, Autonomy, and Rights: Muslim Women and Alternative Dispute Resolution in Britain' in Samia Bano (ed.) *Gender and Justice in Family Law Disputes* (Brandeis University Press, 2017) 60.
8 Lisa Webley, 'When Is Mediation Mediatory and When Is It Really Adjudicatory?' in Samia Bano (ed.) *Gender and Justice in Family Law Disputes: Women, Mediation and Religious Arbitration* (Brandeis University Press, 2017).
9 Ibid.
10 Attorney-General's Department, *New Family Dispute Resolution Services for Aboriginal and Torres Strait Islander Families* (Discussion Paper, January 2022).
11 Ghena Krayem, *Islamic Family Law in Australia: To Recognise or Not To Recognise* (Melbourne University Publishing, 2014).
12 Farrah Ahmed and Ghena Krayem, *Understanding Sharia Process: Women's Experiences of Family Disputes* (Hart Publishing, 2022) 39.
13 Nadav Prawer, Nessen Ainsworth and John Zeleznikow, 'An Introduction to the Challenges and Possibilities of Faith-based Arbitration in Australia' (2014) 25(2) *Australasian Dispute Resolution Journal* 93.
14 Farrah Ahmed and Ghena Krayem, *Understanding Sharia Process: Women's Experiences of Family Disputes* (Hart Publishing, 2022) 120.
15 Ibid 123.
16 Community Leader, interviewed 10 March 2003 and 11 July 2008, cited in Krayem (n 11) 190.
17 Community Member, interviewed 16 December 2007, cited in Krayem (n 11) 190.
18 Mehzabin Farazi, 'Experiences of the Australian Bangladeshi Muslim Community in Family Dispute Resolution' (Masters of Research Thesis, The University of Sydney, 2020); Family Law Council, 'Improving the Family Law System for Clients from Culturally and Linguistically Diverse Backgrounds' (report, February 2012) 28.
19 Susan Armstrong, *Culturally Responsive Family Dispute Resolution in Family Relationship Centres: Access and Practice: A Report for Family Relationship Centres at Bankstown* (2010); Susan Armstrong, 'Good Practices with

Culturally Diverse Families in Family Dispute Resolution' (2013) 92 *Family Matters* 48.
20 Ibid.
21 Family Law Council, 'Improving the Family Law System' 33.
22 Interview 57 (Melbourne, January 2020) cited in Ahmed and Krayem (n 12) 111.
23 Family Law Council 'Improving the Family Law System' 37.
24 Ibid 34.
25 Ibid 34.
26 Antonella Rodriguez, 'Literature Review: Cultural Consideration in Alternative Dispute Resolution' (2018) 28 *Journal of Judicial Administration* 134.
27 Ibid 129.
28 Federal Court of Australia Indigenous Dispute Resolution and Conflict Management Case Study Project, *Solid Work You Mob Are Doing: Case Studies in Indigenous Dispute Resolution & Conflict Management in Australia – Report to the National Alternative Dispute Resolution Advisory Council* (Report, 2009) xv. Also see Attorney-General's Department, *Family Dispute Resolution Services for Aboriginal and Torres Strait Islander Families: Closing the Gap?* (discussion paper, September 2010) Australian Family Relationships Clearinghouse. https://www.ag.gov.au/families-and-marriage/publications/new-family-dispute-esolution-services-aboriginal-and-torres-strait-islander-families-discussion-paper.
29 Attorney-General's Department, *Research/Evaluation of Family Mediation Practice and the Issue of Violence* (Final Report, 1996).
30 Renata Alexander, 'Family Mediation: Friend or Foe for Women?' (1997) 10(1) *Australian Dispute Resolution Journal.*
31 Stephen Ralph and Stephen Meredith, 'Working Together: A Model of Mediation with Aboriginal and Torres Strait Islander Families in the Family Court of Australia' (2002) 40(3) *Family Court Review.*
32 Ibid.
33 Rachel Field, 'A Feminist Model of Mediation: Using Lawyers as Advocates for Participants who are Victims of Domestic Violence' (2005) 1 *DVIRC Quarterly.*
34 Ahmed and Krayem (n 12).
35 Kathy Douglas and Becky Batagol, 'The Role of Lawyers in Mediation: Insights from Mediators at Victoria's Civil and Administrative Tribunal' (2014) 40(3) *Monash Law Review.*
36 Webley (n 8).
37 Field (n 33).

Chapter 13A

Commentary on *Navigating Cultural and Religious Needs in Family Dispute Resolution*

Balawyn Jones

This Bill seeks to amend Division 3 of the Family Law Act in the context of Family Dispute Resolution (FDR) processes which are generally compulsory when a party is seeking a parenting order.[1] There are limited exceptions to this: for example, cases which involve domestic and family violence are excluded from FDR.[2] At its core, the Bill aims to recognise and accommodate cultural and/or religious diversity in Australia. In particular, the Bill seeks to empower FDR practitioners with the discretion to engage 'relevant specialist advisors', including where the parties to a dispute have 'identified cultural and/or religious needs'. There is a wealth of evidence to support the need for increased cultural competency in State legal processes and service provision,[3] particularly where these processes are compulsory. Put simply, FDR processes that are not culturally competent can marginalise, erase and discriminate against parties from culturally and/or religiously diverse backgrounds.[4]

In the context of parties' cultural and/or religious needs, special advisors are further defined as either 'respected community members' of cultural and religious groups or 'representatives' from cultural and religious community support services (CSS).[5] Subject to the discretion of the FDR practitioner, respected community members or CSS representatives may be involved in FDR processes for the purpose of advising the practitioners on issues specific to the culture and/or religion of a party (or parties) involved in the dispute. Some may seek to criticise the inclusion of cultural and/or religious advisors on the basis of a perceived lack of neutrality or challenge the idea that such advisors would be able to provide advice in a 'neutral' manner as suggested in the Second Reading Speech. However, such concerns are often underpinned by imperialist thinking rather than evidence-based critique. Even much feminist scholarship is built upon a presumption of whiteness or cultural 'neutrality'.[6]

It is problematic to assume that existing State systems are value-neutral to begin with, as opposed to being inherently value-laden. As Aftab explains, although State institutions are often conceptualised as neutral, 'the notion of neutrality of state institutions is a fallacy as there are gendered hierarchies

DOI: 10.4324/9781003372462-29

and legacies within formal institutions that shape outcomes for women's agency'.[7] Further, at the intersection of race and gender, Moreton-Robinson identifies institutionalised 'patriarchal whiteness' as 'an invisible unnamed organising principle that surreptitiously shapes the Australian social structure and national culture'.[8] Rather than addressing structural issues that hinder women's meaningful participation in mainstream processes or services, those adopting an imperialist view (explicitly or implicitly) believe that women from diverse cultural and/or religious backgrounds are 'complicit in [the] patriarchal structures of the migrant family' due to their 'supposed inherent passivity'.[9] Such reasoning undermines the agency of women from diverse cultural and/or religious backgrounds to make decisions related to their own lives.[10] Muslim women are, for example, often constructed as 'victims' of their religion.[11]

To clarify, for a variety of reasons, women from diverse backgrounds may or may not wish to involve cultural and/or religious advisors in FDR processes. Significantly, the Bill's drafting makes it clear that the inclusion of cultural and/or religious advisors is contingent on the *consent of both parties*. With respect to concerns relating to the 'informed consent' of parties from diverse cultural and/or religious backgrounds, note the inclusion in the Bill of a right for parties to be supported by a legal practitioner (framed in the same terms as the right to be supported by an interpreter). In addition, the Bill is drafted to ensure that the FDR practitioner retains an overarching discretion to exclude a specialist advisor at any point during the FDR process, in addition to their existing discretion to end FDR processes.[12]

Further, the requirement that a respected community member be recognised as a leader within their cultural and/or religious community could be criticised on the basis that most community-based organisations are dominated by male leadership.[13] While there are broader structural barriers to formal recognition of women in male-dominated leadership structures, the second category of specialist advisor (ie CSS representatives) largely overcomes this concern as women are far better represented in informal leadership positions within community organisations.[14]

Lastly, some may argue that this proposal does not go far enough and that, instead of advisors being included within existing FDR processes, parallel cultural and/or religious FDR processes should be allowed to operate independently outside of the State family law system – that is, an argument for formalised legal pluralism in the family law space. While informal pluralism already exists in practice, the Australian Government has consistently rejected the adoption or endorsement of personal laws for diverse cultural and/or religious groups.[15] The current Australian approach can be described as cultural voluntarism where there is 'tacit acceptance of minority groups following their own ([cultural or] religious) rules without the conferral of State-backed legal authority to minority group institutions'.[16] It is therefore unlikely that the Government would support or implement a shift from cultural voluntarism to legal pluralism in the context of family law for diverse cultural and/or religious communities. The exception to this is, of course, for First Nation communities. While some argue that the colonial State should recognise First Nations law/lore in terms of formalising legal pluralism, others argue that as sovereignty was never ceded by First Nations people, First Nations law/lore 'do[es] not depend on settler law for . . . authority'.[17] The current proposal seeks to regulate the inclusion of cultural and/or religious advisors from diverse communities but does not seek to limit the operation of First Nations law/lore outside of, and in parallel to, the current proposal.

Notes

1 Section 10F of the *Family Law Act* 1975 (Cth), 'definition of family dispute resolution'.

2 Section 60I(9)(b) of the *Family Law Act* 1975 (Cth); Regulation 25(2) of the *Family Law (Family Dispute Resolution Practitioners) Regulations* 2008 (Cth).

3 For example, in the family law context, see Farrah Ahmed and Ghena Krayem, *Understanding Sharia Processes: Women's Experiences of Family Disputes* (Oxford University Press, 2021) Section 6-II. Further, in the context of domestic violence service provision, see Ghena Krayem and Mehal Krayem, 'Muslim Women's Agency in Australian Domestic Violence Services' in Ghena Krayem et al., *Muslim Women and Agency: An Australian Context* (Brill, 2022) 77; Muslim Women Australia, Submission to the Joint Select Committee on Coercive Control (2021) 5; and Rojan Afrouz et al., 'Seeking Help in Domestic Violence Among Muslim Women in Muslim-Majority and Non-Muslim Majority Countries: A Literature Review' (2020) 21(3) *Trauma, Violence and Abuse* 551–66, 563.

4 For more information on the 'importance of FDR services engaging ethically and effectively with cultural and faith communities', see Western Sydney University, *Supporting Culturally Responsive Family Dispute Resolution* (research report, 2012).

5 A proposal for the inclusion of 'cultural advisors' in the context of litigation and court decisions has previously been put forward by Ann Black, 'Cultural Expertise in Australia: Colonial Laws, Customs, and Emergent Legal Pluralism' in Austin Sarat and Livia Holden (eds), *Cultural Expertise and Social-Legal Studies: Special Issue* (Emerald Publishing, 2019) vol 78, 133–55.

6 Contrastingly, this Bill is framed through an intersectional feminist lens. See generally Kimberlé Crenshaw et al. (eds) *The Public Nature of Private Violence* (Routledge, 1994) 93–118; Shakira Hussein, 'Double Bind and Double Responsibility: Speech and Silence among Australian Muslim Women' in Shahram Akbarzadeh, *Challenging Identities: Muslim Women in Australia* (Manchester University Press, 2010).

7 Amira Aftab, 'Muslim Women's Agency Through a Feminist Institutional Lens' in Ghena Krayem, Susan Carland and Balawyn Jones (eds), *Muslim Women and Agency: An Australian Context* (Brill, 2021) 35–58.

8 Aileen Moreton-Robinson, 'Patriarchal Whiteness, Self-Determination and Indigenous Women: The Invisibility of Structural Privilege and the Visibility of Oppression' in Barbara Hocking (ed), *Unfinished Constitutional Business? Rethinking Indigenous Self-Determination* (Aboriginal Studies Press, 2005) 62.

9 Ghena Krayem and Mehal Krayem, 'Muslim Women's Agency in Australian Domestic Violence Services', in Ghena Krayem et al. (eds), *Muslim Women and Agency: An Australian Context* (Brill, 2021) 84.

10 For a critique of the dichotomy between 'choice' and 'force', see Aftab, 'Muslim Women's Agency Through a Feminist Institutional Lens' in Ghena Krayem et al. (eds), *Muslim Women and Agency: An Australian Context* (Brill, 2021) 37, citing Shakira Hussein, *From Victims to Suspects: Muslim Women since 9/11* (NewSouth Publishing, 2016).

11 See Australian Human Rights Commission, 'Freedom of Religion, Belief and Gender: A Muslim Perspective' (Supplementary Paper, 2010) 11. See, more broadly, Lila Abu-Lughod, *Do Muslim Women Need Saving?* (Harvard University Press, 2015) 8 and 88; Saba Mahmood, *Politics of Piety: The Islamic Revival and the Feminist Subject* (Princeton University Press, 2012) 6.

12 See regulation 29(c)(i)–(ii) of the *Family Law (Family Dispute Resolution Practitioners) Regulations* 2008 (Cth).

13 See Feda Abdo and Balawyn Jones, 'Finding a Way Forward: The Revival of Female Islamic Scholarship in Australia' in Ghena Krayem et al. (eds), *Muslim Women and Agency: An Australian Context* (Brill, 2021) 195–209 and Ahmed and Krayem, *Understanding Sharia Processes*, [3.4.6], [4.4.3] and [6.1.5].

14 Abdo and Jones (n 13), 'Finding a Way Forward' [4.1]. A number of Australian Muslim women's organisations represent the interests of women, such as the Islamic Women's Association of Queensland, the Muslim Women's Association of South Australia, the Muslim Women's Council of Victoria, Muslim Women's Support Centre WA, Muslim Women's Welfare Association (ACT) and Muslim Women Australia (NSW).

15 Black (n 5), 152; Malcolm Voyce and Adam Possamai, 'Legal Pluralism, Family Personal Laws, and the Rejection of *Shari'a* in Australia: A Case of Multiple or "Clashing" Modernities?' (2011) 7 *Democracy and Security* 338–53, 341.

16 John Eekelaar and Mavis MacLean, 'Introduction' in John Eekelaar and Mavis MacLean (eds) *Managing Family Justice in Diverse Societies* (Hart Bloomsbury, 2015) 3.

17 Melbourne Law School Indigenous Law and Justice Hub, 'Research Project: Legal Pluralism and Treaty Making in Australia' (2020). https://law.unimelb.edu.au/iljh/research/research-projects/current-projects/legal-pluralism-and-treaty-making-in-australia.

Chapter 14

Family Violence and Migration Law

Protecting Immigrant Women's Legal Status

Heli Askola

Extract from *Hansard* (Commonwealth of Australia)

Migration Amendment (Preventing and Responding to Family Violence) Bill 2024

Second Reading

HON HELI ASKOLA: I move:
That this Bill be now read a second time.

Australia has finally woken up to the seriousness of family violence. This Bill deals with an important aspect of our response to family violence – the role of the victim's migration status.

We have seen a greater awareness of the need to tailor responses to family violence so that they address the specific risks experienced by individuals and groups, such as Aboriginal and Torres Strait Islander women or trans people. This Bill deals with an aspect that has been neglected for too long – the way in which many immigrant women are effectively held hostage by immigration rules that make them dependent on their sponsors, a situation preventing them from leaving a violent partner without compromising their migration status.[1]

How does this happen? Perverse situations, where women stay with violent partners in order to maintain their right of residence, arise because migration law puts women in vulnerable positions where their visa status can be used to threaten and control them. Migrant partners of Australian citizens and permanent residents are initially placed on a two-year temporary Partner visa. To obtain a permanent visa, they must establish that the relationship is still continuing after the 'probationary period'. Leaving a perpetrator therefore risks their visa status, preventing them from seeking help. Women on other temporary visas are often placed in similar dependent situations.

DOI: 10.4324/9781003372462-30

As part of a package of measures aimed at ensuring the safety and integration of migrant women, this Bill overhauls the current system in three ways. First, it amends the federal *Migration Act 1958* and *Migration Regulations 1994*[2] to remove the existing two-stage process for Partner visas to ensure migrant partners are granted direct access to permanent residence, as used to be the case. Second, the Bill lays the foundation for effective visa pathways and institutional mechanisms for survivors of family violence who hold temporary visas. Finally, the Bill clarifies that less well-known forms of family violence that disproportionately affect women from culturally and linguistically diverse backgrounds – namely forced marriage and dowry-related economic abuse – constitute family violence in the migration context.

This Bill and the review accompanying it implement a key action flagged by the *Third Action Plan 2016–2019 of the National Plan to Reduce Violence against Women and their Children* to 'ensure migration rules and eligibility requirements for support services do not disempower victims of violence or discourage them from leaving violent relationships'.[3] Unlike the current rules, which prioritise immigration control at the expense of the lives and safety of migrant women, the Bill strikes an appropriate balance between maintaining the integrity of the immigration system and empowering migrant women.

What Are the Problems with the Current Situation?

In Australia, as in many other states, family migration is both significant in scale and highly gendered. Between 40,000 and 50,000 family visas are granted every year, mostly to partners and spouses of Australian citizens and permanent residents.[4] Two-thirds of these go to women. In addition, tens of thousands of women are granted temporary visas every year as secondary applicants to accompany partners who are primary holders of temporary visas, as students or skilled temporary workers, for instance. Given the high estimated prevalence of family violence in the community, we know that a significant proportion of these women suffer family violence.[5]

The current Regulations require that migrant partners of Australian citizens and permanent residents are placed on provisional visas. A permanent visa is only granted if the relationship is found to be 'genuine and continuing' after two years. This probationary period was introduced in the 1990s in response to concerns about 'sham marriages' and 'serial sponsorship'.[6] There is no support for the claims made at the time that this change would fix those problems – and other measures have been adopted to deal with serial sponsors. Instead, there is plenty of evidence that by making migrants highly dependent on their local partner, the change creates room for abuse of the power differential between spouses.[7]

It is true that the Regulations currently include a so-called 'Family Violence Exception', which allows applicants to continue with an application for permanent residency if they can prove that they (or a family member such as a child) have been victims of family violence perpetrated by the sponsor, even if the marriage or de facto relationship has already ended. But applicants must now meet various cumbersome substantive, evidential and procedural conditions set out in the Regulations.[8] Problems with these requirements have been outlined by several reviews, including by the Australian Law Reform Commission or the ALRC. These include an unduly narrow definition of family violence, poor institutional mechanisms and overly rigid procedural requirements.[9]

The limited nature of this exception – together with obstacles such as fear, shame, trauma, isolation, lack of access to services, linguistic barriers and limited financial resources – means that only a few hundred women per year are able to make use of it.[10] In addition, the rules currently only apply to victims who hold certain classes of visa – most importantly, Partner visa applicants. Women who are not on designated visas, including secondary temporary skilled visa holders, benefit from no similar pathway, regardless of their length of residence in Australia or prospects of obtaining permanent residence. Women on temporary dependent visas are often in particularly precarious situations and typically have limited rights to work, access to medical care or social support.

Finally, the current system is unable to respond to complex forms of family violence, such as forced marriage and dowry abuse. Forced marriage and dowry-related abuse are now recognised in Victoria as family violence.[11] These forms of violence involve manipulation of familial relationships and can be perpetrated by multiple members of the victim's extended family. Yet they are not well understood by decision-makers, which raises problems in relation to the ability of the current family violence provisions to offer sufficient protection.[12] These shortcomings again expose migrant women on temporary partner visas to an unacceptably high risk of visa cancellation.[13]

How Does this Bill Propose to End Dependence and Update the System?

This Bill is part of a suite of measures aimed at providing a genuine opportunity for victims of family violence to leave violent partners without risking the life they have built for themselves in Australia. The Bill amends both the Act and the Regulations, and will be complemented by a subsequent review of the Regulations where visa classes targeted by the changes are set out.

This Bill makes a fundamental change by removing the two-year requirement that currently applies to migrant partners of Australian citizens and permanent residents. Given the compelling force of the argument that women must not feel obliged to remain in abusive relationships due to fears of losing their secure migration status, the Bill directly amends the Regulations by stipulating that partners and spouses immediately obtain permanent residency. The Bill follows the example of Canada, which removed the two-year requirement in 2017.[14] A new provision – that is, section 39B – makes these changes permanent by precluding Partner visas from being made provisional.

With this change, the current Family Violence Exception will no longer be needed to protect future partner migrants. However, we will maintain and expand the exception so that we can offer secondary visa holders in family violence situations, who are already on a pathway to permanent residence, access to permanent status. The government is currently conducting a comprehensive review of the classes that should be eligible for this pathway. The review will also examine the option of introducing a new temporary visa for migrants currently on temporary visas whose partners have perpetrated family violence. Such a visa would make it easier for women to seek help and remain in Australia while applying for another visa.

To establish the foundation for these changes, this Bill inserts new rules on family violence directly into the *Migration Act*. The changes build on the existing system of Family Violence Exceptions, but improve the current framework in the following ways.

First, the definition of 'relevant family violence' currently found in the Regulations is replaced with the definition of family violence from the federal *Family Law Act*. Back in 2011, the ALRC suggested that it was important to establish 'a common understanding of what constitutes family violence across family violence legislation' and that family violence ought to be defined as 'violent or threatening behaviour, or any other form of behaviour, that coerces or controls a family member or causes that family member to be fearful'.[15] The Bill implements this long-overdue change and removes the earlier unduly restrictive definition which relied on the standard of 'causing the victim to *reasonably* fear . . . or to be *reasonably* apprehensive'.[16] The definition of 'relevant family violence' is also broadened in other ways, as I will outline in a moment in relation to forced marriage.

Second, the Bill creates a panel of independent experts to assess cases involving family violence. In the current system, referrals are made to 'independent experts' – usually psychologists or social workers – only in so-called 'non-judicially determined' cases, where the Department of Home Affairs is not satisfied that an applicant has suffered family violence.[17] However, the quality, consistency and transparency of this mechanism have been questioned.[18]

To guarantee uniform application and fairness to applicants, this Bill establishes a panel of genuinely impartial and independent experts, appointed on the basis of their experience in dealing with family violence.[19] The Bill includes detailed provisions on the panel's membership and functions, as well as the legal effects of the panel's determinations. The change brings us in line with other common law jurisdictions, which have increasingly introduced specialised assessments.[20]

Third, the Bill lowers the procedural and evidential hurdles for seeking assistance, especially in relation to so-called 'non-judicially determined' claims.

The new section 91ZD allows a broad range of evidence to be put forward in support of an assertion of family violence, replacing the current overly rigid requirements.[21] The Bill also removes the requirement that the family violence, or part of it, must have occurred 'while the marriage or de facto relationship existed' between the victim and the perpetrator.[22] Proving this has been shown to be overly onerous, given relationships often fall apart over an extended period of time, victims may have to make several attempts to leave, and violence often escalates or begins at the point of separation.[23]

How Does the Bill Respond to Less Common Forms of Family Violence, including Forced Marriage?

I now turn to how the Bill provides further alternatives to migrant victims of complex forms of family violence, such as forced marriage and dowry abuse. These forms of family violence are not considered prevalent in Australia, but are part of immigrant and refugee women's experiences of violence.[24] The family violence provisions must also ensure protection in these cases. I will from here on particularly concentrate on forced marriage, given that is the most well-known of these forms of violence, but much of what I will say also applies, for instance, to dowry abuse.

The essence of forced marriage is that genuine consent of at least one party to the marriage is lacking, typically due to some form of coercion. Coercion can range from physical force to psychological, financial or emotional pressure employed by immediate or extended family members, such as parents.[25] In some cases, young women may seem to consent but only do so because of intense pressure, fear of family estrangement and social isolation. The person is often forced to marry to a member of their extended family, such as a cousin, and women involved in forced marriages are at high risk of further family violence perpetrated by their spouse or in-laws.[26] We know that in the Australian context, forced marriage often involves a migration element.[27] If the person forced to marry is on a dependent visa, they face additional barriers to finding help.

So far, our response to forced marriages has been driven by criminalisation, lumping forced marriage together with serious federal offences such as trafficking and slavery.[28] The support mechanism originally developed for trafficking situations, the Support for Trafficked People Program or STPP, now also provides assistance to people in or at risk of a forced marriage. The Australian Federal Police, which investigates forced marriages, has a central role referring individuals to the STPP. The STPP now has a special Forced Marriage Support Stream, providing intensive support for up to 200 days.[29] Non-nationals may be eligible for the Human Trafficking Visa Framework through this programme, which may help them remain here lawfully.

However, despite an increase in reports, we know that this approach is limited in its ability to reach likely victims of forced marriage. Forced marriage was first criminalised to 'send a clear message to the community', encouraging victims to speak out.[30] Yet individuals in forced marriages are often extremely isolated, unaware of support options and in some cases unwilling to come forward. The role of the Federal Police in screening victims may also discourage reporting among vulnerable women with negative experiences of dealing with authorities. It is therefore likely that some forced marriage victims do not report their circumstances, 'either through fear for their safety or fear for the unity of their family'.[31]

Importantly, women who do seek help in these situations often reach out to family violence services, which 'are not equipped to recognise it in a forced marriage context'.[32] The family violence system must therefore be improved so as to provide women with an alternative avenue for escaping violent relationships. Migrant women's vulnerability is often linked with migration status and temporary visas; the Bill therefore proposes to remedy the known problems with the current Family Violence Exception, with specific provisions recognising forced marriage as family violence, along with other less typical forms of violence. It does so in two main ways.

First, as mentioned earlier, the Bill changes the definition of family violence to the one used in the *Family Law Act*, specifically listing dowry abuse as a recognised form of family violence, removing any doubts about whether it would otherwise be covered. This change also removes the current requirement that the perpetrator must be the sponsoring spouse,[33] which helps address situations where violence may be perpetrated by extended family members such as in-laws or a spouse's siblings. Similarly, the definition covers multi-perpetrator violence in marriages involving domestic labour exploitation.[34] The Bill includes a further provision – section 504A – preventing the Regulations from adopting a narrower interpretation.

Second, the Bill addresses a specific legal problem that arises when a migrant woman trapped in a forced marriage seeks to use the Family Violence Exception, which generally requires a marriage that is 'genuine'. [35] The problem arises because women who seek to apply for the exception under the current Regulations must *first* satisfy the definition of 'spouse' as outlined in section 5F of the *Migration Act.* This definition requires both the existence of a 'marriage that is valid'[36] and a relationship that is 'genuine and continuing'. This issue is considered by the Department of Home Affairs in line with the matters listed in Regulation 1.15A. Current case law suggests that if the Department forms the view that the relationship is not valid or genuine and continuing under section 5F, it is not required to consider whether the person had in fact suffered family violence.[37]

This puts women who are in a relationship founded on a forced marriage in an invidious position. If they raise the fact that the violence perpetrated against them is essentially about, or indeed even *connected* to, entering or remaining in a forced marriage, that marriage will likely be considered either invalid or not genuine. The same conclusion – that a marriage or genuine and continuing relationship never existed – may also be reached in cases involving dowry-related abuse.[38] Likewise, the presence of indicators suggesting an exploitative or servile marriage, where a migrant spouse is effectively treated as a servant,[39] might also lead to a conclusion that there *was* no relationship, leaving women with no recourse.

The Bill removes this outrageous injustice, which compounds the mistreatment of migrant women by treating them as having failed to prove their claim of family violence *because of* the form of family violence perpetrated against them. The Bill ensures that women in such situations can access the Family Violence Exception or would not lose any already-granted permanent residence, because of being unable to satisfy the definition of 'spouse' or 'de facto partner'. The Bill does this in two ways – first, by including provisions that separate the existence of family violence from questions regarding the 'genuineness' of a relationship; and second, by including a new section 5F(4). This section means marriages that are not otherwise recognised as valid are treated as valid for the purposes of the Family Violence Exception.

In conclusion, immigration laws have for far too long incorporated and enforced the dependency of migrant spouses and given excessive power to the sponsor. This Bill is founded on the idea that migration status ought not prevent people from leaving a violent relationship. The removal of the probationary period gives partner migrants the security they need to build a life in Australia that is free of undue power and control. The Bill lays the foundation for new visa arrangements for women who have been subjected to family violence, removing the technical obstacles that have previously resulted in low numbers of migrant women being able to make use of the Family Violence Exception. The Bill will also provide genuine alternatives to those trapped by specific forms of abuse such as forced marriage.

I commend this Bill to the House.

The Parliament of the Commonwealth of Australia

HOUSE OF REPRESENTATIVES

Migration Amendment (Preventing and Responding to Family Violence) Bill 2024

A Bill for an Act to amend the *Migration Act 1958* (Cth), and for related purposes

The Parliament of Australia enacts:

1 Short title

This Act is the *Migration Amendment (Family Violence) Act 2024*.

2 Commencement

(1) Each provision of this Act specified in column 1 of the table commences, or is taken to have commenced, in accordance with column 2 of the table. Any other statement in column 2 has effect according to its terms.

Commencement information		
Column 1	Column 2	Column 3
Provisions	Commencement	Date/Details
1. The whole of this Act	The day after this Act receives the Royal Assent.	

Note: This table relates only to the provisions of this Act as originally enacted. It will not be amended to deal with any later amendments of this Act.

(2) Any information in column 3 of the table is not part of this Act. Information may be inserted in this column, or information in it may be edited, in any published version of this Act.

3 Schedules

Legislation that is specified in a Schedule to this Act is amended or repealed as set out in the applicable items in the Schedule concerned, and any other item in a Schedule to this Act has effect according to its terms.

Schedule 1 – Family violence
Migration Act 1958

1 **Subsection 5(1)**
Insert:

de facto relationship as it appears in sections 4(1AB) and 4(1AC) of the *Family Law Act* in relation to family violence has the meaning given in section 5CB of the *Migration Act*.
family violence has the meaning given by section 4AB of the *Family Law Act 1975*, and includes using coercion, threats, physical abuse or emotional or psychological abuse to demand or receive dowry, either before or after a marriage.
exposed to family violence, in relation to a child, has the meaning given by subsection 4AB(3) of the *Family Law Act*.

2 **After subsection 5CB(2)**
Insert:

(2A) The fact that a person is (or their children are) being subjected to or exposed to family violence by any person is irrelevant to the question of whether that person is in a de facto relationship for the purposes of the Act.

3 **After subsection 5F(2)**
Insert:

(2A) The fact that a person is (or their children are) being subjected to or exposed to family violence by any person is irrelevant to the question of whether that person is in a marriage relationship for the purposes of the Act.

4 **After subsection 5F(3)**
Insert:

(4) for the purposes of determining whether two people are members of the same family in the process of determining whether particular violence is family violence under the *Migration Act* or the *Migration Regulations*, a marriage that is not recognised in Australia as valid because of section 88(2)(d) of the *Marriage Act* is taken to be recognised in Australia as valid despite that provision.

5 **Before section 40**
Insert:

39B Partner visas not to be provisional

Visas granted on the ground that the person is a spouse, de facto partner or dependent child of

(a) an Australian citizen; or
(b) the holder of a permanent visa that is in effect; or

(c) a person who is usually resident in Australia and whose continued presence in Australia is not subject to a limitation as to time imposed by law

must not be provisional.

6 Before Subdivision B of Division 3 of Part 2
Insert:

Subdivision AM – Special provisions relating to family violence
91Z Independent Family Violence Panel

(1) The Independent Family Violence Panel (the *panel*) is established by this section.
(2) The function of the *panel* is to make a determination on whether a person has been subjected to, or exposed to, family violence, where such an assertion is made in relation to an application for a visa that includes a prescribed criterion requiring the applicant for the visa, or another person mentioned in the criterion, to have suffered family violence.

91ZA Membership and appointment

(1) The *panel* consists of:

(a) the Chairperson; and
(b) not less than four other members.

(2) Each member of the *panel* is to be appointed by the Minister by written instrument for a minimum term of three years.
(3) The Minister must not appoint a person as a member of the *panel* unless the Minister is satisfied that the person has:

(a) skills, expertise or experience on family violence, and
(b) skills, expertise or experience in a relevant field, including law, social work, health care and psychology.

(4) A member of the *panel* holds office on a part-time basis.

91ZB Performance of the *panel*'s functions

(1) Subject to this section, the *panel* is to carry out its functions in such manner as the *panel* determines.
(2) In performing its functions, members of the *panel*:

(a) must act with as little formality as possible; and
(b) must act as quickly as is appropriate given the need properly to consider a matter before it; and
(c) may inform itself on anything relevant to the matter before it in any way it thinks fit; and
(d) may, in respect of a matter before it, consult such persons as it thinks fit.

91ZC Processing assertions of family violence

(1) If, as part of an application under this Act, an assertion is made that the applicant, or one of their children, has been subjected to, or exposed to, family violence, the person to whom the application is made must refer the assertion of family violence to the Chairperson of the *panel*.
(2) The Chairperson must assign the assertion of family violence to either themselves or to another member of the *panel* for determination as soon as is reasonably practicable.
(3) A *panel* member must make a determination on an assertion of family violence assigned to them by the Chairperson.
(4) Determinations on assertions of family violence under this Division may only be made by members of the Independent Family Violence Panel.

91ZD Material that can be considered

(1) Material that can be considered in making a determination includes:

(a) judicial findings, including but not limited to:

(i) an injunction granted under paragraph 114(1)(a), (b) or (c) of the *Family Law Act 1975*;
(ii) an order made by a court under a law of a State or Territory for the protection of a victim from family violence; or
(iii) a conviction for offences involving family violence, or a recorded finding of guilt for offences involving family violence;

(b) statutory declarations by or on behalf of the victim or by another person, including but not limited to:

(i) a medical practitioner or nurse;
(ii) a police officer;
(iii) a child welfare authority or protection agency;
(iv) a member of the Australian Association of Social Workers;
(v) a registered psychologist;
(vi) a family consultant under the *Family Law Act 1975* (Cth) or family relationship counsellor;
(vii) a school counsellor;

(c) documents, including but not limited to:

(i) a medical or hospital report or discharge summary;
(ii) a police report, record of assault or witness statement made to a police officer;
(iii) a letter or assessment report from a women's refuge or crisis centre;
(iv) any document detailing an incident of family violence.

91ZE Power to obtain information and documents

(1) If the *panel* has reason to believe that a Department of the Commonwealth or a prescribed authority is capable of giving information or producing documents or other records relevant to the *panel*'s performance of its function, the *panel* may, by notice in writing given to the head of the agency, require the head of the agency, or a person nominated by the head of the agency, to give the information or produce the document or other record to the *panel*.

91ZF Determining an assertion of family violence

(1) A *panel* member to whom a matter has been assigned by the Chairperson must make a determination as to whether the person to whom the referral relates has been subjected to, or exposed to, family violence.
(2) A determination must be made as soon as is reasonably practicable.
(3) The *panel* member must give notice of the finding to the person to whom the application was made and the Chairperson (unless the member deciding the issue is also the Chairperson).
(4) A *panel* member must give full reasons for their determination.

91ZG Legal effect of determination

(1) In making a decision under this Act or the Regulations, the panel member's determination on whether a person has been subjected to, or exposed to, family violence must be taken to be correct for the purposes of deciding whether the person satisfies a prescribed criterion for a visa that requires the applicant for the visa, or another person mentioned in the criterion, to have suffered family violence.

7 Before section 505
Insert:

504A Regulations about family violence

(1) To avoid doubt, it is the intention of the Parliament that:

(a) the definition of family violence established by subsection 5(1) is to be used by the Regulations in connection with family violence as generally or otherwise understood; and
(b) Regulations made under the Act are not to provide differently (whether using the term 'family violence' or otherwise) for violence that constitutes family violence as generally or otherwise understood.

Note: As an example, Regulations must not include provisions in which, for a particular purpose, violence does not constitute family violence if it occurs in the context of a marriage that is not recognised as valid in Australia because of section 88(2)(d) of the *Marriage Act*.

(2) Regulations made inconsistent with this intention are invalid.

(3) Nothing in the section prevents the making of regulations that:

(a) specify circumstances in which family violence is taken to have occurred; or

(b) provide that a question of whether family violence has or has not occurred is to be determined by a particular person or in accordance with a particular procedure, where that procedure is consistent with the definition.

8 **After section 507**
Insert:

508 Transitional Provisions

(1) If, immediately before the commencement of section 39B, a person held a Subclass 100 (Partner) visa, that visa is to be taken to be a Subclass 309 (Partner) visa that permits the holder to remain indefinitely in Australia.

(2) If, immediately before the commencement of section 39B, a person held a Subclass 801 (Partner) visa, that visa is to be taken to be a Subclass 820 (Partner) visa that permits the holder to remain indefinitely in Australia.

Migration Regulations 1994

1 **Division 1.5 – Special provisions relating to family violence**

Repeal the Division.

2 **Heading to Part 309 of Schedule 2**

Remove "(Provisional)".

3 **Clause 309.511**

Replace content with "Permanent visa permitting the holder to travel to and enter Australia for a period of five years from the date of grant."

4 **Heading to Part 820 of Schedule 2**

Remove "(Provisional)".

5 **Clause 820.511**

Replace content with "Permanent visa permitting the holder to travel to and enter Australia for five years from date of grant."

6 **Part 100 of Schedule 2**

Repeal this part.

7 **Part 801 of Schedule 2**

Repeal this part.

Notes

1 ALRC, 'Family Violence and Commonwealth Laws – Improving Legal Frameworks' (final report, 7 February 2012) chapters 20–2.
2 *Migration Act 1958* and *Migration Regulations 1994* as of 1 January 2023.
3 Department of Social Services, 'Third Action Plan 2016–2019 of the National Plan to Reduce Violence against Women and their Children 2010–2022' (Action Plan, 2016) 20.
4 Department of Home Affairs, *Reports on Migration Programs*. https://www.homeaffairs.gov.au/research-and-statistics/statistics/visa-statistics/live/migration-program.
5 See, for example, Australian Institute of Health and Welfare, 'Family, Domestic and Sexual Violence in Australia: Continuing the National Story' (media release, 5 June 2019). https://www.aihw.gov.au/reports/domestic-violence/family-domestic-sexual-violence-australia-2019/contents/summary.
6 R Iredale, 'Patterns of Spouse/Fiance Sponsorship to Australia' (1994) 3 *Asian and Pacific Migration Journal* 547.
7 J Maher and M Segrave, 'Family Violence Risk, Migration Status and "Vulnerability": Hearing the Voices of Immigrant Women' (2018) 3 *Journal of Gender-Based Violence* 503; C Vaughan et al., 'Promoting Community-Led Responses to Violence Against Immigrant and Refugee Women in Metropolitan and Regional Australia' (Research Report, ANROWS Horizons, December 2015).
8 See div 1.5 – Special Provisions Relating to Family Violence.
9 See ALRC (n 1), chapters 20–2; L Gray et al., 'Immigrant Women and Family Violence: Will the New Exceptions Help or Hinder Victims?' (2014) 39(3) *Alternative Law Journal* 167.
10 SBS Punjabi, 'Indians Receive Most Number of Visas Under Family Violence Provisions in Australia' (blog post, 1 October 2018, updated 8 April 2021). https://www.sbs.com.au/language/english/indians-receive-most-number-of-visas-under-family-violence-provisions-in-australia.
11 See s 5 of the *Family Violence Prevention Act* 2008 (Vic).
12 M Segrave, *Temporary Migration and Family Violence: An Analysis of Victimisation, Vulnerability and Support* (report, Monash University, 2017).
13 Australian Institute of Criminology, *When Saying No Is Not an Option: Forced Marriage in Australia and New Zealand* (Research Report No 11, 2018) 58.
14 A Borges Jelinic, 'Australia's Family Violence Provisions in Migration Law: A Comparative Study' (2020) 21(2) *Flinders Law Journal* 259.
15 ALRC, *Family Violence – A National Legal Response* (Report No 114, 11 November 2010).
16 Regulation 1.21.
17 Regulation 1.23(10)(c).
18 ALRC (n 1) ch 21.
19 This solution was discussed in ALRC, *Family Violence and Commonwealth Laws* (Discussion Paper No 76, 2011).
20 Borges Jelinic (n 13).
21 Migration Regulations 1994 – Evidentiary Requirements –IMMI 12/116 (F2012L02237).
22 Regulation 1.23.
23 ALRC (n 1) ch 21.
24 Australian Institute of Family Studies, *Intimate Partner Violence in Australian Refugee Communities: Scoping Review of Issues and Service Responses* (review, December 2018). https://aifs.gov.au/cfca/sites/default/files/publication-documents/50_intimate_partner_violence_in_australian_refugee_communities.pdf; Vaughan et al. (n 6).

25 H Sowey, 'From an Emic Perspective: Exploring Consent in Forced Marriage Law' (2017) 51(2) *Australian and New Zealand Journal of Criminology* 258.
26 Australian Institute of Criminology (n 12).
27 Australian Federal Police, 'Stop Human Trafficking Happening in Plain Sight'. https://www.afp.gov.au/news-media/media-releases/stop-human-trafficking-happening-plain-sight.
28 Divisions 270 and 271 of the *Criminal Code 1995* (Cth).
29 Department of Social Services, Support for Trafficked People Program (Support Program, 2023). https://www.dss.gov.au/women/programs-services/reducing-violence/anti-people-trafficking-strategy/support-for-trafficked-people-program.
30 Attorney-General's Department, *Forced and Servile Marriage* (Discussion Paper, 24 November 2010) 16.
31 Australian Institute of Criminology (n 12) 88.
32 H Askola, 'Responding to Vulnerability? Forced Marriage and the Law' (2018) 41(3) *University of New South Wales Law Journal* 977, 998.
33 This was recommended, eg, by the Victorian *Royal Commission into Family Violence: Report and Recommendations* (Report, March 2016) recommendation 162.
34 Australian Institute of Criminology, *Human Trafficking Involving Marriage and Partner Migration to Australia* (Research and Public Policy Series Report, 2014) 124.
35 Segrave (n 11).
36 With reference to s 12 of the *Migration Act*, which in turn refers to the *Marriage Act* (Cth). According to s 88D(2)(d) of the latter, a foreign marriage is not valid if it lacks real consent, for instance, because of duress or fraud as per s 23B of the *Marriage Act*.
37 *Liu v Minister for Home Affairs* [2019] FCA 1925.
38 Senate Legal and Constitutional Affairs Committee, *The Practice of Dowry and the Incidence of Dowry Abuse in Australia* (Report, 14 February 2019) 54–6.
39 *Shadali* v *MIAC* [2007] FMCA 1230.

Chapter 14A

Commentary on *Family Violence and Migration Law*

Susan Kneebone

Introduction: Gender in Regulation of Migration

This Bill recognises the central importance of gender in regulation of migration in the 21st century. It deals with four examples of female migration: partner migration to Australia of women who are on a pathway to permanent residence; secondary visa holders who are in 'intimate' or marriage relationships with a primary visa holder; forced marriages; and dowry-related exploitation of women in migrant communities.

Family or 'intimate' violence is the common issue in all three circumstances, which requires the state to intervene and to adapt policy responses; such violence can no longer be framed as a private or 'intimate' matter, or as an issue to be determined solely within the family or community. All women have the right to protection as equal members of human society, their international law right to be protected from gender-based violence by the Australian state and their rights to freedom of movement and free choice in marriage. Gendered responses to migration risk resulting in stereotyping and discrimination against women, thus disturbing the supposed neutrality of laws.

In framing policy responses to intimate violence in female migration, the power of the state is paramount. However, we need to guard against double exploitation of female migrants at the hands of both the state and their intimate partners, families and communities. We need to recognise the complex and intersectional background to intimate violence in Australia, which welcomes and celebrates diversity, which, while an admirable goal, can result in unintended consequences. In particular I do not support the removal of the provisional visa in this Bill (s39B) and suggest an expansion of the role of the proposed Independent Family Violence Panel (the 'IFV Panel' – Subdivision AM). However, I support other aspects of this Bill, including the adoption of an extended definition of family violence in s 5(1) and an extension of the role of the IFV Panel to provisional visas in some circumstances.

DOI: 10.4324/9781003372462-31

Extended Definition of Family Violence

I support the adoption of an extended definition of family violence (s 5(1)) as per section 4AB of the *Family Law Act 1975* to remove the inconsistency between the definition in that *Act* and the Family Violence Exception in the *Migration Regulations 1994* (Cth) (Migration Regulations). This is an issue which equally affects secondary visa holders who are victims of family violence. They are also in need of protection, as are women on dependent partner visas.

Removal of Dependency in Partner and Secondary Visa Holder Migration?

The Bill aims to insert a new provision (s 39B) in the Act to preclude the future granting of provisional visas on the basis of a marital or de facto relationship. This provision extends the application of protection in situations of family violence to secondary visa holders through a new Subdivision AM – Special Provisions Relating to Family Violence. In my view, these provisions could be applied to all situations of family violence among migrants, including dowry abuse and forced marriage.

The Second Reading Speech argues that the Bill strikes 'an appropriate balance between maintaining the integrity of the immigration system and empowering migrant women'. I disagree with this 'sledgehammer' approach. Whereas under the Family Violence Exception the (usually female) migrant has to demonstrate subjective fear of the spouse, this reversal assumes that the spouse (usually male) is never 'innocent'. There is a real and plausible risk that some will take advantage of this provision. I have heard anecdotally that there are some unscrupulous women who can and do offer Australian men money in order to obtain a visa. On the other hand, there are some situations where there is no doubt that the probation requirement should be abandoned, including where there are children of the relationship for whom the female migrant is the primary carer. In South Korea, for example, an exception to nationality policy exists in these circumstances, with dual nationality an option available to the foreign spouse.[1]

There is a middle way which avoids the 'sledgehammer' approach. The introduction of the procedural provisions through a new Subdivision AM – Special Provisions Relating to Family Violence provides an opportunity to introduce a transparent and cohesive process to assess assertions of family violence in all situations covered by this Bill.

Subdivision AM – Independent Family Violence Panel

Issues of standard and burden of proof have dogged the application of the Family Violence Exception, which involves establishing 'relevant violence' through a subjective test. The current provisions are unsatisfactory and cumbersome in imposing two standards of evidence – judicial and non-judicial – and in creating an overall discretion as to the 'relevance' of the violence, leading to inconsistent and unfair outcomes. The creation of a panel of independent experts with the power to consider a broad range of evidence put forward to support an assertion of family violence (s 91ZD) will address the well-recognised problems that have arisen in this context.[2] The panel can perform a monitoring role of female visa holders in probationary and secondary temporary situations. It could become an expert panel in scrutinising situations of suspected dowry abuse and forced marriage. Further, the decision-making power under s 91ZC, which is 'quasi-judicial', should be conferred on a panel constituted by no fewer than two members with a mix of skills as well as genders, for example, by a relevant community member, a psychologist, or another relevant professional.

The panel should include persons of all genders from culturally and linguistically diverse backgrounds assigned as appropriate to relevant cases. As the movement for migrant women's rights in Australia demonstrates, the leaders are themselves migrant women and persons with first-hand experience of migration to Australia.

Forced Marriages

I applaud the inclusion of issues of forced marriage and dowry abuse within the scope of this Bill. The criminalised response to forced marriage in Australia is another example of a highly gendered and discriminatory approach to female migrants, which criminalises conduct rather than focusing on the patriarchal and cultural factors in such endogamous practices.[3] The exclusion of forced marriage from the Family Violence Exception through a formalised and legalistic interpretation of 'forced marriage' as involving lack of consent downplays the intersection between gender and power relations in the family and community. It is well-recognised that a focus on consent in this context can be illusory: there is a spectrum of conduct encompassing arranged and forced marriages rather than a clear binary.[4] For this reason, I support the introduction of section 5F(4) and the addition to the definition of 'family violence' in section 4AB of the *Family Law Act 1975* as per the proposed s 5(1). This Bill better encapsulates the experiences of women in culturally diverse communities in Australia and will better promote their safety and integration into the nation.

For these reasons, I commend the Bill subject to the suggested changes.

Notes

1 Susan Kneebone, 'Gender, Race, Culture and Identity at the Internal Border of Marriage Migration of Vietnamese Women in South Korea' in Sriprapha Petcharamesree and Mark Capaldi (eds) *Migration in Southeast Asia: The Interlocking of Vulnerabilities and Resilience* (Springer, 2023) ch 5.

2 M Segrave, *Temporary Migration and Family Violence: An Analysis of Victimisation, Vulnerability and Support* (Melbourne, Monash University, 2017); A Borges Jelinic, 'Australia's Family Violence Provisions in Migration Law: A Comparative Study' (2020) 21(2) *Flinders Law Journal* 259 273–79.

3 Ambika Kohli, 'Forced and Underage Marriages in New Zealand: Some Reflections on Public and Private Patriarchy and Intersectionality' (2015) 1 *International Journal for Intersectional Feminist Studies* 58.

4 Anne Phillips and Moira Dustin, 'UK Initiatives on Forced Marriage: Regulation, Dialogue and Exit' (2004) 52 *Political Studies* 531–51, 537.

Chapter 15

Aged Care, Housing Rights and the Right to Housing

Residents in Aged Care Have Been Patient(s) Too Long

Charlotte Steer

Extract from *Hansard* (Parliament of New South Wales)

Aged Care Rights Bill 2024

Second Reading Speech

HON CHARLOTTE STEER: I move:

That this Bill be now read a second time.

Aged Care is a feminist issue. As well as living longer, women are more likely to be in aged care, to be the primary carers for those in aged care and to be the employed staff. The recent focus on aged care reform has overlooked the fact that residents in aged care have fewer housing rights than occupants in any other form of housing. Residents in aged care deserve the same kinds of housing protections that are available to tenants, occupants of boarding houses, residents in caravan parks and retirement villages and those living in strata titled apartments. An *Aged Care Rights Act* in NSW could give enforceable tribunal remedies for housing harms. This would enhance and protect the human dignity of older people, as envisaged under the proposed United Nations Convention on the Rights of Older People.

The *Aged Care Rights Act 2024* (NSW) will be a powerful tool for the recognition of women's human rights. Women make up two-thirds of the residents in aged care, most of the staff and the majority of the paid and unpaid carers who support the residents. Each of these groups, whether as applicants, respondents or witnesses in the tribunal, deserves the right to have their housing disputes adjudicated quickly, cheaply and fairly by an independent tribunal. It is unfair that aged care, which features so significantly in women's lives, is the one housing jurisdiction which remains unprotected by a tribunal remedy. This is systemic discrimination based on age and gender.

DOI: 10.4324/9781003372462-32

The need for additional remedies for harms in aged care is urgent. Testimonies at the Australian Royal Commission into Aged Care Quality and Safety, held from 2018 to 2021, bear witness to the range of violations, from tragedies to micro-harms, experienced by residents in aged care, and the pain of those who witnessed these. These violations include sexual assaults, force-feeding, rough handling, over-medication, forcible restraint, unnecessary exposure and malnutrition.[1] Micro-harms include

> small oversights, such as a cup of tea placed just out of reach, a request not acknowledged or call bells unanswered. In isolation, these 'oversights' may not be considered significant instances of substandard care. But when repeated over time, they can be more than just unkind; they can amount to neglect.[2]

An additional problem is that, once a facility is subject to sanctions from the Aged Care Quality and Safety Commission, a further complaint about the same type of harm, by a different resident, will have no individual remedy because the relevant sanction has already been imposed.[3]

The Royal Commission recorded the harms experienced by marginalised communities of older people in NSW, such as

> people with culturally and linguistically diverse backgrounds, people who identify as part of the LGBTI communities, care leavers, Aboriginal and Torres Strait Islander people living in major cities and in rural and remote communities, veterans, and people who are experiencing, or are at risk of, homelessness.[4]

These groups are often at extra disadvantage because of the lack of support for their identities in aged care. The Royal Commission attributed this to 'a lack of understanding and respect for people's culture, background and life experiences'.[5] This understates the harms experienced.

As an example, during COVID, a Greek Orthodox aged care facility required a complete staff changeover because 'most residents spoke Greek, and only a minority spoke good English . . . the acting manager was the only Greek-speaking staff member . . . there were several other language groups and, initially, no interpreters'.[6] The independent review found that residents were not only distressed, but 'endangered by their inability to communicate their needs to staff'.[7] Many residents were transferred to hospital, and the independent review recorded that hospital staff reported residents to be 'malnourished and dehydrated on arrival, sometimes with pressure sores; many were semiconscious, distressed and agitated or very ill with COVID-19. Some died soon afterwards'. In 2021, one-third of people using aged care were born overseas, and this proportion is likely to increase, given the high levels of migration over the last decades.[8]

Similarly, the number of Aboriginal and Torres Strait Islander residents will increase in line with the growth in their percentage of the population, and, given the lack of culturally appropriate places in aged care, their younger ages on entry to aged care compared to the non-Indigenous population, and the high need in rural and remote areas,[9] so will the number of harms that they experience, and the need for adequate remedies beyond anti-discrimination law.

There is a lack of adequate remedies for discriminatory conduct against people who identify as, or are perceived as, nonconformist to societal norms of sexuality and gender, because anti-discrimination law has patchy coverage due to exceptions and exemptions. The most startling example is that

> the majority of [aged care] providers are religious organisations, and state-based anti-discrimination exemptions remain for religious providers to potentially discriminate on the basis of gender and sexuality. While some religious organisations are inclusive of [LGBTQI] communities, unfortunately some are not and this . . . needs to be addressed if LGBTI people are to have equitable access to ageing services.[10]

This Bill will address the need for remedies for harms to older people that fall outside the ambit of anti-discrimination legislation.

The testimonies to the Royal Commission inspire a call for radical change to the way Australians conceptualise and respond as a society to harms experienced by older Australians. At the international level, there are calls for a Convention on the Rights of Older People, conceptualising older persons as autonomous, dignified bearers of human rights, entitled to access to justice to promote and enforce their human rights, including the right to adequate housing. This Bill will provide much-needed improvements in access to justice for residents in aged care facilities who experience breaches of their human rights.

This Bill is the first of its kind in Australia, and possibly the world. It reflects a shift in our understanding of the human rights of older people from a protective, charitable model to a model of agency and autonomy. The Bill will give voice and agency to residents in aged care.

The Bill will change the way residents in aged care can enforce their rights under the federal *Charter of Aged Care Rights*, by giving residents the opportunity to apply to the NSW Civil and Administrative Tribunal (NCAT) for adjudication of their disputes.

This legislation is radical in its protection of the human rights of older people, particularly older women, but is soundly based on existing legislation. The Bill adapts provisions from existing NSW laws about housing, guardianship, anti-discrimination and consumer protection, and uses proven mechanisms for effective resolution of disputes at NCAT.

I will now explain the current legislative landscape for aged care.

Australia is a country governed nationally by the federal government, and locally, by state governments. The rights of residents in aged care are currently protected under a federal Act.

Since 1997, aged care facilities in Australia have been subsidised by the federal government under the *Aged Care Act 1997* (Cth). This Act allows aged care corporations who meet quality guidelines to be licensed and receive subsidies. The Act includes a *Charter of Aged Care Rights*, listing the ways in which the rights of recipients of aged care services must be respected.

The *Aged Care Act 1997* (Cth) applies throughout Australia, but only to those aged care facilities who fall within its coverage. Some people who need aged care services may not be eligible, or may face a long waiting time, and therefore choose to pay full fees to an aged care facility that is not funded by the government.[11] Within each state there may be also other requirements under state law, which would apply to all aged care facilities within the relevant state.

The possibilities for co-regulation of aged care by the federal and state governments have not been fully explored. This Bill explores one of those possibilities for co-regulation. The Bill proposes the adoption of the federal *Charter of Aged Care Rights* as State law. Because the *Charter of Aged Care Rights* will be law in NSW, breaches of the *Charter of Aged Care Rights* could be directly enforced through a State Tribunal.

The legal mechanism to adopt the federal *Charter of Aged Care Rights* as State law, and then provide a remedy in a State Tribunal, is a model followed throughout Australia in relation to consumer law. In NSW, the federal Australian Consumer Law is adopted as NSW law by the *Fair Trading Act 1987* (NSW), and remedies for breach are available through NCAT.

I move now to discuss the current remedies for harms experienced by residents in aged care.

There is currently no provision for tribunal or court remedies in the *Aged Care Act 1997* (Cth). Instead, breaches can be reported internally at the aged care facility, or to the federal Aged Care Quality and Safety Commission, an investigative and licensing body.

If the harm is a criminal offence, it may also be reported to the police in the usual way. The harm may also be actionable as negligence, or as a breach of consumer rights.

Some harms may be actionable as breaches of human rights, but there are limited remedies available, because Australia has no federal constitutional or statutory Bill of Rights. Some states and territories have Charters of Human Rights, but not NSW. In NSW, some harms are captured under the *Anti-Discrimination Act 1977* (NSW), or the federal Acts covering race, sex, disability and age discrimination. However, these categories of human rights breaches do not cover all the harms experienced by residents in aged care.

None of the current remedies conceptualises breaches of the *Charter of Aged Care Rights* as breaches of housing rights, despite the fact that the breaches occur in the home of the person concerned, whether that be a private dwelling or an aged care facility. The idea that an aged care facility is a person's home is not part of the way we think about older people or about aged care facilities. This Bill classifies breaches of the federal *Charter of Aged Care Rights* as housing harms, and provides State-based housing remedies through a State Tribunal.

The paternalistic model of complaint resolution for residents in aged care is outdated, ageist and discriminatory. The current complaint mechanisms through the Aged Care Quality and Safety Commission are reportedly cumbersome and unsatisfactory. Residents who complain to the Aged Care Quality and Safety Commission lack the right to see their complaint through. Instead, after the complaint is lodged, the discretion as to enforcement and penalty lies entirely with the Commission. Residents in aged care should have remedies that promote autonomy and choice over the progress of their complaint, as well as the outcome. They should have the dignity of being able to enforce their rights. They should not be subject to structural discrimination by being denied the same rights to access to justice as a resident in any other form of shared housing in NSW, who all have the right to have their dispute adjudicated under specialist housing legislation at NCAT.

For example, residents in retirement villages can make claims under the *Retirement Villages Act 1999* (NSW), which sets out the rights and responsibilities of residents, and the kinds of applications and orders that can be made at NCAT. Similarly, tenants and residents in strata-titled buildings, boarding houses, caravan parks and manufactured home estates, can all apply to NCAT under specific housing legislation. The residents in these other forms of housing can enforce rights and obligations between residents and operators, and, indirectly, among residents themselves, by making an application to the Tribunal.

At NCAT, parties are able to bring a claim, defend a claim, choose to conciliate their claim or choose to have it adjudicated. The parties have control over the evidence that they provide, and whether to withdraw, settle or contest their claim for a remedy. This choice and control is not available for complainants to the Aged Care Quality and Safety Commission, where the complainant's only choice is whether or not to lodge a complaint.

The *Aged Care Rights Act* 2024 (NSW) will give residents in aged care the equivalent housing rights to residents in all other forms of shared housing. Residents in aged care will be able to turn to the flexible and agile methods of dispute resolution available through NCAT. NCAT is designed to be quicker, cheaper and less formal than a court-based process of dispute resolution. The statutory aims of NCAT encourage quick, cheap and just resolution of disputes, with parties representing themselves. Tribunal members resolve the real issues in dispute according to law, with fairness and informality. Application fees are low, and parties are encouraged to settle their disputes with the assistance of a conciliator, or to present their grievance to be adjudicated by the Tribunal. Tribunal members are under a duty to ensure that parties have a reasonable opportunity to present their case, and to be as flexible and informal in their procedures as possible.[12] This Bill provides a comprehensive, contemporary and robust legislative framework for aged care dispute resolution through conciliation and adjudication at the Tribunal.

People who live in aged care deserve the same level of rights protection in relation to their home as residents in any other form of housing. For too long, residents in aged care have been seen as powerless victims who cannot speak for themselves. It is time for this to change. It is time to discard the old ideas of paternalism and protectionism in favour of enforceable human rights. The Bill is built on a model of dignity, autonomy and agency, so that residents have the power to enforce their rights in aged care. The Bill recognises that an aged care facility is home to those who live there.

This Bill recognises residents in aged care as bearers of human rights who are entitled to enforce their rights themselves, rather than rely on investigators at the Aged Care Quality and Safety Commission, or in the police forces, to decide if, and how, any alleged breaches of human rights will be investigated, sanctioned or prosecuted. These remedies will remain, and they are available as additional methods of rights protection and quality assurance in the provision of aged care. However, the current methods of dispute resolution do not allow residents in aged care, or their guardians or carers, to have autonomy in relation to the progress of their disputes. They are instead reliant on the discretion of the investigators.

The Bill specifies a wide range of people who will be able to bring applications to NCAT.

This Bill permits anyone with a genuine interest in the welfare of a resident in aged care to bring an application to the Tribunal. This will include the residents themselves, their guardians and carers and groups of residents. The Bill uses provisions from the laws in relation to retirement villages to permit applications to be made by representatives of groups of residents. The Bill uses guardianship laws as a model to extend the categories of persons who can make applications on behalf of another.

An additional class of applicants is those people who have suffered anxiety and distress as a result of the lack of care provided to their loved ones. This category is loosely based on accident compensation legislation that permits those persons close to the injured or deceased worker to make their own claims for compensation. This is intended to increase the scope of protections, and the deterrent effect of the legislation.

The Bill provides a wide range of remedies in the Tribunal, adding to the remedies that are currently available through the courts and the Aged Care Quality and Safety Commission. NCAT will be able to make orders in NSW for compliance with the requirements of the Commonwealth *Aged Care Act*'s

Charter of Aged Care Rights, to stop breaches of the *Charter of Aged Care Rights* and to order compensation for those breaches.

Monetary compensation is very important in this area, as it provides some recompense for the pain, fear, anxiety and humiliation that can be caused by breaches of human rights. The Bill clarifies that claims for emotional distress are compensable, and not excluded as claims for personal injury under the *Civil Liability Act 2002* (NSW).

The Bill uses anti-discrimination laws as a model for additional remedies by way of apology or retraction, or implementing a programme or policy aimed at eliminating further breaches. These orders are proven to be workable and effective in resolving disputes.

The Bill sets time limits for bringing applications, based on those in anti-discrimination laws.

One of the most challenging areas for dispute resolution is the balancing of competing rights. The Bill addresses the difficult choices that operators of aged care facilities may face. For example, it might be necessary to restrict the freedom of movement of a resident in order to stop the resident entering the rooms of other residents uninvited. This is addressed in the legislation by adapting from the reasoning of the High Court of Australia in relation to the freedom of political communication, which in turn is based on methods of balancing competing international human rights.[13] This is possibly the most contentious and ambitious part of the Bill, as this is not something that has yet been attempted by any other Parliament in Australia. Accordingly, the regulation-making power includes the power to vary the factors that the Tribunal may take into account in determining whether there has been a breach of the *Charter of Aged Care Rights*.

Regulations made under the Act may require the parties to participate, in good faith, in a formal mediation process prior to making an application to the Tribunal. Parties with an aged care dispute already have access to the dispute resolution mechanisms at the Aged Care Quality and Safety Commission. However, it may become apparent that there is a need for a further intermediate mediation process through NSW Fair Trading, as currently exists for retirement villages and strata schemes.

Regulations may also be made to extend the coverage of the Act to all recipients of aged care services. This would provide protection to all people who receive aged care services under the *Aged Care Act 1997* (Cth), including those who live in their own homes. This is a matter that is best determined at a later date, once the community has had an opportunity to experience the operation of the Act.

A final necessity is to provide additional funding to aged care advocates in NSW,[14] so that they can better support residents in aged care to understand and enforce their new rights under the new *Aged Care Rights Act*.

In conclusion, members of the House, I ask you to stand up for equality. The *Aged Care Rights Act 2024* (NSW) will give residents in aged care facilities equality in access to justice for determination of their housing rights. Residents in aged care facilities will have the same rights as residents in all other forms of shared housing in New South Wales, because the Act will provide access to the NSW Civil and Administrative Tribunal for quick, cheap and just resolution of the real issues in their disputes.

Residents in aged care have been treated as patients in hospital, or as powerless recipients of charity, rather than as autonomous, dignified persons with inherent human rights. Residents in aged care have been patients – and patient – for too long. It is time to move forward to a new paradigm centred on the human right to housing.

The former Special Rapporteur on Housing at the United Nations, Ms Leilani Farha, has stated that:

> States cannot hold themselves up as leaders in human rights while leaving increasing numbers of residents . . . with no access to effective remedies. The time for excuses, justifications and looking the other way when access to justice is denied for the right to housing has long passed. Rights must have remedies.[15]

Similarly, the Queensland Supreme Court judge and former President of the Queensland Civil and Administrative Tribunal, Justice Alan Wilson, has declared:

> Individual rights [are] valueless if the means of vindication and adjudication are not also made available through access to courts and tribunals.[16]

This Bill will enact the international human right of access to justice for housing rights into domestic law. The Bill will better promote the autonomy, independence and dignity of residents in aged care facilities. Residents in aged care facilities deserve recognition that where they live is their home.

I am proud to commend the Bill to the House.

New South Wales

Aged Care Rights Bill 2024

A Bill for

An Act to recognise the *Charter of Aged Care Rights* under the *Aged Care Act 1997* (Cth) as New South Wales law; to establish mechanisms for the resolution of certain disputes in aged care facilities in New South Wales; and for other purposes.

The Legislature of New South Wales enacts –

1 **Name of Act**
This Act may be cited as the *Aged Care Rights Act 2024.*

2 **Object of this Act**
The object of this Act is to provide for the promotion and protection of the human rights and wellbeing of residents in aged care facilities in New South Wales, by –

(a) incorporating the Commonwealth *Charter of Aged Care Rights* ('the Charter') into the law of New South Wales, and
(b) providing for the adjudication of disputes arising under the Charter by the New South Wales Civil and Administrative Tribunal.

3 **Act applies to existing and future aged care agreements**
This Act applies to all residents in aged care facilities in New South Wales, and extends to any aged care accommodation agreement, contract or other agreement whenever made.

4 **Contracting out prohibited**

(1) A term of any aged care accommodation agreement, contract or other agreement is void to the extent that it purports to exclude, limit or modify the operation of this Act or the regulations or has the effect of excluding, limiting or modifying the operation of this Act or the regulations.
(2) A person must not enter into any contract or other agreement with the intention, either directly or indirectly, of defeating, evading or preventing the operation of this Act or the regulations.
Maximum penalty – 20 penalty units.

5 **Definitions**
In this Act –

aged care has the same meaning as in the Aged Care Act.

the Aged Care Act means the *Aged Care Act 1997* (Cth)

this Act includes regulations.
Tribunal means the Civil and Administrative Tribunal established by the *Civil and Administrative Tribunal Act 2013*.
the *Charter of Aged Care Rights* means the *Charter of Aged Care Rights* made under the *Aged Care Act 1997* (Cth) s 96-1, found in the User Rights Principles 2014 (Cth) sch 1.
resident means a recipient of residential care as defined in the *Aged Care Act*, and includes a former resident and a deceased resident.
residential care service has the same meaning as in the *Aged Care Act*.
operator means an approved provider of residential care as defined in the *Aged Care Act*.

6 ***The Charter of Aged Care Rights*** **text**
The *Charter of Aged Care Rights* text consists of Schedule 1 to the User Rights Principles 2014 made under the *Aged Care Act 1997* (Cth) s 96-1.

7 **Application of the *Charter of Aged Care Rights***

(1) The *Charter of Aged Care Rights* text, as in force from time to time –

(a) applies as a law of this jurisdiction, and
(b) as so applying may be referred to as the *Charter of Aged Care Rights* (NSW), and
(c) as so applying is a part of this Act.

(2) The *Charter of Aged Care Rights* (NSW) applies to and in relation to –

(a) persons carrying on business within this jurisdiction, or
(b) bodies corporate incorporated or registered under the law of this jurisdiction, or
(c) persons ordinarily resident in this jurisdiction, or
(d) persons otherwise connected with this jurisdiction.

(3) Subject to subsection (2), the *Charter of Aged Care Rights* (NSW) extends to conduct, and other acts, matters and things, occurring or existing outside or partly outside this jurisdiction (whether within or outside Australia).

8 Future modifications of the Charter of Aged Care Rights text

(1) A modification made by a Commonwealth law to the *Charter of Aged Care Rights* text after the commencement of this section does not apply under section 28 if the modification is declared by a proclamation to be excluded from the operation of that section.

(2) A proclamation under subsection (1) has effect only if published or notified no later than two months after the date of the modification.

(3) Subsection (1) ceases to apply to the modification if a further proclamation so provides.

(4) For the purposes of this section, the date of the modification is the date on which the Commonwealth Act effecting the modification receives the Royal Assent or the regulation effecting the modification is registered under the *Legislative Instruments Act 2003* (Cth).

9 Jurisdiction of Tribunal

The Tribunal has jurisdiction to hear and determine an application made under this Act.

10 Application may be made by resident or operator

(1) If a resident (or residents) or the operator of a residential care service claims that a dispute about a breach of the *Charter of Aged Care Rights* has arisen between the resident and the operator, or the operator and one or more residents, the resident (or residents) or operator may apply to the Tribunal for (and the Tribunal may make) an order in respect of the dispute.

(2) Two or more residents who claim that a dispute, as referred to in subsection (1), has arisen may nominate, in accordance with the regulations, any resident as their representative in the dispute.

(3) The nominated representative may apply to the Tribunal for an order in respect of the dispute, and the Tribunal may make an order that applies to the residents who are represented by the nominated representative.

10 Other persons who may make an application

(1) An application alleging that a named person has, or named persons have, breached the *Charter of Aged Care Rights* in relation to a resident in a residential care service may be made by any of the following –

(a) one or more persons –

(i) on his, her or their own behalf, or

(ii) on his, her or their own behalf as well as on behalf of another person or persons, or

(b) a parent or guardian of a person who lacks the legal capacity to make an application (for example, because of age or disability), or
(c) a representative body on behalf of a named person or persons, or
(d) any other person who, in the opinion of the Tribunal, has a genuine concern for the welfare of the person, or
(e) an agent of any of the persons referred to in paragraph (a), (b), (c) or (d).

(2) Nothing in this Division prevents a person from making an application (not being a representative), even though the conduct in respect of which the application is made is also conduct in respect of which a representative application has been made.

(3) Where an application has been made by a person to the Tribunal in relation to a breach of the *Charter of Aged Care Rights*, any other person who is affected by the breach may apply, in writing, to the Tribunal to be made a party to the application, and the Tribunal may, in its discretion, by order, make that person a party to the application.

12 Applications made on behalf of others

(1) When an application is made on behalf of another person or persons (***the other applicants***) –

(a) the person who makes the application is taken to have the same rights, obligations and interests with respect to the resolution of the application as the other applicants, and
(b) the application is taken to have been made by the other applicants on their own behalf.

(2) In respect of an application made wholly or partly on behalf of another person or persons (not including an application made on behalf of a person who lacks legal capacity), the Tribunal may require –

(a) the person or persons on whose behalf the application is made to show that the application has been made with his, her or their consent, or
(b) the person or persons making the application to prove that he, she or they have authority to act at all times in the dispute resolution process, or
(c) both.

(3) In respect of an application made wholly or partly on behalf of another person or persons (including an application made on behalf of a person who lacks legal capacity), if at any time the Tribunal is not satisfied that the person who made the application is acting in the best

interests of the person or persons on whose behalf the application was made or retains the confidence of that person or those persons, the Tribunal may –

(a) appoint another person to act in that behalf, or
(b) dismiss the application.

13 Limitation periods

(1) The Tribunal does not have jurisdiction to hear and determine an application if the cause of action giving rise to the application first accrued more than 12 months before the date on which the application is lodged.
(2) Nothing in this section affects any period of limitation under the *Limitation Act 1969.*

14 Order or other decision of Tribunal

(1) In proceedings relating to an application, the Tribunal may –

(a) dismiss the application in whole or in part, or
(b) find the breach substantiated in whole or in part.

(2) If the Tribunal finds the breach substantiated in whole or in part, it may do any one or more of the following –

(a) order the respondent to pay the applicant damages not exceeding $100,000 by way of compensation for any loss or damage suffered by reason of the respondent's conduct,
(b) make an order enjoining the respondent from continuing or repeating any conduct in breach of the *Charter of Aged Care Rights* (NSW),
(c) order the respondent to perform any reasonable act or course of conduct to redress any loss or damage suffered by the applicant,
(d) order the respondent to publish an apology or a retraction (or both) in respect of the matter the subject of the application and, as part of the order, give directions concerning the time, form, extent and manner of publication of the apology or retraction (or both),
(e) order the respondent to develop and implement a program or policy aimed at eliminating breaches of the *Charter of Aged Care Rights* (NSW),
(f) make an order declaring void in whole or in part, and either ab initio or from such time as is specified in the order, any contract or agreement made in contravention of the *Charter of Aged Care Rights* (NSW), this Act or the regulations, or
(g) decline to take any further action in the matter.

(3) An order of the Tribunal may extend to conduct of the respondent that affects persons other than the applicant or applicants if the Tribunal, having regard to the circumstances of the case, considers that such an extension is appropriate.
(4) The power of the Tribunal to award damages to an applicant is taken, in the case of a complaint lodged by a representative body, to be a power to award damages to the person or persons on behalf of whom the complaint is made and not to include a power to award damages to the representative body.
(5) In making an order for damages concerning a complaint made on behalf of a person or persons, the Tribunal may make such order as it thinks fit as to the application of those damages for the benefit of the person or persons.
(6) If the Tribunal makes an order under subsection (2) (b), (c), (d) or (e), it may also order that, in default of compliance with the order within the time specified by the Tribunal, the respondent is to pay the applicant damages not exceeding $100,000 by way of compensation for failure to comply with the order.

15 Determinations of breach where there are competing rights

(1) In determining whether there has been a breach of the *Charter of Aged Care Rights* (NSW), in a situation where there are competing rights of residents, the Tribunal may take into account the following factors –

(a) suitability: An action is suitable if it exhibits a rational connection to the purpose of the competing right. An action may be seen to have a rational connection to its purpose if the action is capable of realising the right's purpose.
(b) necessity: An action is necessary if it is necessary for the achievement of the competing right. It is only when and if the action lies beyond the range of what could reasonably be regarded as necessary that the action will be adjudged as unnecessary. One circumstance, among others, in which that may appear to be the case is where an affected party can point to an obvious and compelling alternative which is equally practicable and available and would result in a significantly lesser burden on the affected party.
(c) adequate in its balance: An action is adequate in its balance if it presents as suitable and necessary in the senses described unless its effect upon the affected party is grossly disproportionate to, or goes far beyond, what can reasonably be conceived of as justified in the pursuit of the right.

16 Relationship with other laws

(1) The provisions of this Part are in addition to any other duties or other obligations imposed under any other Acts or the common law and do not limit the duties or other obligations imposed under any other Acts or the common law.
(2) This Part does not limit damages or other compensation that may be available to a person under another Act or at common law because of a breach of the *Charter of Aged Care Rights* (NSW).
(3) This Act is subject to the *Civil Liability Act 2002* (NSW), except for any claims for damages for disappointment, distress, inconvenience, anxiety, embarrassment, humiliation, damage to reputation and other like claims, which are not to be considered as claims for personal injury and are therefore not excluded by the *Civil Liability Act 2002* (NSW).

17 Regulations

(1) The Governor may make regulations, not inconsistent with this Act, for or with respect to any matter that by this Act is required or permitted to be prescribed or that is necessary or convenient to be prescribed for carrying out or giving effect to this Act.
(2) Without limiting subsection (1), the regulations may make provision with respect to the following –
    (a) a requirement for the parties to participate, in good faith, in a formal mediation process prior to making an application to the Tribunal,
    (b) the factors which the Tribunal may take into account in determining whether there has been a breach of the *Charter of Aged Care Rights* (NSW),
    (c) the extension of this Act to cover all recipients of aged care.

18 Review of Act after five years of operation

(1) The Attorney-General must cause a review to be made of the first five years of operation of this Act and must cause a copy of a report of the review to be laid before each House of Parliament on or before five years after the date of assent.

Notes

1 Royal Commission into Aged Care Quality and Safety, *Final Report – Volume 1: Summary and Recommendations* (report, 1 March 2021) 68–73.
2 Ibid 71.
3 Emily Doak, 'Aged Care Complaint Upheld, No Further Action taken as Southern Cross Care, Young Already 'Non-Compliant', *ABC Riverina (*online, 2 May 2022). https://www.abc.net.au/news/2022-05-02/aged-care-complaint-about-southern-cross-care-young/101009716.

4 Royal Commission (n 1) 71.
5 Ibid 71.
6 Australian Government Department of Health and Aged Care, *Independent Review of COVID-19 Outbreaks at St Basil's Home for the Aged in Fawkner, Victoria, and Heritage Care Epping Gardens in Epping, Victoria* (report, 30 November 2020).
7 Australian Government Department of Health and Aged Care, *Independent Review of COVID-19 Outbreaks at St Basil's Home for the Aged in Fawkner, Victoria, and Heritage Care Epping Gardens in Epping, Victoria* (report, 30 November 2020). https://www.health.gov.au/sites/default/files/documents/2020/12/coronavirus-covid-19-independent-review-of-covid-19-outbreaks-at-st-basil-s-and-epping-gardens-aged-care-facilities.pdf.
8 Australian Institute of Health and Welfare, 'Aged Care: Overview' (12 August 2022). https://www.aihw.gov.au/reports-data/health-welfare-services/aged-care/overview.
9 Australian Institute of Health and Welfare, 'Aged Care for Indigenous Australians' (31 May 2022). https://www.aihw.gov.au/reports/australias-welfare/aged-care-for-indigenous-australians.
10 National LGBTI Health Alliance, *Aged Care Diversity Framework: Actions to Support Lesbian, Gay, Bisexual, Trans and Gender Diverse and Intersex Elders: Consultation Report* (report, June 2019) 23. https://agedcare.royalcommission.gov.au/system/files/2020-06/NLH.0001.0001.0043.pdf.
11 Aged Care Guide, 'Why Choose Private Home Care?' (undated). https://www.agedcareguide.com.au/information/why-choose-private-home-care.
12 *Civil and Administrative Tribunal Act 2013* (NSW).
13 This is known as 'structured proportionality', addressing 'suitability', 'necessity' and 'adequacy in the balance' to a legitimate end, to assess the proportionality of laws that burden the implied freedom of political communication. See *McCloy v New South Wales* [2015] HCA 34.
14 Older Persons Advocacy Network is the peak body for aged care advocates. https://opan.org.au/.
15 Leilani Farha, Special Rapporteur on the Right to Adequate Housing, *Access to Justice for the Right to Housing: The Report to the 40th Session of the UN Human Rights Council* (report, UN Office of the High Commissioner for Human Rights, 25 July 2018) 18. https://www.ohchr.org/EN/Issues/Housing/Pages/AccessToJustice.aspx .
16 Alan Wilson, 'Procedural Fairness v Modern Tribunals: Can the Twain Meet?' (speech, 7th Annual Government Lawyers' Conference, 31 May 2013). https://www.sclqld.org.au/judicial-papers/judicial-profiles/profiles/awilson/papers.

Chapter 15A

Commentary on *Aged Care, Housing Rights, and the Right to Housing*

Nola Ries and Jessie Hohmann

Introduction

Charlotte Steer's proposed *Aged Care Rights Act* is an important legislative reform in relation to elder law, human rights and access to justice. The legislation offers a neat solution to the lack of rights residents in aged care experience over their home and housing, extending existing housing rights and remedies enjoyed in other tenures to the sector through a novel legal mechanism. In doing so, the legislation sidesteps the politics so often associated with conversations around rights in Australia.[1] At the same time, it brings into play principles that animate pressing 'bigger picture' issues for feminist legislation: autonomy, agency, vulnerability, ethics of care, formal and substantive equality, protection and paternalism, among others.

Elder Law, Human Rights and Access to Justice

A key feature of the proposed *Aged Care Rights Act* is its focus on older people as rights holders. Scholars in the field of elder law have argued for rights-based advocacy, both to raise awareness of the 'indignities and invasions experienced by older adults'[2] and to enable legal action that can drive systemic changes. Framing these issues in terms of rights reflects existing international law, codified with respect to housing specifically in the UN International Covenant on Economic, Social and Cultural Rights (ICESCR). Article 11(1) of the ICESCR enshrines a right to an adequate standard of living, 'including adequate food, clothing and housing'.[3] International law also requires states to ensure the equal rights of men and women to the enjoyment of their rights, in ICESCR Articles 2(2) and 3.

At root, the right to housing protects each person's right to live somewhere in peace, dignity and security. It imposes obligations on States Parties – including Australia – to take concrete steps to respect, protect and fulfil this right, including through legislative measures, and without discrimination.[4] However, efforts to draft a UN Convention on the rights of older persons

DOI: 10.4324/9781003372462-33

demonstrate that they are often not accorded equal dignity, rights and status.[5] This is true in Australia, where the conceptual model for residential aged care by Ibrahim and others notes that 'rights' are 'an aspect which is rarely considered as it is often taken for granted.'[6] However, the needs of people living in residential aged care 'are the same in principle as older persons who dwell in the community.'[7] Steer's legislation implements this principle in practice by giving residents in aged care facilities the same rights as older people in other housing arrangements.

Strengths

Steer's *Aged Care Rights Act* directly responds to key recommendations from the recent Royal Commission into Aged Care Quality and Safety[8] and the Australian Law Reform Commission (ALRC) report on elder abuse.[9] To ameliorate the '[s]ubstandard care and abuse [that] pervades the Australian aged care system',[10] the Royal Commission called for embedding a rights-based approach at the core of aged care legislation. Similarly, the ALRC called for strengthening legal frameworks to give 'greater consumer control'[11] to older people who seek and receive aged care services.

By giving more robust rights to residents, the proposed legislation addresses the serious failings of the national regulator, the Aged Care Quality and Safety Commission.[12] To the extent that the regulator has 'taken its hands off the wheel',[13] Steer's Act empowers residents to pursue legal remedies if their rights are breached. The provisions for representative proceedings are also an essential feature of the legislation. Over half of aged care residents have dementia[14] and live with some degree of cognitive impairment that may affect their capacity in relation to legal matters. The rights of these individuals may be safeguarded through a representative proceeding, or by a guardian or other person with a genuine concern for their wellbeing. The provisions for mediation are also a welcome feature. Australian research demonstrates support for mediation for older people who have experienced elder abuse[15] and lessons from elder mediation[16] can inform supportive and effective processes under the new Act.

Because the Act harnesses existing legislation, giving the NCAT jurisdiction to decide disputes in relation to the federal *Charter of Aged Care Rights*, it cleverly avoids opportunities for grandstanding and the politicisation of human rights which have tended to weaken human rights laws in Australia. At the same time, it in fact protects the human rights of aged care residents, ending the discriminatory exclusion of aged care housing in the current legislative scheme and responding to aged care residents as holders of rights, equally entitled to experience aged care as a home to be enjoyed in peace, dignity and security.

Limitations

While Steer's approach has clear benefits, there are also drawbacks. It carries forward current limitations in the legislative scheme, while doing little to advance human rights discourse in Australia: by avoiding the politics of human rights, it also avoids the potential for a more robust claim to housing as a human rights issue. While this may be a sensible political choice, it also means that many of the structural issues that lie behind poor care and conditions in residential aged care will not be addressed. These include the devaluation of care and other 'women's work', and structural issues in Australia's housing and social welfare landscape, which include a housing affordability crisis coupled with poor social safety nets and social rights. Another legislative approach, which explicitly named and claimed a right to housing, might have capitalised on the current moment of broader housing crisis to engage economic, social and cultural rights for Australia. However, despite a widely acknowledged and deep crisis of homelessness and lack of access to adequate and affordable housing in Australia,[17] recent proposals for a federal human rights act do not include a right to housing per se, continuing Australia's exceptionalism in failing to accept economic, social and cultural rights as of equal status and justiciability to civil and political rights.[18] This reinforces our view that Steer has carefully navigated between practical change and the political pitfalls in invoking human rights in Australia in crafting this legislative proposal.

The proposed Act goes some way to strengthen access to justice for older people, but further work will need to address persistent barriers. For example, compared to younger cohorts, older people are more likely to ignore legal problems, delay seeking professional advice and have 'lower confidence in enforcing their rights and approaching official agencies.'[19] As noted above, residents with cognitive impairment will be reliant on others to assist or represent them, but those individuals may be deterred by power imbalances and fear of retaliation.[20] The Act could be strengthened with explicit attention to supported decision-making, whereby residents are entitled to supports that enable them to exercise their legal decision-making rights, which may include access to a funded scheme of trained support workers.[21] Research also demonstrates the importance of scrutinising how statutory protections are applied in practice to older complainants. The decisions of courts and tribunals reveal varying perceptions and characterisations of older people, which may reinforce ageist 'narratives of extreme vulnerability and pitifulness'.[22]

Strategies to improve the enforcement of residents' rights in residential aged care must be accompanied by improvements in the staffing levels and working conditions for the aged care workforce. This is a key lesson from the Serious Incident Response Scheme, which was implemented to fortify responses to and reporting of specific forms of abuse or violence against residents.[23] In this respect, the rights of residents in aged care to enjoy their housing are interconnected with other economic and social rights: rights to decent work and working conditions, and to social security in particular. These rights, which are protected under the ICESCR, will in turn be better protected when 'women's work' such as care work is revalued, working toward equality and non-discrimination in the enjoyment of all human rights.

Conclusion

In conclusion, we wish to highlight the unique contribution of this legislation, which offers achievable law reform based on a model of dignity, autonomy and agency. In our view, it has the capacity to substantially improve access to justice in housing rights, and thus housing conditions, for residents in residential aged care. Operating in a sphere that is highly feminised, the legislation will provide a powerful and much-needed boost to formal equality for older persons and women. While the legislation does not fundamentally unsettle structural biases and limitations that perpetuate inequalities, it provides an additional mechanism to expose abuses and harms in residential care. Illuminating the problems in current institutional structures will support ongoing advocacy and ambition for different models of care and accommodation that advance choice, dignity and respect for older Australians.

Notes

1 See eg Hilary Charlesworth et al., 'Deep Anxieties: Australia and the International Legal Order' (2003) 25 *Sydney Law Review* 423; John Piccini, *Human Rights in Twentieth-Century Australia* (Cambridge 2019); Louise Chappell et al., *The Politics of Human Rights in Australia* (Cambridge 2009).

2 Nina A Kohn, 'Elder Rights: The Next Civil Rights Movement' (2011) 21(2) *Temple Political & Civil Rights Law Review* 321, 326.

3 *International Covenant on Economic, Social and Cultural Rights*, UNGA Res 2200A (XXI), opened for signature 16 December 1966 (entered into force 3 January 1976).

4 For discussion of the right to housing in international law, see Jessie Hohmann, *The Right to Housing: Law, Concepts, Possibilities* (Hart Publishing 2013) 17–32; see also UN CESCR, *CESCR General Comment No 4: The Right to Adequate Housing (Article 11(1))*, UN Doc E/1992/23 (1992); UN CESCR, *CESCR General Comment No 3: The Nature of States Parties' Obligations (Article 2(1))*, UN Doc E/1991/23 (1990); UN CESCR, 'Non-Discrimination in Economic, Social and Cultural Rights' (art 2 para 2 of the *International Covenant on Economic, Social and Cultural Rights*) (2009) E/C.12/GC/20; Jessie Hohmann, 'The Right to Housing: A Research Agenda' in Markus Moos (ed.) *A Research Agenda for Housing* (Edward Elgar 2019) 18–20.

5 *Towards a Comprehensive and Integral International Legal Instrument to Promote and Protect the Rights and Dignity of Older Persons*, UN GA 'Resolution Adopted by the General Assembly on 20 December 2012: Towards a comprehensive and integral international legal instrument to promote and protect the rights and dignity of older persons' A/Res/67/139 (13 February 2013).

6 Joseph E Ibrahim et al., 'Meeting the Needs of Older People Living in Australian Residential Aged Care: A New Conceptual Model' (2020) 39(2) *Australasian Journal on Ageing* 148, 153.

7 Ibid 154.

8 Royal Commission into Aged Care Quality and Safety, *Final Report: Care, Dignity and Respect Volume 1, Summary and Recommendations* (final report, 28 February 2021). https://agedcare.royalcommission.gov.au/sites/default/files/2021-03/final-report-volume-1_0.pdf.
9 Australian Law Reform Commission, *Elder Abuse – A National Legal Response* (Report 131, 14 June 2017). https://www.alrc.gov.au/publications/elder-abuse-report.
10 Royal Commission into Aged Care Quality and Safety (n 8) 68.
11 Australian Law Reform Commission (n 9) 4.2.
12 Royal Commission into Aged Care Quality and Safety, *Final Report: Care, Dignity and Respect – Volume 2: The Current System* (Final Report, 1 March 2021), 4.14 'Ineffective Regulation'. https://agedcare.royalcommission.gov.au/publications/final-report-volume-2.
13 Ibid 229.
14 Australian Institute of Health and Welfare, *Dementia in Australia, Residential Aged Care* (2023). https://www.aihw.gov.au/reports/dementia/dementia-in-aus/contents/aged-care-and-support-services-used-by-people-with/residential-aged-care.
15 Annie Herro et al., 'Elder Mediation Services Among Diverse Older Adult Communities in Australia: Practitioner Perspectives on Accessibility' (2021) 61(7) *The Gerontologist* 1141.
16 Dale Bagshaw, 'Elder Mediation: An Emerging Field of Practice' in Maria F Moscati et al. (eds), *Comparative Dispute Resolution* (Edward Elgar, 2020) 202–16.
17 See eg Hal Pawson, 'The Housing and Homelessness Crisis in NSW Explained in 9 Charts', *The Conversation* (16 March 2023). https://theconversation.com/the-housing-and-homelessness-crisis-in-nsw-explained-in-9-charts-200523; ACOSS, 'A Secure, Affordable Home for Everybody' (2020). https://www.acoss.org.au/housing-homelessness/; J Hohmann, 'Toward a Right to Housing for Australia: Reframing Affordability Debates through Article 11(1) of the ICESCR' (2020) 26(2) *Australian Journal of Human Rights* 292; J Hohmann, 'A Right to Housing for the Victorian Charter of Human Rights and Responsibilities? Assessing Potential Models under the International Covenant on Economic, Social and Cultural Rights; the European Social Charter; and the South African Constitution' (2022) 48 *Monash University Law Review*.
18 AHRC, 'Free and Equal: Position Paper: A Human Rights Act for Australia' (Position Paper, 2022) 146–65.
19 Law Council of Australia, *The Justice Project: Final Report* (2018) 16. https://www.lawcouncil.asn.au/justice-project/final-report.
20 Royal Commission into Aged Care Quality and Safety, vol 2 (n 12) 148.
21 For further details on supported decision-making models, see eg Royal Commission into Violence, Abuse, Neglect and Exploitation of People with Disability, *Diversity, Dignity, Equity and Best Practice: A Framework for Supported Decision-Making* (Research Program, 24 January 2023). https://disability.royalcommission.gov.au/policy-and-research/research-program.
22 Michal Segal et al., 'The Judicial Construction of Older Consumers' Rights: A Qualitative Case-Law Analysis' (2021) 36(1) *Canadian Journal of Law and Society* 159, 174.
23 Lise Barry and Patrick Hughes, 'The New Serious Incident Response Scheme and the Responsive Regulation of Abuse in Aged Care' (2022) 29(2) *Journal of Law and Medicine* 465.

Part VI

Work, Exploitation and Power

Chapter 16

Women and Flexible Work

Marilyn Pittard

Extract from *Hansard* (Commonwealth of Australia)

Fair Work Act Amendment Bill 2024

Second Reading

HON MARILYN PITTARD: I move:
That this Bill be now read a second time.

This Bill deals with the next tranche of reforms to further promote flexible work and introduce a new employment right – the right to disconnect from work.

Technology is having a major impact on the way employees work. It can enable them to work remotely, including at home and with changed working hours.

Technology also enables employees to be always connected to their workplace, even when they are not present in the workplace.

Undoubtedly, technology has the potential to generate many workplace benefits. Let us make full use of that potential in a way that benefits not only society at large, but also women in particular. For example, a flexible home-based workplace that is not tied to the employer's premises benefits women – it can increase the workforce participation of female workers while improving work-family balance. As the experience of the pandemic has also shown, flexible work is possible across many industries and occupations.

The flexible work provisions in the *Fair Work Act 2009* (Cth)[1] were recently extended by the Secure Jobs, Better Pay amendments in effect since 6 June 2023.[2] In our view, however, they do not go far enough. It is essential that these reforms be taken even further to promote women's

DOI: 10.4324/9781003372462-35

employment and workforce participation, thus expanding flexible work beyond the current provisions.

Unfortunately, benefits of technology may have a downside – namely, it is now possible for employees to be connected at all times to their work via computers, smartphones and other devices. Workplaces commonly expect employees to be constantly connected and available outside their formal work hours. Typically, though, employees do not get paid for these extra hours. To fairly balance the benefits and costs, undertaking flexible work by working from home should not prevent employees switching off from work. I therefore propose that a 'right to disconnect' should be introduced to prevent employees working extended and unpaid hours. This would ensure employees' flexible work is properly supported, without coming at the price of always being connected to work.

I propose amendments to two key areas in this Bill:

- first, to the flexible work provisions, to expand the categories of employees who can seek flexible work, and to amend some of the grounds for employers' denying flexible work requests, which would achieve a more balanced approach between employers and employees; and
- secondly, to introduce a new labour right – the right to disconnect from work after work hours.

Flexible Work

What Does the Law currently Say about Flexible Work?

We recognise that the current law is sympathetic to the right to request flexible working, but does it go far enough? Our answer is *no*!

The law needs to go further to maximise work flexibility and the resultant gains. The *Fair Work Act* already deals with flexible work arrangements in several ways. Beneficial as these mechanisms are, however, they are currently inadequate.

One way the *Fair Work Act* presently deals with flexible work is through individual flexibility arrangements known as IFAs. Of course, we recognise that awards and enterprise agreements must contain flexibility terms to enable an individual employee and their employer to vary the effect of the award or enterprise agreement.[3] However, these take only small steps towards true flexible work, as the variation is permitted for only a limited range of matters. These IFAs do allow changing *when* work is performed, so women who are employees can vary their working hours to fit their family responsibilities, but only if their employer agrees. However, IFA's failure to include the *place* of work makes them of limited use for employees needing to work from home.[4]

More significant then is the right to request flexible work in the National Employment Standards. This is a right given to *some* employees in *some* circumstances to ask their employer for flexible working arrangements.

Let me emphasise that the Act does not give employees an actual *right* to flexible work; instead, it simply allows them to *ask for* flexible work. The request covers working from home and other remote working, but is not limited to requesting changes in the place of work. As the Act notes, examples of changes in working arrangements might include:

- hours of work (for example, changes to start and finish times);
- patterns of work (for example, split shifts or job sharing); and
- locations of work (for example, working from home).

The Secure Jobs, Better Pay amendments took several positive steps to rectify some previous deficiencies in the flexible work provisions. These amendments were part of a multi-pronged approach to remedy, among other things, some deficiencies in women's wages and the gender pay gap, improve bargaining power for the low-paid and prohibit sexual harassment and pay secrecy.

The Secure Jobs, Better Pay amendments also gave employees more effective right to request flexible work, including providing a mechanism for the Fair Work Commission to conciliate and arbitrate flexible work disputes where employers had denied requests for flexible work.

Yet significant restrictions on access to flexible work remain, which now need our focus.

Why Are we Strengthening the Legal Framework for Flexible Work?

We saw that working from home became prevalent during the pandemic due to public health orders or government recommendations. The Fair Work Ombudsman advised employers and employees on their flexible work options.[5] The Fair Work Commission was proactive during this period, issuing information notes on the pandemic[6] as well as temporarily varying some awards to address working conditions for those working at home or remotely.

We see an example in the *Clerks Private Sector Award 2020*, which for a time provided flexibility for an employee working remotely or from home, in such matters as the spread of ordinary hours of work, the employee's ability not to work their ordinary hours continuously, varying start and finish times and arrangements in relation to meal breaks.[7]

This experience of flexible work during the pandemic has the potential to revolutionise how work is conducted in workplaces well beyond the pandemic. It has exploded many myths about which occupations can and cannot carry out work at home.

The government's health orders for people to work at home where possible to protect public health during the pandemic was effectively a 'forced experiment' of working from home.[8] The Productivity Commission estimates that up to 40% of employees worked from home during the pandemic,[9] with some surveys showing that as many as one in two were mostly working from home.[10] This was a revolutionary change: in 2019 only 8% of employees had arrangements to work from home, with 2% of total hours being worked at home.[11] The 'forced experiment' proved it was possible for many more jobs to be undertaken from home than were previously thought feasible, ranging from working in call centres to conducting education online.

This revelation that many jobs could be performed at home, either wholly or in large part, supports the case for the Bill's proposals. Without the pandemic, this catalyst for change in practice and for more flexible work would not have occurred so rapidly. In this regard, Agathe Gross and Sam Mostyn have said:

> The pandemic unlocked a key lever that affects women's participation in the workforce: flexibility. Covid-19 fundamentally changed the way organisations operated. It challenged how companies viewed flexible work, because the need for flexibility affected every worker, regardless of rank, job role, or gender. The pandemic created urgency and accelerated critical changes surrounding flexible work. Now, crucial pieces are lining up to normalise flexibility.[12]

Surveys are now revealing that employees *enjoyed* this flexibility because it improved the home-work balance, enabling them to spend more time with family, reduce travel time and costs and gain more autonomy over their work. These results are telling. For example:

- Deloitte and Swinburne University reported that Australian workers want more hybrid work and more working from home.[13]
- Professor Petrie from the Melbourne Institute's survey revealed that one-third of Australian workers would like to work wholly from home, approximately 90% would like to work partly at home and partly at work, and 64% would like to work at least half their workweek from home.[14]

These statistics decisively support the desire to work from home.

Workplace Gender Equity Agency also reveals: 'Employees are increasingly seeking more autonomy over where, when and how they work. For many employees, flexible working is a highly desirable workplace benefit'.[15]

Although employees are generally free to negotiate enterprise agreements to provide for hybrid working, that depends on their bargaining power. To meet this thirst for retaining working from home for at least part of the workweek, we propose measures in the Bill to strengthen the flexible work framework as a *legislated right*. This will prevent it being traded away in enterprise agreements.

Flexible work, of course, goes beyond working from home to include changed hours and patterns of work. Flexible work can benefit carers, too.[16] Women with caring roles have also voiced the need for flexibility regarding starting times and work patterns. The submission of the Shop, Distributive and Allied Employees' Association to the Senate Committee on Work and Care illustrates the need for flexibility in the voices of workers themselves. One spoke about challenges with work start times and school drop-offs:

> Despite explaining I am a sole parent with primary care responsibilities my manager is very inflexible about my start and finish times. I have a set roster to start at 9 am but cannot get there at that time due to dropping my child at school. I have explained my situation but she acts disappointed that I am 'late' even though I fulfil my hours each week.[17]

Another worker spoke of how difficult it is to deal with family emergencies:

> [Work is] extremely non-understanding when it comes to family emergencies. I have [a] non-English-speaking grandmother with Alzheimer's dementia who still lives at home and is often unpredictable. When extra care is needed I have been told to come to work and find someone else to deal with it.[18]

Studies also show that flexible work promotes health benefits. For example, the Deloitte and Swinburne University study found that

> workers indicate flexible working delivers a direct personal benefit through improved wellbeing. Better work-life balance, less commuting, improved mental health, and more physical activity are clearly the standout benefits for both onsite and flexible location workers.[19]

Regrettably, female workforce participation also clearly needs improving. The OECD tells us that Australian women's workforce participation rate 'is still relatively low when compared with a number of other OECD countries, including our close peers Canada and New Zealand.'[20]

Flexible work is one way of improving female workforce participation. The Workplace Gender Equality Agency, citing the *2015 Intergenerational Report: Australia in 2055*,[21] states:

> To meet workforce needs, the Australian government has acknowledged that it is important to increase female labour force participation rates at a national level. Changing the way Australians work and making the

> balance between work and life more realistic for employees at an organisational level is crucial to achieving this goal.[22]

While improving flexible work for women is important, boosting men's workplace flexibility helps women as well. In this regard, the Workplace Gender Equality Agency has noted:

> Consciously promoting flexibility to men is a good way to promote gender equality as well as employee health and well-being.[23]

Flexible jobs can also expand the recruitment pool to people with caring responsibilities. A study by the United Kingdom's Government Equalities Office found:

> Boosting the supply of flexible jobs is [. . .] key to expanding the pool of jobs available for people with caring responsibilities, which we expect disproportionately to benefit women at the current time. Making flexible working more widely available also has the potential to normalise flexible working for both women and men.[24]

Flexible work's potential to benefit business and the broader economy too has been emphasised by the Workplace Gender Equality Agency, which stated:

> Many studies have identified positive connections between flexible working arrangements, improved productivity and revenue generation. A successful flexibility policy leads to increased employee engagement and performance, which may lead to improved profits for businesses.[25]

Society also benefits from reduced traffic and less congested public transport when people work from home.

As the above examples make clear, there are undoubtedly real benefits from increasing the availability of flexible work.

Expanding Flexible Work by Amending Sections 65 and 65A

Seizing these recognised benefits requires us to expand opportunities for women, along with people who support women and families, to undertake flexible work.

Building on the Secure Jobs, Better Pay changes, this Bill further enhances flexible work for women's benefit while creating a more effective community standard for flexible work to support women. This will place Australia in a better position to improve female workforce participation rates while achieving gender equity.

Given flexible work's many benefits to women and carers – not to mention business, the economy and society – the current law is clearly not fit for purpose. Opportunities for flexible work, including working from home, changing hours or patterns of work, must be strengthened to increase employees' possibility of being granted flexibility.

Surely we do not have to await another pandemic to drive home the necessity for flexibility through overarching public health orders!

The key changes in the Bill would enhance flexibility by expanding the categories of employees who are eligible to make the request, removing some barriers to exercising the right and providing a better balance between the interests of employers and employees in relation to the refusal of the request.

Expanding Categories of Employees Eligible to Make the Request

The Bill proposes expanding the current categories of employees in section 65(1A) who can request flexible work in the following ways:

1. *By expanding the circumstances that can trigger the right to request to include:*

   (a) Helpers – people who support parents or carers or those with a disability
   Currently, employees either over 55, with a disability, who are pregnant or victims of family violence or those who support such victims have the right to request flexible work. Carers, as well as parents and carers of a school-age child or younger, also have the right to request flexible work.
   Often another person – whether a neighbour, another family member, or a family friend – assists those carers and parents, not by directly caring for the children or of the person (say) with a disability, but rather by supporting that carer or parent. For example, they might help with transport for medical appointments or by doing domestic tasks for the carer, parent or person with a disability. These helpers cannot currently request flexible work, yet may need it in some situations.
   The Bill will give these helpers the right to request flexible work. It is similar to current provisions giving a person who supports a victim of family violence the right to request.

   (b) People with a domestic or other pressing necessity
   This Bill adds 'domestic or other pressing necessity' as a circumstance for employees seeking flexible work; this must be the reason for seeking the flexible work, while the 'necessity' requirement must exclude reasons of mere convenience or preference. Special circumstances embracing 'domestic or other pressing necessity' are known in another context – long service leave legislation in various Australian states.

These permit employees in such circumstances to access their long service leave entitlements early.[26]

People with a 'domestic or other pressing necessity' in this Bill could include:

- a woman employee who might otherwise have to resign if she could not work from home, when a family move is necessitated by her husband's work transfer;[27]
- an employee who is transitioning genders and for whom the home is a necessary safe place during this process;[28]
- a First Nations employee who needs to return, maybe for an extended period, to their remote home for community-related reasons;
- an employee who is undergoing medical treatment enabling them to work from home but not attend the workplace.

In these examples, workforce participation of not only women but also of trans and First Nations employees would be improved. Also, if 'pressing necessity' were shown, employees who are 'informal carers' (and thus not carers within the definition in the federal *Carer Recognition Act* 2010 who support people in need) would benefit too.

2. *Eliminating the barrier of qualifying service periods for employees, including for casual employees*

   Employees must currently be employed for a certain time with their employer before they can request flexible work. Although this is generally a period of six months, it is extended to 12 months in the case of casual workers with regular systematic work.

   There is no credible rationale for imposing these qualifying service periods, because the issue triggering the right to request does not vanish during that period.

   Requiring a person to, say, juggle caring duties without flexible work for six months before they can make a flexible work request would discourage that person, from obtaining employment, with negative consequences for female workforce participation. Similarly, offering an employee flexible work from the start of employment may enable a woman or partner to enter or re-enter the workforce.

   Employees should be able to apply at any time during their employment or prior to commencement. Australia is not alone in proposing to abolish a qualifying period, as the UK government announced proposed legislation to permit the right to request from the first day of employment.[29]

We strongly believe that a more meaningful right to request should result in more inclusive, diverse workplaces that also include First Nations people and trans people, while providing increased support for carers and the vulnerable.

When Employers Can Refuse Flexible Work: Improving the Employer-Employee Balance

Currently, employers may refuse a flexible work request only on the 'reasonable business grounds' outlined in the *Fair Work Act*. We propose a second tranche of amendments to further enshrine flexible work in this Bill by increasing the bar slightly regarding the evidence employers must produce to prove 'reasonable business grounds'.

We will make three changes to some of the 'reasonable business grounds' for refusing the flexible work request.

First, the current ground that it is 'impractical' for the employer to alter the working arrangements of other employees, or to recruit new employees in order to agree to the request, will change to being 'very impractical' to make those changes (by amending section 65(5A)(c)).

Secondly, the current provisions that the new working arrangements requested by the employee would be '*likely*' to result in a significant loss in efficiency or productivity would be changed so that the employer must show that the loss of efficiency or productivity would be '*very* likely' to arise if the request were granted (by amending section 65(5A)(d)); and

Thirdly, the ground dealing with the likely impact of flexible work on customer service would be changed to require that the current 'significant negative impact' would be 'very likely' to occur if the flexible work request were granted (by amending section 65(5A)(e)).

These changes will place the employer's refusal on a basis that more confidently addresses the probable impact if flexible work were provided. Coupled with the right to take the employer's refusal to the Commission for conciliation and arbitration, it turns a 'right to request' into a genuine benefit by strengthening the likelihood of flexible work.

The Right to Disconnect from Work

I now turn to the Bill's second and vital aspect – the right to disconnect from work.

We strongly believe that a 'right to disconnect' goes hand in hand with the Bill's enhanced right to request flexible working arrangements. Working from home and flexible hours can result in employees being constantly connected to the workplace through technology. A 'right to disconnect' is a safeguard to avoid this 'always connected' trap. It is also a safeguard against backdoor or informal – and so unrecognised and unpaid – extended work hours. While applying to both women and men, this right has special implications for women.

Helpfully, the *Universal Declaration of Human Rights* Article 24 says:

> Everyone has the right to rest and leisure, including reasonable limitation of working hours and periodic holidays with pay.

Some rights already in the *Fair Work Act* are consistent with Article 24 – the National Employment Standards stipulate maximum working hours of 38 hours per week, plus reasonable additional working hours, ie overtime,[30] and paid holidays of four weeks.[31] In theory, then, employees should only work beyond those hours if undertaking work under the overtime work principles, ie reasonable additional hours,[32] or if they are paid for being on call,[33] as some awards and enterprise agreements provide.

Why We Need a Right to Disconnect

Why, then, do I say that a right to disconnect is needed if the *Fair Work Act* sets maximum working hours and reasonable overtime? It is because digital technology and flexible work have enabled new cultural norms to permeate the workplace. Technology enables employees to be connected with their workplaces at all times, to access emails and other communication platforms used by smartphones and to perform other work enabled by technology, even when they are not physically at the employer's workplace.

The culture of being constantly connected to work through technology is called 'always connected'. Unfortunately, this always-connected *possibility* often leads to practices that create an *expectation* by the employer that the employee will always respond to work emails after hours and work additional hours. Yet this cultural or *de facto* requirement imposed by the employer or expected in the workplace is not readily caught by the current standard provisions about reasonable overtime or being available for 'on call' work. The work appears to be undertaken by employees *voluntarily* responding to out of hours work communications or informally attending to work requests.

We need to avoid giving with the one hand (that is, offering flexible work under the *Fair Work Act*) and taking away with the other, by expecting employees to be always available to work – and without being paid for the additional work performed.

Surveys reveal the serious issue of extended work hours and not switching off. A survey conducted in June 2022 of 2000 Australian workers showed:

> More than half of workers are working more than [the standard] 38 hours a week. Flexible location workers are slightly more likely to be working more hours: nearly three in five (60%) work more than 38 hours a week (54% up to 45 hours and 6% more than 46 hours). Of onsite workers, 53% are working more than 38 hours a week (46% up to 45 hours and 7% more than 46 hours).[34]

The same survey also indicated that '[f]lexible location workers are less likely to be compensated for nonstandard hours – 28% compared to 16% of onsite workers.'[35]

Due to the real risk of flexible work's positive benefits being eroded or undermined if flexible work were accompanied by extended and unrecognised hours of work, the right to disconnect is essential.

We have seen that flexible work promotes physical and mental health.[36] Always being connected to work, however, can have a deleterious effect on health, with longer hours worked, and without the usual checks provided by formal breaks and rest periods.[37]

Being constantly connected affects employees' work-life balance, with particular implications for employees with families, as well as for women who undertake the majority of household and childrearing duties. As the ACTU has observed:

> Working from home brings with it an increased risk of working life impinging on non-working life and the encroachment of work into the personal sphere.[38]

Women with caring duties may be less able to fulfil the expectation of always being available for work after hours, often resulting in negative assessments of, or perceptions of, their performance. According to researchers from the University of Sydney:

> Protection for workers' right to disconnect outside of working hours is necessary not only for workers' mental wellbeing, but to also make sure that workers with caring responsibilities – who are mostly women – don't fall unfairly behind their colleagues in terms of pay, advancement and promotion.[39]

Studies show that women are likely to leave the workforce altogether where the culture of always being connected clashes with their caring duties.[40]

Combined, these factors highlight the importance of introducing a right to disconnect from work.

Discussion of this right has been prevalent in Australia. Supporting the right to disconnect, the ACTU has developed a detailed *Working from Home Charter*;[41] the Senate Select Committee on Work and Care strongly recommended consideration of the right to disconnect;[42] and the right has been discussed and largely supported in academic scholarship.[43]

What Can We Learn from Other Countries?

Many countries have adopted the right to disconnect as a basic labour right.

Several countries in Europe, such as France, Germany, Ireland, Italy and Spain,[44] and in South America, including Chile, Colombia, Argentina and Peru, have adopted a variety of legislative and other models, with some limitations, providing for remote work and a right to disconnect. Other international developments include:

- Ontario, Canada requires some employers to have a written policy dealing with remote work.
- The European Parliament has called on the European Commission to propose a law to enable those working digitally to disconnect outside their working hours; and to establish minimum requirements for remote working while clarifying working conditions, hours and rest periods. A draft European Union Directive is currently under consideration.[45]
- In Ireland, the Workplace Relations Commission Code of Practice provides a right to disconnect.

  'In brief, the Right to Disconnect has three main elements:

  i. The right of an employee to not routinely perform work outside normal working hours.
  ii. The right to not be penalised for refusing to attend to work matters outside of normal working hours.
  iii. The duty to respect another person's right to disconnect (e.g., by not routinely emailing or calling outside normal working hours).'[46]

- In the United Kingdom, the Labour Party in its Employment Rights Green Paper, *A New Deal for Working People*,[47] proposed establishing 'a right to switch off, so working from home does not become homes turning into 24/7 offices. Workers will have a new right to disconnect from work outside of working hours and not be contacted by their employer outside of working hours.'[48]

So while countries approach the nature of switching off in different ways, the idea of ensuring workers disconnect is internationally recognised. Significantly too, the International Labour Organization's 2019 report, *Work for a Brighter Future – Global Commission on the Future of Work*, acknowledged that technology resulted in the blurring of people's private and working lives, and supported a right to disconnect. The report recommended:

> In a digital age, governments and employers' and workers' organizations will need to find new ways to effectively apply nationally defined maximum limits on hours of work, for example by establishing a right to digitally disconnect.[49]

Proposing a New Community Labour Standard: The Right to Disconnect from Work

Neither the *Fair Work Act* nor awards at present provide a right to disconnect. However, the Victoria Police enterprise agreement made under the *Fair*

Work Act adopted the right to disconnect. This innovative approach could inspire other negotiated enterprise agreements to include such a right, particularly for work in high-stress environments.[50]

There is a drawback, though, to using *enterprise agreements* as the vehicle for introducing such a right – namely, employees' ability to negotiate such a term in the agreement varies enormously. In some feminised industries, for example, employees' bargaining power may be quite weak, making it challenging, if not impossible, for employees to successfully negotiate a right to disconnect. For that reason, I propose that legislation should be the source of a *right to disconnect* to ensure the necessary standard for all employees.

The Bill therefore proposes to introduce a right to disconnect as a new National Employment Standard in the *Fair Work Act*. This right will apply to all employees – women, men and non-binary. Conferring the right on all employees regardless of gender will bring family benefits and positive impacts, as I mentioned previously. It will prevent discrimination against women who cannot always be connected; enable women to do paid work as well as their family and caring roles; and enable their partners as well as men to 'switch off' to support families (and therefore women). These benefits would also cover trans people who care for families, and who similarly need time out from being constantly connected.

Some may think that a right to disconnect might operate against those who *choose* to work after hours while reducing business efficiency. This line of thinking is wrong, though. The existence of this right will not stop people working after hours. Instead, the aim is to ensure all work is performed within the National Employment Standards safeguards of reasonable additional hours, breaks and so on, as well as ensuring the 'always connected' culture does not erode basic labour rights.

A 'right to disconnect' safeguards employees against work being excessively flexible and ballooning into extended hours with workers falling into the trap of always being connected and performing their work around the clock. 'Back-door' or informal unpaid extra hours are also diminished.

The right to disconnect will comprise a new section 64A, which will:

- prevent employers from requiring employees to work outside work hours;
- give employees the right to disconnect and not work beyond their expected hours; and
- acknowledge there will still be agreed overtime work or paid on-call work in accordance with the *Fair Work Act*.

The right will be enforced just as other breaches of the National Employment Standards are. An employer expecting an employee to always be connected, or to work outside normal hours of overtime (thus breaching section 64(1)), will be exposed to court-imposed civil penalties (that is, fines).[51]

An employee cannot be prejudiced by disconnecting and not working beyond expected hours of work and reasonable overtime. The legislated 'general protections' will protect a person if their employer adversely affects them (say, by dismissing them) because they have exercised a workplace right – in this case, the right to disconnect.[52]

Conclusion

In closing, I stress that the reforms in this Bill cater for women's and families' needs by improving women's ability to enter and remain in the workforce while promoting gender equity.

The pandemic has shown that many different types of work can be performed at home or remotely and that hours of work can be flexible. While flexible work cannot be guaranteed for every job and worker, employees' flexible work opportunities will be enhanced by expanding the eligibility and circumstances for making the request, while tightening the reasons for employers to legitimately refuse it.

By introducing a right to disconnect from work as an additional National Employment Standard, the Bill also prevents flexible work from morphing into extended hours and employees from being constantly connected to the workplace.

This Bill brings contemporary approaches to work in the 24th year of the 21st century and beyond. Not only will women benefit, but there are also benefits to workers of all genders supporting families, as well as to work-life balance. Businesses, the economy and society are all winners in this Bill.

I commend this Bill to the House.

The Parliament of the Commonwealth of Australia

HOUSE OF REPRESENTATIVES

Fair Work Act Amendment Bill 2024

A Bill for an Act to amend the *Fair Work Act 2009* (Cth), and for related purposes

The Parliament of Australia enacts:

1 After paragraph 65(1A)(b)

Insert:

(ba) the employee provides support and assistance to:

(i) a parent, or person who has the responsibility for the care, of a child who is school age or younger; or
(ii) a carer (within the meaning of the *Carer Recognition Act 2010)*;

2 After paragraph 65(1A)(f)

Insert:
(g) the employee has a domestic or other pressing necessity.

3 Subsection 65(2)

Repeal the subsection, substitute:
(2) The employee, including a casual employee who has a reasonable expectation of continuing employment by the employer on a regular and systematic basis, may make the request prior to commencing employment or at any time during employment.

4 Subsection 65A(5)

Repeal the subsection, substitute:
Grounds for refusing requests
(5) Without limiting what are reasonable business grounds for the purposes of paragraph (3)(d) and subsection (4), reasonable business grounds for refusing a request include the following:

(a) that the new working arrangements requested would be too costly for the employer;

(b) that there is no capacity to change the working arrangements of other employees to accommodate the new working arrangements requested;
(c) that it would be very impractical to change the working arrangements of other employees, or recruit new employees, to accommodate the new working arrangements requested;
(d) that the new working arrangements requested would be very likely to result in a significant loss in efficiency or productivity;
(e) that the new working arrangements requested would be very likely to have a significant negative impact on customer service.

Note: The specific circumstances of the employer, including the nature and size of the enterprise carried on by the employer, are relevant to whether the employer has reasonable business grounds for refusing a request for the purposes of paragraph (3)(d) and subsection (4). For example, if the employer has only a small number of employees, there may be no capacity to change the working arrangements of other employees to accommodate the request (see paragraph (5)(b)).

5 **After Division 3 of Part 2–2**

Insert:
Division 3A – Right to disconnect from work
64A Right to disconnect from work

(1) An employee is entitled to not perform work outside the employee's ordinary hours of work, except in accordance with section 62.
(2) An employer must not require an employee to perform work outside the employee's ordinary hours of work, except in accordance with section 62.
(3) An employee who is on call in accordance with a modern award or enterprise agreement outside the employee's ordinary hours of work is neither performing work outside those hours for the purposes of subsection (1), nor being required to do so for the purposes of sub section (2).

Notes

1 *Fair Work Act 2009* (Cth). https://www.legislation.gov.au/Details/C2017C00323.
2 The *Fair Work Act 2009* (Cth) was amended by the *Fair Work Legislation Amendment (Secure Jobs, Better Pay) Act 2022* (Cth), changing s 65 and adding ss 65A–C.
3 See *Fair Work Act 2009* (Cth) ss 144, 202.
4 The *place* of work is not usually included in award provisions (as an award will not ordinarily include place of work provisions; these are usually provided by the contract of employment): 'Individual Flexibility Arrangements', *Fair Work Ombudsman*. https://www.fairwork.gov.au/employment-conditions/flexibility-in-the-workplace/individual-flexibility-arrangements.

5 See 'Alternative Work Arrangements', *Fair Work Ombudsman*. https://coronavirus.fairwork.gov.au/coronavirus-and-australian-workplace-laws/alternative-work-arrangements.
6 See 'Information Notes'. https://www.fwc.gov.au/about-us/news-and-media/news/covid-19-information-notes-and-updates.
7 *Application to Vary the Clerks – Private Sector Award 2010* [2020] FWCFB 1690, 28 March 2020, sch 1.
8 Productivity Commission, Australian Government, *Working from Home* (Research Paper, September 2021), 2.
9 Ibid 11, quoting Roger Wilkins et al., *Household, Income and Labour Dynamics of Australia in Australia Survey: Selected Findings from Waves 1 to 20* (Research Report, Melbourne Institute, University of Melbourne, 2022), 115–7.
10 *Research Insights: Taking the Pulse of the Nation* (Research Report, Melbourne Institute, University of Melbourne, 14–18 September 2020).
11 See *Working from Home* (n 8) 2, quoting HILDA data.
12 Agathe Gross and Sam Mostyn, 'Equitable Flexibility: Reshaping our Workforce', *Bain and Company* (7 June 2021). https://www.bain.com/insights/equitable-flexibility-in-australia-reshaping-our-workforce/.
13 Deloitte and Swinburne University, *Reset, Restore, Reframe – Making Fair Work FlexWork* (Research Report, June 2022) ('*Reset, Restore, Reframe*').
14 See Melbourne Institute, University of Melbourne, *Taking the Pulse of the Nation: Waves 48–9* (February 2022). https://melbourneinstitute.unimelb.edu.au/data/taking-the-pulse-of-the-nation-2022/wave-48-49.
15 Workplace Gender Equality Agency, Australian Government, *Flexible Working is Good for Business: The Business Case* (Report, February 2019) 3. https://www.wgea.gov.au/sites/default/files/documents/business_case_for_flexibility_0.pdf.
16 Marian Baird et al., *Women, Work and Care in the Asia-Pacific* (Routledge, 2017).
17 Shop, Distributive and Allied Employees' Association (the SDA), Submission by the Senate Committee on Work and Care (15 September 2022) 19.
18 Ibid 20.
19 See *Reset, Restore, Reframe* (n 13) 18.
20 *Flexible Working is Good for Business* (n 15) 4, quoting OECD Statistics, *Labour Force Statistics by Sex and Age 2018*. https://stats.oecd.org/Index.aspx?DataSetCode=LFS_SEXAGE_I_R#.
21 The Treasury, Australian Government, *2015 Intergenerational Report: Australia in 2055* (5 March 2015). https://treasury.gov.au/sites/default/files/2019-03/2015_IGR.pdf.
22 *Flexible Working is Good for Business* (n 15) 4.
23 Ibid.
24 Government Equalities Office UK, *Encouraging Employers to Advertise Jobs as Flexible* (Final Report, 2019) 7. https://assets.publishing.service.gov.uk/government/uploads/system/uploads/attachment_data/file/966407/Encouraging_employers_to_advertise_jobs_as_flexible.pdf.
25 *Flexible Working is Good for Business* (n 15) 3.
26 *Long Service Leave Act 1955* (NSW) s 4(2)(a)(iii). See also other long service leave legislation: *Industrial Relations Act 2016* (Qld), *Long Service Leave Act 1975* (Tas), *Long Service Leave Act 1981* (NT), *Long Service Leave Act 1976* (ACT).
27 In *Kershaw v Electricity Commission of NSW* (1991) *Australian Industrial Law Reports* 91(7) for example, 'domestic and other pressing necessity' was made out (in the context of accessing long service leave entitlements) when the employer's

business was relocating, which would have the effect of forcing a female employee to move house or her husband to change jobs.

28 It has been reported that working from home in the pandemic offered trans employees the privacy and security – see Yvonne Marquez, 'The Employees Who Transitioned Genders During Remote Work', who said: 'People who have recently transitioned report working from home offered opportunities for more control, such as when to appear on camera during video calls, meaning trans people could be more comfortable in their own spaces' (24 June 2022). https://www.bbc.com/worklife/article/20220621-the-employees-who-transitioned-genders-during-remote-work.

29 Department for Business, Energy & Industrial Strategy and Kevin Hollinrake MP, 'Millions of Britons to be Able to Request Flexible Working on Day One of Employment' (press release, 5 December 2022). https://www.gov.uk/government/news/millions-of-britons-to-be-able-to-request-flexible-working-on-day-one-of-employment.

30 *Fair Work Act* (n 2) s 62.

31 Ibid s 87. Shift workers are entitled to five weeks' paid annual leave.

32 Ibid ss 62(2)–(3).

33 That is, the employee is available to attend to work if required by the employer, outside their ordinary hours of work.

34 See *Reset, Restore, Reframe* (n 13) 8.

35 Ibid 12.

36 Ibid 18.

37 For the 'deleterious effect of long working hours' on health of employees see, eg, Kapo Wong et al., 'The Effect of Long Working Hours and Overtime on Occupational Health: A Meta-Analysis of Evidence from 1998 to 2018' (2019) 16(2) International Journal of Environmental Research and Public Health 2102. https://doi.org/10.3390/ijerph16122102.

38 *Working from Home Charter – 3. Work/Life Balance*, Australian Unions (16 January 2022) 5. https://www.australianunions.org.au/wp-content/uploads/2021/01/ACFrOgC5hWP2shJOsnYAE9E3N2bsiRy4-gu9BYM5lrpopeSolUA0J1TzkFED4JwK8obZjV2dUCQeDwoz-WiAPRDqijRHjFrx1NihO71kSg5ehVjU1KZyjdex9NIWAlziPFjEOrJbd3-RAeeU9peU.pdf.

39 'The Right to Disconnect: Allowing Workers to Properly Unplug' (23 February 2022). https://www.australianunions.org.au/2022/02/23/the-right-to-disconnect-allowing-workers-to-properly-unplug/, quoting ACTU secretary Sally McManus.

40 Andrea Constantin et al., 'Looking Beyond Hours of Care: The Effects of Care Strain on Work Withdrawal Among Australian Workers' (2022) 6(3) *International Journal of Care and Caring* 318–34. See also Alexandra Heron et al., 'Australia – The Care Challenge' in Marian Baird et al. Hill (eds), *Women, Work and Care in the Asia-Pacific* (Routledge, 2017) 167.

41 *Working from Home Charter – 3* (n 38).

42 Select Committee on Work and Care, Parliament of Australia, *Interim Report* (Report, October 2022) 103.

43 See Marilyn Pittard, 'Fair Standards and Remuneration' in James Fleming (ed.) *A New Work Relations Architecture* (Hardie Grant Books, 2022) 76, where a right to disconnect was recommended as part of the new architecture for workplace relations; Barbara Pocock, 'As Boundaries Between Work and Home Vanish, Employees Need a "Right to Disconnect"', *The Conversation* (29 April 2021). https://theconversation.com/as-boundaries-between-work-and-home-vanish-employees-need-a-right-to-disconnect-158897; Eliza Littleton and Lily Raynes, The Centre for Future Work at the Australia Institute, *Call Me Maybe (Not): Working Overtime and A Right to Disconnect in Australia* (Report, November 2022).

44 For a discussion of developments in Europe, see Klaus Müller, 'The Right to Disconnect' (briefing, European Parliamentary Research Service, European Parliament, July 2020). https://www.europarl.europa.eu/RegData/etudes/BRIE/2020/642847/EPRS_BRI(2020)642847_EN.pdf.
45 European Parliament resolution of 21 January 2021 with recommendations to the Commission on the right to disconnect (2019/2181(INL) [2021] OJ C 456/161.
46 Workplace Relations Commission Ireland, *Code of Practice for Employers and Employees on the Right to Disconnect* (2021) 4. https://www.workplacerelations.ie/en/what_you_should_know/codes_practice/code-of-practice-for-employers-and-employees-on-the-right-to-disconnect.pdf.
47 Labour UK, *A New Deal for Working People* (Employment Rights Green Paper, 2022) 9. https://labour.org.uk/wp-content/uploads/2022/10/New-Deal-for-Working-People-Green-Paper.pdf.
48 Ibid.
49 International Labour Organization, *Work for a Brighter Future – Global Commission on the Future of Work* (report, 22 January 2019) 40.
50 *Victoria Police (Police Officers, Protective Services Officers, Police Reservists and Police Recruits) Enterprise Agreement 2019* [2020] FWCA 1578 (2 October 2020) cl 59.
51 *Fair Work Act* (n 2) s 44, pt 4–1.
52 *Fair Work Act* (n 2) pt 3–1, div 3.

Chapter 16A

Commentary on *Women and Flexible Work*

Alexandra Heron

Introduction

The proposed amendments to the *Fair Work Act 2009* (Cth) put forward by Professor Marilyn Pittard address two issues of central importance in Australia today – flexible work and the ability to disconnect from work.

The first amendment proposes to strengthen access to flexible work arrangements in Australia through amending the current 'right to request' beyond the amendments made in the *Fair Work Legislation Amendment (Secure Jobs, Better Pay) Act 2022* (Cth) by widening the eligibility criteria to include more employees and tightening the 'reasonable business grounds' employers often use to refuse a request. The second amendment addresses the problem of employees' over-connection with work by adding a new 'right to disconnect' in the National Employment Standards.

It is argued that the changes will primarily benefit women as well as enhancing their attachment to the labour market. This is regarded as a positive outcome for government, as it seeks to increase labour market participation rates. Greater access to flexibility also enhances employees' (mostly women's) ability to balance work and care needs.[1] Enabling flexible working requests prior to or from day one of employment will be significant in this regard.

The proposed changes are timely, as the need for flexible work has grown in importance and the right to request has for some time been regarded as little more than a weak 'right to ask'. Enforced working from home periods during the COVID-19 pandemic (2020–21) disrupted traditional conceptions of flexibility for employees, which had been far more focused on hours of work and scheduling. COVID-19 forced employers and workers alike to work from home.[2] It is in this context, keeping in mind the changes implemented in the *Fair Work Legislation Amendment (Secure Jobs, Better Pay) Act 2022* (Cth), that the amendments should be read.

DOI: 10.4324/9781003372462-36

The Proposed Amendments

Expanding the Right to Request and Abolishing the Qualifying Period

Professor Pittard's first proposed amendment includes two additional circumstances under s65(1A) for (i) those who support parents or carers and (ii) those who have a domestic or other pressing necessity.

While these extensions are welcome, there may be difficulties in putting this amendment into practice. These include resistant workplace cultures, employers being likely to require more convincing to allow supporters of carers to access flexibility and the need for the notion of a 'supporter of a carer' to be adequately defined and fully understood.

The proposal to add 'domestic or other pressing necessity' to the allowable reasons to request flexibility is timely. People's lives are complex, and many domestic or pressing necessities warrant the extension. One example given by Professor Pittard refers to a female accommodating her partner's job move. While this is a conceivable 'real-life' need, the test will have to accommodate a large number of other domestic issues as well.

'Domestic and other pressing necessity' should be interpreted to enable those employees experiencing reproductive health concerns to have access to the right to request flexible work arrangements. This is a growing area of concern, as menstrual- and menopause-related issues and fertility treatments are increasingly being perceived as a workplace issue as much as a personal matter.[3]

Reasonable Business Grounds

Professor Pittard also proposes to further tighten the allowable reasonable business grounds, by adding the descriptor 'very' to the grounds on which an employer may refuse. The addition of 'very' should see employers giving more careful thought to their response.

The Fair Work Commission's General Manager's reports shed some light on the efficacy of the right to request. According to the available (but limited) data, the right is used mostly by women, refusals are uncommon and most requests are either granted or granted after negotiation.[4] Given the lack of more comprehensive data, one area where the amendments could go further is to require keeping a register of requests, recording by whom they are made and for what reasons, and documenting the grounds used for refusal. This would enable policymakers to evaluate where and in what form flexible work changes are happening, and where the formal right is being used. To provide employers and employees with guidance on how to approach requests, it is hoped that the Fair Work Commission will also publish regular analysis of its evolving interpretation of the amended right to request where it arbitrates related disputes.

A New Right to Disconnect

Professor Pittard recommends a new right to disconnect. This is worth including given changes to working arrangements with constant engagement possible through communication technologies. As a National Employment Standard (NES) rather than an enterprise agreement clause, it will apply to all workers one of the general benefits of NES. Not all workers, however, have jobs which can conceivably be undertaken at home, or in a place other than the defined workspace. For these workers, the span of hours and overtime requirements are related issues that need further consideration.

Discussions about a right to disconnect, span of hours and overtime raise the underlying problem of long working hours. A complement to the right to disconnect would be to consider tightening the definition of 'reasonable hours' in the *Fair Work Act*. While the maximum weekly hours for a full-time employee under the NES is currently 38 hours per week, many work longer than this, with 17.7% of men and 8.6% of women working 45–59 hours per week and 7.5% of men and 2.7% of women working 60 hours or more per week in 2022.[5]

The time is right to make changes in the directions proposed by Professor Pittard, especially as strategies to improve female workforce participation and increase gender equality in Australia and globally are at the forefront of government policy-making.

Notes

1 Marian Baird and Alexandra Heron, 'The Life Cycle of Women's Employment in Australia and Inequality Markers' in Russell D Lansbury et al. (eds) *Contemporary Issues in Work and Organisations: Actors and Institutions* (Routledge, 2020) 42–56.

2 Marian Baird and Daniel Dinale, *Preferences for Flexible Working Arrangements: Before, During and After COVID-19. A Report to the Fair Work Commission* (research report, November 2020). https://www.fwc.gov.au/documents/awardmod/variations/2020/am202098-research-report-bd-301120.pdf.

3 Marian Baird et al., 'Mapping Menstrual Leave Legislation and Policy Historically and Globally: A Labor Entitlement to Reinforce, Remedy, or Revolutionize Gender Equality at Work?' (2021) 42(1) *Comparative Labor Law & Policy Journal* 187–225. Also see for example Sydney Colussi et al., 'Menopause Remains Taboo in Most Workplaces. This Needs to Change', *The Guardian* (21 December 2022). https://www.theguardian.com/society/commentisfree/2022/dec/21/menopause-remains-taboo-in-most-workplaces-this-needs-to-change; Australian Council of Trade Unions (ACTU), Senate Inquiry into the: *Secure Jobs Better Pay Bill 2022* ACTU Submission (11 November 2022). https://www.actu.org.au/media/1450209/d45-ir-bill-submission-nov-2022.pdf.

4 Furlong, M, *General Manager's reports – Operation of the provisions of the National Employment Standards relating to requests for flexible working arrangements and extensions of unpaid parental leave under the Fair Work Act 2009, 2018–21*, Fair Work Commission, Sydney (2021).
5 Australian Bureau of Statistics 2023, *Labour Force, Australia, Detailed, July 2023*. https://www.abs.gov.au/statistics/labour/employment-and-unemployment/labour-force-australia-detailed/latest-release.

Chapter 17

Increasing Female Participation in Construction

Legislating for Gender Equity

Rebecca Dickson and Paula Gerber

Extract from *Hansard* (Commonwealth of Australia)

Model Construction Gender Equity (Increasing Female Participation) Bill 2024

Second Reading

HON REBECCA DICKSON and HON PAULA GERBER: We jointly move:
That this Bill be now read a second time.

We rise to speak in support of the Model Construction Gender Equity (Increasing Female Participation) Bill 2024.

This Bill forms a crucial part of the Commonwealth's commitment to increasing female participation and ensuring gender equity in Australia's construction industry. Just like the historic agreement by the members of the former Council of Australian Governments (now National Cabinet) to harmonise work health and safety laws, this Bill demonstrates the willingness of Commonwealth, state and territory governments to work together to achieve nationally harmonised laws, which encourage recruitment practises that promote gender equity within the construction sector.

The Australian building and construction industries generate 7.3% of Australia's gross domestic product[1] and employ 9.4% of Australia's workers.[2] Public infrastructure and construction projects receive $9.6 billion of funding by this government.[3] Yet while this sector makes a significant contribution to our economy, it has one of the worst rates of gender equity in the country. This is a blight on the Australian construction industry. A paltry 13.6% of those working in the construction industry are women,[4] as well as only 2.5% of tradespeople.[5] According to the Women's Gender Equality Agency, '[t]wo-thirds of firms in the construction sector have zero female representation on

DOI: 10.4324/9781003372462-37

their Boards.'[6] Australia prides itself on being the country where everyone gets a 'fair go', but women do *not* get a fair go in the construction industry. The low level of female participation creates an industry that is sexist and 'macho', fuelling a toxic culture which is responsible for poor construction worker mental health.[7] We can no longer ignore this appalling situation. We can no longer make excuses for the industry's lack of female participation, and we can no longer assume that achieving gender equity is inevitable.

Although the regulation of Australia's construction sector is the responsibility of the six state and two territory governments, Australia has a history of adopting uniform laws and regulations in the construction industries. For instance, model work health and safety laws have been enacted in all states and territories, except Victoria, which has similar laws. Another example is the National Construction Code, which sets out uniform minimum standards for the design and construction of certain buildings.[8]

The Bill proposes model laws for the states and territories to adopt to address the lack of women and gender-diverse persons in their construction industries. Like model laws before it, the Bill is intended to be 'mirrored' in all jurisdictions, with separate enabling bills to be introduced into each jurisdiction's parliament to give effect to this Bill.

There are three important elements to this Bill, all of which are consistent with the recommendations made in a 2022 study in New South Wales. That study reviewed the themes of female underrepresentation in 30 prior studies. It found that career advancement and progression, entry into construction-related education and employment opportunities in construction were all likely to improve if Parliament introduced legislation requiring that contractors tendering for government projects included a minimum percentage of women in their tender. [9]

This Bill therefore explicitly addresses the recommendations from the 2022 study. The first important element of this Bill is the introduction of mandatory quotas for the number of women and gender-diverse persons employed or engaged on public construction projects:

50% of the leadership team for the project must be women or gender-diverse persons; and

50% of all individuals engaged on the project must be women or gender-diverse persons.

These quotas are ambitious, but they are not new. The 50% quota is consistent with the target set by this government on 1 July 2016 for the number of women holding government board positions,[10] as well as the overall 50:50 balance between men and women aimed for by the Male Champions of Change promoting women in leadership positions.[11] These quotas are ambitious because quotas work. In Belgium, the Smet-Tobback Law implemented in 1994 stipulated that a maximum of three-quarters of the electoral candidates on a list could be of the same gender.[12] This reform facilitated an increase in female members of parliament from 15% in 1994, to 25% in 1995, 38% in 2007 and 44% in 2017.[13]

The separation of leadership from other roles responds to the hyper-masculine culture of the Australian construction industry. Having higher female participation also makes economic sense. Women are good for business. Women bring diversity and different ideas and skills to companies; there is 'a strong and convincing *causal relationship* between increasing the share of women in leadership and subsequent improvements in company performance'.[14]

The second important aspect of this Bill is its breadth. The Bill – and the quotas mandated in it – apply to all contractors tendering for and delivering public construction projects. The model Bill does not apply only to large-scale projects and large 'tier 1' and 'tier 2' contractors; its application to all contractors ensures that women are encouraged into trades, site roles and the construction professions. The quotas in this Bill are mandatory; they require that contractors wanting to work on public projects address systemic and structural barriers to female participation; they mandate that everyone gets a fair go.

The third important aspect of this Bill is compliance. This aspect of the Bill takes inspiration from Victoria's *Gender Equity Act 2020*, which requires those to whom that Act applies to report on their progress towards achieving gender equity. Reporting drives accountability. The report required by contractors will motivate their compliance with the quotas prescribed in the Bill. Non-compliance attracts a fine, a criminal penalty, which represents this government's high expectations of private bodies to do what they say they will do to achieve gender equity.

For decades, there have been attempts to increase the number of women who participate in Australia's construction industry. The National Association of Women in Construction, whose vision is 'an equitable construction industry where women fully participate',[15] was established in 1995. Other industry associations – such as Roads Australia,[16] Engineers Australia[17] and the Australian Constructors Association[18] – all champion diversity and inclusion and advocate to increase the 'underutilised pool of talent that women represent'.[19] Yet despite the concerted efforts of these organisations, female participation has been *declining* rather than increasing. In 2006, 17% of the construction workforce were women; ten years later, that figure is 12%.[20] Worse, women leave their jobs in the construction sector at a rate that is 39% faster than men.[21]

Considering the worsening position for female participation, this Bill is urgently required. In 2021, the Victorian Government introduced quotas for female participation on government construction projects in the 'Building

Equality Policy'.[22] The response from industry bodies, including the Master Builders Association of Victoria[23] and Incolink,[24] was positive. The Australian Constructors Association, whose members include 'tier 1' contractors such as CPB Contractors, John Holland, Multiplex and Lendlease, has publicly committed to 'attract women from other industries and backgrounds' and 'rebrand construction in the public-eye to share a modern image of the industry [and] tell a positive story that welcomes women to a modern, vibrant workplace and a great career choice'.[25]

Australia's construction industries are suffering from a shortage of skilled workers following the implementation of some of the toughest COVID-19 lockdowns and international border restrictions in the world. We are forecasting a 'severe shortage' of construction workers;[26] roles for workers in the construction sector have increased by 80% since late 2019, and the number of unfilled roles is twice as high as the number of workers qualified to fill them.[27] We wish there was no need for this Bill, but there clearly is. Women are an untapped resource in our construction industries. But those leading our industries appear blind to this; our construction companies are led by blokes who hire their mates. This Bill forces a wider approach to recruitment; it mandates that industry adopt an approach along the lines advocated by the Australian Constructors Association. It compels construction companies to recruit women and gender-diverse persons. We can already hear the cries of construction sector leaders that compliance with these quotas is '*impossible*'. And our response to them is '*try harder*'. The traditional approach to recruiting women into the construction sector sees companies looking for young women finishing school, TAFE or university. But that approach is too narrow, and it is *unsuccessful*. It is time that the construction industry broadens its pool of potential recruits by actively seeking to hire mature-aged women, First Nations women, migrant women, long-term unemployed women, women seeking to retrain, women with disabilities and trans and gender-diverse persons.

Achieving gender equity in the Australian construction sector is no longer optional. It is no longer a mere aspiration. With this Bill, gender equity will become law. This Bill sets out a single set of nationally uniform requirements for the engagement of women and gender-diverse persons in the states' and territories' construction industries. It requires those who seek to deliver public construction projects to make gender equity in construction a reality. To achieve this goal, construction companies will need to set aside their prejudices and unconscious bias, step away from the long history of discriminating against women and finally take concrete steps to ensure that women and gender-diverse persons have real opportunities to work and thrive in this vibrant and important sector.

We commend this bill to the House as a concrete way of ensuring the participation, inclusion and advancement of women in Australia's construction industries. This Bill reflects this government's 'steadfast and ongoing commitment to be at the forefront of efforts to promote gender equity'.[28] It demonstrates this government's promise to advance equity for women and gender-diverse people.

We call on all parties to support this Bill.

Model Construction Gender Equity (Increasing Female Participation) Bill 2024

As released by the Building Minister's Meeting
Published by the Department of Industry, Science and Resources

This is an extract of the *Model Construction Gender Equity (Increasing Female Participation) Bill.* This bill is a national model law and is intended to provide the basis for a nationally consistent approach to the engagement of women in Australia's building and construction industries. This bill does not, by itself, have any legal effect.

A Bill for

An Act to provide the basis for a nationally consistent approach to the engagement of women in Australia's building and construction industries.

The Legislature of [name of enacting jurisdiction] enacts:

Part 1 Preliminary
Division 1 Object

1 Object

(1) This Act provides a model legislative regime that state and territory governments can adopt in order to achieve a nationally consistent approach to redressing gender inequity in their construction industry.

(2) The object of this Act is to ensure equal representation and participation of males, females and gender diverse people in Australia's construction industries by:

(a) requiring that Contractors – being those private entities tendering for and delivering public construction projects in Australia – implement plans to achieve gender equity; and

(b) ensuring appropriate scrutiny by requiring that Contractors make public commitments in relation to gender equity indicators and annually report on their progress achieving the gender equity indictors and gender equity requirements prescribed by this Act; and

(c) securing compliance with this Act and Project Equity Plans through effective and appropriate compliance and enforcement measures.

2 Guiding Principles

It is the intention of Parliament that, in interpreting and applying the provisions of this Act, those to whom the Act applies and the courts are to have regard to the following matters:

(a) the Australian construction industry is plagued by expensive and time-consuming disputes, which are fueled by its adversarial and masculinised culture;

(d) the percentage of female participation in the Australian construction industry is low and there are limited opportunities for women to participate equally in the Australian construction industry;

(e) public infrastructure in Australia's major cities and regions is being upgraded and expanded to cater for Australia's increasing population, and there is a shortage of personnel available in the male-dominated construction workforce to meet this construction demand; and

(f) senior roles – including CEO, director and key management positions – are overwhelmingly held by men.

Division 3 Interpretation

3 Definitions

In this Act:

Contractor means a person (including a body corporate) tendering for or delivering a public construction project.

defined entity means any (*each jurisdiction to specify public bodies to whom the Act applies*).

delivery term means the period on and after the date upon which a Contractor and a defined entity enter into a contract for a public construction project to and including the date upon which such contract expires or is earlier terminated in accordance with its terms.

gender diverse person means a person whose gender identity, role or expression differs from the cultural norms prescribed for people of a particular sex. It includes, but is not limited to, persons who identify as intersex, non-binary, genderqueer and gender non-conforming.

gender equity requirements means, without limiting section 18(2)(c) or any regulations made under this Act:

(a) with respect to employees of the contractor:

(i) 50% of the leadership team of the contractor; and
(ii) 50% of the total number of individuals employed by the contractor and engaged on the public construction project,

must be women or gender diverse persons; and

(b) with respect to other persons engaged or proposed to be engaged by the contractor:

  (i) 50% of the leadership team of the contractor; and
  (ii) 50% of the total number of individuals employed by the contractor and engaged on the public construction project,

must be women or gender diverse persons.

leadership team means the group of persons managing the delivery of the public construction project, including, but not limited to, persons holding the positions of:

(c) director or deputy director;
(d) manager;
(e) lead;
(f) officer;
(g) engineer;
(h) superintendent or supervisor; and
(i) in-house counsel.

Minister means (*each jurisdiction to specify the relevant Minister*).

Project Equity Plan means:

(a) a plan prepared by a Contractor under section 4(1); or
(b) where the context requires, an amended Project Equity Plan prepared by a Contractor under section 5(1).

public construction project includes the construction or carrying out, extension, demolition or removal of a building or works and associated site works, which is carried out by or on behalf of a defined entity.

Part 2 Construction workplace gender equity

Division 1 Obligations of Contractors on public construction projects

4 Requirements for tendering

A Contractor must, when submitting a tender to a defined entity for a public construction project submit a plan (***Project Equity Plan***) that:

(1) demonstrates how the Contractor will, in relation to the public construction project, comply with the gender equity requirements:
(2) addresses any other prescribed matters.

5 Project Equity Plan may be amended

(1) A Contractor may:

  (a) at any time during the delivery term; and
  (b) with the prior written consent of the defined entity; and
  (c) where necessary in order to comply with the gender equity requirements,

amend the Project Delivery Plan.

(2) If a Contractor amends the Project Equity Plan:

(a) the Contractor must promptly submit the amended Project Equity Plan to the defined entity; and
(d) the defined entity must promptly submit the amended Project Equity Plan to the Minister.

6 Requirement during delivery

At all times during the delivery term, the contractor must comply with the Project Equity Plan.

Division 2 Publication and Reporting

7 Publication

(1) The Minister, the defined entity and the Contractor must publish and maintain during the delivery term publication of:

(e) the Project Equity Plan; and
(f) the Contractor's report under section 7(2),

on their websites.

(3) During the delivery term, a contractor must submit a report to the defined entity on or before:

(a) the date which is each 12-month anniversary of the commencement of the delivery term; or
(b) any later date specified by the Minister under sub-section (2).

(4) The Minister, at the request of the defined entity, may extend the time by which a contractor must submit a report under section 5(1)(c).
(5) A report required to be submitted by a contractor under section 5(1)(c) must:

(a) report on the contractor's compliance within the relevant period with the Project Equity Plan; and
(b) address any other prescribed matters.

Part 3 Compliance

8 Non-compliance during tendering

A tender that does not include a plan required to be submitted under section 4(1)(a) is a non-conforming tender and the defined entity must reject such tender.

9 Non-compliance during the delivery term

(1) A contractor commits an offence if the contractor, without reasonable excuse, fails to comply with the Project Equity Plan at any time during the delivery term.

Maximum penalty:

In the case of an offence committed by an individual as a person conducting business as a contractor – $3,000 per day.
In the case of an offence committed by a body corporate – $20,000 per day.

(6) A contractor commits an offence if the contractor, without reasonable excuse, fails to submit a report under section 7(2) within the time required by that section at any time during the delivery term.

Maximum penalty:

In the case of an offence committed by an individual as a person conducting business as a contractor – the person is prohibited from submitting a tender for a public construction project for a period of three months commencing on the date of the offence.

In the case of an offence committed by a body corporate – the body corporate is prohibited from submitting a tender for a public construction project for a period of 12 months commencing on the date of the offence.

(7) A contractor commits an offence if the contractor, without reasonable excuse, fails to publish a Project Equity Plan or any report under section 7(2) in accordance with section 7(1).

Maximum penalty:

In the case of an offence committed by an individual as a person conducting business as a contractor – the person is prohibited from submitting a tender for a public construction project for a period of three months commencing on the date of the offence.

In the case of an offence committed by a body corporate – the body corporate is prohibited from submitting a tender for a public construction project for a period of 12 months commencing on the date of the offence.

(8) The respondent bears the burden of proving any reasonable excuse.

Part 4 Miscellaneous

Division 1 Review of Act

10 Review of operation of Act after two years

(1) The Minister must cause a review to be conducted of the first two years of operation of this Act.
(9) On completing the review, the Minister must cause a report of the review to be laid before each House of the Parliament.

Division 2 Regulations

11 Regulations

(1) The Governor in Council may make regulations for or with respect to any matter or thing required or permitted by this Act to be prescribed or necessary to be prescribed to give effect to this Act.

(10) Without limiting subsection (1), the regulations may prescribe matters for or with respect to the following:

(a) matters to be included in Project Equity Plans and format of Project Equity Plans; and

(b) the method and format for reports under section 7(2).

Notes

1 Reserve Bank of Australia, 'Composition of the Australian Economy Snapshot', *Snapshots* (9 February 2023). https://www.rba.gov.au/education/resources/snapshots/economy-composition-snapshot/.
2 Australian Government, 'Construction', *Labour Market Insights* (7 June 2022). https://labourmarketinsights.gov.au/industries/industry-details?industryCode=E.
3 Department of Infrastructure, Transport, Regional Development, Communication and the Arts, 'Budget Announcements: October 2022–23 Budget', *Budget Announcements* (25 October 2022). https://investment.infrastructure.gov.au/about/budget.aspx.
4 Australian Government, 'Construction', *Labour Market Insights* (7 June 2022). https://labourmarketinsights.gov.au/industries/industry-details?industryCode=E.
5 Paula Gerber, 'Women in Construction: Smashing Down the Concrete Walls that Keep Them Out', *Monash Lens* (7 March 2022). https://lens.monash.edu/@politics-society/2022/03/07/1384504/women-in-construction-smashing-down-the-concrete-walls-that-keep-them-out.
6 Women's Gender Equality Agency, 'More Women at the Top Proves Better for Business', *News* (19 June 2020). https://www.wgea.gov.au/newsroom/more-women-at-the-top-proves-better-for-business.
7 Donna Bridges et al., 'Risky Business: How our 'Macho' Construction Culture is Killing Tradies', *The Conversation* (24 October 2019). https://theconversation.com/risky-business-how-our-macho-construction-culture-is-killing-tradies-122867.
8 Australian Building Codes Board, 'General User', *National Construction Code* (undated). https://ncc.abcb.gov.au/homeowners.
9 Liyaning Tang et al., 'Put Gender on the Tender in Australian Public Projects' (2022) 3(3) *World* 681–91.
10 Department of the Prime Minister and Cabinet, 'Gender Balance on Government Boards — Women's Leadership' (undated). https://www.pmc.gov.au/office-women/womens-leadership/gender-balance-australian-government-boards.
11 Male Champions of Change, '40:40:20 For Gender Balance: Interrupting Bias in Your Talent Processes' (2019). https://championsofchangecoalition.org/wp-content/uploads/2019/11/MCC-40-40-40-Talent-Processes-Toolkit-2019_Web_Final.pdf.
12 D Ghailani, 'The Policy on Gender Equality in Belgium', *European Parliament, Directorate-General for Internal Policies* (2010). https://www.europarl.europa.eu/RegData/etudes/note/join/2010/425620/IPOL-FEMM_NT(2010)425620_EN.pdf.

13 Güler Turan, 'Why Quotas Work for Gender Equality' (*OECD Yearbook 2015*). https://www.oecd.org/gender/quotas-gender-equality.htm.
14 Rebecca Cassells and Alan Duncan, 'Gender Equity Insights 2020: Delivering the Business Outcomes' (March 2020), *BCEC | WGEA Gender Equity Series* 5, 8. https://bcec.edu.au/assets/2020/06/BCEC-WGEA-Gender-Equity-Insights-2020-Delivering-the-Business-Outcomes.pdf.
15 National Association of Women in Construction Australia, 'About Us', *National Association of Women in Construction Australia* (2021). https://www.nawic.com.au/NAWIC/NAWIC/About/About_Us.aspx?hkey=85211aaf-f4fc-447a-9c30-2ec16a5cc3ff.
16 Roads Australia, 'Diversity', *Roads Australia* (2023). https://roads.org.au/diversity/.
17 Engineers Australia, 'Diversity and Inclusion', *Engineers Australia* (26 October 2022). https://www.engineersaustralia.org.au/about-us/diversity-and-inclusion.
18 Australian Constructors Association, 'Time to Attract Women to Construct' (blog post, 2 September 2022). https://www.constructors.com.au/time-to-attract-women-to-construct/.
19 Ibid.
20 Natalie Galea et al., 'The Gendered Dimensions of Informal Institutions in the Australian Construction Industry' (2020) 27 *Gender, Work & Organization* 1214–31.
21 Louise Chappell and Natalie Galea, 'Construction is the Last Frontier for Women at Work', *The Sydney Morning Herald* (6 December 2016). https://www.smh.com.au/opinion/construction-is-the-last-frontier-for-women-at-work-20161206-gt4par.html.
22 Victorian Government, *Building Equality Policy* (9 January 2023). https://www.vic.gov.au/building-equality-policy.
23 Master Builders, 'MBV Welcomes the New Victorian Building Equality Policy', *Master Builders Association of Victoria* (15 December 2021). https://www.mbav.com.au/news-information/news/industrial-relations/mbv-welcomes-new-victorian-building-equality-policy?industrial-relations.
24 Incolink, 'Women to Make Up 20 per cent of Construction Workers by 2040' (15 March 2023). https://www.mbav.com.au/news-information/news/industrial-relations/mbv-welcomes-new-victorian-building-equality-policy?industrial-relations.
25 Australian Constructors Association, 'Culture Pledge' (2023). https://www.constructors.com.au/culture-pledge/.
26 Arcadis, 'The Year of Inflation: International Construction Costs 2022' (White Paper, 2022). https://images.connect.arcadis.com/Web/Arcadis/%7B74c00eae-2295-4b32-8025-54ecb470c178%7D_ICC-Report-2022-Whitepaper_EN.pdf.
27 Infrastructure Australia, 'Infrastructure Market Capacity 2022 – Risks to Project' (14 December 2022). https://www.infrastructureaustralia.gov.au/listing/media-release/Infrastructure-market-capacity-2022-risks-to-project-delivery-increase-as-5-year-investment-climbs-by-%2415b.
28 Department of Foreign Affairs and Trade, 'Australia's International Support for Gender Equality' (undated). https://www.dfat.gov.au/international-relations/themes/gender-equality/Australias-international-support-for-gender-equality.

Chapter 17A

Commentary on *Increasing Female Participation in Construction*

Valerie Francis

This Bill is commended for addressing a long-standing issue within the construction industry, namely the need for more women leaders and workers. Most advocates of women in construction would agree that gender parity is not an issue that will inevitably rectify itself, so some form of intervention is needed for any significant change to occur. The need for mandatory regulation was highlighted by Teresa Medina Arnáiz, who lamented:

> [T]he very limited effectiveness of these [positive discrimination] measures [such as disqualifying a contractor from a tender process where it does not achieve equal treatment and opportunity for men and women] as a stimulus for the observance of gender equality regulations, due to their optional nature for contracting authorities and the practical difficulty of making procurement prohibitions effective.[1]

However, many may argue that a Bill such as this goes against the very nature of probity within public procurement decision-making. They may question if altering procurement practices to this extent will negatively impact the notion of value for money, because this Bill can be seen as privileging one business above another. However, public procurement has been used for several decades as a lever to address discrimination[2] and as a device to strategically advance public policy goals.[3]

Globally, there has been a call to move away from the long-standing practice of positive discrimination measures aimed at 'women-owned enterprises' and to reframe gender-responsive procurement towards companies that are integrating gender equality principles into their policies and workplace practices.[4] The drafters of this federal Bill follow this more current approach, rewarding companies that are gender-responsive. The Bill also reflects recent legislation in other jurisdictions, such as the *Gender Equality Act 2020* (Vic), which provides a framework through which the Victorian Government must work to achieve gender equality. While this legislation is unique to Victoria, other jurisdictions may follow Victoria's direction, a potential further

DOI: 10.4324/9781003372462-38

justifying the proposed federal Bill's introduction of female participation quotas for construction in each state and territory.

The focus of the Bill is ensuring equal representation of men and women or 'gender diverse persons'[5] in the leadership team **and** the proposed labour workforce of contractors (including subcontractors) tendering for the opportunity to deliver government-funded construction projects. Targeting both company leadership and the individuals employed by the contractor and engaged in the public construction project seems sensible, particularly in the context of legislation such as the Victorian *Gender Equality Act 2020*, which requires that public entities (among others) 'make reasonable and material progress' in relation to 'workplace gender equality indicators', including the gender composition of boards of directors.[6] My own research has demonstrated that a higher percentage of women in leadership in construction is associated with many positive workplace attributes.[7]

The drafters have indicated four guiding principles for the proposed Bill.[8] While the principles in proposed sections 2(b), (c) and (d) are factual and defendable, the principle in section 2(a), regarding the industry's adversarial nature, while correct, implies a contributing link to gender. While this principle appears intuitively correct, there is currently no indisputable evidence to support this.[9] However, the adversarial nature of the industry, along with its masculine norms, are cited as hindering industry reform and seen by many as the main barrier to improving working conditions and worsening the growing issue of declining mental health among its workers.[10]

Fifty per cent representation goes significantly further than any current initiatives by state governments within Australia. I commend the drafters' ambition, but wonder what the unintended consequences of an increase to 50/50 might be. For example, what would the impact be on the size of the workforce, and can the sector support this growth? If not, what would the effect be of such a reduction? Could the Bill worsen personnel shortages in other industries that face the same lack of workers? However, in regard to women's overall workforce participation, it should be noted that construction's culture of long work hours currently restricts many domestic partners (typically women) from fully participating in employment.

The equal gender representation within the Bill has been based on a 'headcount' approach, but I believe an 'equal work hours' approach, particularly for site-based personnel, would be preferable and potentially overcome issues that may arise. This approach could, for instance, result in the continuous rotation of female employees around various public projects and/or the development of insecure and unstable employment of women in order to match the number of employed men.

I commend the inclusivity shown by the drafters by including 'women and gender-diverse persons', but worry that some companies, in order to comply, may pressure some individuals to disclose what they may regard as private information (namely, their gender identity or gender expression). I also wonder whether the Bill could be broadened to include other marginalised groups, such as First Nations people and those with disabilities. An extension of the Bill may be to provide some sway over private sector projects by restricting the activity of contractors (and subcontractors) who fail to meet the same requirements across all projects. Any non-compliance on private sector projects would then affect participation in public sector projects.

Reflecting on the Australian Bureau of Statistics (ABS) census data statistics over the past 40 years, it is clear that the representation of women overall, and in the trades in particular, has stubbornly remained at a low level. Practically, it would be almost impossible for any contracting company to meet the requirements set in the Bill in the shorter term. In this context, should the Bill – once enacted – be enforced, this would cause a complete stoppage of most, if not all, public construction work. To address this, the Victorian Government instituted a two-year transition period for achieving quotas of 3% women in trades, 7% female construction workers and 35% female management, supervisory and specialist labour.[11]

With this Bill's more ambitious objectives, it would be appropriate to incorporate a longer transition period and a staged introduction of the legislation to ensure that contracting companies cannot justifiably use a lack of 'supply' of women as a reason for non-compliance. Encouraging a significant number of young and older women into construction training and education and supporting women in leadership will take time. However, regarding the glacial pace of change to date, I am reticent to recommend or suggest a transition period of more than ten years, as this may compromise the proposed Bill's message.

To prepare the industry for such change, short (two-year) and medium (five-year) term targets for different occupational categories (initially higher for leadership, lower for trade roles) on public projects of decreasing construction costs should be established. This is because parity in some roles on public projects may be possible sooner, but this path will be slower for trades (carpenters, electricians, plumbers, concrete workers, etc.) that dominate site activities and the industry overall. This stepwise approach would, therefore, initially involve larger companies using ambitious, achievable targets before the duty becomes enforceable for all projects and companies in ten years.

Some other issues come to mind, too, in terms of implementation. Could the working lives and experiences of women be negatively affected? For instance, will they receive criticism at work and be perceived by competing workers as having unfairly 'got their job' or received a promotion to merely satisfy a quota (rather than meet a skill need)? Will women's employment be more restricted to public projects? Public sector expenditure typically relates to social infrastructure (such as hospitals and schools) and transport (such as road and rail), less so in the domestic sector or specialised projects (such as renewable energy) This is important, because women, like all workers, should have options. Also, domestic building work is less unionised and work hours are generally more flexible. If public construction work declines, will women be first 'out the door' when it comes to retrenchments?

Initiatives to improve women's participation in education and training, upskill older women, promote cultural change within the industry, decrease excessive work hours, reduce (or ban) the use of weekend work and introduce flexible work hours and practices would assist in recruiting women and positively impact all workers in the industry.

Finally, regarding the sanctions – these are necessary for compliance, and while the blanket fixed fee per day amount seems appropriate, it could be calculated as a percentage of the project cost to reduce the impost on smaller contractors. Excluding contractors from tendering for projects for as little as three months appears to be an excessively short period of exclusion and one that would be difficult to manage. A minimum of one year appears more appropriate.

I started this commentary with the observation that optional measures for increasing the number of women in construction have been unsuccessful. The Australian construction industry remains a poor employer of women at all levels, particularly in leadership and the trades. I have identified possible adverse side effects of this Bill and scope for enhancement. However, I commend the authors for proposing a Bill that takes the bold step of imposing mandatory levels of employment and engagement of women and gender-diverse persons and strict penalties for non-compliance. This is a step yet to be taken by the governments of Australia and – if one day enacted – may contribute to a meaningful and enduring change in the number of women having the opportunity to contribute not only to Australia's thriving construction industry, but to a positive, collaborative and inclusive industry culture as well.

Notes

1 Teresa Medina-Arnáiz, 'Integrating Gender Equality in Public Procurement: The Spanish Case' (2010) 19(4) *Journal of Public Procurement* 541–63, at 557.
2 Linda Mayoux, 'Jobs, Gender and Small Enterprises: Getting the Policy Environment Right' (SEED Working Paper No 15, Series on Women's Entrepreneurship Development and Gender in Enterprises, International Labour Office, 1 January 2001).
3 Anna Gollub et al., *Rethinking Gender-Responsive Procurement: Enabling an Ecosystem for Women's Economic Empowerment* (UN Women and the International Labour Organisation, 2021, New York and Geneva).
4 Ibid.
5 This Bill defines a 'gender-diverse person' as 'a person whose gender identity, role, or expression differs from the cultural norms prescribed for people of a particular sex. It includes, but is not limited to, persons who identify as intersex, non-binary, genderqueer and gender non-conforming' (see s 3).

6 *Gender Equality Act 2020* (Vic), s 16(1).
7 Valerie Francis and Elisabeth Michielsens, 'Exclusion and Inclusion in the Australian AEC Industry and Its Significance for Women and their Organizations' (2021) 37(5) *Journal of Management in Engineering* 04021051–040210514.
8 Refer to section 2 of the proposed Bill.
9 Research undertaken by Martin Loosemore and Natalie Galea supports the link between gender imbalance in the construction industry and conflict. However, it involved a small sample size and was conducted over 15 years ago: 'Genderlect and Conflict in the Australian Construction Industry' (2008) 26(2) *Construction Management and Economics* 125–35. Contemporary large-scale research is required to provide indisputable evidence.
10 Talha Burki, 'Mental Health in the Construction Industry' (2018) 5(4) *The Lancet Psychiatry* 30.
11 Victorian Government, *Building Equality Policy* (9 January 2023). https://www.vic.gov.au/building-equality-policy.

Chapter 18

Proposing a Gender-Responsive Reform of the Australian 'Modern Slavery' Act

Voice, disaggregation and accountability

Ramona Vijeyarasa

Extract from *Hansard* (Commonwealth of Australia)

Modern Slavery Amendment (Exploitation in the Supply Chain) Act 2024

Second Reading

HON RAMONA VIJEYARASA: I move:
That this Bill be now read a second time.

I speak in support of the Amendment to the *Modern Slavery Act 2018*. During the past ten years, there has been a surge in recognition that more robust laws are needed to address the exploitation suffered by individuals in the supply chains of medium- to large-scale corporations worldwide.[1] Laws have been enacted in the United Kingdom,[2] France,[3] the Netherlands,[4] the United States of America[5] and the European Union.[6] Australia was among these nations when it enacted the *Modern Slavery Act 2018*.[7]

Despite such regulatory efforts, none of these laws has met the goal of best protecting the human rights of those most affected by supply chain exploitation. In many respects, Australia's opportunity to be a world leader in this space was lost, bringing neither a gender lens nor a human rights framework to the centre of its response.

Today, marginalised and vulnerable groups working in the supply chains of Australian corporations operating nationally or internationally remain unprotected or under-protected. This includes people who experience a higher risk of poverty, social exclusion, discrimination and violence than the general population.[8] Yet although the impact on their lives is dire, it is rare

DOI: 10.4324/9781003372462-39

for research to go far enough in capturing the lived experiences of these individuals. Australia has missed an opportunity to enact a gender-responsive, human-centred legislative approach to eradicating supply chain exploitation. As a result, we have failed to identify the risks facing Uyghur peoples forced to work in the supply chains of garment companies sourcing from China. There are many other examples of vulnerable workers globally. For example, those producing rubber gloves in Malaysian factories face unacceptable conditions,[9] while calls for better working conditions and a basic minimum wage for garment workers in Cambodia remain largely ignored.

Where there have been some examples of compliance with the Act, such reporting has been far from uniform.[10] While nearly 5,000 entities have lodged mandatory statements,[11] clearer reporting standards are needed.[12] Clearly defined and detailed reporting guidelines can help to eliminate the appropriation of human rights language, not dissimilar from the 'greenwashing' we have seen in certain sectors where products are misleadingly promoted as 'sustainable', 'eco' or organic'.[13] To address this, we must move beyond the *appearance* of compliance to *actual* compliance.

Now is the time to address these notable shortcomings. I rise today to propose an amendment to the *Modern Slavery Act* 2018 (Cth). This bill brings a much-needed gender lens to the drafting table. In order to achieve a law that responds to the lived experiences of exploited women, men and non-binary people in the supply chain, three strategies are foremost.

First, we must better understand the ways in which different groups of people and individuals are affected. Attaining such knowledge requires better data collection to improve our understanding of supply chains and their impact.

Second, we must ensure that those most affected, particularly those most vulnerable to exploitation, have an opportunity to speak about their experiences and be part of identifying and designing the response.

Finally, accountability sits at the heart of any human rights-based approach to ending exploitation. This accountability gap must be closed. We can no longer watch as corporations skirt their responsibility with no consequence. A legal regime with no consequences will not catalyse the necessary behavioural change within corporations that is needed to better protect workers.[14] Adopting a gender-responsive approach sets this law apart as a global example of good practice.[15]

Exploitation and its Gendered Dimensions

'Modern slavery' is undefined in international law. As a result, the phrase 'modern slavery' is applied loosely, with limited regard to the meaning of the terms 'slavery' and 'exploitation' in international law.[16] Generally, 'modern slavery' encompasses forced labour, debt bondage and forced marriage.[17]

Australia's *Modern Slavery Act 2018* focused on regulation of corporate supply chains. Such exploitation has particular gendered dimensions.[18] Women workers numerically are dominant in certain sectors. This gender-segregation of labour creates diverse vulnerabilities, with different consequences for particular groups of women and girls as well as non-binary people.[19]

Experiences of inequality manifest in many complex and multi-pronged ways. These can be seen, for example, in gender pay gaps or sexual harassment and violence; lack of access to remedies for violations of women's rights; and lack of protection for human rights defenders who fight for stronger safeguards for the rights of women.[20]

Given this is a gendered problem, our legislative response must be gender-responsive – that is, the law must account for differences in interests, needs and experiences of women, men and non-binary people.[21] A gender-responsive approach to addressing exploitation in the supply chain, for instance, ensures that forms of exploitation that may be less visible come to the fore.[22] Gender-responsive legislative drafting may help to overcome the tendency for reporting to lack nuance as has been witnessed in other jurisdictions such as the UK,[23] and until now in Australia. The goal is to detect and respond to actual exploitation by disaggregating for difference through more comprehensive due diligence, rather than allowing corporations to paper over actual exploitation (or the risk of its occurrence) with a set of standardised responses.

Three Guiding Principles

Three principles guide this amendment: make sure women are heard, make sure women are counted, and make sure that those entities found responsible – either for actual violations or for turning a blind eye to the risks of modern slavery – are held to account.

Ensuring Women are Heard

A due diligence obligation puts an onus on companies to demonstrate that they are taking all necessary measures to identify, prevent and mitigate incidences of modern slavery in their operations and supply chains.[24] Yet what is called for here is gender-sensitive due diligence. Gender-sensitive due diligence is underpinned by the right to gender equality. This concept considers both the positive potential of business as well as the negative impacts of business practices on human rights related to sex, gender, gender identity and sexual orientation. The approach places particular emphasis on the experiences of women and girls and non-binary people, and the multiple intersecting forms of discrimination that influence the realisation of their rights.[25]

Gender-responsive due diligence requires recognition of the embedded gender norms, complex cultural biases and power imbalances at play in corporate supply chains.

Globally, the myth that so-called 'modern slavery' solely or primarily involves women chained to beds has slowly been dispelled.[26] By contrast, nuance is needed to understand where and how women are exploited. In Asia, for example, women dominate the textiles, clothing and footwear (TCF) sector.[27]

Globally, women remain overrepresented in labour-intensive industries, particularly those giving rise to precarious workplace conditions.[28] For instance, women are overrepresented in agriculture in many countries, including India.[29] Gender-sensitive due diligence in these sectors would acknowledge this reality at the outset.

In the garment factories of Cambodia's capital, Phnom Penh, 90% of the workforce are women. These workers are underpaid, work overtime hours under extreme pressure[30] and suffer from lack of hydration and inadequate restroom breaks. These practices increase women's risk of urinary tract infections, a risk exacerbated by a lack of soap, water and sanitary napkins.[31] Many are migrants to Phnom Penh's export processing zones, where they live in overcrowded rental areas with poor lighting, forced to traverse such a significant distance between rental rooms and shared toilets that they encounter an increased risk of gender-based violence.[32]

Meaningful stakeholder engagement with women workers, which must become the new norm, can make visible the power imbalances that drive and sustain such exploitation. Several examples shed light on what this might look like in the global supply chain. Company policies around equal pay, non-discrimination and access to employment benefits often govern only full-time salaried workers while failing to reach informal workers or those on short-term or indirect contracts, areas where women dominate.[33] Female workers are often engaged in home-based work that is less monitored and often involves piece-rate pay.[34] While more flexible – especially for women who prefer to work at home, or who face cultural or religious obstacles to working outside the home – workers with such arrangements are at risk of receiving lower pay and poorer working conditions, while also facing an inability to organise.[35]

The same can be said regarding how corporate practices affect people of different genders differently. Women in rural areas may be affected in particular ways by business activities that restrict access to collective resources including water, fisheries and forestry.[36] Extractive activities and export-orientated agriculture contribute to the forced displacement of Indigenous peoples, exposing them to the risk of being compelled to accept exploitative labour opportunities.

Women and girls, as well as non-binary people, may be placed at heightened risk of sexual and other forms of abuse if businesses lead to an influx of male workers into the local community.[37] These are all essential considerations for Australian businesses operating at home – including those importing from their supply bases overseas – or conducting business abroad.

Gender-sensitive due diligence requires a commitment from corporations to actively ensure that the voices of marginalised groups are heard. This entails facilitating the equal and meaningful participation of women and girls and other non-binary people in consultations and negotiations. Corporations must develop gender-sensitive systems and protections for whistleblowers. Such entities must also actively seek to uncover sexual harassment and gender discrimination while establishing internal mechanisms to provide safe and confidential treatment, services and redress and justice to survivors of sexual harassment and sexual violence. Information must also be provided concerning judicial and other remedies. Companies can play a role in ensuring that all rights holders may freely access these.

Sourcing *malpractice*, which may affect women differently depending on the sector in which they work, also needs attention. Such practices can contribute to aggressive price-setting behaviour, time pressures and short lead times.[38] Ideally, institutions would begin to practise gender-responsive procurement, including prioritising the integration of women-owned and gender-responsive enterprises into the supply chain.

Without interrogating the situation through a gendered lens at the outset, we will be less able to identify the gendered impacts of corporate practices. Australia's legislative response must incorporate gender-sensitive due diligence, to send a clear message to business that failure to considered a gender perspective when investigating harms will prove inadequate and fall short of regulatory requirements.

Ensuring Women are Counted

Despite the overtly gendered nature of global supply, many women's individual and collective experiences are frequently not accounted for. To the contrary, women's participation in senior management is often misleadingly used as a proxy for women's overall participation. Tracking with gender-disaggregated data is therefore essential for us to understand which women are most affected by global supply chains and in what ways they are impacted by them. Since the late 1980s, the Committee on the Elimination of Discrimination against Women (CEDAW Committee) has been calling for the comprehensive monitoring of women's situation in the global labour force.[39]

Such data needs to be collected in a comprehensive manner, and disaggregated, at a minimum, by age, sex, gender, race and nationality. Ideally, corporations would not only collect information broken down by gender, but also ensure that attention is given to the most marginalised women, including those from indigenous, racial, ethnic and sexual minority groups; women and girls and non-binary people with disabilities; adolescents; older and unmarried women; women heads of household; widows, women and girls and non-binary people living in poverty in both rural and urban settings; women engaged in sex work; and migrant women.

Such data can enable entities to ensure that their grievance mechanisms are responsive to the particular needs of workers – be they language- or accessibility-based – and therefore fit for purpose. This level of disaggregation is also needed by all workplace management, human resource and compliance staff to best support workers directly within the corporation but also within its supply; establish benchmarks for improved accountability to gender equality and other human rights standards; and monitor their successes and failings in meeting these benchmarks.

Ensuring Corporations are Held Accountable

Access to justice is a key principle of international law and national legal systems around the world. The right to an effective remedy for violations of fundamental rights was made clear in the Universal Declaration of Human Rights.[40] Holding those responsible is also a core principle of our treasured democracy, because a law without penalties is a law with no teeth. This is an opportune moment for Australia to enact a law that is a global good practice model. Following from the good example set by the French,[41] we must acknowledge that businesses have insufficient incentives to act without facing a serious penalty for failing to do so. An oversight in the *Modern Slavery Act 2018* is that although it refers to 'operations and supply chains', it fails to define either. To address this, the definitions proposed in this revised Bill provide a firm foundation for a system of corporate accountability.[42]

At a minimum, the law must create accountability for a failure to *conduct* due diligence. However, this alone is not enough. The capacity of auditors needs to be strengthened, both to conduct gender-sensitive due diligence and investigate and implement gender-sensitive grievance mechanisms.[43] There must be a clear mechanism for establishing benchmarks and holding entities to account when modern slavery-like practices have been uncovered but no action has been taken. Victims must also be compensated. It is time to right the wrongs of many decades of such global corporate practice and look towards a future where global supply can be more equitable, sustainable and gender-just.

I commend this Bill to the House.

The Parliament of the Commonwealth of Australia

HOUSE OF REPRESENTATIVES

Modern Slavery Amendment (Exploitation in the Supply Chain) Act 2024

A Bill for an Act to amend the *Modern Slavery Act 2018* (Cth) in relation to exploitation in the corporate supply chain, and for related purposes

The Parliament of Australia enacts:

1 Short Title

This Act may be cited as the *Modern Slavery Amendment (Exploitation in the Supply Chain) Act 2024.*

2 Commencement

This Act commences on the day on which it receives the Royal Assent.

3 Schedules

Each Act that is specified in a Schedule to this Act is amended or repealed as set out in the applicable items in the Schedule concerned, and any other item in a Schedule to this Act has effect according to its terms.

Schedule 1 – Amendments

Modern Slavery Act 2018

1 Section 4 – Definitions
Insert:

disadvantaged and vulnerable groups means groups of persons that experience a higher risk of poverty, social exclusion, discrimination and violence than the general population, including, but not limited to, ethnic minorities, migrants, people with disabilities, isolated elderly people and children.

gender-sensitive due diligence means meaningful engagement with women and girls and non-binary people as relevant stakeholders, in order to understand their concrete experiences of global supply chains; measure performance against established benchmarks; and identify and respond to the adverse human rights impacts of work in the sector.

operations means activity undertaken by the entity to pursue its business objectives and strategy in Australia and overseas, including direct employment of workers; processing and production; provision and delivery of products and services; construction; financial lending; financial investments; managed/operated joint ventures; lending of property, products and/or services; research and development; charitable activities; distribution, purchasing, marketing and sales; and religious activities.

responsible data collection means collection of data in a way that specifically seeks to make transparent how different groups are affected, including but not limited to on the basis of sex, gender, indigenous and ethnic status; racial, ethnic and sexual minority status; women and girls and non-binary people living with disabilities; adolescents; older women; unmarried women; women heads of household; widows; women and girls and non-binary people living in poverty in both rural and urban settings; women engaged in sex work; and migrant women.

risk of exploitation report means a report that will replace the previous Modern Slavery Statement.

Note: See Section 16 of this Amendment Act.

supply chains means the products and services (including labour) that contribute to the entity's own products and services. This includes products and services sourced in Australia and overseas and extends beyond direct suppliers.

2 Section 6 – Voluntary Modern Slavery Statements

Repeal the heading 'Voluntary Modern Slavery Statements'; substitute: '6 Compulsory Risk of Exploitation Reports'

3 After Section 12 – Meaning of *Modern Slavery Statement*
Insert:

12A Meaning of *exploit*

(1) For the purposes of this Act, a person is ***exploited*** if:

(a) they are required or coerced to perform labour; and

(b) there is gross unfairness to the person in relation to that labour, whether because:

(i) the requirement or coercion itself is, or is imposed in a manner that is, or in circumstances that are, grossly unfair to the person; or
(ii) the labour itself is to be performed in a manner that is, or in circumstances that are, grossly unfair to the person.

(2) Without limiting subsection (1)(b), circumstances in which there is gross unfairness to a person in relation to their labour include:

(a) that labour being performed for an excessive amount of time;
(b) the magnitude of that labour being excessive in relation to the person;
(c) the labour being performed to meet excessive quotas or other requirements;
(d) the labour being performed for no compensation, or for compensation so low as to be grossly unfair;
(e) compensation for that labour being interfered with or manipulated, including where:

(i) the compensation is given to some other person; or
(ii) amounts are deducted from that compensation in a way that is grossly unfair;

(f) the labour, or the manner in which it is to be performed, being unlawful (including by being in breach of a contract to which the person is a party);
(g) the labour being performed in the absence of a contract; or
(h) the person being denied the ability to access benefits or protection provided by any public authority.

4 Section 16

Repeal the section, substitute:

16 Mandatory criteria for modern slavery statements

(1) In order to prepare a risk of exploitation report, a reporting entity must:

(a) undertake due diligence that includes gender-sensitive due diligence; and
(b) undertake responsible data collection.

(2) A risk of exploitation report must, in relation to each reporting entity covered by the report:

(a) identify the reporting entity; and

(b) describe the structure, operations and supply chains of the reporting entity; and
(c) describe the social, economic and demographic characteristics of workers and consumers of that entity, including data disaggregated by, at a minimum, age, sex, gender, Indigenous and ethnic status, race and nationality; and
(d) describe the efforts of the entity to undertake responsible data collection; and
(e) describe the risks of exploitative practices in the operations and supply chains of the reporting entity, and any entities that the reporting entity owns or controls, with particularly attention to disadvantaged and vulnerable groups; and
(f) describe the actions taken by the reporting entity and any entity that the reporting entity owns or controls, to assess and address those risks, including gender-sensitive due diligence and mediation processes; and
(g) describe how the reporting entity assessed the effectiveness of such actions; and
(h) describe the steps taken to ensure consultation with disadvantaged and vulnerable groups who may have limited access to consultation processes; and
(i) describe the process of consultation with:
    (i) any entities that the reporting entity owns or controls; and
    (ii) in the case of a reporting entity covered by a statement under Section 14 – the entity giving the statement; and
(j) include any other information that the reporting entity, or the entity giving the statement, considers relevant.

(3) In collecting relevant demographic data for the purposes of a risk of exploitation report, the reporting entity must give attention to responsible data collection.

5 Section 16A Explanations for failure to comply etc.

Omit Section 16A(1) and substitute:

(1) If the Minister is reasonably satisfied that an entity has failed to comply with a requirement under Sections 13 and 14 (which deal with requirements to provide a modern slavery report), the Minister may give a Reporting Compliance Notice to the entity to do either or both of the following:

6 Section 16A(4)

Repeal the section, substitute:

Section 16A(4) Explanations for failure to comply etc.

(4) If the Minister is reasonably satisfied that an entity has failed to comply with the remedial action specified in the Reporting Compliance Notice given by the Minister under subsection (1) within six months of receiving the Reporting Compliance Notice, the Minister may request that entity to comply under financial compulsion up to an amount not beyond 0.1% of the entity's annual turnover during the last financial year if appropriate.

7 After Section 16A

Insert:

16B Response to exploitation

(1) If evidence is provided to the Minister that an entity is engaging in exploitation, the Minister may give an Exploitation Compliance Notice to the Reporting Entity to do either or both of the following within a specific period of three months after the request has been given:

(a) provide evidence to demonstrate that no such exploitation is taking place; or
(b) provide evidence of the entity's remedial action to address the exploitation.

(2) If the Reporting Entity fails to provide evidence in conformity with (17)(1), the Reporting Entity will be made liable by the Minister and obliged to pay compensation for the harm that due diligence would have helped to avoid.
(3) Such liability in 17(2) shall accrue within six months of receiving the Exploitation Compliance Notice up to an amount not beyond 0.5% of the entity's annual turnover during the last financial year if appropriate.
(4) An action to establish liability shall be filed before the relevant jurisdiction.

Section 16C Modern Slavery Act Fund

(1) The Modern Slavery Act Fund is established by this section. The Modern Slavery Act Fund will be composed of all funding received pursuant to a Reporting Compliance Notice and an Exploitation Compliance Notice.
(2) The Modern Slavery Act Fund is a victim's compensation fund for the purpose of the *Modern Slavery Amendment (Exploitation in the Supply Chain) Act 2024*. Any individual defined as a victim of modern slavery

pursuant to this Act or another provision of the *Criminal Code* can apply for compensation under the Modern Slavery Act Fund.

(3) The purpose of the Modern Slavery Act Fund is to provide recognition of the harm suffered by victims and is to be used exclusively for the benefit of victims, for medical support, both physical and psychological; housing; social services, including education and childcare; and compensation for lost earnings.

Notes

1 Ramona Vijeyarasa, 'A Missed Opportunity: How Australia Failed to Make Its Modern Slavery Act a Good Practice Global Example' (2019) 40(3) *Adelaide Law Review* 857.
2 *Modern Slavery Act 2015* (UK).
3 *Relative Au Devoir de Vigilance Des Sociétés Mères et Des Entreprises Donneuses d'ordre 2017* (LOI No 2017-399).
4 *Initiatiefvoorstel Wet Zorgplicht Kinderarbeid 2016* (Law No 34506).
5 *California Transparency in Supply Chains Act 2012* (Senate Bill No 657).
6 Regulation (EU) 2017/821 of the European Parliament and of the Council of 17 May 2017, *Laying Down Supply Chain Due Diligence Obligations for Union Importers of Tin, Tantalum and Tungsten, Their Ores, and Gold Originating from Conflict-affected and High-risk Areas* [2017] OJ L 130/1.
7 *Modern Slavery Act (No 153) 2018* (Cth).
8 Definition adapted from the European Institute for Gender Equality, 'Disadvantaged Groups', *European Institute for Gender Equality* (2020). https://eige.europa.eu/thesaurus/terms/1083.
9 Human Rights Law Centre, *Paper Promises? Evaluating the Early Impact of Australia's Modern Slavery Act* (report, 2022) 2. https://opus.lib.uts.edu.au/bitstream/10453/158152/2/Paper%2BPromises_Australia%2BModern%2B_Slavery%2BAct_7_FEB.pdf.
10 David Nersessian and Dessislava Pachamanova, 'Human Trafficking in the Global Supply Chain: Using Machine Learning to Understand Corporate Disclosures Under the UK Modern Slavery Act' (2022) 35 *Harvard Human Rights Journal* 46, 34.
11 Australian Government, 'Modern Slavery Statements Register'. https://modernslaveryregister.gov.au/.
12 Nersessian and Pachamanova (n 10).
13 Ramona Vijeyarasa and Mark Liu, 'Fast Fashion for 2030: Using the Pattern of the Sustainable Development Goals (SDGs) to Cut a More Gender-Just Fashion Sector' (2022) 7(1) *Business and Human Rights Journal* 50–1.
14 Jolyon Ford and Justine Nolan, 'Regulating Transparency on Human Rights and Modern Slavery in Corporate Supply Chains: The Discrepancy between Human Rights Due Diligence and the Social Audit' (2020) 26(1) *Australian Journal of Human Rights* 27, 28.
15 Vijeyarasa (n 1).
16 Ramona Vijeyarasa and José-Miguel Bello y Villarino, 'Modern-Day Slavery – A Judicial Catchall for Trafficking, Slavery and Labour Exploitation: A Critique of Tang and Rantsev' (2013) 9 *Journal of International Law and International Relations* 38.
17 Vijeyarasa (n 1) 857.

18 Miet Maertens and Johan FM Swinnen, 'Gender and Modern Supply Chains in Developing Countries' (2012) 48(10) *Journal of Development Studies* 1412; Genevieve LeBaron and Ellie Gore, 'Gender and Forced Labour: Understanding the Links in Global Cocoa Supply Chains' (2020) 56(6) *The Journal of Development Studies* 1095 ('Gender and Forced Labour'); Ramona Vijeyarasa and Mark Lui, 'Fast Fashion for 2030: Using the Pattern of the Sustainable Development Goals (SDGs) to Cut a More Gender-Just Fashion Sector' (2021) *Business and Human Rights Journal*.
19 Marina Prieto-Carrón, 'Women Workers, Industrialization, Global Supply Chains and Corporate Codes of Conduct' (2008) 83(1) *Journal of Business Ethics* 5; Catherine S Dolan, 'On Farm and Packhouse: Employment at the Bottom of a Global Value Chain' (2004) 69(1) *Rural Sociology* 99 ('On Farm and Packhouse'); Stephanie Barrientos, 'Gender, Flexibility and Global Value Chains' (2001) 32(3) *IDS Bulletin* 83.
20 Maertens and Swinnen (n 19) 1413.
21 Ramona Vijeyarasa, 'Women, Work and Global Supply Chains: The Gender-Blind Nature of Australia's Modern Slavery Regulatory Regime' (2020) 26(1) *Australian Journal of Human Rights* 74, 76.
22 Alexandros Paraskevas and Maureen Brookes, 'Human Trafficking in Hotels: An "Invisible" Threat for a Vulnerable Industry' (2018) 30(3) *International Journal of Contemporary Hospitality Management* 1996.
23 Mark Stevenson and Rosanna Cole, 'Modern Slavery in Supply Chains: A Secondary Data Analysis of Detection, Remediation and Disclosure' (2018) 12(3) *Supply Chain Management: An International Journal* 81.
24 Sharon Burrow, 'Eliminating Modern Slavery: Due Diligence and the Rule of Law', *Business & Human Rights Resource Centre* (blog, 8 August 2017). https://www.business-humanrights.org/en/blog/eliminating-modern-slavery-due-diligence-and-the-rule-of-law/.
25 Office of the High Commissioner for Human Rights, 'Gender-Sensitive Human Rights Due Diligence' (Working Paper, 7th UN Forum on Business and Human Rights, 2018).
26 Ramona Vijeyarasa, *Sex, Slavery and the Trafficked Woman: Myths and Misconceptions about Trafficking and Its Victims* (Routledge, 2016) 25.
27 Joanna Bourke-Martignoni and Elizabeth Umlas, *Gender-Responsive Due Diligence for Business Actors: Human Rights-Based Approaches* (Academy Briefing No 12, The Geneva Academy of International Humanitarian Law and Human Rights, December 2018); Petra Dannecker, 'Collective Action, Organisation Building, and Leadership: Women Workers in the Garment Sector in Bangladesh' (2000) 8(3) *Gender & Development* 31.
28 Erinch Sahan, 'Women in Global Supply Chains: Campaigning for Change' in Kate Grosser et al. (eds) *Gender Equality and Responsible Business: Expanding CSR Horizons* (Taylor and Francis, 1st ed, 2017) 111–113.
29 Business for Social Responsibility, *Gender Equality in Codes of Conduct Guidance* (Report, 2017) 5. https://www.bsr.org/reports/BSR_Gender_Equality_in_Codes_of_Conduct_Guidance.pdf.
30 Kate Hodal, 'Slavery and Trafficking Continue in Thai Fishing Industry, Claim Activists', *The Guardian* (25 February 2016). https://www.theguardian.com/global-development/2016/feb/25/slavery-trafficking-thai-fishing-industry-environmental-justice-foundation.
31 Erika George et al., 'Recognizing Women's Rights at Work: Health and Women Workers in Global Supply Chains' (2017) 35(1) *Berkeley Journal of International Law* 1.

32 ActionAid International, *Women and the City: Examining the Gendered Impacts of Violence and Urbanisation* (report, 2011) 30.
33 Zoe Elena Horn, 'The Effects of the Global Economic Crisis on Women in the Informal Economy: Research Findings from WIEGO and the Inclusive Cities Partners' (2010) 18(2) *Gender & Development* 263.
34 Marilyn Carr et al., 'Globalization and Home-Based Workers' (2000) 6(3) *Feminist Economics* 123.
35 Bourke-Martignoni and Umlas (n 28) 33.
36 Bernadette P Resurrección and Rebecca Elmhirst, *Gender and Natural Resource Management: Livelihoods, Mobility and Interventions* (Routledge, 2012).
37 Katy Jenkins, 'Women, Mining and Development: An Emerging Research Agenda' (2014) 1(2) *The Extractive Industries and Society* 329.
38 Business for Social Responsibility (n 30) 23.
39 Committee on the Elimination of Discrimination against Women, *General Recommendation No 9: Statistical Data Concerning the Situation of Women*, 8th sess, UN Doc A/44/38 (1989) ('General Recommendation No 9').
40 *Universal Declaration of Human Rights*, GA Res 217 A (III), UN GAOR, UN Doc A/810 (10 December 1948), Art. 8.
41 *Relative Au Devoir de Vigilance Des Sociétés Mères et Des Entreprises Donneuses d'ordre* (n 3) 2.
42 The definitions provided in this Bill have been adapted from the *Commonwealth Modern Slavery Act 2018*: Guidance for Reporting Entities produced by the Commonwealth Department of Home Affairs. https://www.homeaffairs.gov.au/criminal-justice/files/modern-slavery-reporting-entities.pd>.
43 Business for Social Responsibility (n 30).

Chapter 18A

Commentary on *Proposing a Gender-Responsive Reform of the 'Modern Slavery' Act*

Jennifer Burn AM

Dr Vijeyarasa's ambitious proposal to reimagine the Australian *Modern Slavery Act 2018* is both insightful and practicable. In the Migration Slavery Amendment (Exploitation in the Supply Chain) Bill 2021 (Exploitation in Supply Chain Bill) and the accompanying Second Reading Speech, Dr Vijeyarasa seeks to address the complexities of exploitation by recognising that the historic and global experience of work has been shaped by gender, power imbalance, inequality and exclusion. While these issues play out in many socio-economic contexts, Dr Vijeyarasa has responded to what has been an inherent and longstanding legal imbalance by creating a new legislative framework crafted to address the root causes of exploitation, such as gender disparities, inequality, race, discrimination and financial precarity.

In the Second Reading Speech, Dr Vijeyarasa identifies multiple global efforts to address exploitation in supply chains and points to the significance of a gender-sensitive due diligence approach as a tool to ensure that corporations have a methodology to both identify adverse human rights impacts and prevent and address such impacts when they occur. The proposed scheme includes a monitoring and evaluation framework, and requires responsible data collection by mandating specific areas of data collection, including data on age, place of work, sex, indigenous status, and racial and ethnic status, and data relating to specific areas of work, such as women engaged in sex work and in settings related to migration.

Recognising the gender dimension of modern slavery, Dr Vijeyarasa sets out three guiding principles to bring a gender lens to the prevention of exploitation – women should be heard and counted, while corporations should be held to account. Practically, these principles could be incorporated into existing business frameworks at the operational level and in the first tier of the supply chain. Beyond the first tier, the complex and multi-layered nature of global supply chains would impose significant practical challenges. While a business may make assertions about compliance, it would be difficult to verify statements made in the absence of a credible global mechanism to audit and review multiple business relations at the contractor and

DOI: 10.4324/9781003372462-40

sub-contractor level. This underscores the importance of well-resourced and credible accountability mechanisms at the domestic level.

I will now turn to a specific part of the Exploitation in the Supply Chain Bill that relates to the establishment of a Modern Slavery Act Fund.

The prevalence of modern slavery is increasing globally, with 27.6 million people reported to be in forced labour on any given day[1] and 73 million children experiencing the worst forms of child labour, including slavery, child trafficking, debt bondage, serfdom and forced labour and sexual exploitation.[2] Increases in such serious exploitation are linked to the continuing impact of the global pandemic, especially the disruption or collapse of global supply chains, civil disruption and the effects of catastrophic climate change. In Australia, the Australian Institute of Criminology has found that only one in five victims of human trafficking and slavery are ever identified.[3] While exploitation is increasing,[4] Australia has not yet provided an effective remedy for victims of human trafficking and modern slavery despite being a signatory to treaties and conventions requiring the provision of access to effective remedies.[5] A national compensation scheme has been recommended by multiple Australian parliamentary committees,[6] and is necessary to ensure that Australia meets its international commitments. Further, the establishment of a national compensation scheme would align with the National Action Plan to Combat Modern Slavery 2020–25.[7] Such a scheme will overcome inconsistencies between the eight Australian states and territories, each of which has a different victims of crime compensation scheme. State and territory schemes are not a good fit for Commonwealth crimes. Across the existing schemes, there is no uniformity or agreement about the nature of particular criminal offences or compensable categories of harm. The existing schemes vary in many respects, including their time limits to make applications, their criteria for assessing harm, their compensable categories and the amounts payable. Importantly, as modern slavery is a federal issue, ultimately the Commonwealth of Australia bears responsibility for the Australian response to the issue. Further, as the crimes of modern slavery are set out in a Commonwealth Act of Parliament,[8] there is not necessarily consistency between the Commonwealth legislative scheme and the statutory victims of crime schemes of each of the states and territories.[9]

Victims and survivors face multiple hurdles that impede access to redress. A person may be exploited in more than one jurisdiction, a situation which would require them to make several applications for compensation. With the time and resources required posing significant barriers to justice for vulnerable people, the reality is that many victims and survivors are not able to access justice in a consistent way.[10] While the definitions of crime vary across states and territories, there is increasing recognition of the role of coercion in exploitation, an element identified by Dr Vijeyarasa in both the Bill and the Second Reading Speech. Coercion may be subtle and is often gender-based, with the effect that vulnerable women and girls are coerced into slavery through threats to their own personal safety or the safety of their families. Not all states and territories recognise the subtle role of coercion in exploitation, a situation which escalates the inequitable outcomes between jurisdictions.

At Anti-Slavery Australia at the University of Technology Sydney, we have developed a model for a national compensation scheme that pays attention to eligibility, limitation period, harm, standard of proof, determination and amount payable.[11] We propose that the funding for the national scheme be provided by direct government grant. Importantly, any person making an application for relief should have access to support for making a claim, and, if needed, access to an appropriate visa to allow them to remain in Australia throughout the process. Similarly, Dr Vijeyarasa has proposed a compensation scheme. The fund would extend a payment to any person who is a victim of modern slavery as defined in the Exploitation in the Supply Chain Bill or set out in the *Criminal Code Act 1995 (Cth)*. The fund would be intended to recognise the harm suffered by a victim of exploitation and compensate them for costs associated with medical issues, including physical and psychological harms; housing; social services, including the provision of education and childcare; and compensation for lost earnings.

For effective public administration, a functional compensation fund must be underpinned by a secure and certain funding source. While the scheme in the proposed Bill would be supported by penalties imposed on entities that fail to meet statutory obligations, funding by direct government appropriation would confer greater certainty. Legislation establishing the scheme could extend to a provision enabling the decision-maker to require those responsible for causing harm to repay to government any amount paid to a survivor, but the payment to the survivor should not be dependent on the capacity of those responsible to provide reparations.

I commend Dr Vijeyarasa on the Migration Slavery Amendment (Exploitation in the Supply Chain) Bill and Second Reading Speech.

Notes

1 International Labour Organization, Walk Free and International Organization for Migration, *Global Estimates of Modern Slavery: Forced Labour and Forced Marriage* (report, September 2022) 85.

2 International Labour Organization, *Global Estimates of Child Labour: Results and Trends, 2012–2016* (report, 2017) 5.

3 Samantha Lyneham et al., Australian Institute of Criminology, *Estimating the Dark Figure of Human Trafficking and Slavery Victimisation in Australia* (Statistical Bulletin No 16, 15 February 2019).

4 Australian Federal Police, 'Reports of Human Trafficking and Slavery to AFP Reach New High' (media release, 30 July 2022). https://www.afp.gov.au/news-media/media-releases/reports-human-trafficking-and-slavery-afp-reach-new-high.

5 Frances Simmons et al., 'Modern Slavery and Material Justice: The Case for Remedy and Reparation' (2022) 45(1) *UNSW Law Journal* 148.

6 See, eg, Joint Standing Committee on Foreign Affairs, Defence and Trade, Parliament of Australia, *Hidden in Plain Sight: An Inquiry into Establishing a Modern Slavery Act in Australia* (report, 2017) 164.
7 Commonwealth, *National Action Plan to Combat Modern Slavery 2020–25* (Action Plan, 9 December 2020).
8 *Criminal Code Act 1995* (Cth) divs 270–271.
9 Simmons et al. (n 5) 166.
10 Ibid 165.
11 'Justice for All: Establishing a National Compensation Scheme for Survivors of Modern Slavery', *Anti-Slavery Australia* (7 July 2022). https://antislavery.org.au/justice-for-all/.

Index

MIX
Papier | Fördert gute Waldnutzung
FSC® C083411

Kolibri 360 GmbH
Ferdinand-Jühlke-Straße 7
99095 Erfurt, Deutschland
produktsicherheit@kolibri360.de